MW00957919

Journal of Vaishnava Studies

IVS

THE INSTITUTE FOR VAISHNAVA STUDIES

The ***Journal of Vaishnava Studies*** (JVS) is the official publication of the Institute for Vaishnava Studies, an interdisciplinary consortium of researchers, educators, public intellectuals, and community leaders academically engaging with Vaishnava traditions. JVS is a biannual, refereed publication dedicated to the in-depth study of the Vaishnava traditions of India, from ancient times to the present. The Journal presents the research of scholars on Vaishnavism and also Vaishnava scholars, thus representing and drawing from both academic and practitioner perspectives and resources.

Subscriber Information: The *Journal of Vaishnava Studies* is published two times a year, Fall and Spring. In the United States, a one-year subscription for individuals is US$40.00; in Canada it is US$65.00 and overseas it is US$80.00. We encourage readers to subscribe two years at a time. Back issues are US$50.00 each. All subscriptions are to be made payable to the "Institute for Vaishnava Studies" and sent to the Institute for Vaishnava Studies, 224 NE 10th Ave., Gainesville, FL 32601 USA.

Submission Information: All manuscript submissions should be sent in electronic format, both in Microsoft Word and as a pdf file. Authors should also send a one-paragraph bio blurb to accompany the article. Direct all correspondence to the Editor-in-Chief at stevenrosen32@yahoo.com.

Manuscript submissions should be in English. If the original is in Sanskrit, Tamil, Hindi, Bengali, or other languages, the author will be responsible for the English translation. Special characters, such as diacritic marks and/or transliteration techniques, are determined by individual authors. In terms of foreign language, then, JVS editors will not attempt to achieve consistency from one article to the next. Words such as Krishna (or Kṛṣṇa) and Braj (or Vraja) will thus be rendered variously. In addition, please note that JVS uses endnotes as opposed to footnotes.

Authors are responsible for all statements made in their work, and for obtaining permission from copyright owners to reprint or adapt a table or figure, or to reprint a segment of an article consisting of 500 words or more. To legitimately obtain such usage, authors should write to the original author(s) and to the publisher or managing editor of the quoted work.

JVS is a refereed publication. All entries are reviewed by at least two (anonymous) qualified scholars in the field prior to publication. For accepted contributions, final editorial decisions, in terms of content and style, rest with JVS editors alone. Opinions expressed in authored articles do not necessarily represent the views of the editors or publisher.

JOURNAL OF VAISHNAVA STUDIES

Volume 32 No. 1 Fall 2023

Introduction

> "We leave it to our readers to decide how to deal with Mahaprabhu. The Vaishnavas have accepted Him as the great Lord, Shri Krishna Himself. Those who are not prepared to accept this perspective may think of Lord Chaitanya as a noble and holy teacher. That is all we want our readers to believe. We make no objection if the reader does not believe His miracles, as miracles alone never demonstrate Godhead. Demons like Ravana and others have also worked miracles and these do not prove that they were gods. It is unlimited love and its overwhelming influence that would be seen in God Himself." —Bhaktivinoda Ṭhākura[1]

Who is Śrī Chaitanya Mahāprabhu (1486–1534)? He has been viewed as everything from prophet and saint to the most confidential of all Krishna Avatāras—indeed, even as the source of all incarnations. Though categorized in various ways, scholars of the tradition are clear about his importance to Vaishnavism as a whole. Edward C. Dimock, for example, asserts that "the intense and unprecedented revival of the Vaishnava faith in Bengal" was due to "the leadership and inspiration of Chaitanya."[2] A. K. Majumdar sees Chaitanya as "the founder of the last great Vaishnava sect."[3] S. K. De describes his contribution as "Vaishnavism par excellence."[4] And there are many more.

Of particular note are the now famous words of Christian theologian John Moffitt, showing that Chaitanya's life and contribution go far beyond the Vaishnava tradition:

> If I were asked to choose one man in Indian religious history who best represents the pure spirit of devotional self-giving, I would choose the Vaishnavite saint Chaitanya, whose full name in religion was Krishna-Chaitanya, or "Krishna consciousness." Of all the saints in recorded history, East or West, he seems to me the supreme example of a soul carried away on a tide of ecstatic love of God. This extraordinary man, who belongs to the rich period beginning with the end of the fourteenth century, represents the cul-

> mination of the devotional schools that grew up around Krishna . . . . Chaitanya delighted intensely in nature. It is said that, like St. Francis of Assisi, he had a miraculous power over wild beasts. His life in the holy town of Puri is the story of a man in a state of almost continuous spiritual intoxication. Illuminating discourses, deep contemplation, moods of loving communion with God, were daily occurrences.[5]

We will allow the above to suffice for now, setting the tone for all that follows. Since there has already been much written about Śrī Chaitanya, what I write here would likely be repetitious. In fact, for this issue of JVS, I have tried to gather together articles on subjects and ideas that, though related to Śrī Chaitanya, do not focus on the more common hagiographical and theological commentary one usually finds in articles and books about him. Instead, I have looked for obscure, almost peripheral aspects, perhaps never commented upon, to round out our conception of his contribution to humanity.

Along these lines, let it be known that as a religious personality in the Indian subcontinent, Śrī Chaitanya's image has been installed as a worshipable deity in grand temples—in both India and around the world—and he has inspired literature, both scholarly and devotional, in the fields of theology, religion, history, and philosophy. But, and this is the point, he has also been the subject of a commemorative postage stamp, a widely read and often reprinted comic book, a series of movies—as will be mentioned in this volume of JVS—and there is now even a museum dedicated to his memory, also celebrated in these pages.

Clearly, Śrī Chaitanya is a consequential religious phenomenon, and, to his followers, even more—he is considered the most esoteric of Krishna's incarnations, a mystical form of Rādhā and Krishna combined.[6]

For this issue of JVS, we begin at the beginning. That is to say, **Ferdinando Sardella** takes us into the world of Mahāprabhu's birthplace, which is not the open and shut case that many think it is—there is debate about the exact location of Chaitanya's birth even today. Indeed, many had long considered Pracin ("old/original") Mayapur in the northern part of Nabadwip (extending to just outside its borders), an area in the environs of Ramchandrapur, to be the actual spot of the divine birth. But in the late nineteenth century (1894), Kedārnāth Datta Bhaktivinoda uncovered an alternative possibility: Mayapur, situated opposite Nabadwip on the Hugli River's eastern shore. Sardella explores the reasoning behind Bhaktivinoda's discovery, and documents its institutionalization by Bhaktivinoda's son, Bhaktisiddhānta Sarasvatī.

Sardella's study also delves into the intricate dynamics of these two rival communities, offering a comprehensive exploration of their historical, cultural, and sociological trajectories while shedding light on their current interrelations.

After this, we include two "first-person" articles about important hagiographic literature: **Tony K. Stewart** writes about his work with Ed Dimock on the Bengali *Caitanya-caritāmṛta*, illuminating their noteworthy and groundbreaking translation and commentary. **Katrin Stamm**, for her part, documents the story of her translation of Walther Eidlitz's German text, *Kṛṣṇa-Caitanya, Sein Leben und Seine Lehre*, which she worked on with several other scholars. Both works are paramount in the study of Śrī Chaitanya, one based on an early 17th-century text by Krishnadāsa Kavirāja Gosvāmī, seminal in the tradition, and the other an early 20th-century retelling, not only of the *Caitanya-caritāmṛta* but of nearly all the early literature on Chaitanya's life.

This is followed by **Gerald Carney**'s article, which, in Carney's own words, "provides short theological snapshots of Kavikarṇapūra's presentation of Śrī Caitanya," using mainly Acts II and III of Karṇapūra's ten-act drama, the *Caitanya-candrodaya-nāṭaka*. In these Acts, Śrī Chaitanya is still known as Viśvambhara, i.e., prior to his taking *sannyāsa*, and Kavikarṇapūra "conveys the Lord's ecstasies, leading to the revelation first of his six-armed form and then his *svarūpa*, or true identity, as two-armed Krishna." In Act III, Viśvambhara and his associates stage a play about Rādhā and Krishna's *dana-līlā*, a virtual drama within a drama, wherein Viśvambhara takes the role of Rādhā and expresses her *bhāva* to the point of actually *becoming* her. Thus, for Kavikarṇapūra, Viśvambhara is Krishna as well as Rādhā, anticipating the truth that will be highlighted in Kavirāja Gosvāmī's later *Caitanya-caritāmṛta*.

Given Carney's unique introduction to Chaitanyite theology, we present a series of seven other articles that dive into diverse aspects of that theology. Although some of these subjects have no doubt been explored elsewhere, we will present them here specifically in the spirit of our current project—offering a new and fresh approach to these same themes. **Guy L. Beck,** for example, gives us an article that focuses on chanting the holy name of Krishna. While this subject is not uncommon in literature about the great Master, who championed the chanting of the name as a central spiritual practice, Beck analyzes the subject in terms of the popular Bengali movies on Chaitanya that have graced the silver screen in India, thus offering a unique look at chanting in the Chaitanya tradition.

Gauḍīya theology solidified more and more from the sixteenth through eighteenth centuries, and as a detailed theology developed regarding Chaitanya and his divinity, so too did sophistication in terms of viewing him as an object of worship. Consequently, he became the focus of praise poetry, a well known genre of Indian literature. In our volume, **David Buchta** examines one such *stotra* written by the 19th-century polymath, Raghunandana Gosvāmī. Among the latter's some 30 works are a few poems in praise of Chaitanya, including his *Gaurāṅgavirudāvalī*, modeled closely on Rūpa Gosvāmī's *Govindavirudāvalī*. Each of these poetic collections contain "alphabet poems"—that is, a series of epithets beginning with each letter of the Sanskrit alphabet in consecutive order. Buchta translates this poem and highlights the difficulty created by letters that do not normally begin words in Sanskrit (or perhaps don't exist in the language at all!) and the grammatical playfulness—befitting Nimāi Paṇḍita—that Raghunandana applies to create such epithets. This grammatical sophistication, Buchta argues, is not a mere show of pedantry, but a way of worshipping Chaitanya with literary embellishments, just as a temple *mūrti* might be adorned with fine jewels and garments.

After this, **Sugopi Palakala** looks to the final chapter of the *Caitanya-caritāmṛta,* as she briefly elaborates on the eight verses (*Śikṣāṣṭaka*) composed by Śrī Chaitanya himself, offering fresh translations. While these verses have been explicated before, here she focuses on how they represent the different moods and identities of Chaitanya, as he intensely experiences various transcendent emotions. In her paper, she offers an overview of the affects generated in the *Śikṣāṣṭaka*, the imagery poetically produced in it, and the subject positions of Chaitanya as they appear in the verses themselves.

For example, in the first and third verses, he seems to assume not only the position of a general devotee praying to God, but also that of a teacher, instructing his followers about the outcomes of *nāma-saṅkīrtana* and the methods for engaging in it. In the second verse, his words aren't directed toward a general, unspecified audience, but toward Krishna himself. Thus, Chaitanya further demonstrates the subject position of a pious, unostentatious devotee in his direct appeal to the Lord. In verse four, once again directly addressing Krishna, his identity/subject position as a *sannyāsī* comes to the fore, in his denial of women, wealth, and fame. In verse eight, we see him fully ensconced in the identity of Rādhā. In this way, before the eight verses come to a close, Chaitanya emerges as a devotee, teacher, *sannyāsī* (renouncer), Krishna, and Rādhā—all at different times and sometimes at once.

The next two papers, by **Cogen Bohanec** and **R. David Coolidge**, respectively, are somewhat interrelated. The first focuses on Śrī Chaitanya's interaction with animals and the natural world, and how this impacts his worldview and movement theologically—from how they view animals rights and vegetarianism to how they see the soul as permeating not just human bodies but that of all living, breathing creatures. One of the episodes in Chaitanya-līlā that speaks to Chaitanya's view of animals involves his interaction with Chand Kazi, the Muslim ruler of the district. Chaitanya chooses to begin his conversation with the Kazi by focusing on vegetarianism and the killing of cows. While Bohanec, as a small part of his analysis, deals with this specific subject, Coolidge, who is well trained in both Gauḍīya *and* Islamic traditions, addresses it as well, but this time allowing the reader to see how a Muslim would view the Chaitanya/Kazi exchange.

We move on to the relationship between the Mādhva and Chaitanya traditions, but whereas many merely look at the connection between these two *sampradāyas* in terms of their theology, **Gerald Surya** looks at it primarily through an incident in Chaitanya's life, i.e., meeting the Tattvavādī branch of Mādhvaism at Uḍupī. Of course, within this context, Surya engages with the theology as well, specifically in terms of *viśeṣa*, a conceptual understanding of God as not only having a form, but explaining that each aspect of that form is absolutely real and ontologically nondifferent from every other aspect. The elucidation of this teaching, Surya claims, is unique to both Mādhva and Gauḍīya traditions, showing a connection between the two.

My own paper, which comes next, deals with the concept of love as found in the Chaitanya tradition, not only in terms of Rūpa Gosvāmī's detailed taxonomy as found in his mammoth literary oeuvre, but in terms of how it applies to Śrī Chaitanya, whom Gauḍīyas perceive not only as fully tasting that love to its highest degree, but also as being the very embodiment of that love. To this end, we explore the esoteric notion of *prema-vilāsa-vivarta*, a term found solely in the *Caitanya-caritāmṛta* (Madhya 8.192), and which indicates the towering limits of love, wherein one finds oneself completely overcome by inner transformation, often with a sense of closeness so profound that one feels nondifferent from the beloved.

Next comes **David Mason**—and Chaitanya as a popular comic book character! "As theorized in the West," Mason tells us, "the concept of popular culture emphasizes the service that it renders capitalism. Anant Pai's Amar Chitra Katha (ACK) comic books certainly demonstrate how a market item can create, shape, and direct a mass population," and this is the subject of Mason's article. ACK's ninetieth title, "Chaitanya Mahaprabhu" does seem to appropriate this historical figure for the sake of ACK's domination of a specific market. "Given the comic's design and function, and given how *bhakti* reads the world," says Mason, "we can see this comic book as appropriating capitalism itself for the sake of something quite apart from the marketplace." However one frames it, Śrī Chaitanya is now known around the world, among theologians and practitioners and no less among scholars and in (albeit a very specific branch of) pop culture.

Which leads us to the Chaitanya Museum. **Måns Broo** and **Sourish Das (Sundar Gopal Das)** have given us an important lens through which to see Chaitanya's significance and popularity in the modern world—not many historical personalities have had a museum dedicated to them, and Śrī Chaitanya is now one of that select few. The contemporary structure currently welcoming visitors in Kolkata, West Bengal, stands as a monument to Śrī Chaitanya's renown, and with this article we are introduced to its history, exhibits, and the bold, visionary efforts of the innovators who conceived and created it.

Finally, **Jeffery Long** creates a bridge between Śrī Chaitanya and Swami Vivekananda, normally conceived as two disparate luminaries on opposing ends of the Hindu spectrum. "Although in some ways seeming opposites," writes Long, "Swami Vivekananda, the modern-day proponent of Advaita Vedānta, and Śrī Caitanya Mahāprabhu, founder of the Gauḍīya Vaiṣṇava tradition, share a number of important affinities."

Though Swami Vivekananda expresses his views in terms of non-dualism, which runs counter to the philosophy of Chaitanya Mahāprabhu, his cosmopolitan school of thought affirms the equal validity of the paths of *bhakti* and *jñāna* as ways to the highest realization. Similarly, Long tells us, Śrī Chaitanya's philosophy of Acintya Bhedābheda is a path that affirms the literally inconceivable truth of the simultaneous duality and non-duality of the individual soul (*jīva*) and the Supreme Being (Īśvara). This essay ultimately argues for the importance of a philosophy that is built on understanding, of seeing ultimate reality as approachable in multifarious ways, thus creating accommodation rather than adversity, harmony rather than dissonance.

—Steven J. Rosen

Endnotes

1. Bhaktivinode Thakur, *Shri Chaitanya Mahaprabhu: His Life and Precepts* (1896; reprint, Madras: Sree Gaudiya Math, 1984), 60–61.

2. Edward C. Dimock Jr., *The Place of the Hidden Moon* (Chicago: University of Chicago Press, 1966), 25.

3. A. K. Majumdar, *Chaitanya: His Life and Doctrine* (Bombay: Bharatiya Vidya Bhavan, 1969), 1.

4. S. K. De, *Early History of the Vaisnava Faith and Movement in Bengal* (Calcutta: General Printers & Publishers, 1942), i.

5. John Moffitt, *Journey to Gorakhpur: An Encounter with Christ Beyond Christianity* (New York, N.Y.: Holt, Rinehart, and Winston, 1972), 129, 135–136.

6. Prominent Gauḍīya Vaishnava scholar Joseph T. O'Connell has articulated it as follows: "During Chaitanya's own lifetime it became axiomatic among his closer devotees that he was in some fashion Hari/Krishna (even Krishna with the feelings and complexion of Rādhā) descended in human form." See Joseph T. O'Connell, "Historicity in the Biographies of Chaitanya," in *Journal of Vaishnava Studies*, Volume 1, No. 2 (Fall 1993), 110.

The Chaitanya Birthplace Controversy

Ferdinando Sardella

The town of Nabadwip is located on the western shore of the Ganges River, approximately 130 kilometres north of Kolkata.[1] The surrounding area is one of the most fertile in Asia, encompassing both West Bengal and Bangladesh, where the waters of the Ganges, Padma, Brahmaputra and other tributaries form one of the largest riverine regions in the world. An arm of the Ganges known as the Hugli (or Hooghly) River flows South to Nabadwip and Kolkata, ending at the Bay of Bengal. From the 15th to the end of the 19th century, Nabadwip gradually rose in public renown, not only for being a major centre of Hindu learning but also for being the birthplace of the *bhakti* saint Kṛṣṇa Caitanya[2] (1486-1534), the most important figure of the pan-India Bengali Vaiṣṇava tradition.

At the turn of the 20th century, however, the local boundaries of the region's sacred geography were challenged and permanently transformed by the apparent discovery and subsequent development of an alternative to Nabadwip as the location of Chaitanya's birth. This alternate birthplace is situated in an area known as Mayapur, which is located on the eastern shore of the Hugli river, almost opposite and within viewing distance of Nabadwip. It was discovered in March 1894 by Kedarnath Datta Bhaktivinoda (1837-1914), solidly established between the years 1918 and 1936 by his son Bhaktisiddhānta Sarasvatī (1874-1937), and has continued to grow in sacred geographical and religious prominence ever since—even to the point of having achieved unprecedented international notoriety, involvement, and monetary support.

From the outset, of course, this development has not been well received by Nabadwip's Vaiṣṇava institutions, which have vigorously contested the authenticity of the Mayapur birth-site while firmly upholding the validity of theirs. Thus, after a century of competition that has fostered the gradual augmentation and popularization of both projects, what we have today is a unique microcosm of religious interactivity that offers a rare opportunity for sociology and history of religion scholars: two adjacent riverside communities, both embracing the same religious tradition, each with its own developmental background, institutional structures, and doctrinal preferences, each displaying markedly different approaches to identity formation, religion, and culture, and each claiming to contain the "real" birth-site of Chaitanya, whose status within the tradition is similar to that of Jesus within Christianity. The remainder of this chapter consists of a historical, cultural and sociological exploration of these two rivalling religious communities, ending with a brief discussion on the current relations between the two.

Nabadwip

The population of Nabadwip stands at approximately 125,000 residents (2011);[3] among these, most are followers of the Vaiṣṇava tradition, some are Muslims, while the remainder follow the Śakta tradition, which includes the worshippers of Śiva, regarded by local Vaiṣṇavas as the protector of this "sacred *dhāma*" (i.e., the town and its surroundings).[4] Naturally, all three traditions are represented by temples (*mandir*) and various holy sites, although those representing Vaiṣṇavism are more numerous. Most of the urban settlement is no older than 150 years due to periodic flooding, which has several times changed the course of the Ganges, forcing the relocation of the indigenous population. Although local historians have concluded that Nabadwip is approximately one thousand years old, it was not until the turn of the 13th century that it became an Indic centre of learning as the capital of the Sena Empire (Mondal 2010, p. 34).

During the late medieval period Nabadwip became an epicentre for the educational study of Sanskrit and philosophy (Chaudhuri 2016, p. 12-13), so much so that by the time of the 19th century European travellers were identifying the city as the "Oxford of Bengal" (Roy 2008, p. 26). This reputation, however, gradually diminished in the 20th century as a result of colonial and later political influences. Despite this, Nabadwip is still regarded by many as the heart of the Chaitanyaite Vaiṣṇava communities of Eastern India and Bangladesh, and continues to attract hundreds of thousands of visitors each year.

The city contains major temple structures, which often include residential quarters for ascetics (*bābājīs*) and itinerant pilgrims. Some examples are:[5] 1) the Mahaprabhu Bari, which contains a wooden deity of Chaitanya, allegedly worshipped by his wife Viṣṇupriyā; 2) the Samaj Bari *mandir*, founded by Radha Raman Charan das bābājī, where the elaborate worship of Rādhā-Kṛṣṇa deities takes place; 3) the Gobindaji *mandir* managed by Chaitanyaite

Vaiṣṇavas from the Eastern states of Manipur and Assam; 4) the Madhan Mohan Mandir, which was established by Madhan Gopal Goswami, among others, and counts thousands of followers from Bangladesh, Tripura, and Assam; 5) the Basudeb Angan, which contains an ancient deity of Viṣṇu; and, 6) the Hari Sabha Mandir, located North of Nabadwip, which contains a dancing deity of Chaitanya.

Throughout the city one can find well-defined Vaiṣṇava communities that have developed around a number of temple structures owned and/or operated by the descendants of Chaitanya's early associates, whose genealogies are meticulously preserved—a class of individuals known as the Goswamis. The esoteric term "*goswami*" literally means "one who controls the senses," and commonly refers to persons that have renounced the world. Those titled Goswami in Nabadwip, however, are not celibates but rather householders that primarily cater to the laity's devotional needs. Those who the Goswamis formally initiate into their Vaiṣṇava tradition (i.e., their disciples) are said to constitute their *paribāra*, or extended family.

Apart from the Goswamis and their laity, Nabadwip contains a small group of spiritual personages known as the *bābājīs*, highly regarded individuals that have entirely renounced the world and taken a life-long vow of celibacy. These senior mendicants (or ascetics) reside in living quarters attached to the temples together with their celibate students (*brahmacārīs*); in total, they represent approximately 800+ Nabadwipians. Finally, there are the highly esoteric, and thus difficult to study, *sahajiyā* tantrics, who come from the poorest sections of society and are involved in the secret performance of various sexual rites (Sarbadhikary 2015).

The Mahaprabhu Bari is the most prominent sacred Vaiṣṇava temple in Nabadwip, located at the site of the home in which Chaitanya's wife (Viṣṇupriyā) is said to have worshipped his image. A brief examination of the workings of this temple will serve to augment the above description by providing a bit more detail. The Bari is currently managed by members of Viṣṇupriyā's hereditary line (*baṁśa*), which currently consists of approximately 200 families, all of which claim to be the fifteenth generation after Yadavācārya, the brother of Viṣṇupriyā, who Chaitanya married prior to his becoming a renunciant. The *baṁśa*, which manages a total of fifteen Nabadwip temples, is comprised of a *brāhmaṇa* class (*varṇa*) that retain the right to worship the Bari's Chaitanya deity so long as they marry a member of the hereditary caste (*jāti*). While women are not permitted to directly worship the deity, they are allowed to assist their husbands by cooking, sewing deity clothes, preparing garlands, and so forth.[6] The Bari is managed by an elected board that is responsible, among other things, for dividing the yearly deity worship among the *baṁśa* families in a way that affords each an equal opportunity to conduct the daily worship and thereby collect donations. Apart from receiving a fee for taking care of the deities, the *baṁśa* accepts large donations for the holding of holiday festivals and the performance of marriage and funeral rites.

The Goswamis of the Viṣṇupriyā *baṁśa* offer initiation to aspiring male students, most of whom come from the *brāhmaṇa varṇa* and *jāti* of Nabadwip's Hindu community. During the initiation ceremony, the guru provides the candidate with the *bīja* (seed) *mantra* "*kliṁ kṛṣṇaya namaḥ*" (adoration to Kṛṣṇa), which he is told to recite in silent meditation each day; the ceremony itself is regarded as the means by which the power of the *mantra* is activated. In addition, the candidate is instructed to recite the Hare Kṛṣṇa *mantra* in order to develop love and devotion to both Rādhā-Kṛṣṇa and Chaitanya, who is regarded as their combined form. The Hare Kṛṣṇa *mantra* consists of the following thirty-two syllables: Hare Kṛṣṇa Hare Kṛṣṇa, Kṛṣṇa Kṛṣṇa Hare Hare, Hare Rāma Hare Rāma, Rāma Rāma Hare Hare. The candidate is told that this *mantra* must be recited at least 108 times each day. After initiation the guru does not necessarily give further guidance to the disciple, who is then free to seek instruction from a teacher of his choice. Formal initiation enables the *brāhmaṇa* disciple to conduct deity worship, perform various temple rites, and minister to the religious needs of Nabadwip's Vaiṣṇava community.

Similar customs (with a number of variations) are found in the other three major *baṁśas* of Nabadwip—i.e., the Nityānanda *baṁśa* (the largest and most popular), the Gadādhara *baṁśa*, and the Advaita *baṁśa*.[7] The Advaita *baṁśa* is only sparsely represented in Nabadwip and is known for its strict adherence to caste and purity rules, thus aligning it with the orthodox *smārta brāhmaṇas* of Bengal. The Nityānanda *baṁśa* is thought to have less standing due it acceptance of disciples from the lower *varṇa* and *jāti* (see also Madsen 2001, pp. 161-62). *Baṁśas* are patrilinear institutions whose women automatically lose their right to worship the family deity if they marry a man from another lineage. Nonetheless, the members of the four *baṁśas* are known to interact on a regular basis, often inviting one another to major religious events.

Most of the families in Nabadwip belong to non-*brāhmaṇa varṇa* and *jāti*, and voluntarily serve the Goswamis by donating money, foodstuffs, and other items, thereby increasing their own ritual status. They also provide for those temples that are under the care of their guru and invite him and his family to their homes to conduct religious ceremonies. The Goswami lineages and the social structures they have created have for centuries provided Nabadwip's Chaitanya Vaiṣṇava community with a high level of stability and continuity, something that has protected its religious traditions from both internal erosion and external intrusion. One modern weakness that has come to threaten this system consists of the fact that the young among the *baṁśas* have tended to move away from Nabadwip for economic reasons, sometimes to as far away as Japan and the United States, thus causing a drain in the number of ritual priests. Another challenge is the growing criticism of the caste system and *brahmāṇism* in the political and cultural life of Bengal, which has gradually eroded the Goswamis' status.

Chaitanya's supposed birthplace in Nabadwip, which is highly respected by the local *brāhmaṇas*, is called Gauranga Janmasthan, which provides residential facilities for approximately twenty *bābājīs* and *brahmacārīs*. The temple belongs to the same *baṁśa* as the Samaj Bari (briefly mentioned above) and contains a deity of Chaitanya as a small child with his mother Śacī. It is regularly visited by Nabadwip's local residents and is popular among the *bābājīs*, who begin an annual Nabadwip pilgrimage from this site to honor the day of Chaitanya's birth (called Gaura Pūrṇimā).

With the exception of three temples that were established on the eastern side of the Ganges, Nabadwip's religious world has remained separate and distinct from the religious world of Mayapur. While this can be readily explained in terms of logistics, the ongoing birthplace dispute between the two communities and the differences between their religious cultures certainly have been contributing factors. The following section examines Mayapur's modern history as well as the manner in which this alternate community has come to challenge the Vaiṣṇava establishment of Nabadwip.

Revival and Reform in Mayapur

During the colonial period, several European nations established trading posts on the Ganges, both above and below the Nabadwip-Mayapur region. On the stretch between Nabadwip, Mayapur, and Kolkata, the Danes, Dutch, French, and Portuguese established the Serampore, Chinsurah, Chandannagar, and Bandel trading posts, respectively; all four posts were located next to each other on the left bank of the Ganges (or Hugli, as it was formerly known). As previously noted, Mayapur as Chaitanya's alternate birthplace was discovered in 1894 by Bhaktivinoda, was then solidly established by his son Bhaktisiddhānta, and has continued to grow in sacred geographical and religious prominence ever since.

Today, Mayapur contains over twenty brightly colored, variously sized Vaiṣṇava Chaitanya Maths, which stand along both sides of the main road, named Bhaktisiddhānta Sarasvatī Marg.[8] They are accessed through large arched gates that are vividly decorated with statues of lions and images of characters from the *Bhāgavata Purāṇa*. The silhouettes of the Maths highlight approximately three kilometres of road, beginning from the docks of the ferries that sail to Nabadwip and continuing north along and beyond the eastern banks of the Ganges. Among these Maths, at one point along the road, one finds the Yoga-pīṭha—a temple building with a tall white dome that marks the spot where Bhaktivinoda discovered the alternate birthplace of Chaitanya. There one can find deities of Chaitanya as both a new-born and an adult, deities of Rādhā-Kṛṣṇa, a Śiva *linga* carved in dark stone, and deities of Chaitanya's parents Śacī and Jagannātha Miśra. The temple belongs to an institution known as the Chaitanya Math, which manages several temples and important landmarks in the area.

Many of Mayapur's Vaiṣṇava institutions were founded during the late colonial period. In 1919, Bhaktisiddhānta re-established one such institution, the *Viṣva-vaiṣṇava-rāja-sabhā* (Royal World Vaishnava Association). The Association was originally founded by Jīva Gosvāmī in Vrindavan during the 16th century and was then revived by Bhaktisiddhānta's father Bhaktivinoda. Under Bhaktisiddhānta's leadership it ultimately came to be known as the Gaudiya Math (Sardella 2013, pp. 92-93). In 1926, Bhaktisiddhānta built the Chaitanya Math, which became the headquarters of his blossoming movement. At the time of his disappearance on January 1st, 1937, the Gaudiya Math encompassed sixty-six *maths*: seventeen in the Mayapur area and its surroundings, forty-six in various parts of South Asia, and one each in Rangoon, London, and Berlin (Sraman 1968, pp. 170-74).

Bhaktisiddhānta had strong faith in the transformative power of personal relationships and the importance of personal example. A self-realized guru, in theological terms, is said to be the transparent medium through which a sincere disciple gains entry to the spiritual realm. While accepting this view in principal, Bhaktisiddhānta questioned the claimed exclusive right of Nabadwip's caste *brāhmaṇas* to be the sole gurus for all other classes and castes (Bhaktisiddhānta 1922). Without directly opposing the rights of the Goswami gurus, Bhaktisiddhānta undermined the legitimacy of their exclusive claim by functioning as guru for all those who approached him (he himself was a *kāyastha* by birth, placed just below the *brāhmaṇas*). To validate this stance, Bhaktisiddhānta argued by reference to various theological texts that a Vaiṣṇava's status was factually higher than that of a *brāhmaṇa* (Bhaktisiddhānta 2000). He also selected from the history of Chaitanya Vaiṣṇavism a disciplic succession (*sampradāya*) that included *śikṣā* (instructing) gurus from various castes, aligning himself with these gurus because they had been recognized by the Chaitanya tradition not on the basis of their birth, but rather on the basis of their character, teachings, and high level of realization. While he also considered *dīkṣā* (formal ritual) initiation to be important, he nonetheless viewed character and quality of instruction as being even more significant.[9]

In 1937 the Gaudiya Math went through a period of institutional crises, which led to schism and a protracted battle in the courts (Sardella 2020). The case concerned the matter of succession, and was fought between opposing groups that had formed around two of Bhaktisiddhānta's closest disciples (Yati 1998, p. 345). The reputation and credibility of the institution suffered greatly, and a period of stagnation ensued during the 1940s and 1950s. At the end, the Gaudiya Math emerged initially as a damaged and divided institution, with many of its leading members and their successors breaking away to establish Gaudiya Math institutions of their own—e.g., B. P. Keśava Goswami, who in 1942 founded the Devānanda Gaudiya Math, and A. C. Bhaktivedanta Swami, who founded the International Society for Krishna Consciousness (ISKCON) in New York in 1966.[10]

In 1971, Bhaktivedanta acquired a Mayapur property with the object of establishing an ISKCON temple and introducing Chaitanya's alternate birthplace to individuals throughout the world. His aim was to fulfill the desire of both Bhaktivinoda and Bhaktisiddhānta (his guru) by transforming Mayapur into a model Chaitanya Vaiṣṇava community, containing a monumental temple that would attract residents, pilgrims, and large numbers of religious tourists from around the world. In the years following the purchase of this property ISKCON gradually became the largest and most visible Vaiṣṇava institution in the Mayapur-Nabadwip area, and its Chandrodaya Mandir became the International Society's world headquarters. For the last several years ISKCON Mayapur has been involved in the construction of the gigantic temple Bhaktivedanta had envisioned, the Temple of the Vedic Planetarium, which when completed will be one of the largest Hindu temples in the world. The temple is scheduled to open for worship in 2024, although it will be only partially completed at that time.[11]

Fuelled primarily by a massive amount of international funding, ISKCON's financial input has revolutionized the area of Mayapur in various significant ways, stimulating a number of social and economic transformations, from new employment opportunities for disadvantaged Muslims and Hindus to increased land prices. At present, ISKCON Mayapur has thousands of married and celibate Vaiṣṇava disciples living on and around its temple properties—disciples originating not only from Bengal and Bangladesh, but also from Europe, North America, Russia, China, Africa, and so on.[12]

An Archaeological Response from Nabadwip

The early controversy surrounding the location of Chaitanya's birth reached a new level of intensity in 1914, the year in which Bhaktivinoda passed away and Brajamohan das (a retired engineer) proposed a precise Nabadwip birthplace, which he dubbed "old Mayapur" (*pracin* Mayapur)—eventually the site of Gauranga Janmasthan. The discovery was delineated in a July 30th, 1917 letter to the Governor of Bengal, which was signed by forty-three respected members of Nabadwip's most prominent *brāhmaṇa* community (Majumdar 1993, pp. 38-41). The letter presented the available evidence for the legitimacy of the Gauranga Janmasthan, and the arguments are summarized herein.

According to eyewitnesses and a number of written reports, the house of Chaitanya's birth had been washed away by the Ganges in approximately 1750, after which a Vaiṣṇava named Dewan Ganga Govinda Singh, who had retired in Nabadwip in 1792, made it his duty to rediscover that home's exact location. As a result of his examination, testimonials, and other forms of relevant evidence he concluded that the exact site was approximately 1.6 kilometres northwest of present-day Nabadwip, on the Ganges' western bank, less than 800 meters northeast of the village Ramchandrapur. Singh then proceeded to erect a temple with nine domes at this location, in which he installed deities of Rādhā and Vallabha (a name of Kṛṣṇa). According to contemporary reports, in the 1820s the temple was destroyed and washed away by the Ganges, but became partially visible for a short period of time in April 1872, when the Ganges took a northern turn. According to the author, this event was personally witnessed by various persons, including Mahamahopadhyaya Ajit Nath Nayratna, a renowned Nabadwip pandit. During the following rainy season, the sandbanks of the Ganges are said to have once again swallowed the temple, this time for good.

In 1916, based on eyewitness testimony, Brajamohan das claimed to have located the exact spot upon which Singh's temple had been built, and there erected a new temple, which he named Gauranga Janmasthan. Brajamohan das' 1917 letter ends by asking the Bengali Government to excavate Singh's old temple and thus unequivocally substantiate the authenticity of the Janmasthan, after which various attempts have been made to initiate such a project. In a six-page report dated April 30th, 1968, P. C. Dasgupta, Director of the Archaeology Department of West Bengal, recommended that an attempt be made to dig in and around the area of the Janmasthan since the issue of Chaitanya's birthplace would remain difficult to resolve without conclusive archaeological evidence (Majumdar 1993, p. 63). Unfortunately, the necessary funds never have been raised, even up to today, despite repeated efforts to solicit help from government officers and potential donors.

Several books have been produced in Nabadwip in an attempt to authenticate the status of Gauranga Janmasthan. One such study draws the following conclusions: The Nabadwip of Chaitanya's time had been a sixteen-mile long peninsula with the Ganges River on its Western shore and the Jalangi River to the south. At around the middle of the 18th century there occurred a significant shift in the course of Ganges that completely destroyed the northwest quadrant of Nabadwip, which consisted of various Hindu localities. At around this same time a shift in the course of the Jalangi River also occurred that similarly devastated the city's northeast quadrant, which largely consisted of Muslim localities. As a result of these natural calamities, Nabadwip's Hindu population migrated to the city's southwest quadrant, where its numbers continued to increase. By the time of the 19th century, the population had become so large that it naturally began spreading to the north once again. Many locals believe that a thorough archaeological exploration of all these regions might very well uncover artefacts that unequivocally establish the true location of Chaitanya's birth (Majumdar 1993, p. 61-62).

Over the last hundred years, Nabadwip's Gauranga Janmasthan theory has received substantial support from figures such as Mahanamabrata Brahmacari, a well-known Vaiṣṇava who had completed a Ph.D. in Vaiṣṇava philosophy at the University of Chicago during the 1930s (Mahanamabrata 1974 [1937]). Moreover, while medieval textual sources such as the *Caitanya Bhāgavata* and the *Caitanya Caritāmṛta* explicitly state that Chaitanya took birth in a place called Nabadwip (or Nadia), they make no mention whatsoever of place called Mayapur (Chaudhuri 2004, s. 106).

An Archaeological Investigation of Mayapur

In 1984 Prof. K. N. Mukherjee published "A Study of Sri Chaitanya's Birthplace" in the University of Calcutta's *Indian Journal of Landscape Systems and Ecological Studies* (Mukherjee 1984). In the article, Mukherjee claims to have surveyed most of the available evidence, including the writings of Chaitanya's contemporaries, cartographical documents, and statistical records as well as archaeological and historical artefacts. Mukherjee's conclusions support Bhaktivinoda's claim that the area of Mayapur contains Chaitanya's factual birthplace. While the scientific examination of documents, texts, and artefacts may be more important in terms of authenticating historical and/or religious sites, we here nonetheless provide a brief summary of Mukherjee's arguments.

Mukherjee first analyzes textual evidence from the *Caitanya-caritāmṛta, Caitanya Bhāgavata*, and *Bhaktiratnākara*—texts written by Vaiṣṇavas accepted by both sides of the dispute—and tentatively concludes that these texts indicate that at the time of Chaitanya's birth the city of Nabadwip had been situated not on the western, but rather on the eastern side of the Ganges (Mukherjee 1984, pp. 39-43). His most compelling evidence, however, is said to have come from archaeological and geological findings, among which was the recovery of an Adhokśaja (Viṣṇu) deity on the site of Mayapur's Yoga-pīṭha (the birthplace of Chaitanya)—a deity carved in black stone much like the one described in various hagiographic texts as having been worshipped in the home of Chaitanya's father, Jagannātha Miśra. This Viṣṇu *mūrti*, measuring approximately twenty centimetres in length, was discovered in 1934 by members of the Gaudiya Math during the construction of the Yoga-pīṭha temple, where it was installed and continues to be worshipped today. According to Mukherjee, since the *mūrti* is extremely rare and apparently more than 500 years old, it is an authentic find and not part of some plot designed to win an argument. The deity's somewhat Mongolian eyes and square jaw is said to indicate that it may have been crafted in the Sylhet district of old Assam, the area from which the Miśra family is said to have originated (Mukherjee 1984, pp. 43–44).

In addition to the discovery of the deity, Mukherjee claims that the cartographical evidence also supports the validity of the Mayapur birth-site. According to him, maps dating back to 1660, drafted by the early Dutch geographer Van den Brouck, indicate that at the time Nabadwip was indeed located on the eastern side of the Ganges and north of the Jalangi river, where Mayapur exists today. This conclusion also appears to be supported by various other maps, including those drafted by Rennel (1780), Gangāgovinda Sinha (approx. 1785), Smythe (1855), and Hunter (1875) as well as both a 1922 and a 1958 Survey of India map that is based upon aerial photographs. This progression of maps enables one to track the gradual shifts of the Ganges, which appear to support the notion that Nabadwip was once located in the area of present-day Mayapur (Mukherjee 1984, pp. 44–51).

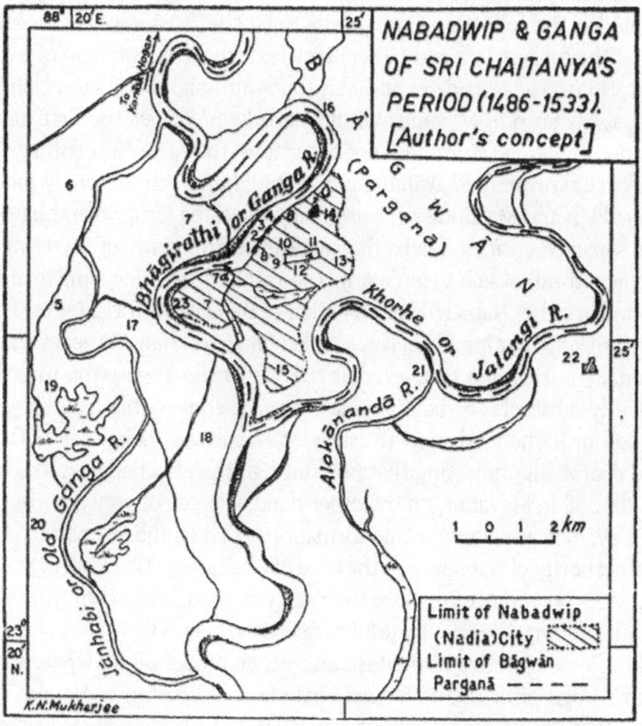

Fig.1. *Nabadwip and the Ganges in the fifteenth and sixteenth century according to Mukherjee (based on a map drafted by Bhaktivinoda)* (Mukherjee 1984, p. 51).

(See map on previous page): 0. Ballal palace ruins (Dhipi) 1. Apan ghāt 2. Mādhāi ghāt 3. Bārakona ghat 4. Nagaria ghāt 5. Janhunagar 6. Purbasthali 7. Rudrapāra 7a. Char Nidaya (Nidaya ghāt) 8. Ganganagar 9. Nimāi's (Chaitanya's, ed.) house (present Yoga-pith) 10. Śrivāsa's house (Angan) 11. Maternal aunt's house (present Śrī Chaitanya Maṭha) 12. Ballāl Dighi 13. Mollāpara 14. Simulia (present Bāmunpukur) 15. Gādigāchha 16. Belpukur 17. Bāblāri 18. Kulia 19. Bidyānagar 20. Samudragarh 21. Subarnabihar 22. Krishnanagar 23. Present location of Ramchandrapur.

For purposes of his analysis, Mukherjee recovered and employed the original map drawn by Bhaktivinoda in 1894, but with slight modifications based upon the 1922 Survey of India map (figure 1, previous page), drawn directly from aerial photographs.

In his article, Mukherjee discusses a total of eleven arguments for his thesis, among which the following four appear to be the most solid: 1) Mukherjee notes that the earliest 15th- and 16th-century texts make no mention of two separate locations—i.e., Nabadwip and Mayapur—although both sides claim that Chaitanya was born in Mayapur within Nabadwip *dhāma*. The first mention of Mayapur in the literature does not occur until the early 18th century, found in Narahari Cakravartī's *Bhaktiratnākara*. To Mukherjee, this strongly indicates that Nabadwip and Mayapur were originally the same location and have only become separate entities due to the eastward movements of the Ganges. 2) The recovered Adhokśaja Viṣṇu *mūrti* is so rare that nothing similar to it has been found in either Nabadwip or any other of Bengal's historical sites. Thus, it is highly unlikely that it had been concealed for more than 400 years and then intentionally buried and recovered at the site of the Yoga-pīṭha in order to fraudulently substantiate Bhaktivinoda's claim, as some critics have suggested. 3) The soil in Ramchandrapur (Northwest Nabadwip) is layered with both fine and coarse silt, indicating that not long ago the area had been the bed of a river; the soil in Mayapur, on the other hand, is made of very compact deep humus clay, indicating an old land formation. 4) The tomb of Chand Kazi, the juridical authority of Nabadwip at the time of Chaitanya, still exists in Mayapur today; a large champak tree, more than 400 years old, has grown through the tomb, thus proving its antiquity (Mukherjee 1984, s. 52–53).

Mukherjee concludes that these and other pieces of evidence point to Mayapur's Yoga-pīṭha as the factual birthplace of Chaitanya. He also notes, however, that the whole of ancient Nabadwip (which includes Mayapur and the Gauranga Janmasthan) must be regarded as sacred space, indicating that there is no real reason for the dispute. According to Mukherjee, Ramchandrapur was located at the far west side of the old city before the shifting river created the divide between Nabadwip and Mayapur (Mukherjee 1984, s. 53–54). While Mukherjee's work requires further corroboration by other independent studies, it nonetheless remains one of the most comprehensive landscape studies produced thus far.

The Dispute of Bhaktivinoda

During the 18th and much of the 19th century mainstream Chaitanyaite Vaiṣṇavism fell into a period of instability and disrepute.[13] Among the factors that contributed to this outcome was the social and political unrest caused by the waning influence of Muslim governance and the establishment of British rule. Beyond this, the patronage that Vaiṣṇavism had enjoyed for centuries among the wealthy Bengali peasantry had been gradually weakened by the more demanding system of land taxation that the British had gradually imposed (Chakravarti 1985, p. 387). At around this time, a form of Chaitanyaite Vaiṣṇavism known as *sahajiyā*, which performed obscure erotic rituals based upon the physical reenactment of Kṛṣṇa's dance (*rāsa-līlā*), had risen to prominence.[14] This "licentious" approach to spirituality came to offend many among a newly created and highly educated indigenous middle-class known as the *bhadralok* (literally "gentle people"), which, on the basis of this particular group's actions, came to regard the entire Chaitanya tradition as sentimental, morally weak, and mostly the religion of the ignorant and illiterate (Sardella and Ghosh 2013, pp. 225-228).

At some point during the latter part of the 19th century, however, Chaitanyaite Vaiṣṇavism gradually came to strike a more positive chord of interest among the *bhadralok*. In 1851, the *Calcutta Review* noted that the Vaiṣṇavas were "the most active of the Hindu sects in Bengal." The Brahmo Samaj also arranged for publication of literature on *kṛṣṇa-bhakti*, and thus is largely responsible for having introduced Vaiṣṇavism to the *bhadralok* on respectable grounds particularly in the early 20th century (Kennedy 1993 [1925], p. 76ff).

Kedarnath Datta Bhaktivinoda came to adulthood amidst this atmosphere of religious and cultural change. Born in 1838 to a non-*brahmaṇa* family of the *śakta* tradition, he received his education in Indian and Western philosophy and went on to become a second-grade Deputy Magistrate in the British administration. At a mature age, he embraced the teachings of Chaitanya and founded a Vaiṣṇava reform movement comprised of both *bhadralok* and villagers from the colonial periphery. One of Bhaktivinoda's aims in founding his institution was to free Chaitanya Vaiṣṇavism from caste boundaries,[15] making religious affiliation and practice dependent on individual merit rather than hereditary privilege. The attempt to deemphasise hereditary privilege was a prominent feature of modern Hindu movements during that period, and it has been observed in other contexts as well.

Bhaktivinoda, however, had an even more fundamental objective—one that ran contrary to the general aims of Hindu modernity. His approach was to reshape the Chaitanya tradition's philosophy on the basis of its original Bengali and Sanskrit texts rather than on the basis of Enlightenment ideas introduced in Bengal by the Europeans—an approach that became more apparent as he grew older.[16] At the same time, he often highlighted traditional elements that he found compatible with Western rationalism and contemporary sociological and philosophical ideas, while also pointing out obvious differences between India and Europe (see for example Bhaktivinoda 1880). In order to stimulate a dialogue between East and West, Bhaktivinoda produced English-language works based on a number of Vaiṣṇava texts. In 1896, for example, he produced a small English pamphlet entitled *Shri Chaitanya: His Life and Precepts* and sent it to prominent Western universities such as McGill (in Canada) and Oxford, seeing this as a first step in introducing Bengali Vaiṣṇavism to educated Westerners (Dutt 1896). It was a revolutionary step at a time when Chaitanyaite Vaiṣṇavas most often lacked vision relative to communicating their religious ideas and practices beyond their regional borders.

This brief introduction leads to a defining chapter in Bhaktivinoda's life: the attempt to solve the centuries-old mystery pertaining to the birthplace of Chaitanya. From a sociological prospective, the controversy that ultimately emerged was not only about sacred space, but also about two further defining issues: 1) challenging the exclusive ritual rights of Nabadwip's Goswami class; and, 2) creating an alternate religious centre for a new cosmopolitan middle-class constituency (Fuller 2004).

In 1894, Bhaktivinoda founded the *Navadvīpadhāma Pracāriṇī Sabhā* (Committee for the Publicity of the Sacred Site of Nabadwip), which promoted Mayapur as Chaitanya's factual birthplace—something that he had also apparently envisioned during a mystical experience.[17] As noted above, this was a period in which Bhaktivinoda attempted to confirm his view by various historical, textual, and archaeological means. To that end, he published the *Śrī Navadvīpa Dhāma Mahātmya* (1890) as well as Prabodhānanda Sarasvatī's *Navadvīpa śataka* (n.d.), and also gained the support of important Nadia landowners such as Nafarchandra Pal Chauduri (1838-1933) and the prestigious royal family of Tripura. At the suggestion of another supporter, Sisir Kumar Ghosh (1840–1911), Bhaktivinoda decided to make his theories public, and thus arranged a gathering at which he presented the evidence for his claim —a gathering that was both well-attended and well-received. Thus, with the support of members of the middle and upper class, Chaitanya's Mayapur birthplace gradually grew as an alternative pilgrimage site.[18]

Despite this promising beginning, Bhaktivinoda's project was firmly opposed by prominent *bhadralok* such as Akshay Chandra Sarkar, who worked for a Hindu revival and edited publications such as the journals *Sadharani* and *Nabajiban* (Bhatia 2017, p. 187). Another opponent was Kantichandra Rarhi, who argued against Bhaktivinoda on the basis of historical-empirical evidence.[19] Undeterred, Bhaktivinoda went on to establish the Mayapur birthplace temple already mentioned above—i.e., the Yoga-pīṭha.

Bhaktivinoda lived at a time when matters of sacred geography were often politically charged. Tony Stewart and Rebecca Manring have already demonstrated this in connection with the case of Sylhet, which 19th century scholar Acyutacarana Chaudhuri considered to be linked to Chaitanya's parents (Stewart and Manring 1996-97, pp. 118ff). As with Acyutacarana, Bhaktivinoda's claims regarding Mayapur's importance were based not only on archaeological evidence, but also on publications and texts that extolled both sacred sites.[20] Bhaktivinoda composed several works in praise of Nabadwip and Mayapur, and also published lost texts such as the above mentioned *Navadvīpa-śataka*.[21]

To an outsider, Bhaktivinoda's interest in the site across the river from Nabadwip seems to be more than purely archaeological; if true, it is certainly convenient, as it allowed him and his disciplic descendants to develop a new community, with a "new" ritual practice, in a place that was somewhat aloof from the old headquarters of the movement at that time, but that still had a claim to the authority of the sacred site. Like Acyutacarana's works regarding Sylhet, Bhaktivinoda's works on the sacred geography of Mayapur clearly enabled him to make that sacred claim. His proposal also indirectly served another purpose: it redefined the Nabadwip area in terms of a new sacred geography, with Mayapur at the center—an outcome that has sustained the creation of a new religious identity for his Chaitanyaite movement that was separate and distinct from the city of Nabadwip, a town with hundreds of years of memories.

Riverside Relations

Bhaktivinoda attempted via various forms of proof to establish Mayapur as the actual location of Chaitanya's birth, and today, regardless of which of the two sites are factual, one thing cannot be denied. Due to ISKCON presence throughout the world, thousands of Indian and non-India Chaitanyaite Vaiṣṇava adherents, from nearly every corner of the globe, have made Ma-yapur their permanent home and Mayapur's national and international reputation as the preeminent centre of the tradition continues to grow, as does its number of residences, businesses, shops, restaurants, schools, and so forth—something that has caused a veritable economic and real estate boom in the Mayapur area, bringing in large sums of both domestic and foreign capital. Undoubtedly, all this development has benefitted not only Mayapur, but Nabadwip as well. Today, largely due to Mayapur's growing international status, both Mayapur and Nabadwip are visited by millions of adherents, pilgrims, and tourists each year.[22] How has all this development influenced the relations between these two rivalling riverside communities?

It appears that a largely silent competition continues to underlie the interactions between Nabadwip and Mayapur, one reason being that Mayapur attracts a far larger number of pilgrims. Differences in doctrine, tradition, and culture also contribute to the divide between the two communities. On various occasions both Bhaktivinoda and Bhaktisiddhānta spoke critically about the Vaiṣṇava communities of Nabadwip and their delimiting caste-conscious approach, and Bhaktivedanta, the founder of ISKCON, expressed such views in his writings as well (see Bhaktivedanta 1975, *Ādi līlā*, 7.48, purport). The Goswamis of Nabadwip, on the other hand, have been critical of what they perceive to be the ritual liberalism of the Mayapur community, which they regard as having deviated from true *brāhmaṇism,* especially because the performances of all types of deity worship and temple ritual are conducted by non-Indic, non-hereditary *brāhmaṇas.*

Moreover, the Nabadwip movement has been challenged not only by Mayapur institutions, but also by political parties that have criticized the *varṇa* and *jāti* system and undermined the authority and religious culture of Nabadwip as a centre of learning and education. On the positive side, one can mention the Gaudiya Math's well-appreciated presence in both Mayapur and Nabadwip as well as the fact that ISKCON members have provided financial assistance for the restoration and repair of important temples in Nabadwip. Beyond this, ISKCON helps to organize Nabadwip's annual pilgrimage tour, during which its members can be seen taking *darśana* of various temple deities, and individuals from the Nabadwip community occasionally visit Mayapur as well. Despite this, tensions between the two sides continue to exist and reciprocal invitations remain rare.

To summarize, in Nabadwip there is a well-established community that draws authority from initiation and strong affiliation to local Hindu families as well as heredity customs that have sustained both the Chaitanya tradition and Nabadwip's birth-site claims for many centuries. This scenario fits well with a traditional model in which authority is transmitted through family lines that have been well-established and enshrined in exclusive priestly forms of access to sanctity and the sacred. On the other hand, Nabadwip's Gauranga Janmasthan community is not caste-dependent, but rather consists of highly respected, completely celebate mendicants and ascetics that reside, along with their celibate students, in living quarters attached to the temple.

In contrast, the Mayapur community adopts a different approach to authority, which is established through charismatic relations of service to a religious community in a way that entirely transcends caste affiliations. The latter approach is distinctly "modern" in regard to community welfare and ritual (with both ascetics and householders), and employs, particularly in ISKCON's case, contemporary administrative and economic tools such as increased institutional employment, commerce, and large financial investments for the building of religious structures. This approach is clearly influenced by Bhaktivinoda's *bhadralok* background along with *bhakti*, theology and mysticism.[23]

Indeed, this paper has shown how two parallel traditions of authority born of the same historical context have grown side-by-side within the same contained geographical space to form two religious communities with distinct features that in meaningful ways add to the complexity and variety found among contemporary Hindu movements.

Endnotes

1. This article is adapted from a chapter published by the author in India with the title "Bhakti and Sacred Sites: The Caitanya Birthplace Controversy" (2023), in Shakuntala Gawde and Ferdinando Sardella (eds.), *Bhakti in Vaishnava Tradition: Exploring Devotional Landscape* (New Delhi: Dev Publishers), 175-198.

2. Kṛṣṇa Caitanya is also known as Śrī Caitanya, Caitanya Mahāprabhu and Gaurāṅga; henceforth, he will simply be referred to as Chaitanya.

3. Govt. of India for Census 2011, https://www.census2011.co.in/census/city/206-nabadwip.html (accessed on January 25, 2023).

4. I wish to thank the following persons who have been among those who have shared their time and knowledge during my field work in Nabadwip and Mayapur in 2002, 2010, 2012, 2015 , 2021 and 2023: Abhirama Gopal Dāsa (Samaj Bari, Nabadwip), Advaita Dāsa (Gauranga Janmasthan, Nabadwip), Bodhayan Swami (Gopinath Gauḍīya Math, Mayapur), Jayapataka Swami (ISKCON, Mayapur), Jaya Rādhā Kṛṣṇa Dāsa (Mayapur Dham Sevak Program, ISKCON, Mayapur), the board of directors of the Mahaprabhu Bari (Nabadwip), Purnānanda das (Samaj Bari, Nabadwip), Rupa Gosvāmī (Mahaprabhu Bari, Nabadwip), Sudin Goswami (Śrī Gouranga Mahāprabhu mandir, Nabadwip).

5. The names of the temples and the persons in these examples are presented in Anglicized spelling.

6. A *mūrti* is an image made of materials such as wood, metal and stone, but it can also be created in the mind. It represents a particular deity and is ritually worshipped as non-different from it.

7. The Advaita *baṁśa* has an important *brāhmaṇa* community in the city of Santipur, located about 28 km South from Nabadwip.

8. The term *maṭha* (Math in English) refers to a monastery with attached *āśrama* for *brahmacārīs* and *saṁnyāsīs*, but also can refer to a temple, as in this case.

9. This and many others topics about Nabadwip and Mayapur were discussed in the daily periodical *Nadīya Prakāśa*, published daily in Mayapur by the Gaudiya Math from the 1930s.

10. In this article only Gaudiya Maths in Mayapur and Nabadwip are considered, since they are most relevant to this topic. They are treated as one unit since they belong to the same institutional family tree.

11. See http://tovp.org, accessed on June 10, 2023.

12. About ISKCON in Mayapur see for example Fahy 2020.

13. Varuni Bhatia deals extensively with the Mayapur controversy and Bhaktivinoda (2017, pp. 161-199). Her analysis complements an earlier one made by Jason Fuller (2004, pp. 241-270), who stresses the ability of the *bhadralok* that favored Bhaktivinoda's position to employ modern fund-raising, organisational and historical-critical methods to establish their point of view. Bhatia, on the other hand, focuses on the role of Bhaktivinoda's mystical experiences as a key legitimising factor in the still ongoing conflict (pp. 188-199). About Bhaktivinoda's theology, see also Shukavak Dasa 1999, p. 105ff.

14. About the *sahajiyā* see also Das (1997, pp. 23-38), and Dimock (1989). About the polemics of *sahajiyā* within Vaiṣṇavism in Bengal during the colonial period see Wong (2020).

15. Here it is important to note that while Bhaktivinoda worked to free Chaitanya Vaiṣṇavism from caste boundaries, he still considered the division of society into four classes (*varṇas*) to be natural and of great social value.

16. Here it must be said that while Bhaktivinoda did not rely upon Enlightenment ideas in his reshaping of the Chaitanya tradition's philosophy, he was well aware of those ideas, and even wrote works analyzing them.

17. *Sajjanatoṣaṇī* 5, no. 11, 1894, pp. 201-207; Sardella 2013: 67-68.

18. A ceremony at that time inaugurated a public sacred site (Bhatia 2017, p. 167). There was earlier also an important large meeting at A. B. School in Krishnanagar for scholarly establishing Mayapur as the birthplace of Chaitanya.

19. Rarhi published in 1884 the *Navadvīpa Mahimā* (The Glories of Nabadwip) (2004).

20. The Bhaktivinoda also relied upon his own spiritual experiences to justify the selection of Mayapur as the location for the development of a Gaudiya Vaiṣṇava community (Bhatia 2017, p.166). Bhaktivinoda quoted an historical verse from the early 18th century *Bhakti-ratnākara* by Narahari Cakravarti translated as: "In the land of Nabadwip there is a place called Mayapur, where Bhagavān Gauracandra was born" (*Sajjanatoṣaṇī* vol. 5 no. 11, p. 221, 1894; Shukavak 1999, p.105). He further elaborates this as a vision in the original work entitled *Śrī Navadvīpa Dhāma Mahātmya*, which greatly praises the area of Mayapur Dhama. A recent English translation of this work describes Mayapur as follows: "Within Antardvīpa is Māyāpura [Mayapur], where Lord Chaitanya [*prabhu chaitanya ṭhākura*] appeared. Devotees know Mahāvana in Goloka to be Māyāpura in Navadvīpa [Nabadwip]" (Bhaktivinoda [1890] 2015, p. 67). This was written at a time when numerous texts praising holy sites were being produced in Bengal.

21. Jan Brzezinski has questioned the authenticity of this text, writing that the *Navadvīpa-śataka* "appears to be a pastiche of Prabodhānanda's style, written to vaunt the glories of Chaitanya's birthplace" (Brzezinski 1992: 54); this charge, however, seems to run counter to one of Bhaktivinoda's primary theological aims, which was to distinguish authentic from inauthentic Vaiṣṇava authors of Sanskrit and Bengali works. Bhaktisiddhānta also noted that he was concerned about the authentic authorship of Vaiṣṇava texts (Sardella 2014, p. 194 and fn 20, p. 202).

22. Morinis (1983) and Nakatani (2003).

23. About Bhaktivinoda's thought in Bengali Vaiṣṇavism and colonial modernity, see for example Wong 2021.

Bibliography

Primary sources

Bhaktisiddhānta, Sarasvatī. 1922. Varṇāśrama. *Gauḍīya* 1, no. 10, pp. 1-2.

———. 2000. *Brahmaṇa o vaiṣṇava (tāratamya-viṣayaka siddhānta)*. Māyāpura: Śrī Chaitanya Maṭh.

Bhaktivedanta, A. C. Swami Prabhupāda. 1975. *Śrī Chaitanya-Caritāmṛta: Ādi līlā*. Los Angeles: Bhaktivedanta Book Trust.

Bhaktivinoda, Kedaranatha Datta. *Sajjanatoṣaṇī*. 1881-1904.
———. 1880. Śrī Kṛṣṇa Saṁhitā. Calcutta: Īśvara-candra Vasu Company.
———. [1890] 2015. *Śrī Navadvīpa-dhāma-māhātmya and Śrī Navadvīpa-bhāva-taraṅga*. Nabadwip: Sri Chitanya Saraswat Math.
Nadīya Prakāśa, daily periodical, Mayapur, West Bengal.

Secondary sources

Bhatia, Varuni. 2017. *Unforgetting Chaitanya: Vaishnavism and Cultures of Devotion in Colonial Bengal*. New York: Oxford University Press.
Brzezinski, J. K. 1992. Prabodhānanda Sarasvatī: From Benares to Braj. *Bulletin of the School of Oriental and African Studies* 55, no. 1, pp. 52-75.
Chakravarti, Ramakanta. 1985. *Vaisnavism in Bengal, 1486-1900*. Calcutta: Sanskrit Pustak Bhandar.
Chaudhuri, Jajneswar. 2004. *Śrī Caitanyadeva o samakālīna navadvīpa*. Nabadwip: Nabadwip Purattatva Parisad.
———. 2016. *Navadvīpa vidyasamājera itihāsa*. Nabadwip: Nabadwip Purattatva Parisad.
Das, Rahul Peter. 1997. *Essays on Vaisnavism in Bengal*. Calcutta: Firma KLM.
Dimock, Edward C. 1989. *The Place of the Hidden Moon: Erotic Mysticism in the Vaisnava-Sahajiya Cult of Bengal*. Chicago: University of Chicago Press.
Dutt, Kedar Nath. 1896. *Srigouranga Smaranamangala or Chaitanya Mahaprabhu: His Life and Precepts*. Calcutta: K. Dutt.
Fahy, John. 2020. *Becoming Vaishnava in an Ideal Vedic City*. Oxford: Berghahn Books.
Fuller, Jason D. 2004. Religion, Class, and Power: Bhaktivinoda Thakur and the Transformation of Religious Authority among the Gauḍīya Vaiṣṇavas in Nineteenth-Century Bengal. Ph.D., University of PA.
Gawde, Shakuntala, Sumanta Rudra and Ferdinando Sardella (eds.). 2023. *Bhakti in India*. New Delhi: Dev. (Needs to be changed later)
Kennedy, Melville T. 1993 [1925]. *The Chaitanya Movement: A Study of Vaishnavism in Bengal*. New Delhi: Munshiram Manoharlal Publishers.
Madsen, Finn. 2001. Social Udvikling i Hare Krishnabevægelsen. Ph.D., University of Copenhagen.
Mahanamabrata, Brahmachari. 1974 [1937]. *Vaiṣṇava Vedānta*. Calcutta: Das Gupta & Co.
Majumdar, Shukumar. 1993. *Mayacchanna Māyāpura*. Nabadwip: Gauranga Mahaprabhu Janmasthan Trust.

Mondal, Mrityunjoy. 2010. *Navadvipera prācina itihasa*. Nabadwip: Nabadwip Sahitya Samsad.

Morinis, E. Alan 1984. *Pilgrimage in the Hindu Tradition: A Case Study of West Bengal*. Delhi: Oxford University Press.

Mukherjee, K. N. A. 1984. A Study for Sri Chaitanya's Birthplace. *Indian Journal of Landscape Systems and Ecological Studies. University of Calcutta* 7, no. 2.

Nakatani, Tetsuya 2003. A Sacred Place or Tourist Spot? Rediscovery of Sri Caitanya's Birth Place and the Development of Mayapur as a Mass Attraction Site. *Journal of the Japanese Association of South Asian Studies*. Vol. 15, pp. 113-141.

Rarhi, Kantichandra, ed. Jajneswar Chaudhuri. 2004 [1884]. *Navadvipā Mahimā*. Nabadwip: Navadwip Purutattva Parishad.

Roy, Sulekha. 2008. *Madhyayugīya vidyācarcā kendra navadvīpa* (1200-1800). Nabadwip: Pusthaka Bipani.

Sarbadhikary, Sukanya. 2015. *The Place of Devotion: Siting and Experiencing Divinity in Bengal-Vaishnavism*. Oakland, CA: University of California Press.

Sardella, Ferdinando. 2013. *Modern Hindu Personalism: The History, Life and Thought of Bhaktisiddhanta Sarasvati*. New York: Oxford University Press.

Sardella, Ferdinando, and Abhishek Ghosh. 2013. Text Migration: The Translation and Modern Reception of the *Bhāgavata Purāna*. In Ravi Gupta and Kenneth Valpey (eds.) *The Bhāgavata Purāṇa: Sacred Text and Living Tradition*. New York: Columbia University Press.

Sardella, Ferdinando. 2014. Colonial Bengal and Bhaktivinoda Through the Lens of Bhaktisiddhānta. In *Journal of Vaishnava Studies*, no. 23.1, pp. 189-204.

———. 2020. Bengali Vaishnavism in Court: the Gaudiya Math's Crises of Succession. In *Journal of Hindu Studies*, vol. 13, issue 1, May, pp. 71-88.

Shakuntala Gawde and Sumanta Rudra (eds.). 2023. *Bhakti in Vaishnava Tradition: Exploring Devotional Landscape* (New Delhi: Dev Publishers).

Shukavak Dasa. 1999. *Hindu Encounter with Modernity: Kedarnath Datta Bhaktivinoda, Vaiṣṇava Theologian*. Los Angeles: SRI.

Sraman, Bhaktikusum. 1968. *Prabhupāda Srila Sarasvati Thākura*. Mayapur: Sri Chaitanya Math.

Stewart, Tony, and Rebecca Manring. 1996-97. "In the Name of Devotion: Acyutacarana Chauduri and the Hagiographies of Advaitacarya." *Journal of Vaishnava Studies*, no. 5.1, pp. 103-126.

Wong, Lucian. 2020. Colonial morals, Vaiṣṇava quarrels: tracing the sources of nineteenth-century anti-Sahajiyā polemics. In Ferdinando Sardella and Lucian Wong. 2020. *The Legacy of Vaiṣṇavism in Colonial Bengal.* Abingdon, Oxon; New York: Routledge.

———. 2021. Devotional Rupture: Bengali Vaiṣṇavism and Colonial Modernity. Ph.D. diss., University of Oxford.

Yati, Mahārāja. 1998. *Ontological and Morphological Concepts of Lord Sri Chaitanya and His Mission.* Mayapur: Chaitanya Math.

Dancing in Shackles†
On Translating the *Caitanya Caritāmṛta* of Kṛṣṇadās Kavirāj

Tony K. Stewart © 2023

The Power of Words

Swiss literary phenomenologist Georges Poulet suggests that in the act of reading, you momentarily allow the author to think your thoughts for you.[1] You do not relinquish your critical faculties, but rather assume a kind of neutral position as the author's ideas play out. But translators take that engagement a step further, for they must make those thoughts their own, to appropriate them, before they attempt to express the author's story, the author's perspective, in a different language. That act sometimes feels like a kind of magical reconstruction from the original as the text moves from the host language to the target. The movement inevitably introduces new ideas—your historical situation is different from the original author. And it loses some of the original—the target language cannot possibly reflect all the lexical and cultural nuances of the host. There is no need to go into the various translation theories about this complicated process. Suffice it say that it is not just the text that is transformed, but the translator as well. My experience is that in both technical and literary translation, this will be the case whether the original text is fiction, poetry, or a theologically profound creation. Such was my experience in working with Edward C. Dimock, Jr. to translate the *Caitanya Caritāmṛta* of Kṛṣṇadās Kavirāj (hereafter *CC*), which was the first regional language text (what used to be commonly called vernacular) published in the Harvard Oriental Series, fulfilling a promise Dimock made to Daniel H. H. Ingalls decades earlier.[2]

Our formal collaboration on the translation stretched over a span of seventeen years. But I am getting ahead of myself because the translation itself led and still leads a kind of double life which has a considerably longer history than that collaborative stretch would suggest. For Dimock that life began more than twenty-five years prior to my formal involvement. For me, now some twenty-four years after its publication, the text continues to exert its presence, sometimes as a lingering backdrop to other inquiries into the intellectual and religious life of Bangla speakers. At other times the text asserts itself more actively as I continue to interrogate its insights into some of the most pressing issues to engage any thoughtful human being.

Given the span of our involvement with the text—each of us logged nearly a half century in dealing with it—the story is inescapably both biographical and autobiographical, sometimes uneasily so. As we sometimes discussed, the truths found in that book exerted their hold on Dimock early on and fueled his own private theology serving as a thrumming undercurrent to the poetics of his publications and professional life. The text's effect on me was, I suspect, equally gripping, but in different ways. In my case, its invasive tentacles shaped my analytical propensities, giving me new ways to look at the world, charging my sense of enchantment at its breathtaking insights into theology and history, insights that not-so-subtly continue to shape Bengali religious and literary sensibilities to this day. The author, Kṛṣṇadās Kavirāj, proved perfectly suited to distill the burgeoning corporate theology of Svarūp Dāmodar and the Gosvāmīs into a flexible framework. By Kṛṣṇadās's own report, the authority of that theology was nearly always attributed directly to Kṛṣṇa Caitanya, or, as Kṛṣṇadās's theology more intimately and appropriately had it, flowing from the mouth of Gaurāṅga, whose golden (*gaura*) limbs (*aṅga*) reflected the presence of Rādhā (whose golden color shone through). I have argued that it was Kṛṣṇadās who shaped the Gauḍīya Vaiṣṇav experience into a tradition, condensing, refining, and synthesizing different theological speculations, ordering the social reality of the different communities spread over Bengal, Orissa, and Braj, imparting ritual instruction, and of course centering the celebratory drama, poetry, and songs that drive devotional experience.[3] As I hope I have shown in *The Final Word*, prior to Kṛṣṇadās's intervention, leadership was decentered, theologically and geographically, with different devotional communities articulating their own version of just who Caitanya was, tending to remain more or less independent of one another. It would seem that Kṛṣṇadās indeed had the final word in consolidating these diverse communities, for no new major hagiographies of Caitanya were composed thereafter, and with the work of the Gosvāmī students—Śrīnivās, Narottam Dās, and Śyāmānanda—the circulation of the book seemed to standardize what being a Gauḍīya-style Vaiṣṇav meant.

When I first began to investigate the Vaiṣṇav literature and history, I was told repeatedly by scholars and *mahants* in Bengal that I did not need to look at any of the other sources portraying the life of Caitanya because everything I needed to know was in the *CC*. Contrary to what those well-intentioned scholars and devotees said to me, as the final word, the *CC* does not end the conversation or argument, to close out the tradition, because the book continues to endure, revalorizing itself and revitalizing its readers, refreshing tradition for each successive generation. That ability to continue to speak as a fully authoritative voice for community is what literary critic Frank Kermode called the quintessential marker for any text we call "the classic."[4] And true to form, the *CC's* propositions and speculations on the æsthetics of love, on the nature of life and death, were poignantly borne out in real life as the translation came to fruition in the last decades of the twentieth century. As some may know, Dimock passed away almost exactly one year after the publication of the translation: its birth, and his death, are forever bound together in my intellectual and emotional life. For this reason, what the text means to me is sometimes fraught and, quite frankly, too personal to share, though I suspect any critical reader can divine some of its power over me in what I write. I will endeavor, however, to focus on the events—the how and why the translation took the shape it did—and attempt to place that in context. That narrative is not linear and will inevitably entail digressions, for which I beg your indulgence.

Wrangling with Words

In 1957, when I was all of three years old, Dimock decided to translate the *CC*. He had been reading the text for his intended dissertation on the second major generation of Gauḍīya Vaiṣṇav history. But the adventures of Śrīnivās, Śyāmānanda, and Narottam Dās would have to wait; his intrigue with the erotically charged mysticism of the *sahajiyās* took precedence and that work would become his dissertation. The formulations of the CC were central to that inquiry, but he felt that simply referring to passages in the text would be insufficient for exploring the ritual theology of the *sahajiyās*. He needed to have translated the *CC* to speak with the kind of confidence those propositions required. As he later observed to me—and which I can confirm through my own experience—one learns the inside and out of a text through translation because there is no way to finesse your reading: you must declare what you understand the text to say. As Gadamer made clear, translation is the ultimate hermeneutical exercise.[5] In so doing you must reach a certain comfort level with your understanding of the text, signaling that you feel you have gained a special mastery sufficient to convey much, if not most, of what the author intended. While authorial intention can never be fully determined, in the case of theologically driven narratives like Kṛṣṇadās's, there are enough markers and intertextual references to increase one's confidence. Unlike many of the texts that were generated in early modern Bengal, the *CC* provides ample opportunity to confirm readings because the sample of writing is so large, some 12,400 couplets (*payār*) and triplets (*tripadī*). Learning the content sufficiently well contributes to one's ability to compare usages, to determine authorial tendencies in context, and eventually to discern the internal logic, all the while remaining skeptical of any author's ability to maintain consistency. So, mastery here does not mean laying claim to THE authoritative reading and interpretation, but rather a deep-seated familiarity that is ultimately a personal perspective, no matter how hard one tries to remain neutral. In fact, practitioners have an obligation not to remain neutral, but to read the text through their own devotional lens. Such familiarity is, of course, different from that which Dimock developed and relied upon for most of his academic career—and the effects of the *CC*'s perspectives can be seen in nearly everything he wrote.

As Dimock conducted his dissertation research in Calcutta, he conferred most notably with S.K. De, but also Suniti Kumar Chatterjee and Sukumar Sen, who pointed him to the extraordinary theological summaries of the Gosvāmī theology found in *CC madhya līlā*, chapters 19-24, and the equally dense opening of the *ādi līlā*, chapters 1-8. Dimock told me that when De was resident at the University of Chicago a few years later, they had long discussions about the theological intricacies of those translations. Dimock reveled in the famous exchange between Caitanya and Rāmānanda Rāya in *madhya līlā*, chapter 8, the celebrated passage that concluded with the disclosure of the androgynous or so-called "dual incarnation." The profound image of Rādhā and Kṛṣṇa fused in the person of Caitanya became the linchpin of the theology widely attributed to Svarūp Dāmodar. That culminating passage (*CC* 2.8.220-242) is the theological climax of the book, as I noted in the commentary. It was this theological assertion that proved so critical to *sahajiyā* perspectives.

Secluded in some unnamed private venue, Caitanya queries Rāmānanda Rāy about the nature of devotion (*bhakti*), the highest forms of love (the apex of which was *prema*), and the tasting of the emotions generated in and through that experience (*rasa*). As they move from the obvious to the more esoteric, Caitanya seems never to be satisfied, but always presses Rāmānanda to "go further still." As they near the climax of the colloquy, Rāmānanda's frustration grows to the point of exasperation, as he tries to make sense of his conflicting perceptions of Caitanya. Addressing him in the endearing form of Lord, Prabhu, the six critical couplets read (*CC* 2.8.229-235):[6]

> 229 And Rāya said, "You are Prabhu! Abandon these wiles. Do not hide your own true form before me. 230 You have embraced the beauty and the *bhāva* of Rādhā; to taste your *rasa*, you have descended. 231 Your own profound duty is the tasting of *prema*, and accordingly you spread *prema* in the three worlds. 232 You yourself came to save me, and now you are deceiving me; what does this mean?"
>
> 233 Then, smiling, Prabhu showed to him his true form: *rasarāja* and *mahābhāva*, the two in one *rūpa*. 234 And when he saw this Rāmānanda fainted with joy; he could not control his body, and fell to the earth. 235 Prabhu with a touch of his hand brought him back to consciousness; and seeing him as a *saṃnyāsin*, [Rāya] was in his mind astonished.

The conceit, of course, hinges on the notion that Rādhā has a more profound experience than Kṛṣṇa. No matter how much their love was magnified in its exchange, what was reflected back to her was always superior to his experience because she was beholding God. To resolve this curious phenomenological impasse, Kṛṣṇa chose to descend to earth in the embrace of Rādhā, the two combined in the single form of Caitanya, a novel solution that allowed him to experience what she did, that is, to taste his own *prema*; they were simultaneously conjoined and yet apart. This is, not surprisingly, an embodiment of the Gauḍīya commitment to the *acintya bhedābheda* philosophy: simultaneous difference (*bheda*) and nondifference (*abheda*), which is cognitively unresolvable (*acintya*). A quick unpacking of this crucial passage with Rāmānanda can serve as a succinct illustration of how Dimock approached the translation and how I interacted as his editor.

As becomes obvious, the untranslated terms abound, but they are, of course, all technical terms with complex histories of their own in Gauḍīya Vaiṣṇav theological discourse. To translate any one of those terms would likely over-determine the meaning, restricting its semantic field, because English does not have easy equivalents. As anyone familiar with the Gauḍīya Vaiṣṇav tradition knows, to translate *prema* as "love" or "pure love" or "highest love" or "refined love" or "sublime love" simply does not do it justice. It is a truism in the translation of religious texts from any culture and language that significant technical terms simply cannot be captured with one-word glosses or even phrases because the full range of meanings is lost. So, for the sake of fidelity, these terms are often left untranslated. In widely read texts, their transliteration might eventually be absorbed into the English lexicon (still with changed meanings, such as *karma*/karma or *guru*/guru), or, as in this case, simply learned by the reader, who, with the aid of the commentary and glossary, will, through repetition, come to appreciate the range of signifieds. So, too, for the terms *bhāva* and *rasa* in the above passage. Leaving these terms untranslated, but glossed, satisfies the academic or devotee who knows enough of the language and who does not then have to guess at what technical term lies behind the translation, but the profusion of technical terms can make for dreary reading as literature (a problem of translating nearly all religious texts in general). At some point, one does have to translate enough to make the passage make sense in English; we never accepted the possibility of the untranslatability of the text, tending to modulate the degree of fidelity along a consistent spectrum, and one of my jobs as editor was to consider readability at every turn.

So, for example, in v. 231 in the passage above, Kṛṣṇadās writes "your own profound duty is to taste the *prema*." In that line, "duty" is *kāryya*," whose meanings cover "business, work, undertaking." Question: is "work" the same as "duty"? We decided in this context it fell within the acceptable semantic range, that is, "work with a mission."

What is translated as "accordingly" in the second half of the couplet is *ānuṣaṅge*. *Ānuṣaṅge* literally means "along with, accompanying, incidental, secondary," which would seem to make the spreading of *prema* in some sense a by-product of Caitanya's primary work, whereas our chosen translation implies another possibility, a causal relation of spreading *prema* in the triple world as necessary for Kṛṣṇa to taste his own *prema*. The ambiguity is potentially significant, and Dimock rightly did not want to foreclose alternate readings by declaring that spreading *prema* in the triple world was simply an after-effect, because the work of any *avatāra* is to save the world (in this case through the spreading of love), so it would have to be a *necessary* element of Caitanya's descent, not just a consequence. The translation thus tries to leave open the options as *avatāra* theory is understood within the tradition.

In v. 232 the word "save" is *uddhār*, "to rescue, deliver, uplift, emancipate." The word "save" can hint at a Christian sensibility, which would then imply western notions of sin and salvation. After discussing it, we felt that there were sufficient numbers of references to Caitanya as the "rescuer of the fallen" (*patita pāban*), and comparable phrases, that context would prevail to guide the reader, reducing the risk of misunderstanding.

In the next line, *kapaṭ* is translated as "deceiving," which implies a willful act by Caitanya to hide the truth. But given the tone of Rāmānanda's exasperation, to my mind he conveys much more a sense of frustration at being "toyed with," which considerably changes, or humanizes the tenor of his complaint by making it more intimate. As I proposed to Dimock, it invokes some of the play of God, his *līlā*, which is often beyond human comprehension and, as such, can be baffling. The range of meanings for *kapaṭ* include "chicanery, deceitfulness, hypocrisy, feigning, insincerity, dissimulation," and given Caitanya's smile in the next verse, the sense of playfulness seems to be indicated. While I argued for the playful reading, Dimock felt the seriousness of the ensuing revelation, and the asymmetry of the relationship of Rāmānanda to Caitanya, made a stronger case for Caitanya deliberately covering over the nature of his divinity and then revealing it. It should be noted that covering and uncovering are common expressions in this text and its predecessors for the rupture of divinity into the world.

The critical statement is, of course, v. 233, where Prabhu shows Rāmānanda his true form as *rasarāja* and *mahābhāva*, theological terms understood to signify Kṛṣṇa and Rādhā respectively. There is no need to unpack those terms here, except to say she, as *mahābhāva*, is the total embodiment of supreme love and he is the king or master (*rāja*) of receiving and savoring that love (*rasa*). The word for "showed" in this couplet is *dekhāilā*, the causative of "to see" in the past tense. Originally, Dimock had translated it as "revealed," which suggests that Caitanya's inherent ontology as Rādhā and Kṛṣṇa is fused into a single form, the two instantiated "in one *rūpa*" (*ekarūp*). That reading is made plausible by how he construes the term *svarūp*, which, even though highly technical, is not left in transliteration, but translated here as "true form," that phrase emphasizing ontology. But *svarūp* can also be read in this and other contexts as "essential nature" or just "nature." If we read *dekhāilā* as "made him to see" or "made him see" Caitanya's "nature"—that is, with the emotional life of Rādhā and the physical form of Kṛṣṇa—it leaves open the question of the ontological reality which is implied if *dekhāilā* is construed as a revelation. Is that vision something Rāmānanda perceives, or, in his devotional fervor, thinks he perceives? Or does he recognize that

Caitanya was living the emotional life of a woman in a man's body? (Given our current discourse on gender issues, I will leave aside whether that might be construed as ontological.) Kṛṣṇadās's expression is somewhat ambiguous, especially since this was a unique event experienced by a single devotee who was already convinced of Caitanya's divinity. That vision occurs nowhere else in the biographical tradition dedicated to Caitanya (some 100,000 lines of text in Bangla and Sanskrit); no one else witnesses such an event. Now, when you look back at the translation, I hope you can see that the choice of "showed" does not foreclose either reading, allowing us to capture both possibilities of "revealed" and "made him to see," or given the common extensions of the verb "to see" in Bangla and in English, "made him realize or understand." The devotees to whom I have spoken about this have a strong preference for the ontological reading, but Kṛṣṇadās, whom I found to be extremely careful in his expression, writes in a manner that allows the reader to decide, and I feel our solution captures that.

For one final observation about the passage, I want to examine when, in v. 235, Rāmānanda is brought back to consciousness after fainting, he sees Caitanya in the form of a *saṃnyāsin*. The choice to render the Bangla word *sannyāsī* as the Sanskrit *saṃnyāsin* is, I think, a vestige of Dimock's training, which was understandably conditioned by his generation's fading Orientalist legacy. As he put it to me, the Sanskrit form was common and would be more easily recognized by a wider audience. Perhaps because I was the product of the new area studies model that emphasized the regional languages, I began to wonder just how much that intervention changed the text—and I note that Kṛṣṇadās most decidedly did not use the Sanskrit term.[7] How much might that seemingly minor shift have changed the reader's perception? I have subsequently been convinced that the semantic field of the classical Sanskrit term does not map perfectly onto the more recent Bangla term, and even less in the case of Caitanya, whose asceticism was distinct. Unlike in the classical model, he took up permanent residence in Nīlācal or Puri to be near Jagannāth, ostensibly at the behest of his mother who did not want him to be far away. He was surrounded by his devotees with whom he sang and danced and shared Jagannāth's *prasād*, participated in glorious feasts, the elaborate culinary preparation for which Kṛṣṇadās waxes eloquent, and so forth. That simple shift elides the divergence of Caitanya's experience from the standard, idealized ascetic forms described in the various Sanskrit *śāstras*. It may seem incidental for some, especially those who wish to see the depiction of Caitanya and the Gauḍīya Vaiṣṇavs in a more stereotyped classical form, but the difference is potentially significant. In this case, that question is not trivial. My additional reading in the unpublished manuscripts from this and the subsequent period makes clear that trying to fathom the seemingly contradictory nature of Caitanya's renunciation generated some very serious concern and speculation,[8] and in talks with devotees today still does. I did not object then to Dimock's choice of *saṃnyāsin* as I would now, but it had a lingering effect and alerted me to a problem that has plagued nearly all translators of religious texts in Indic regional languages.[9]

Fortunately, not every passage required this kind of close interrogation; had it done so we would likely still be translating. But for those who wonder how we adjudicated such disagreements—and most were of this kind of subtle distinction—when we seemed to reach an impasse, I always reminded Dimock that the translation was ultimately his, so I followed Kṛṣṇadās's lead where he writes in *CC* 2.10.167, "In debate between *guru* and disciple, it is true that the disciple is [always] defeated." Dimock always encouraged me to make my case, but in the end, when we could not resolve our differences, I deferred.

Recovering Lost Words

Because almost none of Dimock's initial hand-written and typescript pages were dated, it was impossible later to reconstruct the precise order of those first translated chapters. I can, however, confirm that many of the pages in that set bore the distinctive smudge marks of an old portable Smith Corona electric typewriter he kept in his study on the third floor of his home on South Dorchester in Chicago's Hyde Park where I spent a summer house-sitting and rummaging through the books in his study. A few passages seemed to have been typed on an IBM Selectric typewriter by one of the secretaries (as office administrators were often called) in the Department of South Asian Languages and Civilizations in Foster Hall at the university, while some were typed manually or hand-written during his sojourns on Cape Cod, where he spent summers. In every case the diacritics were inserted by Dimock's own hand in ink. These chapters were usually on legal size paper with handwritten annotations, and in some cases, there were complete rewritings of passages in the margins and on the back of the typescript; when there wasn't sufficient room, emendations would be finished on a scrap of paper taped or stapled to the page. It was the way things were done back then, a manual cut and paste. The order in which this key selection of chapters appeared is ultimately inconsequential, for as a set, they were the first translations that occupied Dimock in the last few years of the 1950s and first five or so years of the 1960s, especially 1961 when he was resident in Calcutta as part of the newly formed American Institute of Indian Studies.

Years later, when I held two different versions of the same chapter, I attempted to discern the latest version using a range of forensic techniques, for example, a question mark in one typescript that led to a change in the other, and so forth. At some indeterminate point, that is, indeterminate from my perspective, since we never had reason to discuss a timeline, J.A.B. van Buitenen, who had been at Chicago from 1957 onwards, agreed to edit or even retranslate the approximately 1500 Sanskrit *ślokas* that are laced through the thousands of Bangla couplets of the text. Van Buitenen's incredibly distinctive hand-written emendations, at times nearly indecipherable, can be found throughout the typescripts that were produced in the sixties. When we were preparing the final manuscript, I was instructed not to alter those unless I had deep concerns, at which point I was to bring them to Dimock's attention. We did, in fact, together revise some small number, but basically those revisions were left as van Buitenen made them. I felt his diction was often as different from Dimock's as the Sanskrit was from the Bangla, so it may well have better captured the bilingual nature of the text. For the next few years, Dimock made draft translations of a haphazard selection of narrative passages, not always in order.

A year after the publication of *Place of the Hidden Moon*,[10] the rewrite of his dissertation, it was clear that his little volume of Vaiṣṇav *padāvalī* translations with Denise Levertov, and which appeared as *In Praise of Krishna: Songs from the Bengali*,[11] similarly hinged on his work with the *CC* for both the introduction and interpretation of the songs. That little volume proved to be especially formative for my own approach to translating, no doubt influencing Dimock's evaluation of my ability to handle the text. Mid-way through my course work at Chicago in 1979-80, I tracked down each source and checked the translations against the original, reading most of them with Dimock. How he and Levertov handled a number of knotty expressions opened my eyes to techniques I had not previously considered and introduced me to what I have come to recognize as the art of translation. It was a kind of prelude to direct involvement with his translation of the *CC*.

For the second half of the decade of the sixties, Dimock began to translate the *CC*'s missing narrative chapters, many of which, when I received them much later, I found were unrevised drafts. There was a flurry of activity in the early 1970s to try and round out the whole. By 1973 he had in hand a more or less complete draft translation of the text, or at least he was convinced he did. But the chapters were scattered between his office, his home study, his home in Centerville on Cape Cod, and embedded in notes for the classes he developed for Bengali cultural and literary history, in which they played a central role. When I assembled them later there were several missing sections and even a couple of whole chapters that had gone astray, which fell to me to remedy. By 1973 he had been working on the translation for no fewer than sixteen years. Then came the first major interruption. For the next thirteen years (1973-1986) Dimock served as President of the American Institute of Indian Studies, which drastically curtailed any work on the *CC*. The lone exception was our private reading classes. For nearly all that time the translation sat idle.

Initiating Words

So how did I come to be involved? I first met Dimock in the spring of 1974 when he and A.K. Ramanujan visited my undergraduate institution, Western Kentucky University, to give a series of talks to Asian Studies faculty and a few select students. I had just begun to study Indian religions and my teacher, Donald R. Tuck, had worked extensively on Bengal religious literature, with a special interest in Tagore. It was during Dimock's visit that I made the decision to go to Chicago to study with him. What spurred me was undoubtedly complicated but crystallized during his moving recitation of Jibanānanda Dāś's poem "Banalatā Sen," a translation that had been invigorated by Clinton B. Seely's work on the author.[12] It was during that talk that I decided to change my course from accounting and business to study Bengali and Indic religions. I petitioned the university to study the Bangla language on my own through an Honors self-study program, since Bangla was not offered in the curriculum.[13] Seely graciously served as my remote mentor and tested me when I visited Chicago before enrolling. So two years later, in 1976, when I finally matriculated at Chicago as a master's student, I understandably favored text over speech because of the nature of my self-instruction, but I was able to take up second-year classes. Having just written a senior paper on *Place of the Hidden Moon*, I was keen to locate myself in the Bangla literature of the early modern period.

In my second year at Chicago, in a class titled "Cultural and Literary History of Bengal," Dimock immersed us in the reading of the *CC* in typescript translations. In his typescript of *ādi* 4, there was a single page missing, so before class, I translated the missing passages that contained both Bengali and Sanskrit. My typed translation filled exactly one page, so when I handed out my version of the missing page, I facetiously announced to the class that my translation had to be correct because it exactly matched the spacing of the missing page, beginning and ending exactly where Dimock's translation left off and picked up again. Dimock chuckled and wryly acknowledged the contribution; of course, I did not point out that he had used a ten-point type and I a larger twelve-point type, making my translation more abbreviated. But it worked well enough and after checking he found no reason to complain, though the eloquence was not quite up to his own. That was my first attempt at something resembling a finished translation of a passage from the *CC*; you can imagine how many hours I spent trying to emulate his style. As the course progressed, I began to read the Bangla and Sanskrit against his translations, which gave me ample opportunity to observe and on occasion challenge, meekly at first, but later more vigorously as my confidence grew. It was during that class that I made my first tentative outline of the *avatār* theory found in the *CC*, which in its final form appears on pp. 142-43 of the translation's introduction.

In 1978-79, I was enrolled in the advanced Bengali language program of the AIIS in Calcutta. During that time, I began to collect and read widely in the Bengali Vaiṣṇav literatures. I found the edition of the *CC* prepared by Rādhāgovinda Nāth,[14] which I knew Dimock had used. I slowly initiated myself into the text and commentary that year, along with many other critical sources, including a nearly complete translation of M. M. Bose's *Sahajiyā Sāhitya*, which for reasons I have explained elsewhere, will remain unpublished, but parts of which I read with Dimock on my return.[15] During that spring, I began to consider a dissertation on the multiple Bangla and Sanskrit biographies of Caitanya. I felt that to understand fully the dominating presence of the *CC* in the discourse on the life of Caitanya, I would have to read the entire corpus. That decision later proved critical to my editing of the *CC*.

Shortly after my return from the AIIS advanced Bengali language program, we were all jolted by the passing of J.A.B. van Buitenen. There was a sense of doom that had fallen on Foster Hall, a sense of mission left unfinished because van Buitenen was only about forty percent of the way through the translation of the *Mahābhārata*. There was palpable relief when James L. Fitzgerald, who had been my first Sanskrit teacher, agreed to assume responsibility for coordinating the remainder of the translation. Given their closeness as colleagues and the parallels between van Buitenen's translation efforts and Dimock's own, it is not hard to imagine the effect van Buitenen's death had on Dimock, whose own translation still lay unfinished.

When I returned to Chicago after the year abroad, I persuaded Dimock to offer a private reading class each quarter in early modern Bangla, which we continued for the next two years. The first year (1979-80) we read broadly in a variety of early modern Bangla genres—*nāth, maṅgal kāvya, vaiṣṇav* hagiographies and poetry—but mainly the *CC*. We first read the thick theological chapters, but then Dimock suggested we read the long narrative passages because those were least refined in his translation. It was during those intense sessions that I began more fully to imbibe Dimock's translation style, his phrasing, how he handled verbal constructions, and so forth. I began to translate sections and, in some instances, whole chapters of the text. And inevitably I began to develop my own style of translating as I began to see different ways of handling expressions that parted from Dimock's. After finishing my master's thesis,[16] I accepted a Fulbright Hays Doctoral Dissertation Research Abroad fellowship for Calcutta to read Vaiṣṇav manuscripts; it would be several years before my dissertation would be finished.[17] But shortly after I returned from my field work, disaster struck.

Sometime in the middle of 1983 as I recall—and I am admittedly a little fuzzy on the precise dates—Dimock was diagnosed with laryngeal cancer. The prognosis was grim, and we all braced ourselves for what seemed to be the inevitable. Reeling from shock, my own work was laid aside, and the time between the announcement of that cancer and his subsequent surgery was and still is a blur. At the last minute it was announced that the surgeons had elected to try a new pioneering technique to remove the cancer and save his voice—and they were successful. Euphoria. After a rough recovery, he had to be careful not to strain his now raspy voice, yet he resumed his work, as did I. He would soon retire from his office as President of the AIIS, but before then, he set about compiling an anthology of his favorite essays, which fell to me to type and proof, and, after some delays, eventually appeared as *The Sound of Silent Guns and Other Essays*.[18] The laryngeal cancer soon made another appearance.

About this time Dimock purchased a boat that was drydocked in a South Chicago boatyard. Named Echo, she was a 33' Stephens-designed full-keel wooden craft, mahogany planked over white oak frames, with teak decks and cabin sole, sloop-rigged with a 42' foot mast above deck. Famous along the Chicago waterfront as a boat that would head out in stormy weather when others ran for cover, she was a classic blue-water yacht, but in neglect. As I was working to finish my dissertation, I would meet him at the boatyard in the morning where we would sand the hull endlessly, caulk the seams with oakum, tinker with the engine, and paint. After an hour or two, if we even lasted that long in the sultry heat, we would sit in the shade cast by the hull, drink dark beer since that was all he could he stomach, and talk, sometimes for hours. Cam, as he was by then known to me, spoke of his plans to sail Echo in Lake Michigan (which we never quite managed, the engine conking out as we made our way up the Calumet River to the lake). We discussed his impending surgery and possible death, stories from his time in Calcutta and Harvard, how my dissertation was developing, and, of course, the *CC*. The surgery was again successful, and he was in remission.

On a particularly cold wintry day in January 1985, with the hoarfrost-covered windows of my apartment rattling from the long zephyrs sweeping in from Canada, Cam telephoned and said the cancer had returned a third time. Would I complete the translation of the *CC* if he was unable to see it through? I asked him if this was really what he wanted and he hesitated, so I suggested that we revisit the issue after a few weeks. As he prepared for that third surgery, he confirmed that he did indeed want me to finish the task and I agreed, albeit reluctantly. Again, the surgery was successful, and we began to work collaboratively on the project. I completed my dissertation in spring of 1985 and during the next year Cam and I co-convened a class to read texts by Narottam Dās, three decades from where his involvement with the Vaiṣṇavs had first begun. With our prerequisites set at two years of Sanskrit and three years of Bangla, Robert D. Evans was our only student. We translated a number of Narottam's short texts, though we never published any of them; but discussion of those texts inevitably hinged on detailed comparisons to the *CC*, which deepened my appreciation for both Narottam and the *CC*. I soon got a job at North Carolina State University in 1986, and the collaboration became remote.

Iterations of Words

I had collected all the typescripts of scattered chapters of the *CC* we could locate, hauled them to North Carolina, and began the process of intense editing. As we worked our way through the text over the next several years, the secretary in my department at NCSU, Ann Rives, began typing the manuscript with a kind of professionalism that was inspiring, a task complicated by the myriad diacritics which we had just discovered could be generated on an early MacIntosh computer. I would periodically fly to Chicago to go over the edits. Resilient as Cam was, his health was still fragile; we would work spiritedly, even feverishly, with a sense of urgency, but sometimes I would have to wait for several days before he was strong enough to respond. As he fought a succession of afflictions generated by other cancers his attitude toward the way the translation was shaping up was sometimes ambivalent, which I soon realized reflected his general health. When he was feeling physically beaten down by the cancers and by the often-harsher treatments of radiation and chemotherapy, he was understandably irritable and wanted the translation left alone; when he was having better days, he seemed delighted at the progress and instructed me to do whatever needed doing. We muddled through the highs and lows. The manuscript was eventually in sufficiently good shape in 1990 or 1991 (again, the date is a bit vague), that it received approval by the Syndics of Harvard University Press for future publication.

In 1993, Cam's close friend and colleague, A.K. Ramanujan passed away during what was supposed to have been a routine surgery, lending an even greater sense of urgency to finishing up the remaining tedious, but necessary, tasks. As I catalogued the remaining work, I belatedly realized that I needed to rectify all the readings of the Sanskrit *ślokas*. The same verse might be quoted a half dozen times and, given the haphazard order of translation stretched over those many years, each rendition was different as were van Buitenen's emendations. Resolving those inconsistencies proved a much more difficult task than it had initially seemed, because we had to revisit each of those translations to establish the preferred reading—and translation by committee presents its own problems. During that process, I generated comprehensive internal cross-references for every Sanskrit verse found in the commentary and an appendix. Then I compiled the Sanskrit citation index, a separate index to the introduction, and of course the subject index for the text, much of that onerous work executed in weeks of solitude in a mountain cabin generously provided by Wild Acres Retreat near Little Switzerland in the western end of North Carolina. Cam and I together produced the glossary and the list of personae, and as a final act, I rounded out the bibliography. When we finally had a viable manuscript, there were puzzling delays in publication queue, but the text finally went to the book designer in late 1998 and was ready for production a year later.[19] During that decade, numerous battles with other forms of cancer ensued, which Cam weathered with a kind of stoicism I did not know was possible. Complaining did not seem to be in his nature, and it was through these episodes that he taught me more about living than anything else could have.

Proofreading was a challenge. The diacritics alone numbered on average sixty to seventy per page, pushing the total to astronomical heights, upwards of 80,000, perhaps more. As Cam and I sat at his dining-room table in Cape Cod, reading out our final corrections and emendations, page by page, line by line, I remember his wife, Loraine, laughing aloud from the adjacent room as we passed the thousandth page of the proofs. The text was officially released in the Harvard Oriental Series in December 1999. Cam held his own for a scant few months before his cancers finally caught up, perhaps no longer held in check by his will to see the *CC* through to completion. His health deteriorated steadily through the rest of the year. He passed away on 11 January 2001.

Last Words

In that last year before Cam met his death, I was able to hand-carry copies of the translation to present to universities and other institutional libraries in Calcutta and Dhaka, a celebration of a life's work to which all of them had in some way contributed.

A number of people have asked me why it took so long for my monograph on the *CC* to appear, twenty-five years after my dissertation and ten years after the publication of the translation. When I agreed to finish the *CC*, I realized I could not put my work before Dimock's. I wanted readers to be able to consult *The Final Word* with the translation in hand, so they could see for themselves the logic of my arguments about the hegemonic nature of the text. And, quite frankly, it proved too difficult to pick up the text in those first years after its publication.

As I write this, Michael Witzel, editor of the Harvard Oriental Series, and I are negotiating an Indian edition of the text. The reprint will be made directly from the master that Harvard used for the original print run, and distribution is planned across the subcontinent.

Endnotes

† "So, the translator needs to be translator, literary critic, and poet all at once—he must read the original well enough to understand all the machinery at play, to convey its meaning with as much accuracy as possible, then rearrange the translated meaning into an aesthetically pleasing structure in the target language that, by his judgment, matches the original. The poet runs untrammeled across the meadow. The translator dances in shackles." R. F. Kuang, *Babel or the Necessity of Violence: An Arcane History of the Oxford Translators' Revolution* (London: Harper Voyager, 2022), pp. 147-48.

I am grateful to James A. Epstein, James L. Fitzgerald, Samira Sheikh, and Lucian Wong for their comments on drafts of this paper.

1. Georges Poulet, "Criticism and the Experience of Interiority" in *Reader-Response Criticism: From Formalism to Post-Structuralism*, edited by Jane P. Tompkins (Baltimore and London: The Johns Hopkins University Press, 1980), pp. 41-49.

2. *The 'Caitanya Caritāmṛta' of Kṛṣṇadāsa Kavirāja*, translated with commentary by Edward C. Dimock, Jr., edited by Tony K. Stewart, with an introduction by the translator and the editor, Harvard Oriental Series no. 56 (Cambridge, MA: Harvard University Press, 1999).

3. Tony K. Stewart, *The Final Word: The Caitanya Caritāmṛta and the Grammar of Religious Tradition* (New York and London: Oxford University Press, 2010).

4. Frank Kermode, *The Classic: Literary Images of Permanence and Change* (Cambridge, MA, and London: Harvard University Press, 1983).

5. Hans-Georg Gadamer, "Language as the Medium of Hermeneutical Experience," in *Truth and Method* (New York: Crossroad,1982), pp. 345-66.

6. It should be noted that Dimock always transliterated following orthography, which included the inherent final vowel on all words in Sanskrit or Bangla, and so it was in our translation of the *CC*. My own preference is to observe appropriate vowel apocope for Bangla terms, but retaining the inherent vowel for Sanskrit, which includes most of the technical terminology, hence what may seem to some as inconsistencies in this essay.

7. *Sannyāsī* is found in the other printed editions of the *CC* that I have checked, and similarly in a half dozen manuscripts I've consulted. For example, see the top three lines of the center folio of the *CC* manuscript on the cover of *The Final Word*, which reads *sannyāsī*.

8. See for example the *Caitanya Ras Kārika* of Yugal Kiśor Dās, MS 580, [n.d.] Bangla Department Manuscript Collection, Calcutta University; and *Caitanya Nityānanda Jāhnavī Tattva* or *Golok Varṇam* of Gopāl Bhaṭṭa, MS 2272 [dtd 1173 (=1766)], MS 3236 [n.d.], MS 3348 (dtd 1072 (=1688)], Bangla Department Manuscript Collection, Calcutta University.

9. *Vide supra* no. 6. My contention about the frequent disjunctions between the Bangla terms and their counterparts in other languages were crystallized when I

began to work on the Musalmāni Bangla of the Sufi tales, the *pīr kathās*. I have now assumed an almost militant stance about the necessity of leaving the Bangla as it is written, which is especially evident when words are imported from Persian and Arabic, for the Bangla writer transliterates them in any number of different ways with a range of meanings frequently unmatched in their apparent sources. For my position today, see "Conventions Regarding Transliteration and Nomenclature" in *Witness to Marvels: Sufism and Literary Imagination* (Oakland, CA: University of California Press, 2019), pp. xxv-xxx.

10. Edward C. Dimock, Jr., *The Place of the Hidden Moon: Erotic Mysticism in the Vaiṣṇava Sahajiyā Cult of Bengal* (Chicago and London: The University of Chicago Press, 1966).

11. Edward C. Dimock, Jr., and Denise Levertov, translators, *In Praise of Krishna: Songs from the Bengali* (Anchor Books, 1967).

12. Seely established himself as a master translator and interpreter of Jībanānanda Dāś's poetry. See Clinton B. Seely, *A Poet Apart: A Literary Biography of the Bengali Poet Jibanananda Das (1899-1954)*, (Newark, Delaware: University of Delaware Press; London and Toronto: Associated University Presses, 1990) and Clinton B. Seely, trans., *The Scent of Sunlight: Poems by Jibanananda Das* (Kolikata: Parabaas, 2019). Dimock's presentation was published that same year as Edward C. Dimock, Jr., "The Poet as Mouse and Owl: Reflections on a Poem by Jībanānanda Dāś," *Journal of Asian Studies*, 33, no. 4 (1974): 603-610.

13. At the time, Dimock told me that his *Introduction to Bengali, Part 1*, done with Suhas Chatterjee and Somdev Bhattacharya (Honolulu: University of Hawaii Press, 1964), was out of print, but he suggested I write to the press to see if they might have a rogue copy somewhere and sure enough, they did, lifting it from the display case in their lobby. They told me I got the last copy, the rest of which had suffered water damage in their warehouse; fortunately, the book was later reprinted (paperback reprint: Delhi: Manohar, 2003), and then digitally remastered by Seely (accessible through the Digital South Asia Library hosted by the University of Chicago: https://dsal.uchicago.edu/digbooks/dig_toc.html?BOOKID=PK1663.D6_1976). Chicago generously sent me a copy of the accompanying cassette tapes. For two years I studied in this manner, and then driving seventy-five miles from Bowling Green, KY, to Nashville, TN, every other Friday night to speak with members of the local Bengali community as we could not locate a single Bengali speaker in Bowling Green at the time.

14. *Caitanya caritāmṛta* of Kṛṣṇadāsa Kavirāj, edited with the commentary *Gaurakṛpataraṅgiṇī ṭīkā* by Rādhagovinda Nāth, 3d ed., 6 vols. (Kalikātā: Sādhanā Prakāśanī, 1355-59 BS [c. 1948-52]; 4th ed, 1369-70 [c. 1962-63]).

15. See Tony K. Stewart, "The Power of the Secret: The Tantalizing Discourse of Vaiṣṇava Sahajiyā Scholarship" in *The Legacy of Vaiṣṇavism in Colonial Bengal*, edited by Ferdinando Sardella and Lucian Wong (London: Routledge, 2020), pp. 125-66.

16. Tony K. Stewart, "Caitanya and the Death Story: Belief, Pattern, Fact," (A.M. Thesis, The University of Chicago, 1981); a truncated version of that thesis was subsequently published as "When Biographical Narratives Disagree: The Death of Kṛṣṇa Caitanya," *Numen* 38, no. 2 (1991): 231-60.

17. Tony K. Stewart, "The Biographical Images of Kṛṣṇa Caitanya: A Study in the Perception of Divinity," (Doctoral Dissertation, The University of Chicago, 1985).

18. Edward C. Dimock, Jr., *The Sound of Silent Guns and Other Essays* (Delhi: Oxford University Press, 1989).

19. After type was set, I nervously enlisted my then student Brian Collins, now holder of the Drs. Ram and Sushila Gawande Chair in Indian Religion and Philosophy at Ohio University, to go through the entire text and count verses. He discovered about twenty couplets that had been skipped or dropped out of the typescript. Much to our relief, the production team was able to incorporate the material.

History of Walther Eidlitz' "Kṛṣṇa-Caitanya" and its Translations

Katrin Stamm

In the following, I will describe the process and the challenges of translating Walther Eidlitz' groundbreaking work on the theology and life of Kṛṣṇa Caitanya, "Kṛṣṇa Caitanya: Sein Leben und Seine Lehre" (1968) (*Kṛṣṇa Caitanya: His Life and His Teachings*) from German into English.[1] To begin with, a short overview of the *content* of the book will be given, including the *genesis* of the *original German* book. Next, the translators and their specific backgrounds and skills and the *history of the translations* will be presented. Both the genesis of the book and the translation process are linked, as the writing of the book as well as the translations were done not only as a scholarly endeavor but also as a service within the Gauḍīya Vaiṣṇava saṁpradāya, or disciplic succession. Consequently, the final part will deal with the specific *challenges* that arose from working within this setting.

1. Content and genesis of the book

Content

Walther Eidlitz' main Indological work, *Kṛṣṇa Caitanya: Sein Leben und Seine Lehre* (1968) was published by the University of Stockholm as part of the Stockholm Studies in Comparative Religion. According to the original book announcement of the German edition, the book gives the "first complete presentation of the life and teachings of Kṛṣṇa Caitanya (1486–1533) who is worshipped as God on Earth by millions of Hindus."[2] The focus here is on the word *complete* as, in 1968, there already existed books in European languages *about* Caitanya, like Kennedy's *The Caitanya Movement* (1925), for example, which provides a short history, but is written from the point of view of a Christian missionary; *retellings* of his life, like Sanyal's *Sree Kṛṣṇa Caitanya* (1933), that also offers a theological and historical introduction into Vaiṣṇavism; or translations of *one* biography, like Stursberg's small thesis "Das Caitanyacaritāmṛta des Kṛṣṇadas Kavirāja: Eine altbengalische Lebensgeschichte Caitanyas" (1907), but never a direct translation and compilation of *all* hagiographical sources merging into *one* storyline.[3]

The book is divided into two parts. The first part deals with "The Indian Concept of the Revelation of God," explaining God's nature, his powers, and realms. It also provides a retelling of some Divine Plays (*līlā*) of the One God as Narasiṁha and Kṛṣṇa according to the *Bhāgavata-Purāṇa* and other sources. Additionally, a concise account of the psychology of Divine Love (*bhakti-rasa*)—"the eternal continuous outpouring stream [. . .] that floods back to its source [God] as serving knowing love (*bhakti*)"[4]—is given. The first part concludes with a chapter about the historical background and the theological and spiritual significance of Kṛṣṇa-Caitanya according to Gauḍīya Vaiṣṇavism. The second part presents extensive excerpts of early hagiographies of the life and precepts of Caitanya. Many of these sources were for the first time translated from Sanskrit and Medieval Bengali into a European language. According to the author, the intention of his work is "to let the spirit of the sources come alive."[5] In the appendix, chronological tables are provided as well as an account of the divisions of the Veda according to the tradition itself, a chapter on the language of the Bengali sources, a bibliography, and a verification of sources. The book also provides an index.

Genesis of the book

The author, Walther Eidlitz (1892–1976), was an Austrian poet and writer who was later initiated into Gauḍīya Vaiṣṇavism and was also known by his spiritual name, Vamandās. He was born into a Jewish family in Vienna but later renounced his Jewish origins and explored new religious movements of his time, like Theosophy and Anthroposophy. He admired the German poets Hölderlin and Brentano and aspired to become a poet of similar rank.

After WWI he publishes his first drama in which he deals with his traumatic war experiences. Travel novels follow that always include a spiritual angle, as Eidlitz interprets his outer journeys as, ultimately, inner journeys. To learn more about ancient Indian wisdom, he manages to procure an official mission from the NSDAP State Department of Culture with the purpose "to explore on the spot the ancient Swastika-Bön religion that had prevailed in Tibet before Buddhism spread" (Mettauer, 2013, p. 121).[6] He departs for India in 1938 and, one year later, when WWII breaks out, becomes a prisoner of war of the British in India. During his internment he meets the German scholar and Gauḍīya Vaiṣṇava, Svāmī Sadānanda Dāsa (Ernst Georg Schulze, 1908–1977). Sadānanda had become the only German disciple of the central representative of Gauḍīya Vaiṣṇavism in India in those days, Bhaktisiddhānta Sarasvatī Ṭhākur, receiving initiation from him in 1934. In Germany, Sadānanda had studied Comparative Religion, Philosophy and various languages like Latin, Hebrew, Sanskrit, Pali and Hindi. He and Eidlitz become fast friends, and he accepts Sadānanda as his guru. In 1946, shortly after Eidlitz and Sadānanda have been released from the British internment camp, Sadānanda writes to Eidlitz: "I trust the time will come when we shall be able to complete a very beautiful book on the Lord of Love (Caitanya) together and to have a *darshan* [the blessing sight] of the *līlā-bhūmi* of the Lord [playground of God on earth]." (letter from Sadānanda (S.) to Eidlitz (E.), 03.03.46). It took another 22 years until the book he envisioned was published.[7]

After the end of WWII and their release from the war camp in India, Eidlitz travels to Sweden, where his family, because of their Jewish origin, had already emigrated to during the Nazi regime in Germany and Austria, whereas Sadānanda stays in India until 1961. After Eidlitz has published his first book on *bhakti*, "Die Indische Gottesliebe" ("The Indian Love of God") in 1955, he starts to work on the Caitanya monograph. In the meantime, Sadānanda, translates not only Caitanya's earliest hagiography, the *Caitanya-Bhāgavatam*,[8] into German, but also supporting theological texts (in parts) like the *Bhāgavata-Purāṇa*, the *Padma Purāṇa* or the *Bhagavadgītā*, and other elementary works of Gauḍīya Vaiṣṇava theology, like Rūpa Gosvāmī's *Bhakti-Rasāmṛita-Sindhu* or the second part (chapters 1-4) of the *Bṛhad-Bhagavatāmṛtam* by Sanātana Gosvāmī.

In addition, he provides Eidlitz with other sources on the life of Caitanya, like central passages from Kṛṣṇadāsa-Kavirāja's *Caitanya-Caritāmṛtam*, the complete *Caitanya-Candrodaya-Naṭakam* by Kavi Karṇapūra and Murari Gupta's *Kadacā*. Moreover, he writes the entire source criticism in the end of the book (see letter from S. to E. 13.10.63). All these texts form the material basis of Eidlitz' book on Caitanya. Eidlitz himself, unlike his teacher, had neither studied Sanskrit nor Bengali in an academic context and could only acquire some knowledge of Sanskrit, Hindi and Bengali in the internment camp under the guidance of his teacher, which he later personally deepened.

After Sadānanda returns to Europe in 1961 and lives in Basel, Switzerland, with friends, he is able to visit Eidlitz in Sweden during the summer months and directly support him in his work. Eidlitz also visits Sadānanda in Basel. In 1963, Sadānanda does the proof-reading of the manuscript—and is very dissatisfied (see letters from S. to E. from 13.10., 14.10., 17.10. and 22.10.63). He writes to Eidlitz' wife:

> From his manuscript it becomes clear that he is inwardly, in his heart and mind, not at all focused on *bhakti*. I don't care if I die and nothing is printed at all, but that he distorts Caitanya and the theology of *bhakti* the way he does and drags them into the dirt, I can't allow that. Should he nevertheless dare to hand over such filth to Hultkrantz,[9] not only will Hultkrantz consider him an idiot and get a justified aversion to all *bhakti shastras*, but I will be forced to write to Hultkrantz that I object to the abuse of my raw translations intended only for Vamandās and tell him that Vamandās has not at all familiarized himself with the matter.

Eidlitz takes this criticism of his teacher to heart, sits down, and writes everything anew. From that time on, Sadānanda not only does *raw* translations, but, according to his own statements, translates in such a way that *there is nothing left to change*. Originally, Eidlitz was only supposed to transform these raw translations into a beautiful German language. However, Eidlitz failed the (maybe too) high expectations of his teacher. (see letters from S. to E., 17.10. and 05.11.63) In 1967, the manuscript is finally printed (see letters from S. to E., 20.12.66 and 30.05.67). But Sadānanda is still not content with this final version:

> The first part, which I worked through, is not so bad, but the second part with the sources from the texts, C.C. [*Caitanya-Caritāmṛta*] etc., is terrible. He has been too lazy to transform the style into a good German in the last 15 years. [. . .]. As sorry as I am—but it goes way beyond my strength to completely rework the 2nd part.

Although the linguistic style of the 2nd part, which mainly consists of translations from the sources of Caitanya's life, may not always be literarily beautiful, there is the advantage that it is as close as possible to the original translation by Sadānanda and thus theologically and linguistically more accurate and reliable.

In total, it took 13 years from the first preparations for this book in 1955 to its completion and publication in 1968, but both, Eidlitz and Sadānanda, never gave up during this difficult process. Sadānanda saw the realization of this joint project with Eidlitz as *service* (*sevā*) to his guru, Bhaktisiddhānta Sarasvatī Ṭhākur, and encouraged his student not to give up despite setbacks. (see letter from S. to E., 14.10.63)

After publication, the book receives very good reviews. The well-known theologian and ecclesiastical historian Prof. Dr. Ernst Benz (1907–1978) from the university of Marburg remarks in a letter to Eidlitz that he particularly appreciates the translations from the sources as they offer a realistic account of the historical personality of Caitanya. He is impressed that Eidlitz managed to render "the teachings of Caitanya into a form that is accessible to our German language and concepts of philosophy of religion."[10]

According to Eidlitz' notes, Prof. Jan Gonda (1905–1991), the celebrated Orientalist and Indologist who taught at the University of Utrecht, considered it a "very valuable work" and Prof. Mircea Eliade (1907–1986), the famous historian of religion, fiction writer, philosopher, and professor at the University of Chicago, spontaneously offered his help to publish an American edition. Friso Melzer, a German Protestant theologian and philologist, praises Eidlitz' book in in the renowned "Theologische Literaturzeitung" (*Theological Literature Journal*) especially for what was in fact *Sadānanda's* contribution:

> The section on references and source criticism (533–549) shows how thoroughly Eidlitz has researched during these 30 years. The final register includes more than 900 terms and names, of which about 700 are Sanskrit words. [. . .] It is very valuable how Eidlitz presents the complexity and ambiguity of the essential Sanskrit terms, such as *akshara* (48, note 4), *asura* (75f., note 1), *atma* (493), *jiva* (39), *kama* (10, note 2), *pada* (46, note 2), *priti* (183 f.). All important Sanskrit terms are derived from the root.[11]

Alf Ahlberg, Professor of Philosophy and Theology at the University of Uppsala, keenly observes in his article "Krishna Caitanya—Indiens dolda skatt" in *Svenska Dagbladet*, Sweden's leading newspaper (October 30, 1968, p. 4) that "in the translations as in all parts of the book, *the scientist and the poet have achieved a happy union.*"[12] (emphasis by me) In fact, the poet and the scientist were the *two authors*, Eidlitz and Sadānanda, who had written the book together.

Even today, the book is still valued for using the hagiographical materials best while remaining "immediately readable." (Stewart, 2014)[13] According to Stewart, it comes closest to a Western style religious biography whereas, e.g.,

De's *Early History of the Vaiṣṇava Faith and Movement in Bengal* (1961) is regarded "the best single-volume introduction to the tradition through an extraordinary mastery of primary sources" by Stewart and remains the main reference book in English. Majumdar's *Caitanya: His Life and Doctrine* (1969)[14] provides, according to Stewart, the most accessible and accurate summary of the life of Caitanya.

2. History of the book's translations

First attempts

Already one year after the book's publication, in 1969, the effort was made to get the book translated into English. Mario Windisch, a central member of the later English translation team, contacted Princeton, Oxford and Harvard University Press. Whereas Princeton declared that Eidlitz' book was indeed scientifically significant but more so to the *German* than to the English readers as most of the translated texts (supposedly) were already available in English, Harvard argued it would be too expensive to produce. The translation from German into English alone would have not been easy, but—and this was their main problem—the Indian texts would have needed to be translated *directly from the sources* by Sanskrit and Bengali experts, as second-hand translations from German would not have been acceptable. (see letter from Harvard to Windisch, 12.02.1969)

When Eidlitz was told the reasons for the decline of his books' translation into English by these renowned publishers he rightfully argued that the main sources of his monograph, the *Caitanya-Bhāgavata*, Caitanya's biography by Murāri Gupta and the biographical Sanskrit drama *Caitanya-Candrodaya* had indeed *not* been translated into any European language by then and Princeton's argument was invalid. Moreover, he severely criticized the available English translation of the *Caitanya-Caritāmṛtam* by Chaudhuri (1959, second edition), as the translator, in his view, omitted several verses he did not understand, was not proficient in medieval Bengali, and, consequently, produced countless mistakes. (letter from E. to W., 20.06.69) But he agreed that a competent translator would require "to be profoundly familiar with the German and English language (English native speaker), to have a genuine relation to German poetry and also know Sanskrit." (letter to W., 17.07.72). Windisch himself did not feel qualified then to accomplish the task himself: "The ever-increasing love for this books, however, does not suffice. One needs a comprehensive knowledge of the English language." (letter from W. to E.,

19.7.72) So Eidlitz gave up trying to find a publisher for an English edition, as it seemed that the obstacles were insurmountable.

In 1975, Vamandas received an honorary doctorate from the University of Lund for his several works on Indian Religion and Philosophy, and in June 1975, eventually, Kurt Leidecker of the University of Mary Washington in Virgina, United States, cabled Eidlitz that he would like to publish an English translation that year. Leidecker was born in Germany in 1902, emigrated to the United States, attended the University of Chicago, where he studied Philosophy and Sanskrit and wrote his Ph.D. dissertation on the *Bhagavadgītā*. However, Leidecker never started the announced English translation. As a result of an inquiry in 2012, the University of Mary Washington explained that after having looked through Leidecker's writings, they could not find any translation of that particular book. They only had the inscribed copy of the book that was given to Leidecker by Eidlitz, along with three pages of handwritten Errata. (personal communication with David Ambuel, 06.06.2012) One year later, in 1976, Eidlitz passed away and it seemed unlikely that anyone would ever give the translation another try.

Translations into Swedish and English

The first actual translation was rendered by Sigvard Sjögren in 1976 into Swedish. It was edited by Eidlitz' son, Günther, though it was a simplified version in two volumes of which only the first volume, "Guds lek. Om indisk gudsuppenbarelse" ("God's Play. About the India Revelation of God") was ever published. The second part was supposed to be called "Kṛṣṇa Caitanya—Indiens dolda skatt" ("India's Hidden Treasure").

The first *complete* Swedish translation was done in 2004 by Kid Samuelsson, who had studied English and German, and Bengt Lundborg, a Swedish physicist, who had studied Sadānanda's translations with Samuelsson for many years and was familiar with the standards of academic publications, too. Already in 1972 Samuelsson had become acquainted with Eidlitz' books on *bhakti*. He read *Livets mening och mål i indisk tankevärld* ("The Meaning of Life in the Indian World of Thought"), which convinced him "that *bhakti*, unadulterated service of Godhead, was the supreme path and goal." (Samuelsson 2022, 2)[15] It so happened that Eidlitz' son was married to an aunt of Samuelsson's wife, and so Samuelsson soon met Eidlitz in person. Through Eidlitz he also came in contact with Sadānanda and they started to write letters. In 1973, during one of Sadānanda's visits to Sweden, they eventually met in person.

Both Eidlitz and Sadānanda felt deep affection and appreciation for Samuelsson. In 1974, when Eidlitz stayed with Samuelsson and his familiy, Sadānanda writes to Eidlitz (10.06.74):

> I am happy to hear that Kid, Maria and Frida-Ananda are fine. Thanks, and Kṛṣṇa's blessings on everyone there, because it is good for them and you to be together in Kṛṣṇa's *seva*. I have a high opinion of Kid—but he does not have to know this, if you think this is the best. (Samuelsson 2022, 6; translation into English by Samuelsson)

At that time, Samuelsson declares his "English was poor" and his German "non-existent." (2022, 16). To overcome the language barrier, Eidlitz advises him to study German and English. In January 1976, Eidlitz bequeaths all his Indological texts in his last will to Samuelsson and Ulla Fjellström. In August 1976, Eidlitz passes away in Samuelsson's home after Samuelsson, his wife and Ulla Fjellström had cared for him at home together with professional help during the last phase of his cancer illness.

Soon after, Samuelsson starts to study English and German at the University of Lund to effectively work with the literary estate he inherited. Starting from the late '80's, he translates many works of Sadānanda into Swedish. In the beginning of the '90's, the later main translator of the Caitanya book into English, the German Canadian author and temporary member of the Hare Kṛṣṇa movement (ISKCON), Mario Windisch, joins the annual disciple meetings of Sadānanda in Sweden. Around 1998, the first website for Sadānanda and Eidlitz is created. (Samuelsson 2022, 20–21) In the beginning of the '90ties, I join the group. As I feel that to understand the texts properly, knowledge of Sanskrit is indispensable, I start to study Indology in addition to Philosophy and German Literature. In this way, I become better qualified to join Samuelsson's efforts to publish and translate more and more texts by Sadānanda and Eidlitz, first on the website, and later in the form of self-published books.

The impulse for the English translation was catapulted forward in around 2010 by Samuelsson to Windisch. He writes: "I think it's a shame that Vamandas' book 'Kṛṣṇa Caitanya' is not available in English. That would be the perfect job for you with your good knowledge of English, don't you think? [. . .] Let's work hard together in our different ways with the common goal of pleasing Svamiji." (undated letter) Mario Windisch accepted the task and—as the (almost) native speaker in the translation team —started to work on the raw English translations that were subsequently refined by the team.

Already in 1969, he had been made chief editor of the translation department in Germany for all ISKCON literature and the "Back to Godhead" magazine of ISKCON by its founder, Bhaktivedānta Svāmī, because of his literary skills, competence in Vaiṣṇava theology, and knowledge of both the German and English language. (letter from Bhaktivedānta to W., 28.05.69) Additionally, Windisch worked as a professional translator and wrote radio features, novels and short stories in German.

Kid Samuelsson, Bengt Lundborg—who had already translated the work into Swedish—contributed the vast experience they had gained regarding both technical and formal aspects, as well as the content. As an Indologist, I added my knowledge of Sanskrit and limited Bengali to the team and checked all the quotations from the sources. Later, Kristina Hedtjärn, a professional translator, who grew up bilingual (German and Swedish) joined the team. So, all together, the translators' team consisted of five members with different skills. And we all had studied the subject theoretically and practically for 25 to 50 years. In this way, the obstacles, e.g., the ones that Harvard University Press had mentioned, like the need to check the translated parts from Sanskrit or Bengali directly, or the combined proficiency in both English and German, could be overcome.

After the English translation had been finished, the initial Swedish translation was completely revised in 2013 to include the improvements of the English translation. Moreover, a revised German edition is in preparation that includes corrections the editors' notes of the English translation.

3. Challenges in the translation process

It is common knowledge that translation cannot be reduced to the literal word-by-word transposition of one text into another, but is rather an act of *transcreation* or rewriting of the original text that effects both the translated text and the translator (cf. Steiner 1998). Consequently, there are always certain degrees of loss of meaning that can be minimized but cannot be totally avoided. Often, no one-to-one translation of a word is possible, and translators need to refer to *compensation strategies* to fill the conceptual (lexical or cultural) gap by paraphrases, loanwords, or translator's notes, keeping a reasonable balance between *fidelity* to the original text and *transparency* regarding the choices within the translation process. These choices always also depend on certain questions that need to be addressed before embarking on translating any text: What kind of text is it? A *poetic* or a *scientific* text? What kind of audience does it target? What is the purpose of the translation? etc. Critical apparatuses, e.g., are the best solution when it comes to transparency and might appeal to an academic audience but could also impede readability and become an obstacle to those who mainly read for personal edification, entertainment, or aesthetic pleasure.

Eidlitz' book on Caitanya was published within an academic series in comparative religion and therefore primarily aimed at an *academic* audience. However, Eidlitz was no academic by education, but a *poet* and novelist. Only his teacher, Sadānanda, had received an academic training in Germany and had written a dissertation, too. As a result, there are more poetic renderings of verses from the Purāṇas or Upaniṣads in the first part that are clearly the work of Eidlitz, whereas the second part is in prose and almost written 100% by Sadānanda. Accordingly, Alf Ahlberg had correctly perceived "a happy union" of poet and scientist in this work. However, this union was not so "happy," despite what Ahlberg had to say. In scientific texts it is important to meticulously define each term, *narrowing down* the meaning to its essence, whereas in poetry, metaphors are preferred that offer a *wide* range of nuances in meaning. In this regard, poetic and academic language are opposites. This also applies to *translations* of academic and poetic texts. Consequently, the German book is a more or less "happy" amalgamation of styles and intentions—which made the choices before and during the translation process difficult: Should we as translators side with the *poet* Eidlitz whose name is on the book—or should we side with the *scientist* and renowned Vaiṣṇava, Sadānanda, who provided all the translations from Bengali and Sanskrit, and was Eidlitz' teacher, too?

It is highly unusual that the co-author of a work intentionally hides, but Sadānanda had planned right from the start to remain in the background, providing the raw translations from Bengali and Sanskrit, and letting Eidlitz write the books, making the translations more readable, compiling them, and providing a beautiful framework. (letter S. to Hedtjärn, 05.11.63)[16] This, however, did not really work out, as we have shown above. Eventually, when the book was published, it was not really finished in the sense that both authors had managed to create *one* coherent text together. It is rather a giant jigsaw puzzle. And it would be worth a dissertation to untangle the different parts and its different authors.

Eidlitz only mentions his teacher in the introduction as an *advisor and assistant*, but not as the main contributor. In a genuinely academic work Eidlitz would have been required to indicate which passages were written by him and which by Sadānanda. Otherwise, it would have been plagiarism. However, in this case, Sadānanda hid *intentionally*, for both practical and for spiritual reasons. On the one hand, Sadānanda had contracted chronic diseases from his time in India and was physically *not capable* to continue his career as an author and academic. On the other hand, he also *preferred* to make people interested in *Kṛṣṇa* instead of himself (letter S. to Hedtjärn, 05.11.63). In another letter (to Hella Eidlitz, 06.05.58), he explains that he intended to follow Seidenstücker's example who introduced Buddhism to the West without trying to convert the West to Buddhism. He preferred an *impersonal theologically correct presentation*, based on the *actual sources*, to a personal profession of faith. In his view, people needed to be convinced by the Word of God itself, not by the *person* who proclaimed it.[17] He explains the reasoning behind this to Eidlitz:

> You are a renowned writer and have a *strong* personality, which implies a great advantage and a great—don't be frightened—disadvantage. The advantage is that when some W. Eidlitz says and writes something, *most* vividly identifies with something, then people will listen where they would have remained unconcerned if an "expert" or someone unknown had done the same. The disadvantage is that Your *personality* carries the message, and the message is interesting because of the *personality*—and when the personality subsides, recedes, then nothing but a weak, personal reverberation of the message will remain. [. . .] This does not only concern You. In the case of Caitanyadeva, for instance, everything rests on *Krishna*, the *Bhagavatam* stands in the foreground and He Himself as Caitanya remains in the background. And thus the *eternal*, impersonal message of the *Bhagavatam* etc. remains—even when He and His Own have left the world. (23.05.58)[18]

As the translation team was equally divided into two parties, the more academic party and the more poetic party, conflicts arose: When was it more important to stay faithful to Eidlitz' poetic style and formulations? When was it more important to stick with literal translation at the cost of aesthetic pleasure? What unified both parties, however, was the fact that *all* considered themselves disciples of Sadānanda and the translation work as *bhakti-sādhana* or spiritual practice and service to their common guru. Due to this unusual setting, most choices in translation were done in favor of *Sadānanda*, not in favor of the official author of the book. Whenever it was unclear how to translate a term, we referred to Sadānanda, his direct translations and letters and corrections to former books by Eidlitz. To make our choices transparent for the reader we decided to introduce *translators' notes*. A complete critical apparatus that identified which part of the book was exactly written by whom or documented the stages of development of the text would have surely been interesting for a purely academic audience, but the original book was intended to be also an accessible introduction to the life and teachings of Caitanya for the interested public. So, we considered translators' notes the best solution and decided to add a glossary in the new revised German edition that is currently written.

After many years of study and translation of Sadānanda's texts into Swedish and English, we had, so to say, gone through Steiner's fourfold "hermeneutic movement,"—the initial act of surrender to the text, the initiative trust, "bringing the meaning home," incorporating the meaning (embodiment) and finally, rebalancing the system through "the enactment of reciprocity"—and had become thereby able to enhance the text:

> Where it surpasses the original, the real translation infers that the source-text possesses potentialities, elemental reserves as yet unrealized by itself. This is Schleiermacher's notion of a hermeneutic which 'knows better than the author did' (Paul Celan translating Apollinaire's Salomé).[19] (318)

The translation in fact offered a great opportunity to *improve* the book. Incalculably valuable was Eidlitz' personal edition, as it contained later handwritten personal corrections and notes by Eidlitz himself. Moreover, we included three handwritten pages of Errata by Eidlitz and two pages of corrections by Sadānanda from 1972. While writing the translation we found many more mistakes: not only spelling mistakes, but also missing lines in verses, wrong verse numbers, etc. Altogether around 200 errors. When we came across "old" mistakes that had already been mentioned by Sadānanda in his 300 pages of corrections to Eidlitz' book *Die indische Gottesliebe* (1955) ("The Indian Love of God") we decided to include, whenever possible, Sadānanda's own words as corrections in the translator's notes. In this way, we tried our best to further integrate the Vaiṣṇava poet's and the Vaiṣṇava scientist's work. The next step will be a new revised German edition that will—thanks to the generous help of Ferdinando Sardella[20]—be published by the publisher PUBLIT, who is working in cooperation with Stockholm University. We hope that both author and co-author, teacher and disciple, would appreciate our efforts to further improve the joint project of their lives.

Endnotes

1. For a list of the different editions and translations of Eidlitz' book on Caitanya see "Bibliography."

2. A transcript of the original book announcement by the author can be found on the website of the Sadānanda Archive under "summary" on the following page: https://Sadānanda.com/#text-downloads (Accessed 22.01.23)

3. A comprehensive bibliography of monographs and studies about Caitanya is given in: Dimock Jr., Edward C. (1999): *Caitanya Caritāmṛta of Kṛṣṇadāsa Kavirāja. A Translation and Commentary.* Cambridge MA, London: Harvard University Press.

4. See book announcement.

5. See book announcement.

6. Mettauer, Phillip (2013). "Um den instinktlosen arischen Wiener vom Besuch jüdischer Buchhandlungen abzuhalten . . ." Das Archiv der Reichsschrifttumskammer. *Biblos* 62 (2), pp. 105–135. Available at: http://data.onb.ac.at/rec/AC14004133 (Accessed 22.01.23)

7. For more information about the life of Eidlitz and his cooperation with Sadānanda please see: Stamm, Katrin (2021): "From Poet to Kavi: Walther Eidlitz' Spiritual Odyssey." *Journal of Vaiṣṇava Studies* 28 (2), pp. 45–67. For a summary of Eidlitz' influence on the Hindu tradition in Sweden, please see *Handbook of Hinduism in Europe*, Vol. I, pp. 811, 1467–68 by Knut A. Jacobsen and Ferdinando Sardella (eds.) (2020).

8. About the *Caitanya-Bhāgavatam* Sadānanda writes in a letter to Eidlitz: "The work is written in an old form of Bengali, very different from C.C. [Kriṣṇadāsa Kavirāja's *Caitanya-Caritāmṛta*] (ca. 1620) and its language, and it presents many difficulties. It gives the whole theology of the Caitanya-līlā, but with *events of His life*, not abstractly. *I have translated it literally, word for word,* with technical words within brackets." (06.08.55, into English by Kid Samuelsson) Available at: https://sadananda.com/txt/en/text_downloads/en/caitanya_bhagavata-en.pdf (Accessed 22.01.23) All letters and manuscripts quoted in this article were provided by the Sadānanda-Archive in Flensburg, Germany, which the author of this article is taking care of. This archive contains both the literary estate of Sadānanda and his disciple Walther Eidlitz as well as other disciples of Sadānanda. All letters were originally written in German and were translated into English by me, if not stated otherwise.

9. Åke Hultkrantz (1920–2006) had a Ph.D. in ethnology and comparative religion and taught at Stockholm University, which was to publish the book on Caitanya.

10. "I can only congratulate you sincerely that you have managed to compose the results of your rich studies in India and your insights into the sources—that are hardly or not at all available in Europe—into such a well-fashioned overview. Moreover, I consider it a very significant achievement that for the first time, as far as my modest knowledge of the matter is concerned, a realistic account of the historical personality of Caitanya is presented. Especially in the Indian history of ideas most often the great

personalities are completely covered by myths. No less rewarding is your successful translation of the teachings of Caitanya into a form that is accessible to our German language and concepts of philosophy of religion." (Undated letter by Benz to Eidlitz in German, quoted in a manuscript by Eidlitz where he listed all positive reviews).

11. Melzer, Friso (1969): Eidlitz, Walther: "Krishna Chaitanya. Sein Leben und Seine Lehre." *Theologische Literaturzeitung* 94 (3) 1969. pp. 190–191.

12. "Lekmannen har det bestämda intrycket att i dessa översättningar och i bokens övriga delar vetenskapsmannen och diktaren ingått en lycklig förening." Ahlberg, Alf (1968): 'Krishna Caitanya—"Indiens dolda skatt."' *Svenska Dagbladet*, October 30, p. 4.

13. Stewart, Tony K. (2014): Oxford Bibliographies: Caitanya. Last modified: 30 June 2014. DOI: 10.1093/obo/9780195399318-0138

14. Majumdar, A. K. Caitanya (1969): *His Life and Doctrine.* Bombay: Bharatiya Vidya Bhavan.

15. Samuelsson, Kid (2022): "Looking back. My Encounters with Sadananda and Vamandas." Available at: https://www.sadananda.com/txt/en/text_downloads/other_text/en/looking-back-en.pdf (Accessed 22.01.23)

16. "I had never thought of ever needing to come to the foreground. I wanted to stay completely in the background and let Vamandas write the books—that is, let the formerly translated texts which I had provided in raw form be given a proper shape. Only my month-long observations at Forshult Gård revealed that it would not work that way. [. . .] Publicity has always been repugnant to me, because I know that only a few can understand Kṛṣṇa's matters anyway, and I prefer people to be interested in Kṛṣṇa and not in me." (letter from Sadānanda to Majstin Hedtjärn, 5.11.63)

17. "It seems to me that it would have been better to present objectively from the beginning what the Vedic religion and Bhakti actually are and seek, without revealing oneself to the listener and reader as a follower of this cult and thus being forced —more or less—to justify oneself to people of other worldviews and religions - and without trying to entice or convince them to adopt a new cult. Classical Buddhism, for example, was first presented in this way in the West (when Buddhist groups formed, it was already going awry), and quite impersonal presentations of these teachings have helped many in the West to honestly worship and love the Buddha, without making it, outwardly, a new cult, without outwardly a dramatic change of faith, a 'conversion'. Where attempts have been made to bring the East close to the West in the 'form' of Western philosophy or comparisons with Christian theology etc. (Otto, Deussen, Dr. Radhakrishnan), everything has gone amiss. [. . .] I think it must end in disaster if one tries to bring the East or India closer to the West, for example. One should offer the eternal and thus first of all the very human in general, to the West as well as to the East." (letter from Sadānanda to Hella Eidlitz, 6.5.58)

18. Available at: https://sadananda.com/txt/en/text_downloads/en/pers-en.pdf (Accessed 22.01.23)

19. Steiner, Georg (1998[3]): After Babel. *Aspects of Language and Translation*. New York, Oxford etc.: Oxford University Press.

20. Dr. Ferdinando Sardella is Associate Professor at the Department of Ethnology, History of Religions and Gender Studies of Stockholm University.

Bibliography

Ahlberg, Alf (1968): 'Krishna Caitanya—"Indiens dolda skatt,"' *Svenska Dagbladet*, October 30, p. 4.

De, S. K. (1942): *Early History of the Vaishnava Faith and Movement in Bengal*. Calcutta: General Printers and Publishers Limited.

Dimock Jr., Edward C. (1999): *Caitanya Caritāmṛta of Kṛṣṇadāsa Kavirāja*. A Translation and Commentary. Cambridge MA, London: Harvard University Press.

Eidlitz, Walther (1972): *Livets mening och mål i indisk tankevärld*. Övers. av Sigvard Sjögren. Stockholm: Aldus/Bonnier.

———. (1974): *Der Sinn des Lebens: der indische Weg zur liebenden Hingabe*. Olten: Walter Verlag.

———. (1976): *Guds lek: om indisk gudsuppenbarelse*. Svensk övers. Sigvard Sjögren. Red. Günther Eidlitz. Stockholm: Natur & Kultur.

———. (2013): *Kṛṣṇa-Caitanya. Indiens dolda skatt. Hans liv och Hans läre*. Till svenska: Kid Samuesson och Bengt Lundborg. Umeå: h:ström.

———. (2014): *Kṛṣṇa-Caitanya. The Hidden Treasure of India. His Life and Teachings*. Mario Windisch, Bengt Lundborg, Kid Samuelsson and Katrin Stamm (transls.). Umeå: h:ström.

———. (1968): *Kṛṣṇa-Caitanya. Sein Leben und Seine Lehre*. Stockholm: Almqvist & Wiksell.

Jacobsen, Knut A., Sardella, Ferdinando (eds.) (2020): *Handbook of Hinduism in Europe*, Vol. I. Leiden, Boston: Brill.

Kaviraja, Krishnadasa (1999). *Caitanya Caritamrita of Krishnadas Kaviraja*. A Translation and Commentary by Edward C. Dimock Jr. With an Introduction by Edward C. Dimock, Jr and Tony K. Stewart. Tony K. Stewart (Ed.). Cambridge MA: Harvard University Press.

Majumdar, A. K. Caitanya (1969): *His Life and Doctrine*. Bombay: Bharatiya Vidya Bhavan.

Melzer, Friso (1969): Eidlitz, Walther: Krishna Chaitanya. Sein Leben und Seine Lehre, in: *Theologische Literaturzeitung* 94 (3) 1969, pp. 190–191.

Mettauer, Phillip (2013). 'Um den instinktlosen arischen Wiener vom Besuch jüdischer Buchhandlungen abzuhalten . . .' Das Archiv der Reichsschrifttumskammer. *Biblos* 62 (2), pp.105–135. http://data.onb.ac.at/rec/AC14004133 (Accessed: 22 January 2023).

Samuelsson, Kid (2022): "Looking back. My Encounters with Sadananda and Vamandas." Available at: https://www.sadananda.com/txt/en/text_downloads/other_text/en/looking-back-en.pdf (Accessed: 22 January 2023).

Stamm, Katrin (2021): From Poet to Kavi: Walther Eidlitz' Spiritual Odyssey, in: *Journal of Vaiṣṇava Studies* 28 (2), pp. 45–67.

Steiner, Georg (1998, third edition): *After Babel. Aspects of Language and Translation.* New York, Oxford etc.: Oxford University Press.

Stewart, Tony K. (2014): Oxford Bibliographies: Caitanya. Last modified: 30 June 2014. Available at: DOI: 10.1093/obo/9780195399318-0138

Svāmī Sadānanda Dāsa (1956). *Corrections*, unpublished manuscript.

Glimpses of Caitanya
From *Caitanya-candrodaya-nāṭaka* of Kavikarṇapūra

Gerald T. Carney

The moon of *bhakti* is newly arisen,
Exciting pure devotion lovelier than the most excellent jewels.
May Gauracandra smite the gloom of the dominion
Of countless darts of pain inflicted by that noxious beast Kali.
—Kavikarṇapūra, *Caitanya-candrodaya,nāṭaka*, Act I, verse 1

This moonrise of *bhakti* is dramatically presented in the *Caitanya-candrodaya-nāṭaka*, a ten-act Sanskrit drama that employs a mixture of allegorical figures and historical personages to celebrate Viśvambhara Miśra, the religious saint known as Kṛṣṇa Caitanya (1486-1533), and regarded as the incarnation of Kṛṣṇa, whose followers still worship him in India and throughout the world.

The author of the play, Paramānanda Sena (b. 1524), was personally blessed by Caitanya and received from him the title Kavikarṇapūra ("the ear-ornament [the most excellent] of poets). His range of Sanskrit works would justify that title. Around 1542, while still a teenager, he composed a *kāvya* hagiography of Caitanya, *Caitanya-caritāmṛta-mahākāvya*. The *Caitanya-candrodaya-nāṭaka* was performed in 1572. The *Gaura-gaṇoddeśa-dīpikā* [1576] describes Caitanya and his disciples and their roles in eternal Kṛṣṇa-līlā come to earth. The *Ānanda-vṛndāvana-campu* retells and interprets the narrative of the *Bhāgavata Purāṇa*, Book X. The *Kṛṣṇāhnika-kaumudi* recounts the daily activities of Kṛṣṇa, the basis for *līlā-smaraṇa*. The *Alaṃkāra-kaustabha* is a treatise on poetics, which is Kavikarṇapūra's contribution to devotional aesthetics.

This article is focused on the distinct aspects of Caitanya that are celebrated by Kavikarṇapūra in Acts II and III of the *Caitanya-candrodaya*. These are "glimpses," moments of seeing Caitanya as Kavikarṇapūra interprets him on the stage.

Context: Young scholar Viśvambhara has journeyed to Gayā to perform the *śraddha* rituals for his deceased father. While there he was initiated by Īśvara Purī and returned home completely absorbed in devotion to Kṛṣṇa that manifested itself in wild chanting and dancing. Gone was his academic career but he quickly attracted a circle of disciples.

About Act I: After the Prologue, the first act opens with a conversation between the allegorical figures Immorality (*Kali)* and Vice (Ādharma), who gloat over their triumph of unrighteousness as they contemplate the threat that Caitanya poses to their total domination. The attractiveness of Caitanya's person from his childhood is a sign that he is the incarnation of Viṣṇu's blissful nature: this blissful nature makes him unconquerable. Through the chanting of the Lord's name (*nāma-saṃkīrtana*), Caitanya is drowning the whole world in an ocean of bliss.

ACT II

Dispassion's Search

The first scene of Act II is the on-stage search by Dispassion (*Virāga*) for authentic religious practice. One after another he considers and rejects each one as insufficient or already corrupted by Kali: yogic discipline; socio-religious duties of the *varṇāśrāma* system; *Nyāya* philosophy (Viśvambara's prior career); absorption in Brahman without qualities (*nirviśeṣa Brahman,* followers dubbed *Māyāvādins)*; followers of *Sāṅkhya, Vaiśeṣika*, Yoga, and *Pūrva-Mimāṃsā* philosophies; other religious groups (Jains, Buddhists, *Kāpālikas, Pāśupatas*); false asceticism; and pilgrimage become just religious tourism. Some do achieve something but their attainment itself creates an obstacle. So, Nyāya philosophy leaves no occasion to think about the Lord. The *Māyāvādins* are free from sorrow and absorbed in *nirviśeṣa Brahman,* but by their identification with impersonal Brahman they reject the concrete visible form of the Lord and kill the joy of worshipping him. None of these paths leads to the truth about the Lord.

> Without sincere devotional service of Viṣṇu, concentrated, prolonged meditation, steadfast application to the task of studying scriptures and to the

> practice of muttering mantras and observing austerities and ritual niceties are but the mock-play of actors, and, however effective, even if carried out with super-abundant skillfulness, serve only to fill up one's pot belly. [9]
>
> Congratulations, Kali! You have brought the whole surface of the earth under your power.
>
> I have seen all this divisive confusion of mind and words, of precept and example, arising from the exhaustion brought about by the myriads of Kali's filthy minions!
> When, oh when, shall we see the Vaiṣṇavas, equally themselves in spirit and appearance,
> coming along with their hair standing on end, shedding tears, worshipping Kṛṣṇa and singing his praises? [11]

He receives his answer from an offstage voice: "Wherever there is devotional love of the Lord, there they may be found." And that place is in Bengal.

> All glorious is the land of Bengal, a territory that is a garland of pilgrimage shrines. It possesses the city called Navadvīpa where the Lord›s incarnation shines with a beauty like a treasure hoard of gold. O Bengal! In its every city the incarnate Goddess of Devotional Love is quivering with life. [12]

Bhaktidevī enters.

She looks with concern at how exhausted her old friend Dispassion seems, how pained he is by all that he has experienced. She consoles him: O, Dispassion, don't you know? Then, listen!

> An exceedingly compassionate one has come for our sake, the Lord whose actions break through the bondage of worldly existence.
>
> Caitanya, *Gauracandra*, has become incarnate among us.
>
> O Dispassion, in this accursed age of Kali, there is no vehicle of dharma anywhere, not even so much as is covered by the tip of a bud. But the religion of the Lord, the true dharma of the right means to realization, overcomes Kali, bondage, and delusion.
>
> The Lord has become incarnate in the form of a devotee, the Lord
> who possesses pure devotional divine love, the Lord who takes

> away sins and destroys the filth of Kali
> and makes the foul stench of passionate and insurmountable
> inclination to evil disappear in each and every one, down to the
> lowest of the outcastes.

Dispassion poses three questions to Bhaktidevī: What are you, Goddess of Devotion, seeking to accomplish here? What does Caitanya strive for? Will he be the help for me who am helpless?

She answers first for herself: "I purify the worst among men. I shake off all traces of impurity, I cast off all the *saṁskāras*, even the most persistent that are connected with the heart. If the Goddess of Compassion (Kṛpādevī) manifests Caitanya's merciful glance, then I cause some devotional sentiment to well up within them." [15] This compassion exists because of Caitanya's constantly renewed grace.

Bhaktidevī then describes the flowering of devotion that Caitanya is creating in Navadvīpa:

> At Navadvīpa, there is no person living in that whole city who lacks a shrine to Hari. And no shrine lacks an image of the Lord. There is no image to be found lacking attentive worship and none of the worship offered is anything less than religious sentiment full of love. Indeed, there can be no religious sentiment in which the communal celebration of the names and actions of Kṛṣṇa and dancing are not a prominent part. [16]

> Each day, as his dear friends would sing, the god would dance, becoming more and more affected by his hair standing on end, free-flowing tears and perspiration, and similar phenomena, [17]

Conversion of the (drunken) Muslim tailor

One day Viśvambhara was engaged in devotion at Śrivāsa's house. He was observed by a tipsy Muslim tailor, "a reveler possessed of consummate arrogance." But, on seeing Caitanya, he became distressed at his state (in the morning!) and his demeanor. "Each time he gazed on Caitanya, his hair stood on end for joy and his whole body shook. . . . A flood of tears left his cheeks and moistened his chest. He began to dance with his hands lifted high." Śrīvāsa said, "Lord, unparalleled is the greatness of your intoxication. Because of it, this man, previously attached to striving for his jars of drink, has not lost his discernment. By that sight he had of you, brief though it was, he was rendered sinless, freed from karmic pain, and was overwhelmed with intoxication." The convert continues the recitation of the Lord's name, even when the local mullah beat him. Asked about this, he replies, "There is no God but Viśvambhara!" Asked how this man of very low origin could come to receive such grace, Bhaktidevī replies:

> This happened because the grace of Hari is not dependent on privilege of birth, conduct, stage of life, fulfillment of religious duties, knowledge, family and all such things. Oh, no! His grace is absolutely spontaneous. He perceives no difference between those worthy and those unworthy of receiving his favor. [19]

Manifestation of the Avatāras in Murāri's Courtyard

On the night of the full moon, "the god was manifested in the form of Balarāma/Saṅkarṣaṇa. As a palpable darkness descended, all sensed a perfume like that of wine and saw a manifestation of the plough and mace. Then Viśvambhara became more intoxicated with the smell of nectar and manifested Balarāma himself. The songs of his gathered friends set him dancing and he "caused to pass before their eyes, one after another, manifestations of all his principal *avatāras*—the Buddha, Nārāyana, Narasiṁha, and so on—and at the end, stirred by impulsive compassion, he showed Nityānanda his six-armed form:

> With two hands he held his pleasant-sounding flute, while with the other four arms, he held the mace, conch, discus and lotus. He was adorned with the diadem, the pearl necklace, the two arm-bracelets, the flower wreath of triumph, and the jewel Kaustubha. [20]

> [Nityānanda] saw such a marvel! One of unsurpassable beauty, and incredible sweetness, great courage, dignity, friendliness and generosity, calmness, abounding in tenderness indeed the noble state of the Undifferentiated Absolute itself. [21]

"When he saw that form, supreme joy welled up in Nityānanda, making his hair stand on end—so that he began to look like a man in a furry robe. He burst into exclamations of praise:"

> You are Viṣṇu! You are Śiva! You are Brahmā! You are the Vasus, Agni, the moon, the sun, the sky, the earth and the wind! I adore you, Murāri! Glory to you, Lord of all! [22]

> Some imagine your six arms to mean that you destroy the six powerful faults of man›s natural state. But, magnanimous Lord, we declare that with those six arms you bestow on us life›s four aims, devotion and love. [23]

Caitanya's Seizure by Ecstatic Devotion

One day some students saw Viśvambhara returning from bathing in the Ganges with his clothes all wet. They began to tease him, one singing a verse on the Lord's name, another on a verse from the *Bhāgavata Purāṇa,* a third a song of love. He fell on the ground in the muddy puddles, his body splattered with mud. The wet clothes, the mud, and his copious tears made him appear as though his body were bound with creepers, "brought to that pass through the agitation of love." But Dispassion had the last word: "How obvious is his inability to control the joy that wells from love."

Refuge of All People: Cure of the Brahman Leper

One day, a Brahman-in-name-only observed him dancing in the middle of the street that passed Ācāryaratna's house. Viśvambhara was dancing, "overwhelmed by the greatest happiness." The Brahman leper, with pus oozing from his body, seeing no other remedy, began to cry out:

> Son of Sacī, Viśvambhara, all men declare you the Lord, the mighty one, the Supreme Being. . . . If you can bring about the cure of a wretch like me, then truly you are none other than the Lord, the lotus-eyed one in person, in essence the happiness of the world.
>
> Then, the Lord, trembling, his body all-aquiver with hair standing on end, felt compassion toward him, that wretch of a Brahman, approached by the noose of death.
>
> Then the Lord said: "Whoever God is, he is inaccessible to all. Why then do you grasp hold of me? Nevertheless, there is a way of curing your own disease. If you follow it, the disease will leave you.
>
> [The cure] "Something that can be a sign. My poor Brahman friend, this man Advaitācārya is the very best of all those sinless men wholly devoted to the love of God, of God who is the friend of all the world. If you but drink of the water that has bathed his feet, then this illness, the result of sin, will recede.
>
> He did this and was cured.

Virāga and Bhaktidevī leave. Viśvambhara enters, with Advaitācārya, Śrivāsa and others

The Lord's Self-Revelation to Advaita (in Navadvīpa)

Advaita's Complaint: "Nityānanda has seen God's six-armed form. But the Lord also promised me: I will show it [the six-armed form] to you to reveal my nature (*svarūpa-darśanāya*). Why is the Lord, my protector, not showing it then? [The six-armed form is revealed.] The Lord: This now is my essential form, the form on which Advaita lavishes such desire.

Advaita's Renewed Complaint (after seeing the six-armed form): "What can I say now? If this is your magnanimous form, your essential nature, then everything has been revealed and our yearning to see your blue and lovely [cowherd] form will be stilled. But if *that* [cowherd] is your true one, then to see *this* one is to make a mockery of love." Śrīvāsa reminds the Lord of his promise to show *his* form to Advaita. Viśvambhara tries to evade this point, citing "madness," but Śrivāsa insists:"

> But, Lord, ordinary madness *is* but a disease. But your madness affects even those who see and hear quite well. It uproots all illness. It is a fact that a person goes out of his mind and loses his composure even after experiencing ordinary joy. Then how can anything restrict the joy coming from God who is joy and knowledge by his very essence. Indeed he *is* Essential Bliss and Essential Knowledge.

Viśvambara surrenders, "What I reveal no longer depends on me. Let him see me with his own inner eye." The Lord is overcome by the insistence of his devotees and reveals his divine form to Advaita with his "inner eye" enlightened by his devotional love.

Advaita's Vision: Advaita is now in an ecstatic trance but Śrīvāsa describes his appearance:

> He has lost the experience of his outer sense organs. His heart has become absorbed in the intensity of his inner joy. Oh! His body is now completely exhausted by the throbbing of his heart. In the enjoyment of that experience, in that highest state, even his soul is dissolved. He breathes heavily

> and reaches out to the object of enlightenment with his hair standing on end for excitement. [25]
>
> We cannot see what *you* don't reveal to us. This form of yours before our eyes is itself the most treasured possession of your devotees. You must now shake him free (of perplexities). Don't any longer, Lord most powerful, cause that form to be hidden from his mind and from his heart.

Caitanya suggests that Advaita tell what he is seeing. Advaita awakens but he seems to see the vision all over again as he gazes at Caitanya.

> Oh! What is this (God of) great brilliance that makes our range of vision disappear? He possesses the fresh fragrance of a cluster of lotuses, of a sudden newly-opening; he glistens like a row of clouds. He is dark like a bunch of Tamāla blossoms, refulgent with a lustre exceeding that of spreading glow of a mass of sapphires. [26]
>
> The Primordial One, the Great Being, appears before my eyes in the center of the dark sun of consciousness, overflowing with sweet nectar and ambrosia in his every limb, skilled in the art of making soft-sounding music on his flute . . . [27]

Śrīvāsa says that Advaita is speaking in present, not past, tense as though "he imagines what is past to be present right now before his eyes." Advaita continues:

> His long hair, dark and thick, is attractively curled. His eyebrows are endearing. His nose is pleasantly curved. His lotus eyes are wide-open, red and rolling. His lovely lower lip, beautifully sloped, has the red glow of the phoenix flower. [28]
>
> He is attended by Śrī and Lakṣmī and adorned with those two precious jewels, Śrīvatsa and Kaustubha. A brilliant garland of pearls hangs on his chest. He is well-adorned with the flower garlands received at his feet; his arms are well-developed, long and strong like staves. [29]

Śrīvāsa asks how Advaita's deep devotion could come about so suddenly. The Lord replies:

> The sort of theophany evoked by meditation and discipline takes long to realize and its nature is accidental to the Lord. But the sudden theophany of

> Hari in the heart, that is the incarnation of the highest Lord. [30]

Śrīvāsa pursues the point, "How then, Lord, without long-lasting yoga practice could his heart be fit for receiving the revelation of the Lord? The Lord replies:

> The Lord's purifying kindness rushed ahead his own unveiling of himself, just as the dawn destroys the darkness before the sun actually rises in the East. [31]

Śrīvāsa raises again the question of a past or present vision. Told by the Lord to ask Advaita himself, he says: "O noble-minded one, are you really seeing this now or are you talking about a vision you have already seen?" Advaita slowly wakes "like someone surfacing on the ocean of happiness" and says:

> Oh! That tremendously great darkness that came forth from the Mighty One entered into the depths of me and in the twinkling of an eye was hidden once more. Now, with my external knowledge restored, my mind is in utter misery, for I seem to see it entering into my depths again. [32]
>
> I saw a divine youth, dark as a garland of blue lotus, with his right thigh placed upon his left. You look like him and he like you. It is just as though there were no difference at all. Oh, tell me please how this trance experience happened to me? [33]

Śrīvāsa sums up the response: "How fortunate indeed is one who perceives *you* in this form." But the point can be clearly stated: It is *you*, Caitanya, who has been seen in this form. And, "Wasn't it *you* who said, "I will show it to you." An offstage voice gets the last word: "Yes, that's the truth."

ALL EXIT

The Drama Speaks: Theological Directions of Act II

* total failure of dharma, yoga practice, intellectual systems, absorption in Brahman, even extreme asceticism; but . . .
*unambiguous affirmation of Viśvambhara's divinity, as the *avatāra* come as devotee (*bhaktāvatāra*), revealer of all the *avatāras*, and then his own form (*svarūpa*) of his identity (non-difference) with Kṛṣṇa
*reliance on the Lord's grace, spontaneous and unconditional, with-

out regard for status or preparation, completely transforming even the most lowly and despised in society (the Muslim tailor, the Brahman leper),
*expressed in the experience of ecstatic devotional practice, singing the Lord's praises with dancing and song (*saṃkīrtana*), participating in his divine *līlā*, entering a practical non-dualism of eternal joy, beyond the six-armed form to the two-armed Kṛṣṇa, from awesome majesty (*aiśvarya*) to intoxicating sweet ness (*mādhurya*)
*Viśvambhara's personal piety (ecstatic rapture from the ruf fians' taunts), an illness that cures
*localized in Bengal, in Navadvīpa, among a devotional com munity of friends and family (Śrīvāsa's house, Murāri's courtyard, disciples Advaita and Nityānanda, mother Sacī)

ACT III "The play about the gifts"

This act consists of three scenes: a conversation between allegorical Maitrī ("Friendship") and Premabhakti ("Ardent Devotional Love" or "Devotion with Rasa"), the prelude conversation between the *sūtradhāra* (stage manager) and the *paripārśvaka* (his assistant), and the *garbhāṅka* (inset play) itself. This play includes preliminary dialogue between the allegorical figures and then the play proper including Rādhā and her friends (Jaratī and Lalitā) and Kṛṣṇa and his (Kusumāsava and Subala).

Maitrī's initial tale of woe mirrors that of Virāga in Act II, but Premabhakti turns Maitrī's attention to the positive effects of Caitanya's appearance, which has countered evil with the arousing of devotional sentiments. Their sweetness and nectar culminate in fully developed devotional love (*prema*) and accompanying bliss (*ānanda*). (vv. 3-5) This is what devotees experience who vicariously share Rādhā's love for Kṛṣṇa, as do those who participate in and observe this play-within-the-play. (vv. 7-9) Just as Caitanya (Kṛṣṇa) was shown in Act II to be the source of all the divine manifestations, so here he is seen to be the cause, possessor, distributor, and Lord of all devotional *rasas*. His *līlā* is portrayed by his participation in the inset-play, playing the role of Rādhā. He tastes her *bhakti rasa* for him, invites his followers to join in taking roles in the play, and extends this invitation to the audience who participate in this līlā. Premabhakti establishes a connection between this play of Rādhā and Kṛṣṇa and their intimate *līlā,* which is the highest reality. Rādhā herself becomes present through *rasa,* according to the receptivity of the audience: there is no comparison between *hearing about* the Lord's loving *līlā* and *seeing it* in this play. Maitrī and Premabhakti then join the audience but continue to interject commentary.

The stage manager introduces the play, extending the parallel between *this* play and the Lord's eternal play. (v 29) People seek delight in ordinary life filled with strife. The reverse is the truth: the play of Kṛṣṇa is the ordinary, bliss-filled reality. When Nārada enters at the start of the inset play, Maitrī comments that although she knows that it is Śrīvāsa playing Nārada, it certainly seems as though it were Nārada himself there. And the setting in Vṛndāvava and *this* play reveal how Kṛṣṇa's own self is manifest in so many different forms. Nārada realizes that these manifestations (the setting and the play) open up an ocean of bliss and intoxicating sweet sentiment, an intoxication that is always complete rather than fading, pleasant rather than debilitating, redemptive rather than destructive. (v. 38)

Thus the play begins. Rādhā (Caitanya) enters, on her way to perform *Gopīśvara pūjā,* making an offering of flower blossoms to Śiva. Nārada emphasizes that these activities are happening here and now in *this* play. And how marvelous it is that Caitanya, the *bhakta-avatāra* of Kṛṣṇa, the Lord himself, *is* Rādhā in the play and in *līlā,* an affirmation of identity even though they appear as different in the play.

In the play itself, an argument develops between Kṛṣṇa and his friends and Rādhā and hers. Kusumāsava asks for the blossoms intended for *pūja* to Śiva with extended banter about the particular "fruit" that Kṛṣṇa wants. Meanwhile, Kṛṣṇa's gaze is hardly directed at the flowers she carries but at the supreme flower, Rādhā. Subala, the more sober-minded of Kṛṣṇa's companions, convinces Lalitā that the blossoms are nothing compared with the women's beauty and hence that keeping them is meaningless. Kṛṣṇa, meanwhile, asks for the blossoms, as Rādhā casts loving looks in his direction. The flowers are handed over and scattered about; now nothing remains for the intended pūja. Kusumāsava tells the crestfallen Rādhā that here in the forest is a Lord who bestows flowers, who is the true Gopīśvara, who shelters all who seek the protection of Vṛndāvana's Lord. The offering is then made at Kṛṣṇa's temple. When Rādhā turns to leave, Kṛṣṇa tries to detain her but receives a fierce tongue-lashing from Lalitā. The actors seem to get carried away in their roles: Kṛṣṇa (Advaita) tries to take Rādhā (Viśvambhara) away by force. She escapes with Lalitā's help, and the play comes to an end. Meanwhile, Premabhakti has been commenting on the significance of this action: this play, seeming so remote from ordinary life, so extraordinary in its bliss, is for Kṛṣṇa most ordinary and natural, extraordinary only its degree of sweet attraction for all.

The inset-play reflects the act's central preoccupation on four levels of *līlā*:

*The *līlā* of Viśvambhara with his companions
*The roles that Viśvambhara and his companions play in the inset-play and the cultivation of the related *rasa*, especially his taking the *rasa* of Rādhā
*The omniscient commentary of Maitrī and Premabhakti who explain what is *really* happening, beyond the surface reality
*The audience of Vaiṣṇava devotees (within the play or reading it) whose cultivated devotional sensibility allows them to participate in the *līlā* and penetrate its levels of mystery.

On all of these levels, the *līlā* serves as a scrim: opaque under the light of ordinary reality, revealing what is hidden as exterior light fades and the inner light takes the audience to deeper and still deeper levels of participation in the *līlā*.

What happened here? To sketch out answers, I turn to two distinguished scholars, Tony K. Stewart and Rembert Lutjeharms, who focus in on this text and probe its meaning. Both see Act III of *Caitanya-candrodaya* as central to understanding the nature and meaning of Caitanya but employ different methods and sensibilities that account for subtle but significant differences in approach and conclusion.

Tony K. Stewart's treatment of Kavikarṇapūra in *The Final Word* fills only a dozen pages but he highlights the important contribution of this Act III within the development of the Bengal Vaiṣṇava tradition. Stewart begins his use of *Caitanya-candrodaya* against the background of three earlier hagiographies of Caitanya: Murāri Gupta's *Kṛṣṇa-caitanya-caritāmṛta*, Vṛndāvana Dāsa's *Caitanya-Bhāgavata*, and Kavikarṇapūra's earlier work *Kṛṣṇa-caitanya-caritāmṛta-māhakāvya*.

> From this point, the issue was not to establish Caitanya's divinity, for by the fourth decade of the sixteenth, all Vaiṣṇavas seemed to agree in a general way that he was Kṛṣṇa as *svayam Bhagavān*, and all that entailed. These three and subsequent biographies took the practicing community for their

> primary audience. The concern of the remaining biographies was to work out the implications of these assertions, rectifying inconsistencies where they were deemed significant, exploring how the community itself participated in his divinity, and explaining what Caitanya meant to the community and the world, for the world was fast changing in the territories occupied by Bengali Vaiṣṇavas in the mid-sixteenth century. (Stewart 120)

Not the least of these questions concerned how Caitanya was not just identified with Kṛṣṇa but was the Lord *as Caitanya* in his activities or *līlā*. After reflecting back to the revelations of Act II, Viśvambhara revealed as Kṛṣṇa himself in his *bhakta-avatāra*, Stewart argues that Kavikarṇapūra arranges the critical moment for the play as a whole in Act III. There Caitanya and his followers stage a play about Kṛṣṇa and Rādhā that concerns the *dāna līlā*, the demand for "toll" payment for passing through; the opportunities for playful banter make this subject an audience favorite as *rāslīlā*. It serves as the tool to reflect *Rādhā-bhāva* and *gopī-bhāva* in the context of the drama.

Stewart points out that "Kavikarṇapūra chose to reveal in a formal drama what he deemed to be the final truth of Caitanya's descent, that is, his assumption of the *bhāva* of Rādhā." That intimate play is displayed in *this* play and especially in "the climax, in which Caitanya's true identity was presented, [that] came in the *garbhāṅka*, the 'play within the play,'" a strategy of three-fold distancing that kept the "secret" that "Gaura is Rādhā" from the uninitiated but revealed it to "experienced devotees." (Stewart 168) "Kavikarṇapūra's allegory is but a frame to explain how Caitanya and his companions have come to reveal the secret by which they will rid the world of *adharma* in this final age." (Stewart 167) The allegorical figures provide commentary and context for the historical figures, thus revealing the third dimension of transcendence. The play provides an immediate experience of devotion that is more delightful and compelling than any theoretical argument: it moves the audience to attentive participation in that experience. Stewart identifies Kavivarṇapūra's use of dramatic strategies of *replication* and *identity* within this act. Caitanya is so many figures: devotee Viśvambhara, *bhakta-avatāra*, as Kṛṣṇa, then as Rādhā, then absorbing Advaita's play of Kṛṣṇa, and then that of Lalitā as well—all complicating but revealing his identity as Kṛṣṇa *and* Rādhā. Caitanya and his companions "discover that they are enacting in history a reality that is timeless and transcendent: the eternal love of Rādhā and Kṛṣṇa." (Stewart 170) Stewart summarizes, "Up to now we have only glimpsed the bits and pieces of these strategies as the devotional community sought to explain what they had experienced; with Kavikarṇapūra's drama the serious work of consolidation was begun in earnest . . ." (Stewart 169)

The dramatic development of Act III harkens back to the conclusion of Act II. Viśvambhara has manifested all of the *avatāras* with himself as *svayam Bhagavān*, Kṛṣṇa. Now he comes to enter the *līlā* of Rādhā. In Stewart's translation of the dialogue between allegorical players Maitrī and Premabhakti (Stewart 171-173), Premabhakti explains: "Today he wishes to manifest the *līlās* of Rādhā . . . to act in the *bhāva* of Rādhā. He has entered into the *līlā* of [Vṛndāvana's queen], the *rādhā-bhāva*, in order to make available this experience to every great *bhakta*'s heart."(171) As the various actors appear to *become* the roles they are playing, and in fact they *do*, Premabhakti concludes: "What you see is precisely what you are supposed to believe you are seeing."(172) The climax of this act is expressed by Premabhakti when Rādhā enters (that is, Viśvambhara as Kṛṣṇa playing Rādhā, experiencing *rādhā-bhāva*, being Rādhā, while being Kṛṣṇa, appearing as Viśvambhara): "He has assumed this form [of Rādhā] in order to perform the actions appropriate to Rādhā in the descent of Kṛṣṇa this time around. In the *līlās* of Kṛṣṇa he has a *śakti*, and that *śakti* is not differentiated from him or his parts; and now he has appeared in a male and female form, the part of which are not divided even though the body is." (Stewart 173)

Kavikarṇapūra includes in Act III a kind of genealogy of *bhakti*, the background of Premabhakti. *Prema* is devotion as intense emotional love that is lived, experienced, intoxicating (devotion with *rasa*). This is the highest expression of love. It is characteristic of Rādhā's love. And it is "the preferred form Kṛṣṇa chooses to experience when he takes on two forms as the taster and tasted, lover and beloved, Rādhā and Kṛṣṇa." (Stewart 173) Viśvambhara is *bhakta-avatāra*, non-different from Kṛṣṇa. He is playing Rādhā in this *līlā* so profoundly that she is really there, no difference at all. Then *who* is he? The not-so-much-later tradition will respond that Caitanya is both Rādhā and Kṛṣṇa, not acting in a play, much less play-acting, but the divine nature itself. Stewart continues to discuss the second "almost-revelation" of this truth in Act VII where Caitanya pushes Rāmānanda Rāya further and further toward a realization of his full identity, in Stewart's summary: "the ultimate object of worship is not Kṛṣṇa, but the divine couple Rādhā and Kṛṣṇa together" and the audience's recognition that "Caitanya is that Rādhā and Kṛṣṇa mysteriously fused." (Stewart 175)

> Some few years later it would fall to Kṛṣṇadāsa Kavirāja finally to state explicitly what many devotees had come to believe, and he would expand the conversation between Rāmānanda and Caitanya to do it in the eighth chapter of the *madhya līlā* of the *Caitanya caritāmṛta;* but it was Kavikarṇapūra who first located that specific revelation in the conversation between Rāmānanda and Caitanya.

But all of this was anticipated dramatically, devotionally, in the play-within-the-play of Act III.

Rembert Lutjeharms' *A Vaiṣṇava Poet in Early Modern Bengal: Kavikarṇapūra's Splendor of Speech* adds additional layers to the understanding of Caitanya as well as of Caitanya Vaiṣṇavism in Bengal during the mid- to late-sixteenth century. His focus is on Paramānanda Sena, the youngest son of Śivānanda Sena--Kavikarṇapūra. Śivānanda was the devotee from Kumārahaṭṭa who organized and supported from 1512 onward the annual pilgrimage of Caitanya's Bengali disciples to Puri.

There they encountered him anew and sought to re-establish their devotional nexus during a short visit or a relatively long summer sojourn. According to various narratives, Paramānanda as an infant was presented by his father to Caitanya. The master allowed him to suck on his toe; later he received the mantra "Kṛṣṇa" from the Lord as *dīkṣā*, and, when he improvised a couplet in praise of Kṛṣṇa, received the title "Kavikarṇapūra" as "the adornment of poets" from Caitanya himself. His subsequent works amply fulfilled the promise of the title. Thus Kavikarṇapūra, born in 1524, personally encountered Caitanya and participated in the inner circle of his Bengali disciples prior to the master's death in 1533.

Lutjeharms' book has a broad scope as he is concerned with all six of the works attributable to Kavikarṇapūra. But beyond the two distinctly hagiographical works, *Caitanya-caritāmṛta-mahā-kāvya* (1542) and *Caitanya-candrodaya-nāṭaka* (1572), Lutjeharms emphasizes, as his title suggests, Kavikarṇapūra's treatment of poetics (*Alaṃkāra-kaustubha*) and his realization of the full range of "splendor of speech" in his "poetic masterpiece" *Ānanda-vṛndāvana-campū.* (40-45)

Kavikarṇapūra's theology is developed in tandem with that of his guru, Śrīnātha Paṇḍita, as presented in *Caitanya-mata-mañjuṣā*, his commentary on the *Bhāgavata Purāṇa.* Lutjeharms' discussion of their theology is therefore essentially a conversation between the two. This text "could be the earliest commentary on the *Bhāgavata* from the Caitanya tradition. More importantly, it is one of the few comprehensive theological texts of the early movement to have emerged from Bengal, far from the intellectual center in Vraja, and as such reflects the early intellectual developments of the Caitanya movement in Bengal."(50) Śrīnātha's strategy is to show that the *Bhāgavata* teaches what Caitanya embodies and teaches; its meaning is directed to him and Caitanya completes the purport of the *purāṇa*. In Lutjeharms' development of this dialogic theology between *Caitanya-candrodaya* and the *Bhāgavata*, passages from the *purāṇa* are explicated by reference to the drama and vice versa so that the two voices, guru and chela, drama and commentary, blend together. Lutjeharms concludes his initial treatment of Kavikarṇapūra's contribution in the following fashion:

> I highlighted the importance of Kavikarṇapūra for our understanding of the early history of Caitanya Vaiṣṇavism. Kavikarṇapūra furthers the teachings of his guru Śrīnātha, whose thought seems to have developed independently of the Vṛndāvana Gosvāmīs, and, in some sense, that tradition ends with Kavikarṇapūra, whose ideas have been overshadowed by the works of the Gosvāmīs which arrived shortly after he completed his main works. Kavikarṇapūra and Śrīnātha taught a theology that is distinctly Caitanya Vaiṣṇava and not, fundamentally, at odds with those ideas taught by their contemporaries (including the Gosvāmīs of Vṛndāvana), yet there are some ideas unique to them, or uniquely articulated by them . . . which no later author further developed, as Rūpa's and Jīva's magisterially systematic exposition of Caitanya Vaiṣṇava theology became the foundation for all later theological thought in the tradition. (Lutjeharms 67)

Lutjeharms' development of the theology implicit in this conversation between guru and chela, between the *Bhāgavata* and the lived experience with Caitanya leads him to coin a phrase that serves to resolve the tension between the other worldly reality (*alaukika*) of Kṛṣṇa and this ordinary world (*laukika*): everything has been transformed by the entry of the otherworldly reality of Kṛṣṇa into this world as Caitanya. The world has been irrevocably changed into an *other-worldly worldly world*. (Lutjeharms 71-72) Viśvambhara is Kṛṣṇa descended as a devotee (*bhakta-avatāra)* bringing with him all his associates that are described in Act I of *Caitanya-candrodaya-naṭakam* and in the *Gauragaṇoddeśa-dīpikā*. He reveals himself to his devotees, draws them into his devotional practice and, in Act II, reveals all the divine forms until finally, in respose to Advaita's demand, he reveals as his own *svarūpa*—the two-armed cowherd lover Kṛṣṇa. "Caitanya can do all this only because he is Kṛṣṇa himself, the complete manifestation of divinity, just as only the full moon can dispel the darkness of night." (113)

The third act, as we have seen already, shifts its focus to Rādhā. Friendship [Maitrī] and Devotion-with-Love [Premabhakti] come to witness the extraordinary play which Caitanya and his followers are staging that morning. They lead the audience "to the play of Rādhā and Kṛṣṇa that Caitanya and his companions have brought to earth." (Lutjeharms 115) There he will play her role and give joy to the whole world by revealing the intensity of her passionate love. "Through *rasa*, Śrī Rādhā herself will very soon appear before our eyes." (121) "It is *rasa* by which the audience of Caitanya's performance can absorb themselves in the divine play and come to understand Rādhā's pure love, as Rādhā herself will appear in the improvised theatre of Ācāryaratna's courtyard through *rasa*." (122)

As background, Lutjeharms explains that "though Caitanya is indeed God, he would rarely reveal his divinity but instead act as his own devotee, thereby teaching the world the way of devotion but also, through his own devotional experience, affecting that world and bringing others into that passionate devotion." (101)

> Kavikarṇapūra teaches that Caitanya is none other than Kṛṣṇa as his devotee (*bhakta-rūpa*). . . . When Kṛṣṇa appears as Caitanya, hiding his divinity under his identity as his own devotee, it is thus particularly Rādhā's love that he reveals. He "wishes to see the passion of Vṛndāvana's queen," Kavikarṇapūra explains, "and through spontaneous play revealed . . . the irreproachable wisdom of the great emotions of the cowherd maidens' crown jewel." Kavikarṇapūra brings out *this dual identity of Caitanya as both Rādhā and Kṛṣṇa subtly but clearly in act three of the Caitanya-candrodaya, in which Caitanya and his associates stage a short drama about Rādhā and Kṛṣṇa's play.* (101 emphasis added)

As the play unfolds, initially Caitanya plays Rādhā, Advaita Kṛṣṇa, Śrīvāsa Nārada, and Gadādhara Lalitā, but Premabhakti and Friendship comment on how the characters are played with an intensity that is more than acting; portrayal reveals reality, their real presence on that courtyard stage. Caitanya's emotional attachment overflows as he incorporates not only Rādhā but Kṛṣṇa and Lalitā together as well, male and female but without conflating, non-different but still different. Lutjeharms notes how all these dimensions are revealed simultaneously by Caitanya, in Caitanya: Caitanya is Kṛṣṇa, Rādhā, and the gopīs as well. And the audience—Friendship and Premabhakti, the disciples that morning, his subsequent readers—participate in that play, they live in it and from it. They "come to realize that Caitanya is not just Kṛṣṇa but embodies Rādhā and the *gopīs* too. The unique character of Caitanya is such that when he acts as his own devotee, his divinity is most vividly revealed." (102) It is revealed as both intimate and transcendent, another dimension of the dynamism of devotional transformation brought by Kṛṣṇa's *bhaktāvatāra.*

Kavikarṇapūra tells us about Viśvambhara's experience, his devotional practice with his Bengali disciples, and the powerful dynamism of devotion let loose in Caitanya Vaiṣṇavism. In this play, this *līlā,* Caitanya experiences Rādhā's yearning and love for Kṛṣṇa so deeply that there is no difference between him and her, only the depths of devotion experienced with *rasa.* This experience was communicated in Kavikarṇapūra's drama and Śrīnātha's *Bhāgavata* commentary. It was experienced anew in devotional practice by the community of disciples in Bengal and in Purī. His disciples, his audience, his readers can cultivate this experience of heart so well that they are enabled by this deep devotion to participate in the divine *līlā* itself.

In the conclusion of his book (and drawing on other texts), Lutjeharms returns to the relationship of Caitanya with Rādhā and the *gopīs*: "Kavikarṇapūra can thus not think of the *gopīs'* love for Kṛṣṇa without thinking of Caitanya." (319) He and Śrīnātha presented a re-reading of Rādhā's character, "profoundly shaped by their understanding of Caitanya. Since Caitanya is Kṛṣṇa 'who wishes to see the passion of Vṛndāvana's queen' we can only understand *her* through *him.*" (320 emphasis added)

> Śrīnātha's and Kavikarṇapūra's personal relationship with Caitanya frames their interpretation of the *Bhāgavata* narrative . . . and it is through their encounters with Caitanya that they re-read the narrative of the *rāsa* dance. Indeed, Kavikarṇapūra specifically refers to this *rāsa* dance to explain Caitanya's dual identity in both the *Caitanya-caritāmṛta-mahā-kāvya* and the *Gaura-gaṇoddeśa-dīpikā.* It is therefore through him, who is "a golden mountain of true Love" that Kavikarṇapūra understands Rādhā's devotion to Kṛṣṇa and the nature of love. Caitanya's desire to deliver the world and bring his devotees to Vṛndāvana, as Kavikarṇapūra describes at the end of the *Caitanya-candrodaya,* is therefore an expression of Rādhā's desire to lead the *gopīs* to Kṛṣṇa, as we see here in the *Ānanda-vṛndāvana.* Indeed, as the *Ānanda-vṛndāvana* suggests, *it is because he experienced Rādhā's love that he desires the deliverance of others, by granting them what he himself experienced as his own devotee.* And that experience of Rādhā's love draws all devotees together in mutual friendship, so that they can dance around

> the divine couple, whom Caitanya embodies, while they are all simultaneously embraced by the dark splendor of Vṛndāvana's cowherd prince. (320 emphasis added)

A futile struggle indeed to find words to describe this intimate relationship between Caitanya and Kṛṣṇa, and Rādhā, and the *gopīs*, and their devotional communities. In Act II Caitanya reveals his *svarūpa* as Kṛṣṇa: "you look like him and he like you: it is just as though there were no difference at all." In Act III he enters into *rādhā-bhāva* and becomes her, and the *gopīs* for added measure. The dramatic play of Caitanya and his substantive relationships with Rādhā, Kṛṣṇa, and *gopīs* cannot be limited to "androgyne" or "joint incarnation," true as they are in stating the "secret" identity. There is so much more "secret," more mystery. Kavikarṇapūra recounts a *līlā* that is eternal but brought into time, that "other-worldly worldly" world of Caitanya. Caitanya, Kṛṣṇa, Rādhā are non-different, but not identical. The devotion of Kṛṣṇa's *bhakta-avatāra* as experience, as substantive relation, as indwelling, as co-inhesion is simply an echo of that dark splendor. The *kīrtana* recalls that on the threshold of the worst of time, an exceedingly compassionate one came for the sake of all, even those least deserving. And that drama is sketched out in these two acts of Kavikarṇapūra's play with that mystery made visible with *rasa*: memories of ecstatic dancing at Śrīvāsa's house, a revelation in the heart, and the love of Rādhā realized in Ācāryaratna's courtyard, moments when the divine became palpable with a glimpse of Caitanya that penetrates the depths of the heart.

Caitanya's Bengali associates, like Śivānanda Sena and his son Kavikarṇapūra, could make the annual journey to Purī to see Caitanya and reinforce their memories. Now, in this play, many years after Caitanya left his body, the narrative of this *līlā* provides an opportunity for the audience to have an experience of Caitanya, indeed to participate in his *līlā*. Caitanya is always the devotee, in every situation he reveals himself as the *bhakta-āvatāra* and empowers deeper devotion. There is so much at stake in sustaining this memory as both experience and the underlying relationship, "[Kavikarṇapūra's] own works on Caitanya—and the *Caitanya-candrodaya* in particular—were then also an attempt to preserve the memories of Caitanya and his devotees for future generations and, by the rich theological contextualization of his life, help them understand their significance."(51) That journey continues . . .

It is best to close with poetry, a final couplet of Kavikarṇapūra's, adapted from Lutjeharms work (102)—

May that golden moon
Drive away the darkness of the world

Bibiography

Sanskrit Texts

Caitanya-candrodayam nāṭakam of Kavivarṇapūra [Paramānanda Sena]. Edited with Hindi commentary *Prakāśa* by Ācārya Rāmacandra Miśra. Haridāsa Sanskrita Granthamālā, 267. Vārāṇasī: Chowkhamba Sanskrit Series Office, 1966.

Caitanya-mata-mañjuṣā of Śrīnātha Cakravarti. Edited by Purīdāsa Mahāśaya. Vṛndāvana: Haridāsa Śarmā, 1955. (Sanskrit in Bengali Script) Available online: https://archive.org/details/chaitanya_mata_manjusha/page/n3/mode/2up [Accessed 4/20/23]

Critical Studies

Lutjeharms, Rembert (2018): *A Vaiṣṇava Poet in Early Modern Bengal—Kavikarṇapūra's Splendor of Speech.* Oxford: Oxford University Press.

Stewart, Tony K. (2010): *The Final Word—The Caitanya Caritāmṛta and the Grammar of Religious Tradition.* Oxford: Oxford University Press.

Previous Publications on Caitanya-candrodaya nāṭaka of Kavikarṇapūra:

Carney, Gerald T. (1979): "The Theology of Kavikarṇapūra's Caitanyacandrodaya, Act II." Doctoral Thesis. Fordham University.

———. (1989): "Caitanya and his Mother Saci Discuss Sannyāsa: A Note to Kavikarṇapūra's Caitanya-candrodaya 4.1," in Tony K. Stewart (ed.), *Shaping Bengali Worlds, Public and Private.* East Lansing: Asian Studies Centre, Michigan State University [South Asia Series Occasional Papers no. 37].

———. (1992): "Caitanya in Vraja: Another Construction." *Journal of Vaiṣṇava Studies* 1(1): 134–45.

———. (1996): "Entering the Dynamics of Vaiṣṇava Devotion: The Inset Play in Act III of Kavikarṇapūra's Caitanyacandrodaya." *Journal of Vaiṣṇava Studies* 5(1): 53–63.

Sacred Soundtracks: Chaitanya and Kīrtan in Classic Bengali Cinema

Guy L. Beck

Prior to the 1960s, the name of "Chaitanya" was virtually unknown in the Western world except among members of the Indian community and a handful of academics. My first encounter with the story of Chaitanya was in New York in 1970 through the International Society for Krishna Consciousness (ISKCON), a spiritual movement that entered the culture of America in 1965. The beautifully produced books by Founder/Ācārya, His Divine Grace A. C. Bhaktivedānta Swami Prabhupāda (1896–1977), provided the first compelling narratives and devotional teachings of Śrī Chaitanya Mahāprabhu (1486-1534 CE) of Bengal and Orissa, one of India's greatest saints of the past five hundred years, in the English language. The writings and lectures of His Divine Grace were so profound and uplifting that it seemed amazing how such a divine manifestation as Chaitanya had appeared and walked on this Earth at that time. Avoiding many of the difficulties and controversies associated with the life of Jesus more than two thousand years ago, Chaitanya's life occurred on the cusp of modernity, and fortunately offered a better chance for authentication of sources both artistic and literary. Indeed, Chaitanya's life and teachings have been carefully preserved in medieval Sanskrit and Bengali texts, including especially the *Caitanya-Caritāmṛta* by Krishnadās Kavirāja. As part of my research on Bhakti devotional music that included the Vaishnava religion of Chaitanya, I spent part of the 1970s in Calcutta (Kolkata). To my surprise, between visits to libraries, concerts, and scholars, I discovered that the West Bengal film industry had released three full-length feature films on Chaitanya that were produced years before the creation of ISKCON and its arrival in the West.

At first, the idea of reducing a spiritual icon like Chaitanya to the movie screen with the aid of professional actors and cinematographers seemed unserious at best and perhaps a sacrilege, as not a few earnest followers had expressed doubts about its feasibility. But after attending a screening of the inspiring film *Nilachale Mahaprabhu* at Bharati Cinema Hall in South Calcutta in 1978, my suspicions quickly vanished. According to my developing knowledge of Indian music, the songs, musical instrumentation, and choreography appeared quite authentic. Indeed, the music director who oversaw all the arrangements, Shri Rai Chand Boral (R. C. Boral), came from a renowned family of classical musicians and was considered a pioneer in Indian film music. In the movie hall, I was impressed that several members of the audience were brought to tears of joy and ecstasy at the singing and dancing of the cinematic Chaitanya and his disciples. Moreover, outside the hall and before the film began, patrons had offered up incense, bowed down before the posters, and affectionately touched each step as they entered the building. In 1980, my Bengali wife Smt. Kajal Dass introduced me to the landmark film *Bhagwan Shri Krishna Chaitanya,* noting that it has been a favorite of conservative upper-class Bengalis. And after viewing *Nader Nimai,* I was delighted to find several Padāvali-Kīrtan songs arranged and directed by one of my own teachers, Shri Rathin Ghosh. Thus, while there were reservations about Chaitanya and cinema, it was incumbent upon me and my positive experiences with these films to delve deeper into the medium and uncover more interesting details.

The theme of Chaitanya and Kīrtan in classic Bengali cinema is explored in this essay by taking a listen to the "sacred soundtracks" of three films, *Bhagwan Shri Krishna Chaitanya* (1953), *Nilachale Mahaprabhu* (1957), and *Nader Nimai* (1960). All three are in black & white and extend for more than two hours each. But while these films have not been studied seriously by scholars, ethnomusicologist Eben Graves (2014) has discussed Kīrtan in the latter two films in relation to Indian politics and Bengali national identity and explored the role of Gaudīya Vaishnava Kīrtan in the emergence of modern economic life in Kolkata (Graves 2022). My approach differs by highlighting the religious dimension and context of specific songs and chants in the films according to the historical sources. Though recognizing the rich body of musical material in each film, this account cannot be exhaustive due to space limitations—it is hoped that future work will be more comprehensive. As such, with brief references to the narrative, this essay is focused on Sanskrit recitations, songs in the form of Kīrtan or Padāvali-Kīrtan, as well as a few items of classical music. Sanskrit and Bengali lyrics, with English translation, are either given or referenced so that viewers (see film links in References) may more fully appreciate the devotional depth and artistic production. Before proceeding, I take note of new directions in the study of religion and film, music and Indian cinema, and the historical context of Chaitanya and his association with Kīrtan according to the sacred biographies.

Religion and Film: "Film as Religion"

The study of religion and film is ideally viewed in the wider context of the gradual re-alignment between religion and the arts. While religion and the arts were closely affiliated in ancient times, a dichotomy arose between religion and culture in modernity that has tended to separate the study of religion from the arts. When the eighteenth-century philosopher Kant postulated a separate realm of aesthetics from religious experience, he forged a distinction that has endured among many intellectuals. Accordingly, religion and aesthetics were to be considered as separate domains—the temple and the theater hall as venues for different experiences, one for religious and the other aesthetic.

However, early nineteenth-century philosophers like Schelling and Hegel began to reject the Kantian separation and postulated that the arts are ways of discovering or revealing the Absolute. Following this direction, twentieth-century theologians and historians of religion have argued that the element of the sacred is manifest in all dimensions of human experience including culture and the arts. As such, the arts and religion are now understood to be integrated at primary levels of meaning, necessitating the current reunification of religion and aesthetics. Moreover, the combined study of theology and the arts, known as "theological aesthetics," has witnessed an upsurge in recent decades, based upon the Greek idea of the ascent to divinity through beauty.

As a corollary to the Western union of religion and the arts, Indian philosophy contains an ancient sacred principle that underlies all visual and performing arts. Rasa ("essence," "flavor") is proclaimed to have divine status in the Upanishads, wherein Brahman (the Absolute or God) is stated to be full of aesthetic delight or Rasa. James Alfred Martin (1990: 146) explained how Rasa is tied directly to the highest metaphysical reality, Brahman: "The experience of the joy of Brahman as Ānanda. As such, it is the goal and guide of poetic instruction, musical composition and performance, painting, and all the other arts." According to Susan L. Schwartz (2004: 97-98), the divine realm and the performing arts are closely bound together through Rasa: "Religion *is* the performance, and the performance *is* religion, not in its character or setting, its plot or content, but in its essence . . . India's diffuse and diverse religiosity makes this approach to performing arts viable and unique. To the extent that music, dance, and drama retain their divine association, their Rasic character continues to resonate and compel." This view aligns well with twentieth-century Indian art historian and philosopher Ananda K. Coomaraswamy (2014: 62), who proclaimed the unity of religion and art in 1934: "Art is religion, religion art, not related, but the same." In 1943, Coomaraswamy (1956: 51) even introduced the notion that religious art embeds a 'visual theology': "Religious art is simply a visual theology." As a counterpart to visual theology, music as 'sonic theology' is discussed in Beck (1993). Religious film, combining the visual and the sonic, encompasses both perspectives.

In the wake of these developments, the study of religion and film has experienced a noticeable rise in recent years along with the elevation of popular culture as a locus of scholarly attention. Hence, film as "art" is now recognizable as part of religious studies and theological analysis. Originally published in 2003, John Lyden's *Film as Religion: Myths, Morals, and Rituals* (2019: 35) argues that film conveys higher "spiritual" truth regardless of the perception of it being a human construct: "The fact that a cultural phenomenon---such as religion or film---is humanly constructed does not take away from its power to express another reality, even when people are aware of the constructed, 'imaginary' nature of the phenomenon. . . Filmgoers . . . know that films are not 'real,' but the imaginary constructions within them can still serve to convey real truths about the nature of reality and how it is believed to be."

In a pivotal observation, Lyden (2019: 36) describes the viewing of a religious film as a ritual experience, whereby myth is capable of elevating human consciousness above profane reality: "In the ritual context of viewing a film, we 'entertain' the truth of its mythology and ethos as a subject of consciousness even as it 'entertains' us. It presents a reality that differs from that experienced in ordinary profane time and space just as the reality depicted in religious myth and ritual differs from the empirical world of our everyday lives---and yet that alternative reality is still integrally connected with the world of the everyday, and hence its vision is relevant to it."

Cinema and Religion in India

Religion and film studies in India had been underdeveloped until very recent times. Rachel Dwyer, in her pioneer work, *Filming the Gods: Religion and Indian Cinema* (2006: 5), clearly bemoaned the situation whereby social and political issues have taken center stage in Indian film criticism: "Film theory has also given little space to the study of religion. The concerns of many film critics are mostly with the modern and postmodern forms of subjectivity, audience, and the dominance in recent years of psychoanalytic and feminist criticism. Scholars of Indian cinema have examined the form of film, its history, its social context and its relation to politics, in particular its relation to nationalism, but rarely discussed the spiritual realm; in fact, there has been almost no research on religion in cinema in India." This may be due to misunderstandings about the wide definitions of religion in religious studies that include, besides beliefs and doctrines, customs, behaviors, artefacts, and relationships that permeate nearly all of society.

Nonetheless, Dwyer (2006: 2) has made a strong case for film studies and religion in India: "The study of religion in Indian film studies is long overdue as it has been ever present as the dominant worldview of Indian cinema, not just represented directly by divine presences or by religious communities, but also manifested in ways of creating an ideal world through the individual, the family and society." Dwyer (2006: 5) has underscored the religious dimension of many Indian films: "Cinema is almost a form of religion, as, like religion, it presents and examines images, relationships, ideas, beliefs, desires, fears, and brings to them its own specific forms such as the quasi-divine figures of the stars. . . Very few films show an absence of the religious, and many that seem to have some 'secular' patterning of divine order through the operation of fate, virtue and redemption reshape these into meaningfulness by their divine or superhuman qualities, while also emphasizing the spirituality of the individual."

The arrival in Bombay in 1896 of Auguste and Louis Lumiere from France with their short silent films marked the beginning of the Indian film industry. The intriguing story of the development of Indian cinema is a tale with many overlaps between religion and the portrayal of human and divine characters on the screen. Without recounting the various stages in its history here, I refer the reader to the useful summary introduction of N. Ramaswamy, *History of Indian Cinema* (2022). Over the years, the cinematic creations of "Bollywood" have eclipsed the production of film industries of other nations, as portrayed in the voluminous reference work of Ashish Rajadhyaksha and Paul Willemen, *Encyclopedia of Indian Cinema* (1999). And while there is a presence of religion in many Indian films, the first few decades of Indian cinema witnessed the production of a proportionately large number of films encompassing religious themes.

The contribution of West Bengal to Indian film is significant, such that over the years the film industry in Calcutta has also produced a series of quality religiously based films, including those involving Chaitanya. The first Bengali language movie was the silent feature *Bilwamangal,* also known as *Bhagat Soordas,* based on the life of a South Indian Bhakti saint named "Surdas" (not to be confused with the Hindi poet). It was produced by the Madan Theatre Company of Calcutta in 1919. With the advent of the "talkies," B. N. Sircar (1901-1980) founded the studio at Tollygunge in South Calcutta in 1931 called New Theatres Ltd., which became legendary.

New Theatres' first film was the Bengali talkie, *Dena Paona,* released in 1931. As a prominent film producer in Bengal, Sircar presided over New Theatres for twenty-four years, producing more than 150 films in various languages including Bengali, Hindi and Tamil. Devaki Kumar Bose (1898-1971), a confessed Vaishnava, was the film director at New Theatres, releasing several groundbreaking films based on religious theses: *Chandidas* (1932) followed by the Hindi version directed by Nitin Bose in 1934 starring singer K. L. Saigal, *Meerabai/Rajrani Meera* (1933) based on the life of the woman saint Meera Bai, *Seeta* (1934) on the tales of Rāma, *Bidyapati* (1937), based on the life of Bhakti poet Vidyāpati starring Prithvraj Kapoor, *Nimai Sannyas* (1940), directed by Phani Burma and starring Chhabi Biswas, and *Bhagwan Shri Krishna Chaitanya* (1954), starring Basanta Choudhury.

The music director and composer at New Theatres was Shri Rai Chand Boral (1903-1981), son of classical musician Lal Chand Boral and credited as the "pioneer of Indian film music." Boral was the music director of two important Chaitanya films, *Bhagwan Shri Krishna Chaitanya* (1953) and *Nilachale Mahaprabhu* (1957).[1]

Cinema and Music in India

More than other movie industries, Indian films contain significant elements of music and dance, whether as part of the plot or for amusement. Ethnomusicologist Alison Arnold, in "Film Music: Northern Area" (2000: 534), describes the historical context of devotional music in Indian films: "The popular devotional bhajan, ubiquitous among the majority Hindu population in India and prevalent also among Sikhs and other religious groups, has been commonly included in Hindu-oriented commercial films, particularly up to and during the 'golden age of melody' (1950s-1960s)." In a variety of situations, music is presented in multiple formats (2000: 534): "As in real life contexts, film bhajans offer praise to Hindu deities and may be solo, group, or solo-group responsorial songs. They are often sung in a Hindu temple or a worship area within a home." Rather than amateurs or non-musicians, according to Arnold (2000: 536), "Throughout the history of Indian sound film, most music directors have been trained musicians or singers."

When audiences consume the finished product in the movie halls, they are generally overwhelmed by the theatrical effects, and may be oblivious to the many layers of production involved in creating a film. While the names of actors as star performers become household names after the film's release, the complicated processes of direction, especially regarding the musical numbers, often remain unacknowledged by the wider public. In this regard, Arnold (2000: 537) provides a concise overview of the production of film music: "The film music director is the creative force behind the production of all music for a film, including background music, songs, and dance compositions. The music director creates the song melody, envisions the final recorded product, and oversees the process by which this is reached.

The process requires a production team including a lyricist, singer(s), studio musicians, music assistants, sound recording engineers, and sound editor, each member of which makes his or her contribution to the song recording." Unlike many artists in the West who can act, sing, and dance at professional levels, in India the practice of "playback singing" in films has become the norm, whereby songs are sung by another vocalist and placed into the footage at the editing stage. This process is described by Arnold (2000: 538): "'Playback singing' is the term used in the Indian film industry to refer to dubbing voice-overs in film songs. Professional singers record the songs, which are then inserted into a film soundtrack and matched to the frames showing the actors mouthing the lyrics. At the film shooting, the song recording is played back through loudspeakers to ensure correct timing by the screen artist, hence the term *playback*." The result is a union of the best image with the best music.

The above steps form part of creating an Indian religious film as an "artefact" that includes music as a central focus, that is, as an aesthetic creation infused with Rasa capable of delivering a unique human experience of the divine. Moreover, the close connection between music and religions around the world confirms the potentiality of music in films as a spiritual vehicle: "Music plays an important role in all the major world religions. While it often accompanies the performance of religious ritual, it is also considered to be a spiritual expression in itself" (Sheldrake 2014: 24).[2] Thus in religious films we have "sacred soundtracks."

Who was Chaitanya, and what was unique about his teachings and Kīrtan music that could be successfully represented in film?

Chaitanya and Kīrtan

Śrī Chaitanya Mahāprabhu spent most of his adult life striving to establish a devotional religion in India. Originally a student of logic, he renounced all scholastic activity and dedicated himself to the emotional side of religion in the form of Bhakti that included spreading love of Krishna through chanting, dancing, and teaching all those who would receive his message. Krishnadās Kavirāja, as the author of Chaitanya's authorized biography known as *Caitanya Caritāmṛta* (CC), recounted Chaitanya's life and provided an intellectual foundation to this new devotional movement. As the founder of the Gauḍīya Vaishnava Sampradāya, Chaitanya spent his ministry performing Kīrtan ("devotional music"), teaching followers, debating among scholars, traveling to holy sites, and assigning writing and temple establishment to his prominent disciples. Chaitanya became a staunch advocate of Nām-Kīrtan or Nām-Sankīrtan, the practice of publicly chanting divine names so that maximum exposure to God may be obtained, with the compassionate goal of deliverance of the population from the miseries of the decadent age of Kali Yuga.[3]

Despite his critics, Chaitanya's practice of Kīrtan was based on firm theological ground, namely, the Sanskrit literature of Bhakti including the *Bhagavad-Gītā*, the *Bhāgavata-Purāṇa*, and the *Gīta-Govinda*. The *Bhāgavata-Purāṇa* (BP) is the premier text that endorses Kīrtan as a near compulsory practice in devotional worship. In BP 7.5.23, Kīrtan is mentioned as one of nine prescribed activities: hearing and glorifying/chanting [*kīrtanam*] about the sacred name, form, qualities, paraphernalia and pastimes of Lord Vishnu, remembering them, serving the feet of the Lord, offering worship to the image of Lord, offering prayers to the Lord, becoming His servant, considering the Lord one's friend, and surrendering everything unto Him; these nine processes are known as pure Bhakti service. The effectiveness of Nām-Sankīrtan (Nam-Kīrtan) for destroying all sins (*pāpa*) and suffering (*duhkha*) is declared in the final verse, BP 12.13.23:

> *nāma-saṅkīrtanaṁ yasya, sarva-pāpa praṇāśanam*
> *praṇāmo duḥkha-śamanas, taṁ namāmi hariṁ param*

> "I offer my adoration to Hari, the Supreme, the recital of Whose names destroys all sins, and humble submission to Whom brings surcease of sorrow" (N. Raghunathan 1976: II, 698).

In all three feature films, two types of Kīrtan are presented: Nām-Kīrtan and Padāvali-Kīrtan. Nām-Kīrtan refers to the singing or recitation of specific names of God or Krishna, often performed outdoors as walking Nām-Sankīrtan (also called Nagar Kīrtan). These forms are performed through loud articulation of the names of Krishna accompanied by the strong rhythms of the Khol (clay drum) and Kartal (hand cymbals). Chaitanya and his followers proclaimed that the singing or chanting of God's names was most effective in obtaining salvation along with the Bhakti sentiments required for the highest spiritual experience, namely, love of God. Accordingly, in addition to escaping the suffering of the Kali age, as in the BP above, the chanting by Chaitanya of the divine names of "Hari" and "Krishna" invokes a deeper meaning connected to Rādhā's passionate separation from Krishna, as described in the 12th century medieval Sanskrit poem of Jayadeva, *Gīta-Govinda* (8.17), "Destined to die through the unbearable pain of separation, she [Rādhā] moans, chanting passionately [*japati*] 'Hari, Hari,' hoping to attain thee in her next life" (Mukhopadhyay 1990: 40-41). As an earthly manifestation of Krishna in the loving mood of Rādhā, Chaitanya and his Kīrtan fulfilled this double role that is well portrayed in the films.

The other form of Kīrtan in the films is Padāvali-Kīrtan (or Pāla-Kīrtan), a distinctive style of devotional music found in Bengal and Orissa. Originally influenced by the late medieval songs of poets Vidyāpati (1352-1448 CE), and Chandidās (ca. 1390-1450 CE), who were each inspired by Jayadeva, Padāvali-Kīrtan was later modified according to the classical forms of music in Vraja by Narottam Dās (ca. 1531-1587 CE).

Padāvali-Kīrtan combines religious narratives with songs in various tempos and rhythms composed by Bhakti saints in Bengali and Brajbuli. A typical session revolves around a theme from the pastimes of Rādhā and Krishna. The songs include short improvisatory phrases called Akhar that are inserted into the lyrics of the original songs by the singers using colloquial expressions for the benefit of local audiences. The performers include vocalists, Khol (double-headed clay drum) players, hand cymbal (Kartal) players, and sometimes a violinist or flautist.[4]

What were the principle Kīrtan songs utilized by Chaitanya that are mentioned in the Gauḍīya literature? As mentioned in the CC, there are three compositions of Kīrtan or Nām-Kīrtan in the Sanskrit language, numbered below, which also appear in the three films in connection with Chaitanya's movement: [1] Mahā Mantra, [2] *Hari Haraye namah Krishna*, [3] *Krishna Keśava pāhi mām*. While there is little or no textual information on their authorship, these three chants or songs represent a core element in terms of the musical expression of Chaitanya's mission. The Bengali songs listed as [4] and [5] in the films, while not appearing in the biography, are also significant because they represent oral tradition. The Sanskrit verses listed as [6] [7] [8] also appear in various places throughout the films. Additional songs or chants cited are left unnumbered---they may be sourced, unsourced, or composed especially for the film.

[1] The Mahā Mantra is the most popular form of Kīrtan in the Gauḍīya tradition. It is a Nām-Kīrtan that contains sixteen names, Krishna, Hari, Rāma, in succession in the form of a Sanskrit *śloka* in Anustup meter of four lines of eight syllables each.

> *Hare Krishna, Hare Krishna*
> *Krishna Krishna Hare Hare*
> *Hare Rāma Hare Rāma*
> *Rāma Rāma Hare Hare*

Part of a collection of 108 Upanishads which are of South Indian provenance, the short *Kali-Santarana-Upanishad* (ca. before 1500 A.D.) contains the earliest presentation of the entire Mahā Mantra. Although the human author of the text is uncertain, the spiritual context is an instruction to sage Nārada by Lord Brahmā in response to his question about how to best avoid the degradation of the present age of Kali Yuga. Nārada learns that there are no rules or purity requirements for chanting the Mahā Mantra, making it suitable for distribution to all humankind. In *Kali-Santarana Upanishad* (5-6), it is stated: *Hare Rāma, Hare Rāma, Rāma Rāma, Hare Hare, Hare Krishna, Hare Krishna, Krishna Krishna, Hare Hare. Iti ṣoḍaśakam nāmnām kali-kalmaśa-nāśanam nātah parataropāyah sarva-vedeṣu dṛśyate.* The translation of the passage is as follows (Srinivasa Ayyangar 1953: 19): "This collection of sixteen names [O Hari, O Rāma, O Krishna, etc.] is destructive of the baneful influences of Kali [Kali Yuga]. Beyond this there is no other better means to be found in all the Vedas."

While it appears from the text that the sixteen names refer to Nārāyaṇa as Hari, Rāma, and Krishna, according to Gauḍīya Vaishnava interpretation the expression "Hare" is the vocative form of "Harā," referring to Rādhā as the Śakti (female energy) of Krishna. The biographies mention a ten-syllable Mantra that Chaitanya received upon his initiation in Gayā by Ishvara Puri (i.e., the shortened form of the 18-syllable Gopāla Mantra, *Gopījana-vallabhāya svāhā*). Many believe that the Mahā Mantra was also given at that time. And while there is no mention of the term "Kīrtan" in this text, only the practice of *japa* (counting on beads), the Mahā Mantra has become a staple of Chaitanya Nām-Kīrtan.[5]

Although the order of the lines differs in the original text of the *Kali-Santarana-Upanishad* (note above), the normal practice today, and in the films, is as [1] above. The Mahā Mantra is in fact cited with the "Hare Krishna Hare Krishna" part first in an earlier biography of Chaitanya, *Chaitanya-Bhāgavata* (Ādi 14.145 and Madhya 23.74-78, 82); and two passages refer to it (but neglect to mention it directly) in the CC, as part of Chaitanya's ministry. In the CC, Ādi-Līlā, Vol. 2, Chapter 7, verse 83 (pp. 66-67), we find the reference: *krishna-nāma-mahā-mantrera ei ta' svabhāva yei jape, tāra krishna je upajaye asty*. According to the translation, "It is the nature of the Hare Krishna Mahā Mantra that anyone who chants it immediately develops his loving ecstasy for Krishna." In the CC, Antya-Līlā, Vol. 3, Chapter 9, verse 56 (pp. 155-156), we find another: *se kahe – 'Vaninātha nirbhaye laya krishna-nāma hare krishna, hare krishna' kahe avisrāma*. In the translation: "The messenger replied, 'He [Vaninātha] was fearlessly, incessantly chanting the Mahā Mantra." In the next verse (57), it is indicated that Vaninātha was chanting this Mantra on his beads in the form of *japa*. Moreover, the previous verse is also suggestive of the practice of *japa* and, noticeably, the terms 'Kīrtan' or 'Nām-Kīrtan' are not mentioned in either verse.

[2] The next Kīrtan song or chant was very important for Chaitanya's devotees, such that its very name is "Nāma-Sankīrtana," with its popular version below:

Hari Haraye namaḥ Krishna Yādavāya namaḥ
Yādavāya Mādhavāya Keśavāya namaḥ
Gopāla Govinda Rāma Śrī Madhusūdana
Giridhārī Gopīnātha Madana Mohana

In the CC, Madhya-Līlā, Vol. 9, Chapter 25, verse 64 (pp. 331-332), only the first and third lines are given: *Hari Haraye namaḥ Krishna Yādavāya namaḥ Gopāla Govinda Rāma Śrī Madhusūdana.* In the translation: "They chanted, 'Hari Haraye namaḥ Krishna Yādavāya namaḥ, Gopāla Govinda Rāma Śrī Madhusūdana.'" It is noteworthy here that in the commentary by A. C. Bhaktivedānta Swami, the singing of "Hari Haraye" is essentially equated with the Mahā Mantra: "This is another way of chanting the Hare Krishna Mahā Mantra. The meaning is: 'I offer my respectful obeisance unto the Supreme Personality of Godhead, Krishna. He is the descendant of the Yadu family. Let me offer my respectful obeisance unto Gopāla, Govinda, Rāma and Śrī Madhusūdana.'" This equivalency is also suggested in the translation of the previous verse (63): "There were four people accompanying Śrī Caitanya Mahāprabhu, . . . They were all chanting the Hare Krishna Mahā Mantra in the following way." In the CC, Ādi-Līlā, Vol. 3, Chapter 17, verses 121-122 (pp. 322-323), another reference is made: *nagariya loke prabhu yabe ajna dili ghore ghore sankīrtana karite lagili.* In the translation (verse 121): "The Lord [Chaitanya] ordered all the citizens of Navadvīpa to chant the Hare Krishna mantra, and in each and every home they began performing sankīrtana regularly;" followed by *'Haraye namaḥ Kṛṣṇa Yādavāya namaḥ Gopāla Govinda Rāma Śrī Madhusūdana.'"* In the translation (122): "All the devotees sang this popular song along with the Hare Krishna Mahā Mantra, *'Haraye namaḥ Krishna Yādavāya namaḥ Gopāla Govinda Rāma Śrī Madhusūdana.'"*

The commentary by A. C. Bhaktivedānta Swami instructs devotees to sing this Nām-Kīrtan, considered a "favorite of Chaitanya Mahāprabhu," in addition to the Mahā Mantra twenty-four hours a day in Mayapur. As stated, these Kīrtans "should go on so perfectly well that no one there hears any other vibration than the chanting of the holy names of the Lord. That will make the center spiritually all perfect." The history of its composition is described in a letter to disciple Ekayāni Dāsī, dated May 3, 1970, where A. C. Bhaktivedānta Swami explains: "The first two lines of the song 'Haraye namah Krishna' were sung by Lord Chaitanya and His followers, but the other lines of song were composed later on by Śrīla Narottam Dās Thākura." (Letter to: Ekayani (vedabase.io) For the complete song, see SVA (pp. 64-65).

[3] In at least three places in the CC, Chaitanya is described as chanting the following Nām-Kīrtan comprising names of Krishna and Rāma in repetitive sequences, as represented below:

Krishna Krishna Krishna Krishna Krishna Krishna Krishna he

Krishna Krishna Krishna Krishna Krishna Krishna rakṣa mām
Krishna Krishna Krishna Krishna Krishna Krishna pāhi mām
Rāma Rāghava Rāma Rāghava Rāma Rāghava rakṣa mām
Kṛishna Keśava Krishna Keśava Krishna Keśava pāhi mām

In the CC, Ādi-Līlā, Vol. 2, Chapter 8, verse 26 (p. 181), there is a description before the chant: "Caitanya Mahāprabhu has also taught us this. While passing on the road, He used to chant." In the CC, Madhya-Līlā, Vol 3, Chapter 9, verse 13 (p. 298), a part of the chant is given. In the CC, Madhya-Līlā, Vol 3, Chapter 7, verse 96 (pp. 47-48), the chant appears in translation: "0 Lord Krishna, please protect Me and maintain Me. . . . That is, O Lord Rāma, descendant of King Raghu, please protect Me. O Krishna, O Keśava, killer of the Keśī demon, please maintain Me."

[4] The Bengali song below is a staple among Vaishnavas of Bengal, especially in the villages. Though not mentioned in the CC, *Bhaja Gaurāṅga* is claimed, without reference, to be a composition of Krishnadās Kavirāja (see Bhajans By Krsnadasa Kaviraja Goswami | Vaishnav Songs (iskcondesiretree.com). It is sung in what is called the "morning melody" in ISKCON. Appearing in all three films, the song is a plea to "worship Gaurāṅga," and was thus not sung by Chaitanya himself but believed to have been taught by Nityānanda (Nitāi):

Bhaja Gaurāṅga, kaha Gaurāṅga, laha Gaurāṅger nāma re
Je jana Gaurāṅga bhaje se hoya āmār prāṇa re

"Worship Gaurāṅga, sing Gaurāṅga, take the name of Gaurāṅga!
One who thus worships Gaurāṅga is my heart and soul."

In a lecture in Mayapur on the CC, Ādi-Līlā, Chapter 7, verse 5, A. C. Bhaktivedānta Swami explained: "Nityānanda Prabhu is teaching how to worship Śrī Chaitanya Mahāprabhu. This is Nityānanda Prabhu's business." (Śrī Caitanya-caritāmṛta, Ādi-līlā 7.5 (prabhupadavani.org)

[5] Despite uncertain authorship, another popular Bengali Kīrtan appears in two of the films, *Nilachale Mahaprabhu* and *Nader Nimai*. While not mentioned in the CC, this song is sung by Chaitanya in the former film and by itinerant musicians in the latter.

Hare Murāre Madhu-Kaitabhāre, Gopāla Govinda Mukunda Saure

Nāme būka bhore jāya peyāsa metāya
Je nāmer guṇe Kaṁsa kāndāye Ālo hoye uṭhe, dvāra khule jāya
Dvipada bārana, Śrī Madhusūdana
Vāsudeva je nāmera kavaca vakṣye dharia tāra
jharera āñdhāre adhīra Yamunā hoye jāya pārāpāra

"O Lord Hari, Enemy of Mur, Defeater of the demons Madhu and Kaitabha
O Protector of cows, Bestower of pleasure, Giver of Liberation, O Hero of Heroes.
My heart fills up with your holy names and quenches my thirst.
Such is the power of your Holy Name that it brings the demon Kaṁsa to tears, heralds a new dawn, and opens up the bolted door.
He who wears the Talisman of the Name of Vāsudeva close to his bosom in the darkness of the storm, when the Yamunā is turbulent and overflows its banks."

In addition to the Kīrtans and songs above, there are specific verses in Sanskrit recited in the films that are unique to Gauḍīya Vaishnavism.

[6] In the CC, Ādi-Līlā, Vol. 2, Chapter 7, verse 76 (p. 61), there is a verse chanted by devotees that speaks to the missionary zeal of the Chaitanya movement: that chanting the Holy Name is the only means of overcoming the decadent age of Kali Yuga. While the authorship is uncertain, it is featured in *Nader Nimai* and *Nilachale Mahaprabhu.*

Harer nāma Harer nāma
Harer nāmaiva kevalam
Kalau nāsty eva nāsty eva
Nāsty eva gatir anyathā

"In this age of Kali there is no alternative, there is no alternative, there is no alternative for spiritual progress than the holy name, the holy name, the holy name of the Lord."

[7] Sung by devotees in the film *Bhagwan Shri Krishna Chaitanya* (verse

7), and as the opening background music of *Nilachale Mahaprabhu* (verses 2, 3, 7, 8), several verses from the famous eight-verse *Jagannāthāṣṭakam* of Śankarācārya are heard in attractive musical arrangement. The signature fourth line of each verse requests the vision of Lord Jagannāth:

> *Jagannāthaḥ svāmī nayana-patha-gāmī bhavatu me*
>
> "May that Jagannātha Swami be the object of my vision."
> Full text and translation: https://www.devshoppe.com/en-us/blogs/articles/shri-jagannath-ashtakam-with-meaning

[8] While not cited in the CC, and of uncertain authorship, there is a famous Sanskrit prayer to Krishna present in all three films that is called Śrī Krishna Praṇām in SVA (p. 19). Like a Wagnerian *leitmotiv* in the films, the sound of this prayer indicates the arrival of Chaitanya on several occasions, who appears chanting it in a distinctive melody. The verse also serves to close each film as Chaitanya either leaves his home as a renunciate, or ultimately reaches out for Krishna at the end of life. While it has been chanted on occasion by A. C. Bhaktivedānta Swami accompanied by Khol and Kartal, in the films it is chanted without rhythm, and functions as a personal "Namaste" to Krishna by Chaitanya in the mood of Rādhā.

> *He Krishna, karuṇā sindho*
> *Dīna bandho jagatpate*
> *Gopeśa Gopikā Kānta*
> *Rādhā Kānta namo 'stu te*
>
> "O Krishna, Ocean of Mercy. Friend of the fallen, Father of the universe. O Master of the Gopas, O Lover of the Gopīs. O Lover of Rādhā, I bow down before thee."

Regarding musical instrumentation, all three films adhere to period practices. Without harmonium, which was introduced in the nineteenth century, there is only employment of the clay *mṛidanga* drum (Khol) and hand bells or cymbals (Kartals) as described in the CC, Ādi-Līlā, Vol. 3, Chapter 17, verse 123 (p. 323): "When the Sankīrtan movement thus started, no one in Navadvīp could hear any other sound than the words "Hari! Hari!" and the beating of the *mṛidanga* [Khol] and clashing of hand bells [Kartal]."

Each of the three films are now discussed separately, noting the inclusion of items numbered [1] through [8] above, as well as other Sanskrit chants, songs, and Bengali Kīrtans.

Bhagwan Shri Krishna Chaitanya

The first Bengali film discussed is *Bhagwan Shri Krishna Chaitanya* (128 minutes), produced in 1953 and directed by Devaki Bose of New Theatres in Calcutta. The young Basanta Choudhury acted as Chaitanya, with Suchitra Sen as Vishnupriyā. Under the musical direction of Shri Rai Chand Boral, several local musicians including Dhananjaya Bhattacarya and Sucitra Mitra lent their talents to the sacred soundtrack. What is noteworthy is the singing of famous blind vocalist Krishna Chandra De.

The film focuses entirely on Chaitanya's life as a householder, married to his second wife Vishnupriyā. Chaitanya ultimately leaves home at the end of the film as a renunciate.

After the singing of [7] *Jagannātha svāmī*, the film opens with a scene whereby a lower caste man is denied access to the deity in a procession.

The saint Ishvara Puri then enters, singing a Sanskrit prayer from the *Mahābhārata* (Pāndava Gīta) in which Queen Gandhari says to Lord Krishna that He is everything, "my Gods of gods."

> *Tvam eva mātā ca pitā tvam eva,*
> *tvam eva bandhuś ca sakhā tvam eva |*
> *tvam eva vidyā dravina tvam eva*
> *tvam eva sarvam mama deva deva ||*
>
> "You truly are my Mother and you truly are my Father.
> You truly are my Relative and you truly are my Friend.
> You truly are my Knowledge and you truly are my Wealth.
> You truly are my All, my God of gods."

Ishvara Puri explains to the devotees that Navadvīp is now a "Nava Vrindāvana," a "New Vrindāvana." Nitāi then sings a Kīrtan of Vidyāpati (VP: 100-101) about the new Vrindāvana: *Nava vrindāvana nava nava tarugana.*

Next, two wandering singers, a man and a woman, enter singing [7]

Jagannathāstakam, verse 7; *na vai yāce rājyaṁ na ca kanaka-māṇikya-vibhavaṁ* . . . *jagannāthaḥ*: "I do not pray for a kingdom, nor for gold, rubies, and wealth . . . I simply pray that Jagannātha Swami, . . . be the constant object of my vision." Chaitanya and Vishnupriyā listen to the verse, then Vishnupriyā repeats the refrain several times with heartfelt devotion.

After several scenes including with devotees at the house of Śrīvās, there is a skillful performance of Khol playing accompanied by Kartal and the singing of "Hari Bol, Hari Bol." But this is interrupted by Jagāi and Madhāi who break the Khol and threaten to ban Kīrtan. However, the situation changes dramatically. Prefaced by a devotee reciting the *Bhagavad-Gītā* verse anticipating the coming of a savior or avatar (*yadā yadā hi dharmasya*), Chaitanya appears chanting [8] *He Krishna karuna sindho,* followed by K. C. De reciting [2] *Hari Haraye namah Krishna*, and then a Padāvali-Kīrtan sung by Nitāi.

Then, after Chaitanya collapses at a temple upon seeing a vision of Krishna, the same wandering singers enter and offer portions of a beautiful Sanskrit devotional prayer (Stotra), slightly modified, known as the *Madana-Mohana-Aṣṭakam*.

Jaya śaṅkha-gadādhara nīla-kalevara, pīta-paṭāmbara dehi padam
Jaya bhakta-janāsraya nitya-sukhālaya, antima-bāndhava dehi padam
Jaya durjana-śāsana, keli-parāyaṇa, kāliya-dāmana dehi padam
Jaya bhakta-janāśraya dīna-dayāmaya, cinmaya-acyuta dehi padaṁ
Jaya pāmara-pāvana, dharama-parāyaṇa, daitya-nisūdana dehi padam

> "All glory to the holder of the conch shell and *gadā* weapon, to the one of bluish bodily hue wearing yellow garments. Glory to you who is the shelter of the devotees, an eternal reservoir of happiness, and the ultimate friend of all. Glory to the slayer of miscreants and demons like Kāliya who is also sportful, to the one who is merciful to the fallen, purifies the sinful, and is devoted to righteousness."

Vishnupriyā then repeats three of the above verses and sings another, *jiya veda-vimocana śrī-rādhā-ramaṇa vrindāvana-dhana dehi padam,* in honor of Krishna and Vrindāvana. The Stotra is repeated by the devotees later in the film with additional verses.

Full text: https://sanskritdocuments.org/doc_vishhnu/madanamohana8.html
Full text with rendition: https://www.youtube.com/watch?v=KUvUwn9qUFM

After the residence of Śrīvās is attacked by adversaries who pronounce a ban on Nām-Kīrtan, Chaitanya pacifies his followers by singing [8] *He Krishna karuṇā sindho,* and Nitāi enters Chaitanya's house singing a Kīrtan. Next, K. C. De sings a Kīrtan. Vishnupriyā offers a song to Chaitanya out of love. Then the scene changes to a procession of Chaitanya and devotees singing [3] *Krishna Keśava pāhi mām.* Undeterred by guards sent by Jagāi and Madhāi to stop them, the group continues, singing [1] Mahā Mantra. Nitāi then preaches to Jagāi and Madhāi, singing [4] *Bhaja Gaurāṅga,* followed by a variation of [2] *Hari Haraye namaḥ Krishna* until Chaitanya arrives and both Jagai and Madhai surrender and chant '*Krishna Keśava.*' There follows a procession singing [3] again. At home, Chaitanya and Vishnupriyā sing '*Bhaja Śrī Krishna*' to the melody of [4] *Bhaja Gauranga,* which is also sung by Nitāi as he enters Chaitanya's house.

After tender moments between Chaitanya and Vishnupriyā, Chaitanya shares his plan to leave family life and preach Bhakti to the world. In an emotional scene, both his wife and mother are shocked and lament his immanent departure. Following the sounds of "*yadā yadā hi dharmasya,*" Chaitanya (as Nimāi) requests Pandit Keśava Bharati to grant him the order of *sannyāsa* (renunciate), taking the name "Shri Krishna Chaitanya." Then, placing a flower garland on his wife and touching the feet of his mother, Chaitanya walks into the wilderness to the repeated singing of [8] *He Krishna karuṇā sindho.* The film closes with the opening refrain of [7] *Jagannātha svāmī.*

Nilachale Mahaprabhu

Nilachale Mahāprabhu (133 minutes), produced in 1957, provides a sequel to the first film by portraying Chaitanya in his life as a renunciate. The film was directed by Kartik Chattopadhyay and starred Asim Kumar in the title role. The musical director was Rai Chand Boral who provided several original songs with the assistance of Pranab Roy and Baishnab Mahalanabis. Nilachala refers to the holy town of Puri in Orissa where the famous temple of Lord Jagannāth attracts pilgrims from all over India. The film is set in Puri and focuses on Chaitanya as a devotee of Lord Jagannāth. The opening scene shows the plight of lower caste men who are treated unfairly and forced to fight in battles overseen by King Pratāparudra. But a follower of Chaitanya soon announces the arrival of a new King (Chaitanya) who does not employ weapons but who will wake up Lord Jagannāth with a new song and dance in the name of acquiring love of God as a panacea for the ills of social injustice.

As part of the introduction, eight verses (2, 3, 7, 8) of [7] *Jagannāthāṣṭakam* are heard accompanying footage of Chaitanya searching for Krishna and entering the temple of Jagannāth.

The film opens as Chaitanya, now shaven headed, is discovered unconscious due to his devotional ecstasies. His followers carry him to the home of Sarvabhauma Bhattācārya, who considers Chaitanya a madman who does not know Vedānta. After singing a solo song, and declaring the equality of human beings, Chaitanya mobilizes his followers for Nām-Sankīrtan, singing and dancing to [5] *Hare Murāre Madhu-Kaitabhāre*. Witnessing the Kīrtan, Sarvabhauma states that it is improper for a *sannyāsa* like Chaitanya to dance and sing.

However, adversaries in the form of impersonalist scholars, pandits, and local administrators challenge Chaitanya's religion of devotion. After curing a leper, Chaitanya enters the temple of Jagannāth and sings a song by Vidyāpati. Sarvabhauma teaches Chaitanya the philosophy of Advaita Vedānta, but he is unsatisfied. Then an associate breaks out in song about the Holy Name. Hearing Sanskrit verses in praise of Krishna in a vision, Sarvabhauma accepts Chaitanya as his spiritual guide. Chaitanya recites [6] *Harer Nāma Harer Nāma*, followed by devotees and Sarvabhauma singing *Govinda bol jaya Govinda bol, Mukunda Mādhava Govinda bol*. Despite royal opposition, Chaitanya leads a Kīrtan with [2] *Hari Haraye namaḥ Krishna.*

Appointing Sarvabhauma as his "standard bearer" in Puri, Chaitanya embarks on a tour of south India where he meets Ramānanda. King Pratāparudra suddenly returns to Puri and arrests the sitting Prime Minister for conspiracy, and then hears about Chaitanya from Rāmānanda. Shown chanting [3] *Rāma Rāghava,* followed by [1] Mahā Mantra in procession at the Ratha Yātrā festival, Chaitanya accepts the King as his follower. At first hesitant, Chaitanya then agrees to return to Bengal to offer respects to his mother. But his wife Vishnupriyā, shown decorating a statue of Gaurāṅga and singing [4] *Bhaja Gaurāṅga,* is disappointed as their meeting is forbidden due to the regulations of a renunciate.

Back in Puri, Chaitanya displays ecstatic symptoms in his search for Krishna, chanting [8] *He Krishna karunā sindho* and *Hā Krishna* ("Oh Krishna!"). For safety reasons, he is placed in a locked room, but later his followers discover he has vanished, leaving an 'empty room' reminiscent of the empty tomb of Jesus. Chaitanya has wandered outside singing and hugging a tree, believing it to be Krishna who then disappears. A fisherman on the beach then finds Chaitanya in a fishnet, who is returned to his room. Yet again, lost in ecstasy, Chaitanya walks out with arms outstretched---the doors open mysteriously—in search of Krishna. Singing [8] *He Krishna karuṇā sindho,* Chaitanya departs for the spiritual world.

Nader Nimai

Nader Nimai (138 minutes), released in 1960, is a film about the birth, childhood, and household life of Chaitanya. It was directed by Bimal Roy with Asim Kumar as "Nimāi," the name of Chaitanya who was "born under a Neem tree." The musical director was Satyen Chatterjee with added direction of Padāvali-Kīrtan songs by Kīrtan musician Shri Rathin Ghosh. Vocalists include Hemanta Mukherji, Chinmaya Lahiri, Dhanañjaya, and Mānabendra.

During the opening credits, a verse from the Sanskrit prayer, *Śrī Gopāla-Sahasra-Nāma* (One Thousand Names of Krishna; verse 29 of the Introduction) is chanted by radio artist Virendra Krishna Bhadra. set in Rāga Bhairava and accompanied on the Pakhavaj drum. This verse is repeated later when Chaitanya visits Gayā:

> *Oṁ phullendivara-kāntim indu-vadanam barhāvatamsa-priyam*
>
> "I worship Lord Govinda, who is splendid like a blossoming blue lotus, whose face is like the moon, who is charming with a peacock-feather crown." (Full text: Sri Gopala-sahasra-nama (stephen-knapp.com)

This is followed by a Padāvali-Kīrtan song of Narottam Dās, with Akhar.

> *gaurāṅgera duṭi pada, jār dhana sampada, se jāne bhakati-rasa-sār*
>
> "Anyone who has accepted the two lotus feet of Gaurāṅga can understand the true essence of *bhakti*, or devotional service."

Akhar:

Hridaya nirmala bhelo tāra
Tāra manera añdhāra jāya je dūre

"Gaurāṅga's feet will at once purify their hearts
The darkness of their minds is dispelled"

The film begins with the announcement of the birth of Viśvambhara, known affectionately as "Nimāi." According to the family astrologer, Nimāi is an avatāra of Krishna for the purpose of ridding Navadvīp of the corrupt practices of Tantrism. A scene of Goddess Kālī worship ensues with a young woman being held and forced to drink alcohol as part of Tantric ritual. Hearing about the prediction, local Tantric leaders fear that Navadvīp will become a Vaishnava haven.

A woman playing an ektara instrument along with a young boy enter, singing [5] *Hare Murāre Madhu-Kaitabhāre.*

The plot against the family begins by the kidnapping of young Nimāi, who, being lured by a toy, stuns the predator by revealing his form as Vishnu. Then, after the opening verse of *Brahmā-Samhitā,* there is a musical arrangement by Rathin Ghosh of a Padāvali-Kīrtan song lamenting the departure of Krishna from Vraja and a plea for his return:

Emana sundara binā vraja āñdhi, āja Krishna, Krishna boli śabe kare hāhākāra
Kothā gelo nanda kula chañd Vraja adhara kore nanda kula chañd kothā gelo

"Bereft of its Beauty, Vraja is now covered by darkness
Everyone is calling out to Kṛṣṇa in utter despair
"O where is the bright moon of the Nanda dynasty?"
"O where did the moon of the Nanda dynasty go, plunging the whole of Vraja into darkness?"

Saba saṅginī gheri baithata gāvata Harināme gāvata Harināme

"All the dear friends of Rādhārāṇī surrounded her and sang the holy names of Hari."

Āja bheṅge gelo, sukhera hāta bujhi bheṅge gelo
Sukhera hāta bujhi bheṅge gelo
Morā boro sādhe petechilām
Sukhera hāta bujhi bheṅge gelo. Sukhera hāta bujhi bheṅge gelo.

"Today it is destroyed—our marketplace of pleasure has been destroyed.
Our marketplace of pleasure has been destroyed.

We had set it up with great enthusiasm and effort. But now our marketplace of pleasure has been destroyed. We think that our marketplace of pleasure has been destroyed."

Sakhi Lalitā cried and said these words again . . .

Nidoya hoye lukiye keno Dekhā dāo murāri

"Why this cruelty to us? Why do you hide? Please come back to us, O Enemy of Mur."

As the young Nimāi begins his education, Sarvabhauma Bhattācārya assigns a teacher in Nyāya logic. Finishing his studies, Nimāi marries Lakshmīpriyā and starts teaching yet declares Nyāya 'dry speculation.' But alas, adversaries appear, threatening to expel the Vaiṣhṇavas from Navadvīp by the power of Mantra. After the death of Lakshmīpriyā by snakebite, Chaitanya marries Vishnupriyā, who sings, *He Govinda He Gopāla Yashodā nayana avirāma;* "O Govinda, O Gopāla, eternally beheld by the eyes of Yashodā."

Chaitanya goes to Gayā to meet Ishvara Puri. The scene in Gayā is accompanied by a repeat of the opening verse followed by a classical Dhrupad in Rāga Bhairava in praise of Hari, *Bhava ārādhya deva-ari sādhya, asura nara jana vandyam*: "Worshipped by the whole world, the goal of the demigods as well as their enemies."

A Sanskrit verse is also chanted: *Gayo gachyānkuṣa-paṅkaja-kalitam*: "His pure and beautiful feet at Gayā with markings of elephant goad and lotus." Chaitanya appears overwhelmed with emotion as Ishvara Puri whispers a Mantra in his ear, after which Chaitanya expresses a desire to go to Vrindāvana, and sings a Kīrtan before a vision of Krishna with flute:

> *Krishna varṇa śiśu eka. muralī bājāya muralī bājāya*
> *Nayana samukhe mora nāciyā beḍāya.*
>
> "A child known as Kṛishna who plays the flute, who plays the flute before my own eyes and dances about."

Chaitanya then chants three items in sequence: [8] *He Krishna karuṇā sindho,* [6] *Harer nāma Harer nāma,* and [3] *Krishna Keśava pāhi mām.* These are followed by a poem of Dvija Chandidās (VP: 49), sung by Mukunda: *Rādhāra ki halo antare byathā*: "O what pain of separation did Rādhārāṇī feel?" Chaitanya continues by singing another song of Chandidās.

Several Kīrtans follow when Nityānanda (Nitāi), appearing in the form of Balarām, meets Chaitanya: *Ke tāre bol cinte pare, tāra līlāra sīmā nāi;* "O tell me who can know the One, whose pastimes are unlimited." Balarām sings a song about the Holy Name: *Hari nāme dūba debe bhāi, thakbe nā āra bhaya;* "If you drown yourself in Hari Nām, you will have no fear anymore." After Balarām reveals himself as Nitāi, Chaitanya addresses him as "dādā" (elder brother). Chaitanya then leads Balarām and the devotees in a Kīrtan.

> *Jaya jaya Govinda Gopāla Gadādhara*
> *Krishna candra kara kripa karuṇā sāgara.*
> *Jaya jaya Govinda, Gopāla Vanamālī*
> *Śrī Rādhāra prāṇa dhana Mukunda Murāri*
>
> "O Krishna Candra, O Ocean of Compassion, please have mercy upon us.
> Glories to Govinda, Glories to Gopāla, Keeper of the Forest.
> O Treasure Chest of Śrī Rādhā's heart, O Mukunda,
> O Killer of the Mura demon."

The saint Advaitācārya, after a vision, proclaims: "I think Lord Nārāyaṇa has appeared in Navadvīp in person." Then, after he offers Sanskrit prayers, verses from the *Madana-Mohana-Aṣṭakam*, beginning with *Jaya śaṅkha-gadādhara nīla-kalevara, pīta-paṭāmbara dehi padam,* are sung in classical Dhrupad style in Rāga Malkosh accompanied on the Pakhavaj drum.

Then, in the home temple of devotee Śrīvās, a Kīrtan of Govinda Dās is sung by Nitāi and the devotees, with alternating verses sung by Chaitanya as all circumambulate the Deity in the central shrine (VP: 581; SVA: 94-95): *Bhajahū re mana, Śrī Nanda-nandana, abhaya-caraṇāravinda re.* "O mind, just worship the lotus feet of the son of Nanda, which make one fearless."

After a confrontation with an adversary, Chaitanya sings a poem by Vidyāpati (VP: 111): *Mādhava! Bahuta minati karu toya:* "O Mādhava, I plead with you again and again." Chaitanya and his devotees then circumambulate the Deity, singing [2] *Hari Haraye namaḥ Krishna* and *Haribol bāhu tule nece nece:* "Raise your hands, dance and sing Haribol."

The scene abruptly shifts to a royal palace where a courtesan woman sings to an audience headed by Jagāi and Madhāi. Hearing a classical Khayal song, they reject it in favor of something more erotic. She continues but is interrupted by the procession of devotees singing [1] Mahā Mantra, appearing to lose herself in the sound by swaying her head back and forth, ultimately singing along. Jagāi and Madhāi are visibly upset and decide to confront the devotees, threatening and attacking Chaitanya as he pleas for them to recite the name of Hari. To ease the tension, Nitāi sings a song of consolation, forgives them, and sings [4] *Bhaja Gaurāṅga* with all the devotees.

Chaitanya then visits his mother and wife. Vishnupriyā sings to Chaitanya, "You are my Life Partner from a hundred births." But while she sleeps peacefully, he places a flower garland near her and quietly departs the home and household life; slowly walking, arms outstretched, as he recites [1] Mahā Mantra. She awakens to find that her husband has gone! Not responding to calls of "Nimāi" from his wife and mother, Chaitanya has taken the life of a renunciate in search of Krishna. Like the other films, this film closes with [8] *He Kṛishna karuṇā sindho.*

Conclusion

The current climate in the study of religion is one that embraces culture and cultural productions as embedded within or reflecting religious experience. This includes the arts like music, poetry, literature, painting, sculpture, and architecture, but also film. As understood, a religious film is an artefact that has the capacity to convey religious or metaphysical truths beyond the ingredients of material production regardless of the perception of it being a human construct. As human imaginary constructions, religious films partake of the sacred in their function of creating units of ritual space and time that elevate human consciousness above everyday profane reality. Religious studies scholar John Lyden has indeed emphasized that the visual representations of religion in film offer a reality that is not dependent upon ordinary existence yet integrated with it in multiple levels.

In this way, the images and sounds of Chaitanya in classic Bengali cinema, as represented, create an alternative reality that acts as a "window" into the sacred reality of the transcendental Vaishnava experience of love of Krishna. As "sacred soundtracks," the chants and songs in the films, as Kīrtan, are "authentic" as far as it is possible for musicians to reconstruct them from the available biographies and lineages. The arrangements of the Sanskrit prayers as well as the songs and poems of Chandidās and Vidyāpati also reveal the superb craftmanship of well-trained composers, singers, and instrumentalists according to established musical traditions. But while the music is traditional in execution, it is also infused with a sense of devotion capable of moving audiences to tears, as reported by many viewers. These films may thus be considered "scripture," in the sense that they embody and preserve the essence of the Vaishnava musical tradition surrounding Chaitanya and his early followers.

We close with a verse by Śrīla Rūpa Goswami in praise of Chaitanya as cited in the CC, Madhya-Līlā, Vol. 7, Chapter 19, verse 53 (p. 272). This prayer of obeisance, sometimes heard as background in the films, perfectly captures the identity of Chaitanya:

> *Namo mahā-vadanyāya*
> *Krishna-prema-pradāyate*
> *Krishnāya krishna-chaitanya*
> *nāmne gaura-tviṣe namah*

> "O most munificent incarnation! You are Krishna Himself appearing as Śrī Krishna Chaitanya Mahāprabhu. You have assumed the golden color of Śrimatī Rādhārānī, and You are widely distributing pure love of Krishna. We offer our respectful obeisance unto You."

Endnotes

1. This author had the honor of meeting R. C. Boral when he was affiliated with the ITC Sangeet Research Academy in Calcutta in the late 1970s.

2. Inspired by the ubiquity of music in religious life, this author has introduced the new field of "musicology of religion" (Beck 2023).

3. For a general introduction to Kīrtan, see Beck (2010).

4. For more information on Padāvali-Kīrtan, see Ray (1985: 3-53), Chakraborty (1992: 199-224), and Chakrabarty (1996). For Narottam Dās, see Beck (1996).

5. For more information on the Mahā Mantra, see Beck (2004).

Bibliography

Arnold, Alison. 2000. "Film Music: Northern Area." In *Garland encyclopedia of world music*, vol. 5, Indian subcontinent. Edited by Alison Arnold. New York and London: Garland Publishing, 531-541.

Beck, Guy L. 2004. "The Hare Krishna *Mahāmantra*: Gauḍīya Vaishnava Practice and the Hindu Tradition of Sacred Sound." In *The Hare Krishna Movement: The Postcharismatic Fate of a Religious Transplant*. Edited by Edwin F. Bryant and Maria L. Ekstrand. New York: Columbia University Press, 35-44.

———. 1996. "An Introduction to the Poetry of Narottam Dās." *Journal of Vaiṣhṇava Studies* 4. 4: 17-52.

———. 2010. "Kīrtan and Bhajan in Bhakti Traditions." In *Brill's Encyclopedia of Hinduism*. Edited by Knut A. Jacobsen. Leiden: Brill Academic Publishers, Vol. II, 585-598.

———. 2023. *Musicology of Religion: Theories, Methods, and Directions*. Albany, NY: SUNY Press.

———. 1993. *Sonic Theology: Hinduism and Sacred Sound*. Columbia, SC: University of South Carolina Press.

Caitanya-Caritāmṛta of Kṛṣṇadāsa Kavirāja. 1974-75. 17 vols. Translated with text and commentary by A. C. Bhaktivedānta Swami. Los Angeles, CA: Bhaktivedānta Book Trust.

Chakrabarty, Ramakanta. 1996. "Vaiṣṇava Kīrtan in Bengal." *Journal of Vaishnava Studies* 4.2: 179-199.

Chakraborty, Mriganka Sekhar. 1992. *Indian Musicology: Melodic Structure*. Calcutta: Firma KLM Private Ltd.

Coomaraswamy, Ananda K. 1956 (1943). *Christian & Oriental Philosophy of Art*. New York: Dover Publications

Coomaraswamy, Ananda K. 2014 (1934). *The Transformation of Nature in Art*. New Delhi: Munshiram Manoharlal.

Dwyer, Rachel. 2006. *Filming the Gods: Religion and Indian Cinema*. London and New York: Routledge.

Graves, Eben. 2014. *Padāvali-Kīrtan: Music, Religious Aesthetics, and Nationalism in West Bengal's Cultural Economy*. Ph.D. dissertation. University of Texas-Austin.

———. 2022. *The Politics of Musical time: Expanding Songs and Shrinking Markets in Bengali Devotional Performance*. Bloomington, IN: Indiana University Press.

Lyden, John. 2019 (2003). *Film as Religion: Myths, Morals, and Rituals*. New York: New York University Press.

Martin, James Alfred. 1990. *Beauty and Holiness: The Dialogue between Aesthetics and Religion*. Princeton, NJ: Princeton University Press.

Mukhopadhyay, Durgadas, ed. and trans. 1990. *In Praise of Krishna: Translation of Gita Govinda of Jayadeva*. Delhi: B.R. Publishing Corporation.

Raghunathan, N., trans. 1976. *Śrīmad Bhāgavatam*. Madras and Bangalore: Vighneswara Publishing House, Vols. I & II.

Rajadhyaksha, Ashish and Paul Willemen. 1999 (1994). *Encyclopedia of Indian Cinema*. New Revised Edition. New Delhi: Oxford University Press and London: British Film Institute.

Ramaswamy, N. 2022. *History of Indian Cinema*. Lansing, MI: Independent Publisher.

Ray, Sukumar.1985. *Music of Eastern India: Vocal Music in Bengali, Oriya, Assamese and Manipuri with Special Emphasis on Bengali*. Calcutta: Firma KLM.

Schwartz, Susan L. 2004. *Rasa: Performing the Divine in India*. New York: Columbia University Press.

Sheldrake, Philip. 2014. *Spirituality: A Guide for the Perplexed*. London: Bloomsbury.

Srinivasa Ayyangar, T.R., trans. 1953. *The Vaiṣṇava Upanishads*. Madras: Adyar Library.

[SVA] *Songs of the Vaiṣṇava Ācāryas: Hymns and Mantras for the Glorification of Rādhā and Kṛṣṇa*. New York: Bhaktivedānta Book Trust, 1989 (1974).

[VP] *Vaiṣṇava Padāvalī*. Edited by Śrī Hare Kṛṣṇa Mukhopādhyāy. Kolkata; Sahitya Samsad, 1961.

Film Links:

BHAGWAN SRIKRISHNA CHAITANYA (https://www.youtube.com/watch?v=TOUuAzD6JTo)

NILACHALE MAHAPRABHU (https://www.youtube.com/watch?v=ZVOUi__D4ps)

NIMAI OF NADIYA-NADER NIMAI (https://www.youtube.com/watch?v=Y8qbMDxniSg)

An "Alphabet Poem" for Caitanya: The *Akṣaramayī kalikā* in Raghunandana Gosvāmin's *Gaurāṅgavirudāvalī*

David Buchta

Even amongst his immediate followers, the 15th-16th century Vaiṣṇava religious leader, Caitanya, came to be regarded not just as a model of devotion, but as an object of devotion himself, ultimately as a manifestation of Rādhā and Kṛṣṇa jointly in one embodiment. The substantial scholarship on the theological doctrines regarding Caitanya and the history of their development, especially the contributions of Tony Stewart including *The Final Word* (2010), will be well-known to the readers of this journal. Understood in this way, Caitanya has frequently been the focus of *stotras* (praise-poems) from the time of his direct followers to the present. In fact, I have argued (Buchta 2014: 70-75) that a lack of attention to these *stotras* is one of the few shortcomings in Stewart's work, who claims, wrongly I think, that the *stotra* literature "has never had much impact because of its form." (2010: 101) The current paper examines a section of a *stotra* from much later in the tradition, the *akṣaramayī kalikā* in Raghunandana Gosvāmin's *Gaurāṅgavirudāvalī*. As its name suggests (*akṣaramayī* = "consisting of letters"), this text can be loosely called an "alphabet poem" – that is, a poem wherein the lines begin with each letter of the language, in the standard order in which they are arranged. In Sanskrit, of course, this is not strictly speaking an "alphabet," but rather the basic *varṇa-krama* or sequence of sounds.

In what follows, I will introduce the author, Raghunandana Gosvāmin, and the *Gaurāṅgavirudāvalī* in which this "alphabet poem" appears. I will then briefly situate this poem in relation to the *virudāvalī* genre of Sanskrit *stotra* poetry, specifically discussing its relationship to Rūpa Gosvāmin's (16th century) *Govindavirudāvalī*.[1] Following this, I will provide the text of Raghunandana's *Akṣaramayī kalikā* with a translation.[2] Finally, I will consider the question of why the format of an alphabet poem is used for praise-poems such as this. Scholarship on alphabet poems, or alphabet literature more broadly, often identifies a pedagogical or mnemonic purpose in such texts or highlights mystical associations with each letter. As for *akṣaramayī kalikā*s in Sanskrit *virudāvalī*s, however, I instead suggest that these poems may be seen as akin to the highly ornate *citra-kāvya* ("poetry of astonishment") style, and I offer an interpretation of their motivation involving the literary ornamentation of the object of devotion, rather than a poet's mere self-aggrandizement.

Raghunandana Gosvāmin and his Gaurāṅgavirudāvalī

Born into a family in the lineage of Caitanya's close associate Nityānanda in the latter part of the 18th century,[3] Raghunandana was a scholar of wide range and voluminous output. William Adam, in his 1838 *Third Report on the State of Education in Bengal*, called Raghunandana "the most voluminous native author I have met with" and lists 37 works by him in Sanskrit and Bangla, ranging from *stotra*s and theological tracts to works on grammar, medicine, and the art of letter writing. Of particular interest in this list is mention of a *stotra* praising Caitanya included in his *Stavakadamba*. It is also worth noting that many of the *stotra* are in the *citra-kāvya* style, including a pair of *ālāta-cakra-bandha* verses (verses inscribed in a whirling firebrand), "so framed that each *sloka* contains materials for 64 *slokas* by the transposition of each letter in succession from the beginning to the end, first the thirty-two syllables from left to right, and afterwards the thirty-two from right to left." (Adam 1838: 50-52) Haridāsa Dāsa gives a partially overlapping, but much shorter list of nine works by Raghunandana including his *Gaurāṅgavirudāvalī* as well as his *Gaurāṅgacampū*,[4] suggesting that these two undated works were likely written after Adam's 1838 report. Raghunandana lived at least until 1849, when he completed the *Rādhāmādhavodaya*.[5]

Raghunandana's *Gaurāṅgavirudāvalī* is the most recent (or possibly second most recent) of five poems in the *virudāvalī* genre composed by poets in the Gauḍīya Vaiṣṇava tradition, beginning with Rūpa Gosvāmin's *Govindavirudāvalī*.[6] In addition to composing a poem in this genre, Rūpa Gosvāmin also wrote a textbook enumerating the highly complex features of the genre, his *Sāmānyavirudāvalīlakṣaṇa* (General Characterization of *Virudāvalī* Poetry), or simply, *Virudāvalīlakṣaṇa*. Rūpa's is the oldest extant full example of a poem in this genre, leading some scholars to assume that Rūpa gave the genre its form, though I have demonstrated that this assumption is mistaken, and that the genre likely developed from antecedents in South India, especially in the context of song composition and reached its full form somewhere in either Andhra Pradesh or Odisha over a century before Rūpa.

The details are beyond the scope of this paper, so I will offer here only a broad outline. According to Rūpa's description and the model he presents, *virudāvalī* poems consist of three main components: 1) verses (*ślokas*) in classical meters, which precede and follow 2) *kalikās*, passages composed of segments called *kalās* with distinctive structures, usually involving sustained patterns of rhythm and rhyme, followed finally by 3) *virudas*, shorter strings formed on the same principles as *kalikās*. Additionally, he notes that both *kalikās* and *virudas* should end with a word like *dhīra* (sage) or *vīra* (hero). Rūpa specifies that a complete *virudāvalī* composition should contain between five and 30 of such units, with no fixed order for the various types of *kalikās*. While most complex *kalikā* types involve distinctive phoneto-metrical structures, Rūpa calls one of the major *kalikā* types, alternately, *kevala* ([metrically] simple) or *gadya* (roughly, "prose" or "non-metrical"). The *akṣaramayī kalikā* is one of the two subtypes in this category. Yet, while Rūpa's partial example in the *Virudāvalīlakṣaṇa* is non-metrical, in his *Govindavirudāvalī* he instead uses a moric meter with eight beats per *kalā* segment (with one segment for each letter) and end-rhyme in each pair of *kalās*.

After Rūpa, we find his nephew Jīva Gosvāmin's incomplete *Gopālavirudāvalī*, Viśvanātha Cakravartin's *Nikuñjakelivirudāvalī* composed in 1678, and the otherwise unknown Kṛṣṇaśaraṇa's *Kṛṣṇavirudāvalī*, in addition to Raghunandana's poem. All four of these poems are closely modeled on Rūpa's *Govindavirudāvalī*, especially Raghunandana's *Gaurāṅgavirudāvalī*. From beginning to end, Raghunandana follows the structure of Rūpa Gosvāmin's poem almost exactly, employing the same sequence of *kalikā* types and sub-types. A close comparison showed only four very minor structural differences between the two poems. Even in small details, Raghunandana follows the model of Rūpa's *Govindavirudāvalī* very closely. In his *akṣaramayī kalikā*, for example, Raghunandana follows the same moric metrical and rhyme structure found in the *Govindavirudāvalī*. As I will indicate in the footnotes through the next section, Raghunandana followed Rūpa's model quite closely especially in formulating epithets with sounds that rarely, if ever occur at the beginning of Sanskrit words, including *ḷ*, *ḹ*, *ṅ*, and *ñ*.

Their indebtedness to Rūpa Gosvāmin is made explicit in the concluding *maṅgala* (invocatory) verses of each of these poets except Jīva, whose incomplete *virudāvalī* does not, of course, contain such concluding verses. The penultimate verse (123) of Raghunandana's *Gaurāṅgavirudāvalī* is particularly striking:

govindasya prakāśo'bhūd yathā śrī-gaurasundaraḥ.
govindavirudāvalyās tatheyaṃ virudāvalī.

Just as Śrī Gaurasundara [Caitanya] was a *prakāśa* manifestation of Govinda,
So this *virudāvalī* is [a *prakāśa* manifestation] of the *Govindavirudāvalī.*

Rūpa Gosvāmin uses the word *prakāśa* as a technical term in his *Laghubhāgavatāmṛta* (1.20-24) where he defines it as "a manifestation of a single form in many places at one time which is completely identical with that [one form]."[7] Thus, identifying Caitanya as a *prakāśa* manifestation of Kṛṣṇa, as the tradition came to do, is to assert the fullest level of identity.[8] By this analogy, then, Raghunandana presents his poem as ontologically identical with Rūpa's. I turn now to Raghunandana's "alphabet poem."

The *Akṣaramayī Kalikā* from Raghunandana's *Gaurāṅgavirudāvalī*: Text and Translation

adbhuta-guṇa jaya	With wonderous virtues, triumph!
āhita-kali-bhaya	Setting aside fear of the age of Kali,
iṣṭa-janāvaka	Protecting people dear to you,
īśvara-sevaka	Servant of god (or Īśvara Purī),[9]
uddhata-daṇḍana	Punishing the arrogant,
ūḍha-sumaṇḍana	Bearing beautiful ornaments,
ṛju-jana-saṃśrita	Refuge for honest people,
ṝṣi-gaṇa-stuta	Praised by sages and by the gods' mother,[10]
ḷD-iva ṛtāmita	Honest and immeasurable, as *ḷ* becomes *ṛ*,[11]
ḹvad asādhita	Not effected, like long *ḹ*,[12]

ejita-durjana	Causing the bad people to tremble,
aiśya-niketana	Abode of Power,
oḍra-sadṛg-adhara	Your lower lip like a butterfly rose,
aujjvalyākara	Repository of beauty,[13]
aṃśuka-bhūṣaṇa	Adorned [only] by your clothing,[14]
asta-ga-dūṣaṇa[15]	With all critique vanished
kanaka-sama-prabha	As radiant as gold
khala-jana-dur-llabha	Difficult for wicked people to attain,
gaṇanā-virahita	Beyond enumeration,[16]
ghana-kaca-vilasita	Beautiful with your hair dark as a raincloud,
ṅuti-jita-kokila	Defeating the cuckoo with your music,[17]
cūḍita-vicakila	With jasmine flowers for a crown,
chalita-kamala-mada	Making a fool of the lotus's arrogance,
jagatī-priya[18]*-pada*	With feet that delight the world,
jhanad-iti-nūpura-	With tinkling ankle-bells...
ñoṅūyā-kara	Making abundant music,
ṭīkana-nistala	Fathomless in exposition,
ṭha-jayi-nakhāñcala	Defeating the cresecent moon with the edge of your nails,[19]
ḍamaru-dhṛg-īśvara[20]	Lord of Śiva who hold the *ḍamaru* drum,
ḍhuṇḍhya[21]*-kṛpā-bhara*	With great compassion that ought to be sought out,
ṇa-rūpa-vigraha	With a form that is joy embodied,[22]
tattva-vid-āgraha	Affectionate towards those who know the truth,

thut-kṛta-muktika-	With liberation spat upon...[23]
dara-pada-bhaktika	By even a bit of devotion to your feet,
dharma-hṛd-ādara	With respect in your heart for piety,[24]
narma-rasākara	Repository of the ecstacy of play,
padma-vijayi-kara-	With hands that defeat lotuses...
phulla-kamala-dhara	Bearing a blossomed lotus,
bandha-vimocana	Liberating from worldly entanglement,
bhāskara-rocana	Radiant like the sun,
madhuratarānana	With the sweetest face,
yama-jayi-sevana	With service to you conquering Death,
rasa-bhara-dāyaka	Bestowing the great ecstacy of *rasa,*
lalita-vidhāyaka	Granting what is desired,
valad-anupama-daya	With ever-increasing, unparalleled mercy,
śamita-bhuvana-bhaya	Quelling the world's fear,
ṣaḍ-bhuja-vīkṣaka	Appearing with six arms,
san-mata-śīkṣaka	Teaching the doctrines of the wise,
hari-guṇa-kathana-	With narration of Hari's virtues...
kṣaṇa-nandita-jana	Delighting the people with festivity,
deva	O Lord!

The Challenge and Purpose of Akṣaramayī Kalikās

An author of an ABC book for children has to contend with the paucity of word other than xylophone and zebra for X and Z, among other challenges. But it quickly becomes clear that the difficulty of composing an *akṣaramayī* is substantially greater. To conclude this paper, I will consider why, given this difficulty, a poet like Raghunandana might choose to praise their object of devotion in this format.

As noted in the introduction, the small body of scholarship on this type of literature focuses on its pedagogical, mnemonic, or mystical purposes. Nyr Indictor offers these three suggestions:

> Firstly, alphabetic texts are relatively easily committed to memory. Psalm 119, which is a lengthy description of Jewish law, renders a complex body of knowledge more accessible through its alphabetic structure. Secondly... the use of an alphabetic structure may have implicitly symbolized completeness. Then too, there is the possibility of viewing these texts as early children's alphabets, although generally it is felt that the level of sophistication of the texts is too high to have been intended for children. (Indictor 1995: 132)

Victoria Symons similarly summarizes the reasons for composition suggested in scholarship on the Old English *Rune Poem*, with some arguing that it "served as a mnemonic device, helping students to remember the correct order of the letter of the fuþorc"; some, that it "preserves traditional wisdom associated with each of the runic letters" or "preserves traces of cultic or divinatory practices." (Symons 2016: 157-58) And Charles Wright and Stephen Pelle discuss the Latin *Alphabet of Words*, wherein "each letter of the alphabet is written in order in the left margin, next to which (in nearly all cases) is placed a word or phrase beginning with that letter; the spiritual significance of this word or phrase is then explained." (Wright and Pelle 2017: 62)

An examination of Raghunandana's poems makes clear that none of these explanations will suffice for his *akṣaramayī kalikā.* Though it is possible that the *akṣaramayī kalikā* type's antecedents may have had a pedagogical function, Raghunandana's (and Rūpa's) metalinguistic puns and obscure derivation are hardly child's play, ruling out this poem's having a pedagogical purpose. They are too difficult to read without already having a deep knowledge of the language. And while the poem characterizes Caitanya and proclaims his divinity in a variety of ways, there is nothing like an essential and systemic theological account here that would need memorization.

One might expect a Vaiṣṇava "alphabet" *stotra* to invoke mystical identifications between the letters and various manifestations of the divine. From Kṛṣṇa's statement in the *Bhagavad Gītā* (10.33) that, among letters, he is the first letter *a* (*akṣarāṇām akāro'smi*) to the syllable by syllable analyses of *mantras*, especially the Gāyatrī and Kāma-Gāyatrī *mantras*, in Vaiṣṇava commentaries,[25] and practices of *mātṛkā-nyāsa* where letters with sacred associations are inscibed on the body,[26] such identifications are pervasive in Vaiṣṇava literature.[27] In fact, Haridāsa Dāsa refers to the practice of *mātṛkā-nyāsa* in his commentary on the epithet for long ḹ, "As the long sound ḹ is not brought into being [i.e. derived through *sandhi*] ... but is in fact eternally established in contexts such as *mātṛkā-nyāsa*, so similarly, you [Caitanya] are not born, but are eternally established."[28] Nevertheless, the connection between Caitanya and the sound ḹ here is metaphorical, not mystical. Caitanya's nails are identified with the shape of the letter *ṭha*, but again, the connection is metaphorical.[29] And Caitanya is said to be the embodiment of *ṇa* (joy or knowledge), an association known to Vaiṣṇavas from analyses of the name *kṛṣ-ṇa*, but the connection here is etymological.[30] Aside from these possible partial exceptions, Raghunandana's poem does not focus on the significance, mystical or otherwise, of the letters of the language.

Indictor's mention of "implicitly symbolized completeness" is perhaps the most helpful line of analysis here. Raghunandana's *akṣaramayī kalikā*, like Rūpa's, contains the entire set of Sanskrit sounds, even the long ḹ which arguably doesn't even exist in the language. It is this completeness which thus leads to the poem's difficulty, in both composing and reading. But I want to suggest that the difficulty is a feature, not a bug, of these praise-poems. One might think that the motivation to compose intentionally difficult poems is the opportunity it affords the poet to show off their erudition. The ever-curmudgeonly S. K. De, evaluating our poet's place in Bengali literature, writes, "Raghunandan is by no means a slovenly writer but in his striving after technical perfection, he is often elaborate and artificial. His writings display faultless execution and a great command over the language; but ingenuity and verbal or rhythmic dexterity can never supply perennial nutriment for art." (De 1919: 432) While such a potential motivation cannot be discounted, the devotional context of this poem and Raghunandana's protestation of humility[31] perhaps gives scope to consider a more charitable analysis of the poet's motivation.

The difficulty of this poem structure created by the self-imposed constraint of starting each line with the letters of the language in order parallels the constraints seen in *citra-kāvya*. *Citra-kāvya,* one finds, is particularly common in *stotras*.[32] I have argued previously that *stotras* are quite an appropriate context for *citra-kāvya* where the ornate figures of speech can be understood as offering to a deity, just as elaborate offerings of food, clothing, and other items are made before a temple icon. Raghunandana, like Rūpa, certainly had a great wealth of erudition, as the volume and range of his literary and scholarly output demonstrate. The colonial administrator, William Adam, was impressed. His profound learning would have been apparent to any who encountered him; he did not need the context of a *stotra* in praise of Caitanya to demonstrate it. As a devotee, he offered to Caitanya his possession of greatest value, his skill with language.

One further motivation deserves consideration: Gary Tubb (2014) and, following him, Hamsa Stainton (2019: 223-224) argue that, while highly ornate poetry may not be conducive to evoking *śṛṅgāra* (the erotic *rasa*), it can be effective for evoking *abdhuta* (the wonderous). It is noteworthy that, rather than end with one of Rūpa's two suggested words, *vīra* or *dhīra*, Raghunandana ends his *kalikā* with *deva* (god), proclaiming Caitanya's divinity, not as widely accepted as Kṛṣṇa's. And many of the epithets speak directly to Caitanya's divinity, from his conquering fear of Kali to his appearance with six arms. It is thus reasonable to think that complexity of his poem should contribute to evoking *adbhuta.* It is, indeed, a wonder of a poem.

Endnotes

1. Numerous similar "alphabet poems," have been composed in other literary contexts in Sanskrit, and indeed in many languages around the world going as far back as the Hebrew Bible. For the present study, however, I will restrict my contextualization of this poem in praise of Caitanya to its most immediate precedents, namely the other Gauḍīya Vaiṣṇava *virudāvalīs*. The final section of this paper, considering the purpose of the *akṣaramayī* format, will briefly consider the broader context of alphabet poems. I am currently preparing a thorough study of all available *akṣaramayī kalikās*, including a royal praise-poem (reportedly in honor of Shah Jahan), which will engage in broader comparison. The most comprehensive study of alphabet poems in world literature is a playful article by Nyr Indictor (1995).

2. The entirety of the *Gaurāṅgavirudāvalī* has been translated into Bangla around the turn of the 20th century by Śrīvaikuṇṭha Nātha Ghoṣāla Bhaktitattva Vācaspati (originally published in Bhaktivinoda Ṭhākura's periodical *Sajjanatoṣaṇī*), commented on in Sanskrit and translated into Bangla by Haridāsa Dāsa in 1942, and translated into Hindi (presumably by Haridāsa Śāstrī in whose 1984 edition the translation appears). This *Akṣaramayī* section has been translated into English by Hari Parshad Das in a 2013 issue of *Sri Krishna Kathamrita Bindu.* I have benefited by consulting each of these sources. Still, I will indicate in the footnotes a few particularly tricky places where the various translations warrant improvement and will offer justification for my divergent translations. I will also note discrepancies between the Sanskrit text as published in the various editions, arguing for the best reading or emendation. Note: for Vācaspati's edition and commentary, I rely on an undated pamphlet, "Printed by Jogendra Nath Chakraburti At The 'Hari Press'" in Calcutta, acquired by the Harvard University Library in 1957, which states on the inside of the front cover that it was originally "Published

in SAJJAN TOSHANI Vol XV & XVII." I do not know the year of these volumes, but the *Sajjanatoṣaṇī* ran from 1881 to 1904. I am indebted to Anand Venkatkrishnan at the University of Chicago for assistance acquiring Haridāsa Dāsa's edition.

3. De (1919: 428) notes an edition of his *Rāmarasāyaṇa* that lists his date of birth as 1786, while Haridāsa Dāsa claims that he was born "in the last part of the 17th century of the Śāka era (*sapta-daśa śaka-śatābdīra śeṣa-bhāge*)," (1957: 1324) placing him at least nine years earlier.

4. It is noteworthy that, just as Jīva Gosvāmin composed both a *Gopālavirudāvalī* and a *Gopālacampū*, so likewise Raghunandana composed both a *Gaurāṅgavirudāvalī* and a *Gaurāṅgacampū*. The latter work certainly warrants study, particularly in relation to Jīva's poem.

5. *śāke'bde kṣamā-sapta-sapta-kṣā-mite*

6. The following paragraph summarizes details of the history of Gauḍīya Vaiṣṇava *virudāvalī* poems discussed in Buchta 2014: 259-357. Kṛṣṇaśaraṇa's dates are unknown, but Haridāsa Dāsa suggests that he may have lived prior to Raghunandana. I hope to publish a thorough examination of the history of the *virudāvalī* genre soon.

7. *anekatra prakaṭatā rūpasyaikasya yaikadā. sarvathā tat-svarūpaiva sa prakāśa itīryate..*

8. Haridāsa Dāsa understands the term in this technical sense, citing *Laghubhāgavatāmṛta* 1.20 in his commentary on this verse.

9. I follow Vācaspati's straightforward translation for my first interpretation here. Haridāsa Dāsa offers the alternate reading of Īśvara as a proper name here, but also gives yet another sense of this compound as a bahuvrīhi, meaning, "one who has kings for servants," perhaps alluding to figures such as Pratāparudra.

10. Vācaspati translates this with simply, "*he ṛṣi-gaṇera stabanīya* (Fit to be praised by the sages)," But it is noteworthy that the Sanskrit text in this edition, written in the Bangla script, has *ṛṣi* in place of *ṝṣi*. This is not surprising since the sound *ṝ* does not occur as the initial sound of any normal words. The printer may not, in fact, have been able to print the Bangla character for *ṝ*. Hari Parshad Das similarly has "who is worshipped by the sages," though he has the correct reading *ṝṣi*. It is perhaps possible that Raghunandana understood *ṝṣi* as simply an alternate spelling of *ṛṣi*, though I have found no evidence for this as an attested alternate spelling (including, for example, in Puruṣottamadeva's lexicon of words with two spellings, his *Dvirūpakoṣa*). Rather, I follow Haridāsa Dāsa here in interpreting *ṝṣi* as a compound *ṛ-ṛṣi*, where the two short *ṛ* sounds coalesce into a single long *ṝ* sound according to normal *sandhi* rules. The monosyllabic word *ṛ* in the sense of "mother of the gods" is widely attested in classical Sanskrit lexicons such as Puruṣottamadeva's *Ekākṣarakoṣa* (verse 3c: *ṛ-kāro deva-mātā syāt*), presumably a back-derivation from the word *ṛbhu* meaning "god." Rūpa Gosvāmin begins his corresponding epithet with *ṝbhu*. Though his commentator, Baladeva Vidyābhūṣaṇa presents this as just and alternate spelling of *ṛbhu*, I suspect that Rūpa intended a similar compound, *ṛ-ṛbhu*, and that Raghunandana likely took inspiration from this.

11. This epithet and the next involve metalinguistic puns. Here, Caitanya is compared to the short *ḷ*, in that both can be said to be *ṛtāmita*. For Caitanya, this is a pair of adjectives, *ṛta* and *amita*. The short *ḷ* is here called *ḷT*, adding the Pāṇinian code-letter *T* according to *Aṣṭādhyāyī* 1.1.70 *(ta-parasya tat-kālasya)* to distinguish it from long *ḹ*. (Note: In contemporary scholarly literature, these code-letters are capitalized to distinguish them from the linguistic units which they mark.) For this short *ḷ*, the phrase *ṛtāmita* breaks down to *ṛtām ita*, "gone to the state of being *ṛ*." This is an allusion to the verb root √*kḷp*. The *ḷ* in this root may be said to "become *ṛ*" insofar as the Pāṇinian *Dhātupāṭha* instead lists this root as √*kṛpŪ* (and Patañjali's *Mahābhāṣya* gives it as √*kṛpA*), with the *ṛ* restored to the proper sound *ḷ* (and its substitutes) by *Aṣṭādhyāyī* 8.2.18 (*kṛpo ro laḥ: l* is the substitute for the *r* of [the root] √*kṛp*). This pun is similar to the corresponding epithet in Rūpa Gosvāmin's *Govindavirudāvalī*, *ḷD-iva kṛpeṣkita*, where Kṛṣṇa is said to be seen through his mercy (*kṛpā-īkṣita*) just as *ḷ* is seen [only] in the root √*kṛpA* (*kṛpA-īkṣita*). Alternatively, Raghunandana may be referring to the shift in some dialects of Sanskrit where *ḷ* comes to be pronounced the same as *ṛ*.

Unfortunately, Haridāsa Śāstrī's edition has an incorrect reading of this line as *ḷdiva ṛtāmiva*, not recognizing that the end rhyme thus fails, and despite the fact that he includes Haridāsa Dāsa's commentary indicating the correct reading. The accompanying Hindi translation is a somewhat incoherent attempt to translate Haridāsa Dāsa's commentary. Hari Parshad Das follows Haridāsa Śāstrī's incorrect reading of the text and likewise offers a translation that is not fully coherent and is grammatically untenable. Vācaspati offers a translation of this and the next epithet that strays completely from the basic sense of the text.

12. The sense regarding Caitanya is clear: that he is eternal, not brought into being. As for the long *ḹ*, I understand Raghunandana to be alluding to discussions about *Aṣṭādhyāyī* 1.1.9 and 6.1.101 in Patañjali's *Mahābhāṣya* and in the *Kāśikāvṛtti* of Jayāditya and Vāmana, where the juxtaposition of a final *ṛ* and intial *ḷ* would result in substitution of either long *ṝ* or short *ḷ*, but not long *ḹ*. Thus, it is not that long *ḹ* does not exist; only that it is not brought into being (*asādhita*) through *sandhi* rules. Haridāsa Dāsa offers an interesting interpretation: "As the long sound *ḹ* is not brought into being, because of becoming *ṛ* [sic; presumably: *ṝ*], but is in fact eternally established in contexts such as *mātṛkā-nyāsa*, so similarly, you [Caitanya] are not born, but are eternally established. (*dīrgha ḹ-kāro yathā sādhito na syāt ṛtva-prāpteḥ kintu mātṛkā-nyāsādau nitya-siddho'sty eva tathā tvam api janyo na kintu nitya-siddhaḥ.*)" *Mātṛkā-nyāsa* is a meditative technique involving imprinting sacred syllables on various parts of the body. Hari Parshad Das translates, "who cannot be attained by material endeavors, just like the elongated *ḷḷ* [sic] cannot be pronounced by the material senses." The sound *ḹ* can, in fact, be pronounced, and is recognized in a number of Sanskrit grammatical traditions. In fact, its inclusion in alphabet poems such as this, which were intended for recitation, necessitates its being utterable. Again, Raghunandana's epithet for Caitanya closely mirrors Rūpa's epithet for Kṛṣṇa: *ḹvad alakṣita*.

13. Or, a repository of *ujjvala-rasa,* i.e., the *rasa* of erotic devotion. Each prior commentator and translator includes this interpretation.

14. Here, I follow Haridāsa Dāsa's line of interpretation (*bhūṣaṇādi-rahiteti bhāvaḥ*), which highlights Caitanya's renunciation. Hari Parshad Das, on the other hand, translates, "who wears fine decorated cloth," though this does not seem to be a grammatically tenable translation of the compound.

15. This is supposed to be the epithet starting with *visarga,* i.e., *aḥ.* However, Raghunandana, like Rūpa, includes a sibilant, as though it were the result of a *sandhi* substitution for a *visarga.*

16. The sense of this epithet is opaque. My translation is intentionally open to varying interpretations. Vācaspati paraphrases this as "singing [Kṛṣṇa's] name non-stop (*avirata nāma-kīrttaka*)," while Haridāsa Dāsa and those after him take this as a reference to the lack of inclusion of Caitanya in the enumeration of *avatāras* in the *Bhāgavata,* stating that he is the "hidden" *(pracchanna) avatāra.* I suggest a more straightforward interpretation of this epithet as simply meaning something like *ananta* (limitless). Consider *Caitanyacaritāmṛta* 3.9.109, which says of Caitanya's mercy, "A calculation of it [can]not come into anyone's mind (*tāhāra gaṇanā kāroṁ mane nāhi āise*). Or it could mean that he is free of accounting, i.e., the accumulation of wealth.

17. Both here and in the later epithet beginning with *ñ*, Raghunandana follows Rūpa, creating a nominal derivate from the root √*ṅu*, and then from its intensive derivate root √*ñoṅūya.*

18. All editions read *priyaka*, but this breaks the meter and the word does not make sense in the context.

19. Sanskrit lexicons widely list "moon" or "the orb of the moon" (Puruṣottamadeva's *Ekākṣarakoṣa* 17ab: *bṛhad-dhvanau ca ṭhaḥ proktas tathā candrasya maṇḍale*), presumably based on the shape of the letter in *Nāgarī.* Rūpa draws on this sense in his poem, describing Kṛṣṇa as "having a fine face like the orb of the moon (*ṭha-nibhānana-vara*). I believe Raghunandana is being quite clever here, drawing the sense of *ṭha* not from the Nāgarī letter, but from the Bangla letter. Thus, he uses the crescent moon rather than the full moon as a vehicle of comparison for the white edge of Caitanya's fingernails and toenails.

20. Vācaspati's edition for this line is completely unmetrical and so was not considered.

21. Vācaspati's edition is correct, but Haridāsa Śāstri has, erroneously, *ḍhuṇḍya.* The root √*ḍhuṇḍh* from which Raghunandana derives this word is extremely rare, appearing only in the *Dhātupāṭha* in the traditions of Kāśakṛtsna and Vopadeva, but not in the *Dhātupāṭha* of Pāṇini or other traditions. See Palsule (1953:166).

22. Alternatively, *ṇa* can mean "knowledge."

23. Raghunandana follows Rūpa here in using *thut-kṛta...*, though Rūpa's poem spells the onomatopoeic word with long *ū.*

24. I consider this translation tentative, but have departed from all previous

interpreters here, who read this as "causing great perturbation (*ā-dara)* for those who remove (*hṛt*) *dharma.*" My main hesitation with this reading is that I can find no attestation of *ādara* used in this sense, while it regularly has the meaning "respect."

25. Much of this was discussed in issue 24.2 of this journal.

26. See Chapter 5 of Sanātana Gosvāmin's *Haribhaktivilāsa* in Broo (2023: esp pp 6624-635), and the discussion of Jīva Gosvāmin's *Bhaktisandarbha* in Ch. 6 of Holdrege (2015).

27. Schemes of mystical associations with letters is prominent in Tantric contexts. As a rather stark example, Somadeva Vasudeva (2007) discusses a series of text which identify each letter (in a distinctive order) with a particular goddess and a body part, such that an icon of the goddess Mālinī is constructed from the written form of the letters.

28. See note 12.

29. See note 19.

30. See note 22.

31. In his opening *maṅgala* verses, for example, Raghunandana describes himself as having a poor speech and a corrupted mind, and compares himself to a blind *cātaka* bird with an unpleasant song, but asks Caitanya, as a cloud of mercy, to hear him.

32. For some examples outside of a Vaiṣṇava context, see Ingalls (1989), Vose (2016), and Stainton (2019).

Bibliography

Adam, William. 1938. *Third Report on the State of Education in Bengal; Including Some Account of the State of Education in Behar, and a Consideration of the Means Adapted to the Improvement and Extension of Public Instruction in Both Provinces.* Calcutta: G. H. Huttmann, Bengal Military Orphan Press.

Broo, Måns (ed. and tr.). 2023. *Haribhaktivilāsa of Sanātana Gosvāmin, Volume One.* Leiden: Brill.

Buchta, David. 2014. "Pedagogical Poetry: Didactics and Devotion in Rūpa Gosvāmin's *Stavamālā.*" Ph.D. Dissertation. University of Pennsylvania, Philadelphia.

———. 2016. "Evoking *Rasa* through *Stotra:* Rūpa Gosvāmin's *Līlāmṛta,* A List of Kṛṣṇa's Names." *International Journal of Hindu Studies* 20: 355-71.

Das, Hari Parshad. 2013. "All Alphabets in Service of Gaura." *Sri Krishna Kathamrita Bindu* 297: 1-4.

Dāsa, Haribhakta (ed.). 1989. *Śrī-śrī-Laghubhāgavatāmṛtam, Śrīla Rūpa-Gosvāmi Pādena Viracitam: Śrīmad-Baladeva Vidyābhūṣaṇa Kṛta Sāraṅgaraṅgadā Ṭīkā Śrīmad-Vṛndāvanacandra-Tarkālaṅkāra-kṛta Rasika-raṅgadā Ṭīkā cā bhāṣānuvāda-sametam*. Vṛndāvana: Harināma Presa [Press].

Dāsa, Haridāsa (ed.). 1941. *Sāmānya Virudāvalī-lakṣaṇaṃ tathā Śrī-Gopāla-virudāvalī*. Navadvīpa: Haribola Kuṭīra.

———. 1942. *Śrīśrīgaurāṅgabirudābalī*. Navadvīpa: Haribola Kuṭīra.

———. 1957. *Śrīśrīgauḍīya-Vaiṣṇava-Abhidhāna*. Parts 2, 3, and 4. Navadvīpa: Haribola Kuṭīra.

De, Sushil Kumar. 1919. *History of Bengali Literature in the Nineteenth Century 1800-1825*. Calcutta: University of Calcutta.

Durgāprasād, Paṇdit, Kāśīnāth Pāṇdurang Parab, and Paṇdit Śivadatta (eds.). 1889. *The Abhidhāna-Sangraha or A Collection of Sanskrit Ancient Lexicons. Nos. 2, 3, 4, 5. The Trikāṇḍaśesha, the Hārāvalī, the Ekāksharakosha, and the Dvirūpakosha of Purushottamadeva*. Bombay: Nirṇaya Sāgara Press.

Gosvāmī, Madanagopāla (ed.). 1905. *Śrīśrīrādhāmādhabodaya: Mahātmā Raghunandana Gosvāmī Praṇīta*. [2nd edition]. Kalikātā: Vidyāratna-yantra.

Holdrege, Barbara A. 2015. *Bhakti and Embodiment Fashioning Divine Bodies and Devotional Bodies in Krsna Bhakti*. London: Routledge.

Indictor, Nyr. 1995. "Alphabet Poems: A Brief History," *Word Ways* 28.3: 131-135.

Ingalls, Daniel H. H. 1989. "Ānandavardhana's *Devīśataka*." *Journal of the American Oriental Society* 109.4: 565-75.

Palsule, G. B. 1953. "A Concordance of Sanskrit *Dhātupāthas*." *Bulletin of the Deccan College Post-Graduate and Research Institute* 15.1/2: i-iv, 1-203.

Śāstrī, Bhavadatta and Kāśīnāth Pāṇdurang Parab (eds.). 1903. *The Stava-mālā of Śrī-Rūpadeva: With the Commentary of Śrī-Jīvadeva* [*sic*]. Kāvyamālā 84. Bombay: Nirṇaya-Sāgara Press.

Śāstrī, Haridāsa (ed.). 1984. *Śrī-Raghunandana Gosvāmi-viracitā Śrī-Gaurāṅgavirudāvalī*. Mathurā: Śrī-Gadādhara-Gaurahari Presa [Press].

Stainton, Hamsa. 2019. *Poetry as prayer in the Sanskrit hymns of Kashmir*. New York: Oxford University Press.

Stewart, Tony K. 2010. *The Final Word: The Caitanya Caritāmṛta and the Grammar of Religious Tradition*. New York: Oxford University Press.

Symons, Victoria. 2016. *Runes and Roman Letters in Anglo-Saxon Manuscripts*. Berlin: de Gruyter.

Tubb, Gary. 2014. "Kāvya with Bells On: *Yamaka* in the *Śiṣupālavadha*; Or, 'What's a flashy verse like you doing in a great poem like this?'" In *Innovations and Turning Points: Toward a History of Kāvya Literature*, edited by Yigal Bronner, David Shulman, and Gary Tubb. Delhi: Oxford University Press: 142–194.

Vācaspati, Śrīvaikuṇṭha Nātha Ghoṣāla Bhaktitattva (tr.). No date. *Śrī-Gaura-virudāvalī: Śrī Raghunandana Gosvāmī Kṛta, Sajjanatoṣaṇī Patrikāya Prakāśita*. Calcutta: Hari Press.

Vasudeva, Somadeva. 2007. "Synæsthetic Iconography: 1. Nādiphāntakrama." In *Mélanges tantriques à la mémoire d'Hélène Brunner*, edited by Dominic Goodall and André Padoux. Pondicherry : Institut français de Pondichéry: 517-50.

Vose, Steven M. 2016. "Jain Uses of *Citrakāvya* and Multiple-Language Hymns in Late Medieval India: Situating the *Laghukāvya* Hymns of Jinaprabhasūri in the 'Assembly of Poets.'"

Wright, Charles D. and Stephen Pelle. 2017. "The *Alphabet of Words* in the Durham Collectar: An Edition with Two New Manuscript Witnesses." *Traditio* 72: 61-108.

The *Octet of Teachings*: Subjectivities in Śrī Caitanya's *Śikṣāṣṭaka*

Sugopi Palakala

Introduction

Several Gauḍīya Vaiṣṇava communities understand the *Śikṣāṣṭaka*[1] as the sole composition left behind by their founder, Śrī Caitanya (1486-1534).[2] Thus, despite its brief nature, the octet occupies a weighty position in the tradition's theological canon; practitioners view it as providing the rare opportunity to encounter Caitanya's message in his own words. Over time, practitioners' engagement with the *Śikṣāṣṭaka* formed a rich reception history, partially evidenced by the written record they created and preserved.

The earliest exegetical remarks on the *Śikṣāṣṭaka* appear in Kṛṣṇadāsa Kavirāja's *Caitanya Caritāmṛta,* a 17th century sacred biography of Caitanya. Three centuries later, the first extensive commentary on the *Śikṣāṣṭaka* materialized: the *Bhajana Rahasya* of Kedarnath Datta Bhaktivinod (1838-1914).[3] Since the publication of the *Bhajana Rahasya,* the *Śikṣāṣṭaka* attracted significant commentarial attention. Consequently, numerous traditional expositions have arisen in Sanskrit, Bengali, and English, presenting diverse takes on its import. The *Śikṣāṣṭaka*'s reception history is not limited to literary production, however; it also enjoys an oral dimension. While this oral facet is harder to track throughout past centuries, it can be claimed that the *Śikṣāṣṭaka's* verses have received frequent mention in Gauḍīya Vaiṣṇava discourses for at least the past three decades. Even to the present day, the *Śikṣāṣṭaka* constitutes an integral part of lived Gauḍīya Vaiṣṇavism, with many practitioners reciting it as a daily spiritual *sādhana* (practice).

Throughout its verses, the *Śikṣāṣṭaka* engages with multiple modes of being, providing entry into the concept of devotional subjectivity in the Gauḍīya Vaiṣṇava tradition. Dynamic agentive subjects appear during the *Śikṣāṣṭaka*'s course, and along with them emerge the varied realms of identity they occupy. Those realms of identity serve as vessels for a range of emotions, including jubilation, grief, and earnestness.

The following essay will reflect on the *Śikṣāṣṭaka* and a few of its traditional interpretations, placing special attention on the notion of subjectivity. I will argue that the *Śikṣāṣṭaka's* literary feature of shifting subjectivities plays the dual role of revealing the multifaceted identity of Gauḍīya Vaiṣṇavism's founding figure, Caitanya, and connecting him with its primary religious practice and its devotees.

Translations and Reflections[4]

(1)
ceto-darpaṇa-mārjanaṃ bhava-mahā-dāvāgni-nirvāpaṇaṃ
śreyaḥ-kairava-candrikā-vitaraṇaṃ vidyā-vadhū-jīvanam
ānandāmbudhi-vardhanaṃ prati-padaṃ pūrṇāmṛtāsvādanaṃ
sarvātma-snapanaṃ paraṃ vijayate śrī-kṛṣṇa-saṅkīrtanam

Supremely victorious is the proper chanting of Kṛṣṇa's names, which cleanses the mirror of the mind, extinguishes the vast wildfire of worldly existence, spreads forth moonlight on the white lotus of fortune, enlivens the wife who is scholarship, increases the ocean of happiness, engenders the relishing of pure nectar at every step, and bathes the entire self.

The *Śikṣāṣṭaka* opens celebratorily, setting the glories of *saṅkīrtana*[5] into a framework of royal allusions. The Sanskrit root "*viji*"—from which ensues the verb "*vijayate*"—frequently connotes successful military conquest for establishing a harmonious and flourishing reign. Accordingly, the grammatical subject of the verse, *śri-kṛṣṇa-saṅkīrtana*, juxtaposed with the main verb "*vijayate*" ("is victorious") could be read as personifying *saṅkīrtana* as a powerful sovereign. What stands before "*vijayate*" and "*śrī-kṛṣṇa-saṅkīrtanam*" could then indicate *how saṅkīrtana* is victorious in terms of "*viji*'s" two facets in Sanskrit literature: subduing the enemy and generating stability and prosperity. Firstly, *saṅkīrtana* fully triumphs over the evils of cyclical worldly entanglement and the clouding of the heart. The two specific phenomena that *saṅkīrtana* purges indicate the versatility of its prowess. *Saṅkīrtana* dispenses with plaguing elements that operate both on the micro level of the individual heart *and* the macro level of the entire world. After doing so, *saṅkīrtana* realizes an abundance of pleasant effects for its partakers, which could be considered the hallmarks of its prosperous reign.

Among the favorable conditions *saṅkīrtana* produces, the imagery of it casting moonlight on a lotus of fortune remains particularly vivid. Similar to a closed night-blooming Kairava lotus, people's fortunes might seem closed and their potentials invisible like the lotus's inner petals. However, having eliminated calamities from their lives, *saṅkīrtana* unleashes the potential of their fortunes. It spreads invigorating moonlight on the closed lotus and thereby allows auspiciousness to bloom uninhibitedly.

Traditional commentator Swami B. V. Tripurari points out a sensory interpretation. He writes that after the sweltering conflagration of worldly existence abates, *saṅkīrtana* diffuses the moon's cooling rays onto the devotee's heart, which by now has become as spotlessly pure as a white lotus.[6] Ultimately, this introductory verse presents the lifeblood of the Gauḍīya Vaiṣṇava movement—the chanting of Kṛṣṇa's names—in heroic and potent terms using a victorious king's subjectivity. It sets a backdrop against which the remaining seven verses rest as they explicate Caitanya's meditations on the divine names and his experiences of devotion to Kṛṣṇa.

> (2)
> *nāmnām akāri bahudhā nija-sarva-śaktis*[7]
> *tatrārpitā niyamitaḥ smaraṇe na kālah*
> *etādṛśī tava kṛpā bhagavan mamāpi*
> *durdaivam īdṛśam ihājani nānurāgah*
>
> Your complete and inherent power has been multiplied among the names and invested in them. For their recollection, no specific time is enjoined. O lord, although your grace upon me is so great, now such is my misfortune that no passion for them has arisen.

This verse prompts a shift in literary ambiance through its tone and structure. In contrast to its previous exultant style, the *Śikṣāṣṭaka* now takes on a confessional spirit. Furthermore, making Caitanya the main subject, *saṅkīrtana* shifts from the subject position to the object position. Caitanya gravely reflects on two divergent parts of his being in a private address to Kṛṣṇa (God in Gauḍīya Vaiṣṇavism). He begins by exploring the marvel of divine grace upon him: Kṛṣṇa imbues something as simple as his names with his full power and mandates no specific time for their remembrance, unlike several Hindu rituals. Thus, instead of limiting access to his undiluted power due to its utmost value, Kṛṣṇa expands access to it by easing restrictions. Despite possessing such great divine favor, Caitanya mourns his misfortune that he has no loving attachment to the sacred names. Though Gauḍīya Vaiṣṇavas revere Caitanya as God, here he inhabits the subjectivity of an imperfect practitioner. He places fallibility at the forefront and gives expression to an inner conflict ordinary worshippers might experience, being unable to invest as fully into devotion to God via *saṅkīrtana* as God invests into bestowing compassion to them.

In his *Anuvṛtti* commentary, Gauḍīya teacher Bhaktisiddhanta Sarasvati (1874-1937) expresses that a layer of professorial subjectivity undergirds this verse. By emphasizing this subjectivity, Bhaktisiddhanta provides an explanation for why Caitanya would have authored the verse. He writes that Caitanya communicated the verse's last two lines to *instruct* materially conditioned individuals about the method of worshipping the divine names.[8] Thus, according to Bhaktisiddhanta's analysis, Caitanya seems to adopt a pedagogical method of showing rather than telling. He takes on and lives the persona of a spiritual neophyte to illustrate the reason why their relationship with Kṛṣṇa's names fails to achieve fruition.[9]

Delving deep into this reason, Bhaktisiddhanta Sarasvati claims that "*durdaiva*"[10] (which I have translated generally as "misfortune") denotes a living being's aversion to the Lord and to service.[11] This interpretation awards more agency to the practicing devotee's subjectivity than the common sense of "*durdaiva*" as "destiny," which represents a force outside one's control. Implied by Bhaktisiddhanta's analysis of "*durdaiva*" is that regardless of how liberally Kṛṣṇa facilitates a connection with an individual, until they consciously choose to fully turn towards him, that connection will not be securely established, and the above-mentioned discordance will remain.

Ultimately, this verse links Caitanya and *saṅkīrtana* (the central topic of the previous verse) by establishing a relationship of devotion between them. Moreover, the question of Caitanya's subjectivity or identity elicits a discussion in commentarial literature that brings the commonplace religious aspirant into the picture. By so doing, the commentarial tradition engenders a connection between the aspirant and Caitanya, demonstrating his ability to understand the imperfect devotee's situation and, catering to their needs, provide a template for prayer. Lastly, the commentarial tradition also connects devotees and *saṅkīrtana*. If Caitanya produced this verse in the persona of a follower of Gauḍīya Vaiṣṇavism, that would imply that attachment to the names of Kṛṣṇa (*saṅkīrtana*) is an objective all Gauḍīya Vaiṣṇavas should be concerned about achieving, rather than an activity reserved only for Caitanya due to his elevated status as founder of Gauḍīya Vaiṣṇavism.

(3)
tṛṇād api sunīcena
taror api sahiṣṇunā
amāninā mānadena
kīrtanīyaḥ sadā hariḥ

Hari[12] should always be glorified by he who is more insignificant than grass, more forbearing than a tree, self-effacing, and simultaneously, an offeror of respect.

Like its second verse, the *Śikṣāṣṭaka*'s third verse also contemplates the capability of engaging in *saṅkīrtana*, but in a positive sense. Additionally, compared to the previous verse's focus on Caitanya, this verse's subjectivity of interest becomes explicitly generalized, applying to any person wishing to embrace *saṅkīrtana*. The subjectivity's nuances are conveyed through an inversion of an intuitive understanding of notability. The *Śikṣāṣṭaka* suggests that it is not a conspicuously accomplished person who earns the right to one of Gauḍīya Vaiṣṇavism's most elevated religious states. Instead, it is one who remains *down* to earth like grass, which the verse *up*lifts and endows with the everlasting ability to chant Hari's names. Thus, a clear message comes across: *there is significance in insignificance.*

Next, espousing the absence of pride and tolerance, the verse encourages one to turn attention away from the self in positive and negative situations. First, tolerance includes not concentrating on how troubling circumstances affect the self and remaining steady amidst them. Second, being pride-free involves restraint from meditating on the praiseworthy aspects of one's personality. In the end, both thinking less of oneself (*sunīcena*) *and* thinking of oneself less (*sahiṣṇunā, amāninā, mānadena*) are spotlighted as central spiritual virtues of a Gauḍīya Vaiṣṇava follower who enjoys a sustained connection with *saṅkīrtana*.

(4)
na dhanaṃ na janaṃ na sundarīṃ
kavitāṃ vā jagad-īśa kāmaye
mama janmani janmanīśvare
bhavatād bhaktir ahaitukī tvayi

O lord of the universe, I do not wish for wealth, a following, a lovely woman, or poetry.[13] Let there be devotion to you, the lord, without any motive, in every one of my lives.

Among other identities, the lexicon of this verse evokes *Caitanya, the renouncer*. For approximately the last two decades of his life, Caitanya inhabited the social position of a *sannyāsin*, broadly definable as a Hindu monk.[14] The term *sannyāsin* derives from the verbal root "*as*"—"to throw," combined with the prefixes "*ni*"—which possesses a downward directionality—and "*sam*," which conveys a sense of togetherness or completeness. Cumulatively, the prefixes and verbal root mean "to throw down together" or to "throw down completely." By extension, "*sannyāsin*" signifies one who thoroughly relinquishes.

Reminiscent of his *sannyasin* identity, Caitanya rejects common markers of success and pleasure. He disallows those elements from defining his subjectivity and instead prays that pure devotion to Kṛṣṇa becomes his lasting possession. In addition to the mood of detachment from worldly matters that Caitanya's words reflect, his specific disinterest in beautiful women and riches speaks to two essential characteristics that form the heart of the *sannyāsin* subjectivity: poverty and celibacy. In the end, abandoning material multiplicity, Caitanya aspires toward a spiritual exclusivity that transcends even the temporal boundaries of the human life span.

(5)
ayi nanda-tanuja kiṅkaraṃ
patitaṃ māṃ viṣame bhavāmbudhau
kṛpayā tava pāda-paṅkaja-
sthita-dhūlī-sadṛśaṃ vicintaya

O son of Nanda![15] Please, think of me, the servant who has fallen into the terrible ocean of worldly existence, as tantamount to the dust situated at your lotus-like feet.

Remaining the primary subject, Caitanya continues his supplication to Kṛṣṇa.

Therein, smallness forms a salient feature of the subjectivity he constructs. Caitanya's utilization of oceanic imagery portrays the enormity and overwhelming power of *bhava*—the treacherous cycle of death, rebirth, and suffering. As opposed to such a massive ocean and its raging tides, the individual who has fallen into it (and is presumably drowning in it) stands out as utterly minute and incapable of saving themselves. Having described this turbulent situation, however, Caitanya does not wish for liberation from a position of minuteness. Instead, he embraces smallness of another kind, vis-à-vis the largeness of Kṛṣṇa. He appeals for being like the dust on Kṛṣṇa's feet. Once again, the juxtaposition of something appearing negligible—dust—in the face of something much larger—Kṛṣṇa's human-like body—surfaces. While Caitanya negatively characterizes the former experience of finitude, describing the ocean of worldly existence as terrible (*viṣama*), he places the latter condition of finitude within a traditionally positive landscape. Straightforwardly, the latter finitude directly connects to Kṛṣṇa. Beyond that, lotuses, with which Kṛṣṇa's feet, the abode of the dust, are compared, often symbolize beauty and purity in Hinduism.[16] Lastly, Caitanya frames the second situation of diminutiveness as something that Kṛṣṇa would occasion out of grace (*kṛpā*), which is considered a beneficial phenomenon in Gauḍīya Vaiṣṇavism and across religions.

(6)
nayanaṃ galad-aśru-dhārayā
vadanaṃ gadgada-ruddhayā girā
pulakair nicitaṃ vapuḥ kadā
tava nāma-grahaṇe bhaviṣyati

When will, at the mention of your name, my body be full of horripilation, my mouth be filled with speech hindered by faltering, and my eyes be full of streams of flowing tears?

The sixth stanza re-evokes Caitanya's eagerness from the second verse to achieve an intense connection with chanting Kṛṣṇa's names. In so doing, it also verbalizes the Gauḍīya Vaiṣṇava tradition's conception of religious ecstasy. Theologically, Gauḍīya Vaiṣṇavas believe that a devotee attains the lofty stage of ecstatic connection with the divine after the meticulous practice of scripturally regulated routines.[17] In this verse, Caitanya looks forward to the moment he can achieve such a stage and fill the gap he perceives in his spiritual practice. As they do for other verses where Caitanya demonstrates fallibility or a desire for religious improvement, commentaries on this verse emphasize Caitanya's role of a teacher in the garb of a devotee.[18]

When performing *saṅkīrtana*, Caitanya aspires to partake in an ecstatic subjectivity that ruptures composure. The descriptions in the verse suggest that the devotee's internal spiritual feelings become so fervent that they can no longer be contained in the invisible mental sphere. They burst forth, manifesting themselves physically. Typically, the somatic experiences described here are universally relatable but episodic: they occur at defining moments when encountering something extremely shocking, pleasantly surprising, or bitterly painful. However, this verse implies that every time an advanced practitioner chants the divine names (as the *Śikṣāṣṭaka* hinted to earlier, constant chanting is ideal), those names should trigger emotions of ultimate intensity. Thus, while poise is commonly prized, uninhibited expression in connection with Kṛṣṇa occupies a coveted position in this stanza. Ultimately, like the *Śikṣāṣṭaka*'s third verse, the sixth verse elevates an attribute considered undesirable in the material world as highly desirable in the context of *saṅkīrtana*.

(7)
yugāyitaṃ nimeṣeṇa
cakṣuṣā prāvṛṣāyitaṃ
śūnyāyitaṃ jagat sarvaṃ
govinda-viraheṇa me

Due to my separation from Govinda,[19] my eyes appear like heavy rains, a moment appears like an eon, and the whole world appears as if it is void.

The *Śikṣāṣṭaka*'s theme of spiritual exclusivity makes a re-appearance. Like in the fourth verse, Caitanya here highlights that Kṛṣṇa is his all-in-all. Caitanya communicates this point by analyzing how the absence of Govinda mediates his perception of time and place. He claims that the whole world is as if it is empty. This statement somewhat parallels the sentiment in colloquial English phrases like "you mean the world to me" and "you are my world." To elaborate, though there is a shared world that all beings inhabit, each person also lives in their own world, animated by people and objects they value. Without those defining components of their world, both the general world and their specific world can lose meaning for a person. In this verse, Caitanya depicts

Kṛṣṇa as his world. When Kṛṣṇa is absent, the world feels vacant, despite whatever else it might be full of, as those things hold no worth for Caitanya. Additionally, Caitanya claims that Kṛṣṇa's absence renders time difficult to pass and causes incessant tears. Even the minutest amount of time it takes to blink an eye (*nimeṣa*) resembles thousands of years (*yuga*) to him. By mobilizing spatial and temporal experience, Caitanya implicitly signifies that Kṛṣṇa is the defining factor that provides meaning and fulfillment to his being.

(8)
āśliṣya vā pāda-ratāṃ pinaṣṭu mām
adarśanān marma-hatāṃ karotu vā
yathā tathā vā vidadhātu lampaṭo
mat-prāṇa-nāthas tu sa eva nāparaḥ

> After embracing me, let him trample me who is devoted to his feet, or let him make me one whose limbs are afflicted by his disappearance. In whatever manner that libertine behaves, he alone is still the lord of my life, par excellence.

At its culmination, the *Śikṣāṣṭaka* zeroes in on Caitanya's subjectivity of vulnerability. In absolute surrender to Kṛṣṇa, Caitanya willingly renders himself defenseless in the face of however Kṛṣṇa might treat him. To elucidate the terms of this relationship, the verse evokes scenes of bodily closeness between Caitanya and Kṛṣṇa. On the one hand, Kṛṣṇa might embrace Caitanya, demonstrating affection, but on the other, he might bruise and crush him, expressing negative emotions. In either case, Caitanya affirms Kṛṣṇa's agency as *the* unparalleled lord of his life. Due to this verse's emphasis on such unconditionality, traditional commentator A. C. Bhaktivedanta Swami (1896-1977) quotes it in numerous theological expositions as an illustration of what it means to be a true lover of God.[20]

The final verse embeds conjugality into its overarching theme of steadfast loyalty. The expressions "libertine" (*lampaṭa*) and "lord of one's life breath" ("*prāṇa-nātha*"), which is often used in the context of a husband, suggest that Caitanya is visualizing Kṛṣṇa in conjugal terms. Furthermore, Caitanya referring to himself in feminine grammatical forms supports such a reading. Traditional author Kṛṣṇadāsa Kavirāja explores this conjugal feature in his *Caitanya Caritāmṛta*. He describes that during an ecstatic experience, Caitanya recited this verse while inhabiting the emotional world of Rādhā, whom

Gauḍīya Vaiṣṇavas revere as the Divine Feminine and topmost among the *gopīs*, Kṛṣṇa's female lovers.[21] Commentator Bhaktisiddhanta Sarasvati is careful to note that the reader must never aspire to become identical to Rādhā (as Caitanya is traditionally considered).[22] Instead, he advises one to strive to become one of her followers.[23] In this way, Bhaktisiddhanta reinforces Gauḍīya Vaiṣṇavism's crucial distinction between God and an ordinary being while simultaneously preserving Caitanya's identity as a teacher-devotee in the *Śikṣāṣṭaka.*

Conclusion

While the *Śikṣāṣṭaka* has often been approached as a repository of key Gauḍīya Vaiṣṇava doctrines, I have attempted to show that it also provides a wealth of information on spiritual subjecthood. The *Śikṣāṣṭaka* serves as a confluence where the three subjectivities of Caitanya, his devotees, and the primary religious practice he taught (*saṅkīrtana*) meet. As its verses progress, the literary device of shifting subjectivities, along with the commentarial interpretations it elicited, unveils Caitanya's multivalent identity in the Gauḍīya Vaiṣṇava tradition. Caitanya emerges as a devotee, teacher, *sannyāsin* (renouncer), Kṛṣṇa, and Rādhā. In particular, commentarial emphases on Caitanya's teaching role in the *Śikṣāṣṭaka* create a bond between him and Gauḍīya Vaiṣṇava devotees, demonstrating his capacity to intimately relate to humanity despite being fully divine. As a teacher, Caitanya shows the centrality of *saṅkīrtana* as a spiritual practice for Gauḍīya Vaiṣṇavas and illustrates its potency by setting it in a royal subjectivity.

Ultimately, not only is the *Śikṣāṣṭaka's* feature of shifting subjectivities distinctive, but the manner in which the octet develops those subjectivities also remains noteworthy. It utilizes powerful tropes like smallness, spiritual exclusivity, inversion, and unconditional love to illustrate the inner world of Kṛṣṇa's devotee. Additionally, it evokes vivid visual imagery from nature and palpable sensory experience to elucidate the effects of *saṅkīrtana,* the subjectivity of one who performs it, and the esoteric religious states of ecstasy and conjugal interaction with the divine.

Thus, though the *Śikṣāṣṭaka* fundamentally deals with devotional ideas beyond the material sphere, it mobilizes tools from the material realm to explicate those extramundane concepts, thereby rendering its message more relatable for readers of this world. Nevertheless, through the subtle changes of subjectivity it conducts and the demanding spiritual ideals it presents, the

Śikṣāṣṭaka continues to retain a mystery that stands in intriguing tension with its intelligibility.

Endnotes

1. Traditional author Kṛṣṇadāsa Kavirāja seems to be the first one traceable to have brought these eight stanzas together and designated them with the title "*Śikṣāṣṭaka*" (the octet of instructions) in his 17th-century *Caitanya Caritāmṛta*. Though these eight verses appeared previously in Rūpa Gosvāmin's *Padyāvali*, they did so as individual verses disconnected from one another.

2. Śrī Kṛṣṇa Caitanya (1486-1533), also known as Viśvambhar Miśra, was the founder of the Gauḍīya Vaiṣṇava movement. Gauḍīya Vaiṣṇavas worship him as Kṛṣṇa in the form of a devotee; "Caitanya," Oxford Bibliographies, accessed January 10, 2023, https://www-oxfordbibliographies-com.ezproxy.lib.utexas.edu/display/document/obo-9780195399318/obo-9780195399318-0138.xml; Jan Brzezinski, "Śrī Caitanya's Śikṣāṣṭakam: Comparing the original with two translations," *Journal of Vaishnava Studies* 12, no. 1 (Fall 2003): 87.

3. Brzezinski, "Śrī Caitanya's Śikṣāṣṭakam," 89.

4. All the translations included in this paper are my own.

5. "*Saṅkīrtana*" has traditionally been interpreted in two ways. First, it can refer to *kīrtana* performed communally, wherein the prefix "*sam*" means "together." Second, it can refer to *kīrtana* conducted well if "*sam*" is taken to stand for "*samyak*" or "properly." Importantly, Sanskrit allows both meanings to function simultaneously in a way English does not.

6. B. V. Tripurari Swami, *Śikṣāṣṭakam of Śrī Caitanya* (San Rafael: Mandala Publishing, 2005), 18.

7. The adverb "*bahudhā*" combined with the verbal root "*kṛ*" can mean to divide one entity into many or to multiply it into many, such that it exists in its complete form in several places simultaneously. I have chosen the latter meaning in this verse due to the presence of the adjective *sarva*—"all." If the power were divided amongst the names, with each name having a part of that power, the word "*sarva*," indicating that the *full* divine power was "made many" amongst the names, would likely be unnecessary.

8. Bhaktisiddhanta Sarasvati, *Śrī Śrī Śikṣāṣṭakam Anuvṛtti Sahitam* (Kolkata: Gaudiya Printing Works), 7.

9. *Caitanya Caritāmṛta, Ādi Līlā,* 7.6 contains a helpful traditional statement about Caitanya's identity as both Kṛṣṇa and Bhakta (devotee).

10. The word "*durdaiva*" is composed of the prefix of negation "*dur*" and the adjective "*daiva*," which derives from the noun "*deva*" or "god."

11. Bhaktisiddhanta Sarasvati, *Śrī Śrī Śikṣāṣṭakam Anuvṛtti Sahitam*, 6.

12. Another name for Kṛṣṇa.

13. Although it is not common, the Sanskrit word "*kavitā*," which I have translated

as "poetry," can also be interpreted as an abstract noun that denotes the state of being a learned person.

14. Joseph O'Connell, "Caitanya," in *Encyclopedia of Religion,* ed. Lindsay Jones (Gale Ebooks, 2005): 1345.

15. The *Bhāgavata Purāṇa,* the key scripture of the Gauḍīya Vaiṣṇavas, describes Nanda as the father of Kṛṣṇa.

16. Ryan Adams, "Lotus," in *Encyclopedia of Global Religion,* eds. Mark Juergensmeyer and Wade Clark Roof (Sage Publications, 2011).

17. David Haberman, *The Bhaktirasāmṛtasindhu of Rūpa Gosvāmin* (Delhi: Motilal Banarsidass Publishers, 2003), 99; Haberman, *The Bhaktirasāmṛtasindhu,* 117.

18. B. V. Tripurari Swami, *Śikṣāṣṭakam of Śrī Caitanya,* 97; The title of the work itself suggests that the tradition understands Caitanya's professorial identity to be implicitly present throughout the octet. The appellation "*Śikṣāṣṭaka*" renders each verse a teaching (*Śikṣā*) and, by extension, underscores Caitanya as the teacher conveying each of the eight teachings, in addition to the other subjectivities he adopts.

19. Another name for Kṛṣṇa.

20. Bhaktivedanta Swami, "*Bhagavad-gītā* 9.27–29" (lecture, New York, December 19, 1966). https://vedabase.io/en/library/transcripts/661219bg-new-york/.

21. Edward C. Dimock, *Caitanya Caritāmṛta of Kṛṣṇadāsa Kavirāja* (Cambridge: Harvard University Press, 1999), 995.

22. Bhaktisiddhanta Sarasvati, *Śrī Śrī Śikṣāṣṭakam Anuvṛtti Sahitam,* 16-17.

23. Ibid; In his Bengali translation of the *Śikṣāṣṭaka,* the *Gītāvalī,* Kedarnath Datta Bhaktivinod articulates a more specific and personal analysis of the eighth stanza. Adopting the verse as a prayer, Bhaktivinod envisions himself as a maidservant of Rādhā and Kṛṣṇa rather than Rādhā herself. Thus, he aligns with the principle of eternal distinction between the Divine and human that Bhaktisiddhanta outlines. At the same time, he particularizes his identity as a female devotee of Rādhā and Kṛṣṇa, as compared to Bhaktisiddhanta's general directive for practitioners to adopt the temperament of Rādhā's followers.

Acknowledgements

I thank my Sanskrit teachers, Aaron Sherraden, Aleksandar Uskokov, Donald Davis, and Manasicha Akepiyapornchai, for sharing their insights on the *Śikṣāṣṭaka*'s grammar. I owe a special debt to Donald Davis for reading early drafts of this essay and providing valuable suggestions for its improvement.

Bibliography

Adams, Ryan. "Lotus." In *Encyclopedia of Global Religion,* edited by Mark Juergensmeyer and Wade Clark Roof. Sage Publications, 2011.

Brzezinski, Jan. "Śrī Caitanya's Śikṣāṣṭakam: Comparing the original with two translations." *Journal of Vaishnava Studies* 12, no. 1 (Fall 2003): 87-111.

Dimock, Edward, C. *Caitanya Caritāmṛta of Kṛṣṇadāsa Kavirāja: A Translation and Commentary*. Cambridge: Harvard University Press, 1999.

Haberman, David. *The Bhaktirasāmṛtasindhu of Rūpa Gosvāmin*. Delhi: Motilal Banarsidass Publishers, 2003.

O'Connell, Joseph. "Caitanya." In *Encyclopedia of Religion*, edited by Lindsay Jones. Gale Ebooks, 2005.

Sarasvati, Bhaktisiddhanta. *Śrī Śrī Śikṣāṣṭakam Anuvṛtti Sahitam*. Kolkata: Gauḍīya Printing Works, n.d.

Stewart, Tony. "Caitanya." In *Oxford Bibliographies Online*. Last modified June 30, 2014. https://www-oxfordbibliographies-com.ezproxy.lib.utexas.edu/display/document/obo-9780195399318/obo-9780195399318-0138.xml.

Swami, Bhaktivedanta. "Bhagavad-gītā 9.27–29." Lecture. New York. December 19, 1966. https://vedabase.io/en/library/transcripts/661219bg-new-york/.

Swami, B. V. Tripurari. *Śikṣāṣṭakam of Śrī Caitanya*. San Rafael: Mandala Publishing, 2005.

Śrī Caitanya's Implicit and Explicit Regard for Animals

Cogen Bohanec[1]

Introduction

Since for Gauḍīya Vaiṣṇavas Śrī Kṛṣṇa Caitanya Mahāprabhu (1486-1533, hereafter "Caitanya") is an exemplary figure, his attitudes towards and relationships with animals in the *Caitanya-caritāmṛta* (CC) can be understood didactically. Followers of the Caitanya tradition might properly understand these episodes as implying animal personhood (see Bohanec 2023), animal rights, a robust ecotheological ethic (see Bohanec 2018), biophilia (Bohanec "Dialogical" 2021), and vegetarianism and veganism (Bohanec "Bhaktivedānta" 2021). Elsewhere I have argued that for the tradition love of God necessarily implies love for all living beings—including and *especially* animals (see Bohanec 2024), a concept that is instantiated by several key episodes of Śrī Caitanya's life as conveyed in the CC.

Entering Caitanya's Līlā

Ādi[2] 1-16 includes Caitanya's miraculous childhood (Ādi 13-14), and his education when he eventually becomes renowned as a *paṇḍita* due to his impressive scholarly abilities (Ādi 15-16). But by Ādi 17 he begins something of a transformation away from his academic erudition after he becomes initiated by Īśvara Purī (1.17.9-10) into the chanting of the holy names of Śrī Kṛṣṇa. His mood shifts from that of a scholarly *paṇḍita* to a true *bhakta* who pined with separation from Kṛṣṇa, and he expressed that mood by calling out in song or instructing his students to chant in a way that became infectious, initiating the populist *saṅkīrtana* movement of public congregational chanting. Caitanya's *saṅkīrtana* movement ignites the public in West Bengal with an episode that is akin to a political protest, involving a confrontation between Caitanya and the local Muslim magistrate, the Chand Kājī (Ādi 17). It is during that episode that we see Caitanya's demonstrable care for the welfare of animals, cows in particular.

Cow-killing and the Chand Kājī, Ādi 17

Initially the *saṅkīrtana* was held in private in the house of Śrīvāsa Ṭhākura (Ādi 17.34-35), but the participants were harassed by "non-believers" (*pāṣaṇḍi-pradhāna sei durmukha vācāla*, Ādi 17.37 ff.) who created a spectacle to turn them against "respectable *brāhmaṇas*" (*brāhmaṇa-saj-jana*, Ādi 17.42). Sometime after, "the Lord [Caitanya] gave the instruction (*ājñā*) to all the people of the city to perform saṅkīrtana in every single home"[3] (CC Ādi 17.121). Soon "nothing else could be heard other than the sound of drums and cymbals and the great saṅkīrtana vibration sounding 'Hari, Hari ('hari' 'hari')!'"[4] (CC Ādi 17.123).

As the movement grew in the city of Navadvīpa, the Muslim magistrate, the Chand Kājī, was petitioned with a complaint from some angry local Muslims (*yavanas*, CC Ādi 17.124). The Kājī responded by going to one home *kīrtana*, breaking a *mṛdaṅga*, and declaring that *kīrtana* was forbidden in the city (CC Ādi 17.127), threating to confiscate the wealth and caste-status (*jāti*) of those who failed to comply (CC Ādi 17.128). Caitanya again repeats his instruction to perform public *saṅkīrtana*, (CC Ādi 17.130) organizing something of a peaceful protest[5] (CC Ādi 17.135) to fill the city with *saṃkīrtana* in defiance of the Kājī. They approached his home (17.141 ff.) and the Kājī came out and spoke with Caitanya in a respectful and friendly way (17.144 ff.).[6]

After briefly and amicably discussing their shared familial relationships, the Kājī asks Śrī Caitanya to "instruct" (*ājñā*) him as to what is on his mind (CC Ādi 17.152). It is notable that despite the source of the initial grievance being the ban on public *saṅkīrtana*, Caitanya's initial grievance is the Kājī's allowance for the killing of cows. Caitanya protests, that since "you drink the milk of the cow, the cow is your mother" and since "the bull produces grains, therefore he is your father"[7] (CC Ādi 17.153). Therefore, "you eat and kill the father and mother. What kind of religion, what kind of dharma, is this? On what authority do you engage in such immoral, negative karma (*vikarma*)?"[8] (CC Ādi 17.154).

It is worth keeping the words of Doniger in mind that "nonviolence, pacifism, compassion for animals and vegetarianism are not the same thing at all" (Doniger 2009, 192) and we certainly might add Hindu taboos against killing cows to that list.[9] There are plenty of examples where those who promote *ahiṃsā* may support human warfare or exploitation (such as caste discrimination), where those who purport to practice *ahiṃsā* might not be vegetarian, and of course we have seen the horrific human violence inflicted against the Muslim community by modern Hindus in the name of cow-protection. But the CC brings all of these virtues together as something of a composite animal ethic.

Nevertheless, this episode demonstrates a care and a concern for at least this one type of animal, and it gives a theological basis—as well as an ethical basis—regarding the intersection between concern for animals and cow-protection. For example, the argument that likens the cow and bull to one's parents invokes an important South Asian virtue of filial piety that should also include one's relationship to animals (cows in particular). This filial affection for cows further invokes the kind of system of virtue ethics characteristic of the Gauḍīya tradition (for more on Gauḍīya Vaiṣṇavism as a systematic virtue ethic see Bohanec 2024) as well as the other related issues of animal personhood (see Bohanec "Personhood" 2023), vegetarianism, animal rights (Bohanec 2018), biophilia, ecotheology, etc.

If Caitanya's life is didactic, then perhaps modern Hindus might learn something about the way that Caitanya, a Hindu, approaches the issue of cow-killing with the Muslim Kājī, an approach characterized by respect and a palpable sense of mutual goodwill between both parties. The Kājī notes that according to Muslim scriptures killing cows is not problematic (CC Ādi 17.157), and he makes a legitimate point that the killing of cows is even allowed in the Vedas (CC Ādi 17.158). Moreover, we can see that cows are allowed to be eaten in various Hindu dharma-śāstras if their meat comes from sacrificial cows (e.g., the *Āpastamba Dharma-sūtra*, the *Vāiṣṭha Dharma-sūtra*, and the *Kauṭṭalya Arthaśāstra*), and the *Suśruta-saṃhitā* allows that cows, amongst other animals, be eaten for medicinal purposes[10] (Alsdorf 2010, 65-66).

However, Caitanya responds that actually "Cow killing is prohibited by what is said in the Vedas" and therefore "no Hindu engages in the killing of cows"[11] (CC Ādi 17.159). Caitanya may have been referring to restrictions on killing cows that may date as far back as to the time of the *Ṛg* and *Atharva* Vedas, texts which use the term *aghnya* "not-killed" as a designation for cows. But Alsdorf is skeptical of taking this term as conclusive evidence for taboos against cow killing in the Vedas, because this designation may simply mean that one cannot kill a cow, that is to say, as a sacrificial offering the sacrificial cows go to heaven and are therefore not killed at all (Alsdorf 2010, 69-73). Certainly, by the time of the *Śatapatha-brāhmaṇa* there begins to be clearer injunctions against eating cows or bulls.[12]

But the possible meaning of *aghnya* as an animal that is brought back to life is perhaps alluded to by Caitanya when he says that, "In the Vedas and the Purāṇas there are written instructions (*ājñā-vāṇī*) such that if one is able to bring a being back to life only then can one kill a living being"[13] (CC Ādi 17.160), broadening the discussion to a prohibition against killing animals in general. He notes that in olden times "there was a class of sages who killed elderly cows that were subsequently brought back to life with Vedic mantras"[14] (CC Ādi 17.161), a position that is found throughout the literature (e.g., *Manu-Smṛti* 5.39-44[15]). Therefore, in the days of yore, Vedic sacrifice would not be considered an act of killing; rather it was considered as an act of beneficence (*upakāra*, CC Ādi 17.162). And since in "the age of Kali there is no such power amongst *brāhmaṇas*,"[16] the killing of cows is now prohibited (CC Ādi 17.163-164).

Therefore, Caitanya concludes with a standard Hindu refutation of the viability of animal sacrifice, that since one "cannot bring a being back to life, it is essentially nothing but killing"[17] even if such killing is done in accordance with Muslim scriptures (from CC Ādi 17.155) or if one were to attempt to perform a Vedic sacrifice of animals. Thus, "there can be no deliverance from hell"[18] for the sin of killing cows (CC Ādi 17.165). Caitanya cites a common idea in Hindu literature that "one who kills a cow perpetually is cooked within a hellish realm called 'Raurava' for as many hairs as there are on the cow's body or for up to a thousand years"[19] (CC Ādi 17.166). A similar idea occurs also in *Manu-smṛti* which goes further to even recommend consumption of faux meat rather than meat from dead animals (5.37-.38),[20] a prescription that might have ethical implications for modern vegetarian culinary trends. Moreover, since texts such as the *Manu-smṛti* attach this karmic argument against the killing of animals to vegetarianism and non-violence (*Manu-smṛti*, 5.48-49),[21] we might rightly assume that Caitanya's arguments against cow killing becomes a synecdoche for a composite ethic of cow-protection, animal advocacy, vegetarianism, and nonviolence, all of which I have elsewhere related to virtue ethics, feminist care ethics, and theological voluntarism (see Bohanec 2024).

The episode concludes with Caitanya asserting that the Kājī's scriptures that allow for cow killing (and, arguably, meat eating, as per 17.160) are mistaken (CC Ādi 17.167). The Kājī accepts defeat (CC Ādi 17.168), admitting the fault of the scriptures (CC Ādi 17.169), and acknowledging that he only follows them because of his "communal obligations" (*jāti-anurodhe*, CC Ādi 17.170). Caitanya asks that the Kājī no longer oppose the *saṅkīrtana* (CC Ādi 17.221), to which the Kājī agrees, declaring that "All of the descendants who take birth in my lineage shall be given this warning: *kīrtana* is never to be obstructed"[22] (CC Ādi 17.222).

By the end of Ādi 17, Caitanya accepts *sannyāsa* in 1510 at the age of 24 when he becomes known as Śrī Kṛṣṇa Caitanya. The Madhya-līlā begins with him living as an itinerate preacher. He departs for Jagannātha Purī (Madhya 1-6), and then leaves on an extensive tour of South India, where he endeavors to further spread the *saṅkīrtana* movement. When he returns to Jagannātha Purī for the Ratha-yātrā festival, his followers and the public are astonished upon witnessing his incredible spiritual ecstasy (Madhya 7-15).

Loving Animals as Persons in the Jhārikhaṇḍa Forest: Madhya 17

Towards the end of the 16th chapter of the *Caitanya Caritāmṛta's Madhya Līlā*, Caitanya is in Śāntipur (Madhya 16.216-249) and departs for Jagannātha Purī (16.250-252) and again from there to Vṛndāvana (Madhya 16.256). He decides to be as low-key as possible, appropriate to the atmosphere of Vṛndāvana (Madhya 16.270-275), and to go with only two attendants (17.15-17).

To avoid drawing crowds, Caitanya decided to cut through the Jhārikhaṇḍa forest. As he travelled, he chanted the holy name as a strategy to keep him safe from the animals of the forest (Madhya 17.25-26). But rather than being a threat, the animals seem to have been attracted to the force of his spiritual practice, and there are several episodes where they begin to display human-like characteristics. For example, as Caitanya's foot brushes a tiger, that tiger began to dance and sing the name of Kṛṣṇa (17-28-29). Elephants also sang and danced when they were attracted to his ceaseless chanting, exhibiting advanced symptoms of *bhakti* (e.g., *vātsalya-rasa* of Madhya 17.195, *prīti-rasa* of 17.203) that few human practitioners might ever attain (17.31-33). He befriended and petted the deer and they joined with the tigers in the singing and dancing, and even began to hug and kiss each other (17.37-43) as the birds and even the plants joined in (17.43-46). Caitanya cites a verse that is similar to the Christian idea of the Peaceable Kingdom (Isaiah, 11:1-9),

> "Vṛndāvana is the transcendental abode of the Lord. There is no hunger, anger, or thirst there. Though naturally inimical, human beings and fierce animals live together there in transcendental friendship"[23] (BhP 10.13.60).

As I have argued elsewhere (Bohanec "A Theocentric Argument for Animal

Personhood" 2023), anthropocentricism, or the belief in human exceptionalism as a self-serving human devaluation of animals and the natural world, is often cited as a paradigmatic underpinning that enables the exploitation of animals socially, culturally, and individually. To reverse this pattern, we might seek to enhance, underscore, and articulate cultural resources that disanthropocentrize, such as those that underscore human likeness with animals, as we see in this episode. One way of doing this is by asserting models of non-human personhood, evidenced here in the Jhārikhaṇḍa forest. Such likeness between humans and non-human animals is also supported by modern scientific findings where animals are now believed to have many of the same capacities as human beings (Beckoff 2001, 616). Here, this idea of human-likeness as a basis for non-human personhood is particularly prominent in the fact that these animals achieved very advanced states of *bhakti* rarely achieved by humans.

This juxtaposition between the advanced spiritual attainment of the animals in comparison to the lack of advancement for some humans is underscored when, after the Jhārikhaṇḍa episode with the animals, Caitanya arrives in Kāśī (17.82) only to find that rather than being populated with Vaiṣṇava *bhaktas*, it was a learning center for *māyā-vādin*, theological impersonalists, who inappropriately, from the Gauḍīya perspective, subordinate *bhakti* to philosophical *jñāna* and were indifferent to *bhakti* discourses about Kṛṣṇa (*kṛṣṇa-kathā*, 17.91-96). The implication of the chapter is clear: the animals of Jhārikhaṇḍa were capable of a level of spiritual advancement that even the Kāśī *paṇḍitas* were not able to achieve.

The juxtaposition of elevated animals and stagnant human *paṇḍitas* continues when Caitanya gets to Vṛndāvana, and we see a similar reaction on the part of animals to what we saw in Jhārikhaṇḍa. The cows followed him, licking him as he pets them. Of particular note is the *vātsalya-rasa*—the divine affective state of parental affection usually spoken of in relationship to God—that Caitanya felt for the cows (17.194-197). Like in Jhārikhaṇḍa the deer began chanting and licking him, while the bees sounded the note that represents the esoteric sound that Kṛṣṇa used to call the *gopīs* (17.197-199). The plants also displayed symptoms of *bhakti* (such as *ānandita*, 17.200-202), and parrots recited verses about Kṛṣṇa's loving pastimes with the *gopīs* (17.208-217). Indeed, all beings in the vicinity cried out "Hare Kṛṣṇa" as Caitanya cried with them in complete ecstasy (17.206-207). All of this seems to have intensified Caitanya's own mood of ecstatic emotions (e.g. *prīti-rasa*) and physical symptoms of *bhakti* (17.203-205), for the sight of peacocks, which undoubtedly reminded him of Kṛṣṇa's *līlās* in Vraja, caused him to faint (17.218-222).

For the teleology of Gauḍīya Vaiṣṇava reincarnation and karma theory, personhood is not necessarily a matter of species distinction as it often is in Western notions of personhood. For GV theology, all living entities are qualitatively and ontological alike, irrespective of species, and are all equally capable of developing personhood as they reincarnate through higher forms of life. But what is notable in Madhya 17 is that advanced degrees of personhood, commensurate to spiritual advancement, are displayed by animals beyond even that which many humans are capable of, despite the superior intellectual capacities of humans, such as we see with the Kāśī *paṇḍitas.*

Moreover, attaining the status of personhood involves advancement relative to a goal, and for GV theism, that telos is achieving a personal relationship with God, with Kṛṣṇa—which the animals easily achieve through their association with Caitanya as God incarnate. For GV theology all value is in relationship to God theocentrically, rather than based on being a human species anthropocentrically. Thus, this amounts to what I've referred to as a theocentric account of personhood that includes animals as persons, and therefore as citizens of a much broader moral community than human exceptionalism would otherwise allow (Bohanec "A Theocentric Argument for Animal Personhood" 2023).

Vegetarianism, and Nārada and the Hunter, Madhya 24

On the way back to Vṛndāvana, Caitanya instructs Sanātana Gosvāmī who asks about the so-called *ātmārāma* verse of the *Bhāgavata-purāṇa* (BhP) 1.7.10 (CC Madhya 24.5). Sanātana begs for an explanation (Madhya 24.4), which Caitanya proceeds to give by explaining each word in the verse and its multiple possible meanings (Madhya 24.10 ff.). In the process, Caitanya delivers an edifying parable about the standard connection between Vaiṣṇavism and vegetarianism.[24]

The term *nirgrantha* from the verse in question becomes of particular interest. Apart from a variety of other meanings (CC Madhya 24.17, 147), Caitanya says that "the word '*nirgrantha*' refers to a hunter (*vyādha*) who is without wealth but due to good association is able to engage in worship of Kṛṣṇa"[25] (24.227). To illustrate, Caitanya relates a story in which Nārada visited the confluence of the Ganges, the Yamunā, and the Sarasvatī to bathe (*triveṇī-snāne*, Madhya 24.230). At that time, he came across a "deer that was lying on the ground, pierced by an arrow, with broken legs, and writhing in pain"[26] (24.231). Next, he saw a boar in a similar condition (Madhya 232), and finally a rabbit (24.233). He discovered the culprit was a hunter (our soon-to-be *nirgrantha*) who was hiding and intending to hurt more animals (24.234), appearing "like Yama, the God of death, bearing a rod that is symbolic of the application of violence" (*yena yama daṇḍa-dhara*, CC Madhya 24.235). Nārada asked him why he would leave the animals suffering without killing them (24.241), and the hunter replied, "If a living being writhes in pain, then my inner happiness increases"[27] (24.243).

Despite his urge to treat Nārada abusively, the hunter was so impressed by the Muni that he only shows the sage deep respect (CC Madhya 24.237). The hunter offers Nārada anything that he desires (24.244-245), and Nārada begs him that, "whatever animals you kill, please just make sure that you kill them immediately, and please do not leave them only half dead"[28] (24.247). When the incredulous hunter asks him what is wrong with "half killing" (*ardha mārile*, 24.248), Nārada replies, "Half killed beings feel severe anguish. Since you inflict suffering upon living beings, you must therefore also endure the same"[29] (24.249). Moreover, "killing animals as a hunter is a lesser transgression" but "unnecessarily torturing them is infinitely more sinful (*pāpa*)"[30] (24.250). Therefore, by the laws of karma, "all of the living entities that you have killed and tortured will likewise kill you life after life repeatedly"[31] (24.251), which is what the *Manu-smṛti* tells us is implied by the etymology of the Sanskrit word for meat (*Manu-smṛti* 5.55),[32] an idea expressed elsewhere such as in the *Jaiminīya-brāhmaṇa* (1.43) and the *Śatapatha-brāhmaṇa* (12.9.11), for example (Olivelle 2009, 254).

Afraid, the hunter asked Nārada what he could do to avoid such a fate (Madhya 252-253) and accepted Nārada as his guru by "falling down at his feet" (*paḍoṇ tomāra pāye*, CC Madhya 24.254). Nārada instructed him that to become "liberated" (*mocana*, 24.255) he would have to break his bow (24.256) and allow Nārada to supply him with food (24.257, 262), assumedly, because of context, only vegetarian food. He then instructed the hunter to give away whatever wealth he had to *brāhmaṇas*, to depart his home with his wife, carrying no possession other than a single cloth each (24.259); and to go and build a hut (*kuṭīra*) by the river where he would care for a sacred *tulasī* plant (24.260) and live like a Vaiṣṇava (24.266). Demonstrating the true spirit of a Vaiṣṇava, Nārada then revived the injured animals (24.263).

Nārada seemed to test the ex-hunter by bringing enough food for many people, with Caitanya noting that the ex-hunter and his wife ate abstemiously (Madhya 24.267, 280), again demonstrating the proper attitude of restraint of a Vaiṣṇava. Moreover, when Nārada returned with his friend Parvata Muni (24.268), the ex-hunter demonstrated an exemplary attitude that Vaiṣṇavas should have towards living beings when he hesitated from prostrating on the ground due to the presence of ants, not wanting to cause even a tiny ant any harm (24.270), whisking them away before he finally prostrated (24.271). Caitanya then tells us, through the voice of Nārada, that,

> "This is not unusual since a devotee of Kṛṣṇa is without any impulse to cause harm (*hiṃsā-śūnya*) and in so doing becomes a preeminent *sādhu*[33] (CC Madhya 24.272). O hunter, these amazing qualities that you possess such as nonviolence (*ahiṃsā*), etc., are characteristic of those who are engaged in *bhakti* towards Hari such that they would never the cause of suffering for others"[34] (CC Madhya 24.273).

Thus, the parable illustrates that Caitanya's attitude towards animals included a standard composite of non-violence (*ahiṃsā*) and vegetarianism as being essential to Vaiṣṇava identity, praxis, and belief. Moreover, the tone with which he describes the suffering of the animals elicits a sense of empathy on the part of the reader, where we are encouraged to, like Caitanya, have a deep sense of sympathy and care for the suffering of animals, perhaps even invoking emotions towards those animals in a way that is not dissimilar to his affect towards the animals of the Jhārikhaṇḍa forest.

Śivānanda Sena & The Dog, Antya 1

The text of the Madhya-līlā ends with Caitanya feasting on *prasāda* at the temple of Jagannātha, and the Antya-līlā begins with devotees from all over India converging on Jagannātha Purī to see Śrī Caitanya. One devotee, Śivānanda Sena, met with the devotees at Kulīna village (Antya 1.15) and he was put in charge of arranging the journey to Jagannātha Purī (1.16). Śivānanda became attached to a certain dog that he had been caring for (1.17), and he even went through some trouble to pay extra for the dog's fare to a ferryman who initially refused to ferry the animal (1.18-19).

Once, when Śivānanda was away, the devotees forgot to feed the dog (Antya 1.21) and the dog disappeared and could not be found (1.22-24). They went to see Caitanya in Jagannātha Purī (1.25) and found that the dog was with him (1.28) being fed by Caitanya while he encouraged the dog to chant the holy names (1.29), which the dog amazingly was able to do (1.30), not dissimilar to the chanting and singing of the animals in Jhārikhaṇḍa. In a species reversal that symbolized the elevated status of the dog-cum-devotee, Śivānanda was inspired to offer his obeisance to the dog so that the dog might forgive his offence (1.31). Then, "the following day they did not see that dog because he had attained a spiritual body (*siddha-deha*) whereupon he went to Vaikuṇṭha"[35] (1.32).

This is a relatively short episode compared to the others, but it is particularly noteworthy that the dog achieved not only liberation, but an actual *siddha-deha*. For the GV tradition, spiritual advancement is realized by following vaious prescriptive practices and behaviors; this is known as the "path of prescriptions" (*vaidhī mārga*) and is enacted by the "body of the practitioner" (*sādhaka-deha*). But on a more advanced level there is the realization of one's "perfected body" (*siddha-deha*) through the "path of following one's loving attachment" (*rāgānugā mārga*) by which one "enters into" (*āveśa*) the spiritual world.

The effect of *bhakti-sādhana* involves the transportation of the practitioner —in a spiritual body (*siddha-deha*)—to Kṛṣṇa's eternal spiritual realm. Here, in this instance, it is a dog who attains this extremely advanced level, underscoring the potential of even non-human animals to achieve advanced states of personhood beyond what many humans may ever achieve. The ramifications of this, and the episodes above, for the inclusion of animals as full members of an ethical community cannot be overstated.

Conclusion

Thus, it is important to note, as many scholars have (e.g. Alsdorf 2010, Doniger 2009), that often themes of cow protection, vegetarianism, and non-violence (*ahiṃsā*) are *not* necessarily connected in South Asian traditions. Those who are advocates for cow protection need not necessarily be vegetarian or follow nonviolence (as we seen with communal violence against Muslims); those who are vegetarian may not be forceful advocates of cow protection (as in the case of dairy consumption where dairy cows are often killed for meat, their calves are taken away at birth, etc.), and those who purport to follow nonviolence may not be advocates for cow protection or vegetarianism (e.g., in the case of Indian Buddhists who generally eat meat).

However, the life of Śrī Caitanya brings all of these themes into an aggregate ethic for animal care and advocacy that allows for significant status of non-human personhood and inclusion of animals as full members of a moral and spiritual community alongside of humans, and even at times surpassing humans, in their capacity for spiritual attainment expressed in a loving relationship with God, as Kṛṣṇa incarnate in the person of Śrī Caitanya.

Endnotes

1. Research for this project was supported by Arihanta Institute (ArihantaInstitute.org). Translations are my own, unless otherwise stated.

2. The CC is divided into three sections based on the life of Śrī Caitanya Mahāprabhu during his "early pastimes" (Ādi-līlā, hereafter just "Ādi"), the "events of the middle part of his life (Madhya-līlā, hereafter just "Madhya"), and the "occurrences towards the end of his life" (Antya-līlā, hereafter just "Antya").

3. CC Ādi 17.121: *ghare ghare saṅkīrtana karite lāgilā*

4. CC Ādi 17.123: *mṛdaṅga-karatāla saṅkīrtana-mahādhvani |'hari' 'hari' — dhvani vinā anya nāhi śuni ||*

5. On the analogy between this action and non-violent peaceful protest, see Rosen 2023, 63 ff.

6. The same episode described in the *Caitanya-bhāgavata* is decidedly more intense.

7. CC Ādi 17.153: *prabhu kahe, — go-dugdha khāo, gābhī tomāra mātā | vṛṣa anna upajāya, tāte teṅho pitā ||*

8. CC Ādi 17.154: *pitā-mātā māri' khāo — ebā kon dharma | kon bale kara tumi e-mata vikarma ||*

9. "[W]e have no basis or indication for vegetarianism to have originated from cow-veneration or started from abstinence from beef" (Alsdorf 2010, 70).

10. Alsdorf cites *Śarīrasthāna* 3 that says (by his translation), "Beef is a good remedy for asthma, cough, catarrh, chronic fever, exhaustion and for quick digestion; it is purifying (Pavitra) and alleviates wind" (Alsdorf 2010, 66).

11. CC Ādi 17.159: *prabhu kahe, — vede kahe go-vadha niṣedha | ataeva hindu-mātra nā kare go-vadha ||*

12. *Śatapatha-brāhmaṇa* 3.1.2.21 (Translation by Julius Eggeling, 1882): "He (the Adhvaryu) then makes him enter the hall. Let him not eat (the flesh) of either the cow or the ox...Such a one indeed would be likely to be born (again) as a strange being ... let him therefore not eat (the flesh) of the cow and the ox."

13. CC Ādi 17.160: *jiyāite pāre yadi, tabe māre prāṇī | veda-purāṇe āche hena āj̃ñā-vāṇī ||*

14. CC Ādi 17.161: *ataeva jarad-gava māre muni-gaṇa | veda-mantre siddha kare tāhāra jīvana ||*

15. *Manu-Smṛti* 5.39-44 (translation by Olivelle 2009, 87-88): "Within the sacrifice, therefore, killing is not killing. When plants, domestic animals, trees, beasts, and birds die for the sake of a sacrifice, they will in turn earn superior births ... a sacrifice, an offering to gods or ancestors—at no other occasion than these, Manu has declared,

may animals be killed ... a twice-born man who is self-possessed must never, even in a time of adversity, carry out a killing that is not sanctioned by the Veda. When a killing is sanctioned by the Veda and well-established in this mobile and immobile creation, it should be regarded definitely as a non-killing; for it is from the Veda that the Law has shined forth."

16. CC Ādi 17.163: *kali-kāle taiche śakti nāhika brāhmaṇe | ataeva go-vadha keha nā kare ekhane ||*

17. CC Ādi 17.165: *tomarā jīyāite nāra, — vadha-mātra sāra |*

18. CC Ādi 17.165: *naraka ha-ite tomāra nāhika nistāra ||*

19. CC Ādi 17.166: *go-aṅge yata loma, tata sahasra vatsara | go-vadhī raurava-madhye pace nirantara ||*

20. *Manu-Smṛti* 5.37-38 (translation by Olivelle 2009, 87): "If he gets the urge, let him make an animal out of butter of flour; but he must never entertain the desire to kill an animal for futile reason. When a man kills an animal for a futile reason, after death he will be subject in birth after birth to being slain as many times as the number of hairs on that animal."

21. *Manu-Smṛti* 5.48-49 (translation by Olivelle 2009, 88): "One can never obtain meat without causing injury to living beings, and killing living beings is an impediment to heaven; he should, therefore, abstain from meat."

22. CC Ādi 17.222: *kājī kahe, — mora vaṁśe yata upajibe | tāhāke 'tālāka' diba, — kīrtana nā bādhibe ||* "

23. Translation by Bhaktivedānta Swami (1975): *yatra naisarga-durvairāḥ sahāsan nṛ-mṛgādayaḥ | mitrāṇīvājitāvāsa-druta-ruṭ-tarṣaṇādikam ||*

24. "In practice, Vaishnavas in the tradition of Chaitanya have in fact for the most part been vegetarians ... [O'Connell 58] ... Vaishnavas typically are vegetarian and shy away from occupations and activities that of their nature breed or depend upon violence" (O'Connell, 60).

25. CC Madhya 24.227: *nirgrantha-śabde kahe tabe 'vyādha', 'nirdhana' | sādhu-saṅge seha kare śrī-kṛṣṇa-bhajana ||*

26. CC Madhya 24.231: *vana-pathe dekhe mṛga āche bhūme paḍi' | bāṇa-viddha bhagna-pāda kare dhaḍ-phaḍi ||*

27. CC Madhya 24.243: *ardha-mārā jīva yadi dhaḍ-phaḍa kare | tabe ta' ānanda mora bāḍaye antare" ||*

28. CC Madhya 24.247: *kāli haite tumi yei mṛgādi māribā | prathamei māribā, ardha-mārā nā karibā" ||*

29. CC Madhya 24.249: *nārada kahe, — "ardha mārile jīva pāya vyathā | jīve duḥkha dite-cha, tomāra ha-ibe aiche avasthā ||*

30. CC Madhya 24.250: *vyādha tumi, jīva māra — 'alpa' aparādha tomāra | kadarthanā diyā māra' — e pāpa 'apāra' ||*

31. CC Madhya 24.251: *kadarthiyā tumi yata mārilā jīvere | tārā taiche tomā māribe janma-janmāntare ||*

32. *Manu-smṛti* 5.55 (translation by translation by Olivelle 2009, 88): "'Me he (*māṃ sa*) [where *māṃ* means "me" and *sa* means "he"] will eat in the next world, whose meat (*māṃsa*) I eat in this world'—this, the wise declare, is what gave the name to and discloses the true nature of 'meat' (*māṃsa*)."

33. CC Madhya 24.272: *nārada kahe,— "vyādha, ei nā haya āścarya | hari-bhaktye hiṁsā-śūnya haya sādhu-varya ||*

34. CC Madhya 24.273: *ete na hy adbhutā vyādha tavāhiṁsādayo guṇāḥ | hari-bhaktau pravṛttā ye na te syuḥ para-tāpinaḥ ||*

35. CC Antya 1.32: *āra dina keha tāra dekhā nā pāilā | siddha-deha pāñā kukkura vaikuṇṭhete gelā ||*

Bibliography

Alsdorf, Ludwig. 2010. *The History of Vegetarianism and Cow-veneration in India*. New York: Routledge.

Bekoff, Marc. 2001. "The Evolution of Animal Play, Emotions, and Social Morality: On Science, Theology, Spirituality, Personhood, and Love." *Zygon*, vol. 36, no. 4: 615-655.

Bhaktivedānta, A.C. Svāmī Prabhupāda. 1975. *Śrī Caitanya Caritāmṛta: The Pastimes of Lord Caitanya Mahāprabhu*. Fourth printing, 2011. Vols 1-9. Los Angeles: The Bhaktivedānta Book Trust.

Bohanec, Cogen. 2024. *Bhakti Ethics: The Role of Emotions and Love in Gauḍīya Vaiṣṇava Metaethics*. New York: Lexington.

———. 2023. "Bhaktivedānta, Gandhi, and the Social Implications of Nonviolence." *Ahiṃsā in India: Diverse Traditions of Nonviolence*. Forthcoming, Lexington.

———. 2023. "A Theocentric Argument for Animal Personhood in the *Caitanya-caritāmṛta*." *Journal of Dharma Studies*.

———. 2021. "Bhaktivedānta Swami and Buddhism: A Case Study for Interfaith Dialogue and Peacebuilding." *The Journal of Dharma Studies*. New York: Springer.

———. 2021. "A Dialogical Encounter between Christian Ecotheological Ethics and Gauḍīya Vaiṣṇava Theology." *Sustainable Societies: Interreligious, Interdisciplinary Responses*. New York: Springer.

———. 2018. "Ecotheology, Animal Rights, and the *Śrīmad Bhāgavatam*." *Journal of Vaishnava Studies*. Volume 26, NO.2, Spring 2018, 17-33.

Doniger, Wendy. 2009. *The Hindus: An Alternative History*. New York: Penguin Press.

O'Connell, Joseph T. 2011. "Chaitanya Vaishnava Devotion (*bhakti*) and Ethics as Socially Integrative in Sultanate Bengal." *Bangladesh e-Journal of Sociology*. Vol. 8, no. 1, January 2011.

Olivelle, Patrick. 2009. *The Law Code of Manu*. Oxford: Oxford University Press.

Rosen, Steven J. 2023. *Chaitanyology: A Collection of Essays on Śrī Chaitanya*. Charlottesville, VA: Bookwrights Press.

What Should We Do With Chand Kazi? *Caitanyacaritāmṛta* and Vaiṣṇava-Muslim Dialogue

R. David Coolidge

Not all historical figures from the premodern past are still revered today. For example, Īśvarakṛṣṇa, who lived approximately in the range of 350-450 CE, is respected for authoring the text *Sāṃkhyakārikā*, but it would be a stretch to say that he is revered.[1] On the other hand, it would be an understatement to say that Caitanya (1486-1533) is revered, when the truth is that he is unambiguously worshipped.[2] Due primarily to the efforts of A. C. Bhaktivedānta Swami Prabhupāda (hereafter, Prabhupāda), the worship of Caitanya has become a global religious phenomenon. One can find *mūrti*-s of Caitanya throughout the world, as he is seen by Caitanya Vaiṣṇavas as "a combined manifestation of Rādhā and Krishna, a unique dual incarnation of God in the mood of his own devotee."[3] Anyone who wants to understand the Caitanya Vaiṣṇava tradition must make sense of Caitanya's life and teachings, as well as his impact on those who carried his message to future generations. On this latter point, it seems that above all it was being in the physical presence of Caitanya in the 16th century that transformed the lives of those who devoted themselves to elucidating and embodying his understanding of *bhakti*.[4]

A human being in the 21st century who wants to know Caitanya cannot recreate those past events. As with many other people in history, the facts of Caitanya's life are mediated through narrative structures that impute meanings to them.[5] For example, the study of the biography of Muḥammad (d. 632) takes into account both the dominant Muslim accounts of his life as well as the less well-known accounts created by authors outside of the Islamic tradition.[6] A historical fact of Muhammad's life may take on different meanings depending on who is narrating his biography, and different historians may even disagree on what constitutes the facts. In the case of Caitanya, he is known almost exclusively through devotional works written by his followers, as well as their followers in the next generation. Those works, written in Sanskrit and Bengali, are focused heavily on narrating the meaning of Caitanya's life through already well-established frameworks of Hindu belief and practice.[7] We have no accounts of his life from a non-Hindu perspective, and that means that it is important to recognize the ideological foundations upon which his biographies were constructed by their authors.

As has been argued by scholars of Caitanya's biography, the dominant text that influences later generations' perceptions of Caitanya is Kṛṣṇadāsa Kavirāja's *Caitanyacaritāmṛta,* which was perhaps completed in 1615, roughly 82 years after Caitanya's disappearance.[8] It brought together various strands contained in the previous biographies and became "the final word" on who Caitanya was.[9] As such, it is not inappropriate to posit that for Caitanya Vaiṣṇavas, Caitanya is who the *Caitanyacaritāmṛta* says he is. It is also clear that discussions of what happened in Caitanya's life proceed first and foremost from the accounts related in *Caitanyacaritāmṛta.* As such, anyone endeavoring to approach Caitanya through that text must have a grasp of certain basic features of its compositional structure. For example, the previously cited quote about Caitanya being the dual incarnation of Kṛṣṇa and Rādhā is a central theme of the text. Previous biographers had put forward various interpretations of who Caitanya was, utilizing the pan-Hindu theological concept of *avatāra* ("divine descent") as the basis for theological discussion.[10] However, Kṛṣṇadāsa Kavirāja effectively won the debate, and his theology became orthodoxy.

He also structured the text in such a way that Caitanya has theological debates with various opponents in the model of a "conqueror of all directions (*digvijaya*)," a "wider premodern hagiographical pattern" in Hindu religious literature.[11] So, for Kṛṣṇadāsa, Caitanya was not only a unique incarnation in the history of the Hindu tradition, but was also actively trying to demonstrate that theology to others and overwhelm their false and/or incomplete religious worldviews. This phenomenon can be seen, to give two prominent examples, in the dialogue with Sarvabhauma Bhaṭṭācārya that is clearly meant as a critique of Advaita Vedānta, and the dialogue with Chand Kazi, which contains a critique of Islam. In this regard, it is appropriate to state the Kṛṣṇadāsa wanted to work out the universal implications of Caitanya's life and teachings. Even though his discussion was deeply rooted in Hindu texts/practices/thought, he wants to show how Caitanya is not just for Hindus, but for all people. In 17th century India, the most obvious non-Hindu Other that could potentially be won over were Muslims. Later Caitanya Vaiṣṇava gurus also followed through on that universal impetus in Kṛṣṇadāsa's thought, such as when Bhaktivinoda Thakur (d. 1914) sent letters and books to Ralph Waldo Emerson (d. 1882) in hopes of spreading Caitanya's message beyond India.[12] Prabhupāda's global missionary work, and the many transnational gurus who followed in his wake, brought about the full blossoming of this aspiration.

The dialogue with Chand Kazi is an important document of premodern engagement between Hindu and Muslim discursive frameworks. Caitanya was born and raised in Bengal under the Bengal Sultanate, and the beginning of his preaching career coincided with the reign of 'Alā al-Dīn Ḥusayn Shāh (r. 1494-1519), generally considered a tolerant Muslim ruler who even patronized Sanskrit works about Kṛṣṇa.[13] As with other Muslim rulers in South Asia, magistrates (*qāḍī*-s) were appointed in various localities to deal with disputes. According to the *Caitanyacaritāmṛta*, at some point there was push back against the public performances of devotional music, chanting and dancing (usually referred to as *sankīrtan*), and the local magistrate was involved.

The following analysis of the encounter is rooted in the translation and commentary on the *Caitanyacaritāmṛta* by Prabhupāda, since it is the most widespread of all versions and thus the most suitable to serve as a starting point for crosscultural and interreligious scholarship. The story is narrated in chapter 17 of the *Ādi-Līlā* section, the first of three major divisions that structure the biographical narrative. All verse numbers correspond with Prabhupāda's version, beginning with verse 123, which states evocatively, "When the *saṅkīrtana* movement thus started, no one in Navadvīpa could hear any sound other than the words 'Hari! Hari!' and the beating of the *mṛdanga* and clashing of hand bells."[14]

In response to this situation, Chand Kazi became angry, broke someone's drum (*mṛdanga*), asked who was responsible, and threatened further punishment if it continued. (124-128) When Caitanya's followers inform him about what happened, he tells them to keep doing what they have been doing and declares, "Today I shall kill all Muslims!" (129) Of course he doesn't actually do that, but leads his followers on a torchlight *saṅkīrtana* procession to Chand Kazi's home in defiance. (133-140) Those who get there early are so mad that they start destroying some of his property, but when Caitanya arrives they settle down. (141-143) In this way, the stage is set for the dialogue.

The first aspect of the dialogue is an acknowledgement by both parties that they share family ties. (148-152) This establishes that this is not meant as a dialogue between a foreign occupier and an indigenous activist, but actually is centered squarely on what we would now call purely religious matters. This is made more clear by the fact that immediately Caitanya puts Chand Kazi on the defensive by making an argument for vegetarianism, namely that since cows provide milk and bulls help plow the fields for grain, they are like mothers and fathers to humanity and should not be slaughtered. (153-154) Vegetarianism does not hold any particular spiritual value across Muslim societies, whereas for Caitanya Vaiṣṇavas it is essential to spiritual advancement.[15]

Through appeal to a matter of Vaiṣṇava orthopraxy, Caitanya confronts the divide between the two spiritual traditions head on. Chand Kazi does not offer a strong counterargument, but instead makes a broad assertion that the Qur'an can be interpreted according to the Sanskrit concepts of *pravṛtti* ("increasing the propensity to enjoy," in Prabhupāda's rendering) and *nivṛtti* ("decreasing the propensity to enjoy"). If one looks at the issue from the perspective of *nivṛtti*, then he concedes that, "the killing of animals is prohibited." (156) Yet, if looked at from the standpoint of *pravṛtti*, one can enjoy meat without sin as long as the "killing is done under the guidance of scripture." (157) Then Chand Kazi brings up the animal sacrifices mentioned in the Vedas, but Caitanya contends that such acts were for a bygone age, and it is now the case that no such acts can be performed due to the spiritual devolution inherent in Kali Yuga. (158-164) Caitanya goes further and states, "therefore you are going to hell; there is no way for your deliverance. Cow-killers are condemned to rot in hellish life for as many thousands of years as there are hairs on the body of the cow." (165-166) More than that, he states flatly that, "there are many mistakes and illusions in your scriptures. Their compilers, not knowing the essence of knowledge, gave orders that were against reason and argument." (167) Chand Kazi agrees with Caitanya, and states that he only accepts the legitimacy of Muslim scriptures for the sake of his community. (168-171)

At this point, it is already clear that the dialogue is not meant for a Muslim audience. Chand Kazi emerges not as a learned Muslim scholar, but as a paper tiger. He half-heartedly uses Sanskrit concepts to try to justify his behavior and interpret the Qur'an, while already conceding that not eating meat is a higher spiritual path. When Caitanya makes a threatening theological pronouncement about the consequences of his actions, Chand Kazi concedes almost immediately by declaring that he does not even really believe in the

Qur'an. At this point, the dialogue doubles down on preaching to the choir by having Chand Kazi explain how he had a threatening dream of the *avatāra* Nṛsiṃha, and reveals claw marks that were left on his chest when he awoke, which understandably elicits wondrous gasps from the Vaiṣṇava onlookers. (174-187) The entire dialogue simply demonstrates the obvious truth of Kṛṣṇadāsa's theology, and denigrates Muslim perspectives as both a likely path to Divine punishment and severely lacking in intellectual merit.

Kṛṣṇadāsa and other early followers of Caitanya were living in a time of Muslim political supremacy, and in various ways the texts they produced help us to understand how Vaiṣṇavas constructed the Muslim Other. Previous biographers of Caitanya had presented Muslims in an unfavorable light, and while Kṛṣṇadāsa perhaps does a better job than his predecessors, his remarks about Islam barely hide a "condescending tone."[16] Even Prabhupāda, despite numerous statements in other texts that show an appreciation for the spiritual value of Islam, contributes to this phenomenon. In his purport on verse 128, he implies that none of the conversions to Islam in Bengal were based on the spiritual merits of Islam, but rather a combination of government oppression, tricks that took advantage of Hindu rules of ritual purity, and economic incentives.[17] Obviously, the conversion of hundreds of millions of Bengali speakers over the centuries has been based on something more.[18] Perhaps it is easier in such a socio-political context to represent the Other as not actually a theological rival but rather as the conveyor of a flimsy edifice of myth and confusion that will fall apart at the slightest touch. But if Caitanya's goal was to spiritually conquer Islam in the *digvijaya* model, then the dialogue with Chand Kazi in *Caitanyacaritāmṛta* barely begins the process from a Muslim perspective. All that it potentially achieves is providing an uninformed Vaiṣṇava with a feeling of vindication that such an eminent Muslim personality as Chand Kazi was so easily subdued. That being said, it is acknowledged by a Bengali Muslim historian that Caitanya's movement did slow down "the progress of Islām to a considerable extent."[19]

Caitanya eventually settled as a renounced ascetic (*saṃnyāsī*) in the town of Puri, on the coast south of Bengal. This meant that he left the environs of the Muslim Ḥusayn Shāhī dynasty in Bengal, and settled in the Hindu kingdom of the Gajapati dynasty in Odisha. In the biographies of Caitanya this is presented as being done at the behest of Caitanya's grieving mother, who wants her newly renounced son to not be too far away from his family home in Bengal. But given that his prominent disciples Rūpa and Sanātana may have left their jobs under Ḥusayn Shāh both to join Caitanya's movement and in protest against military tensions between Bengal and Odisha, it may also indicate a preference for living in a Hindu kingdom.[20] But at no point does Caitanya suggest that all of his disciples need to emigrate away from Muslim kingdoms, even when, according to the biographers, the Gajapati king Pratāparudra (r. 1497-1540) became Caitanya's disciple.[21] But it should be noted that this Hindu kingdom was not only occasionally at war with the Muslim Sultanate in Bengal, but also the neighboring Hindu kingdom of Vijayanagar.[22] South Asian history is rarely as black and white as contemporary polemicists would like us to believe.[23]

So what do we do with the Chand Kazi dialogue, if we actually want Muslims and Vaiṣṇavas to understand each other in the 21st century? The first option is to surmise that whoever Chand Kazi actually was (because his name was obviously not "Moon Judge," the literal meaning), he was a government functionary who had scant religious knowledge (*'ilm*) of Islam. This might be historically true, but it is probably impossible to know for sure without the discovery of other Bengali or Persian sources that shed light on the event. But even if it were historically true, it would defeat a narrative purpose of the dialogue in the text. It would mean that Caitanya had defeated an uniformed Muslim in debate, who just happened to have a government position in that particular time and place. That seems like an unlikely interpretation, given what was stated earlier about the larger purposes of the text.

Another possibility is that Kṛṣṇadāsa perhaps did not know enough about Islam to properly construct a literary representation of a debate between two worldviews, or that he did know enough but chose to describe the debate in a way that would primarily be meaningful for Vaiṣṇavas. This scenario could be seen as casting Kṛṣṇadāsa in a somewhat negative light, but it doesn't necessarily have to be so, for a Vaiṣṇava *ācārya* is not required to be an expert in other faith traditions, nor does he have to be able to write for potential Muslim readers. Put simply, he did his best, but his presentation of the dialogue needs to be critiqued and supplemented for contemporary purposes of inter-religious scholarship.

Lastly, one could surmise that perhaps the dialogue never happened at all, and was embellished in the transmission of the story. This also could be possible, but would cast doubt on the authenticity of Kṛṣṇadāsa's work. If Kṛṣṇadāsa unknowingly transmitted false words from Caitanya and events about his life, then that opens up the possibility of critical readings of

Caitanyacaritāmṛta in a proverbial "quest for the historical Caitanya." But if Caitanya Vaiṣṇava tradition maintains simultaneously that Caitanya was a universally relevant dual incarnation, and also that *Caitanyacaritāmṛta* is an accurate representation of Caitanya's life and teachings, then resorting to that interpretive strategy seems unlikely to bear fruit. Exploring the second option seems the most beneficial hermeneutical approach for scholarly conversations between Vaiṣṇavas and Muslims.[24]

At the core of Caitanya Vaiṣṇava faith is the belief that Caitanya was far more than just another human being walking the planet Earth approximately 500 years ago, just as the core of Islamic faith is belief that Muhammad was far more than just another human being walking the planet Earth approximately 1400 years ago. This paper cannot adjudicate the ways in which Muslims and Vaiṣṇavas either attain faith in these historical individuals, nor lose it. Rather, it can acknowledge that certain possibilities of interpretation may be pursued for the sake of interreligious scholarship. It would be unacceptable for a follower of Caitanya to assume that Caitanya did not have the knowledge necessary to defeat a real Muslim scholar.

Similarly, no knowledgeable Muslim would accept that Chand Kazi does an adequate job as a representative of the Islamic scholarly tradition. So in order for Caitanya to retain his theological status as capable of winning a real debate, and for Muslims to accept the terms of the debate, the most suitable hermeneutical option is to state that Kṛṣṇadāsa was unable, or possibly unwilling, to render the debate in terms that would do the Islamic tradition justice.[25]

As stated earlier, a Vaiṣṇava *ācārya* is not expected to be an expert in other religious traditions. As Akshay Gupta has argued, the statements of the *ācārya* can be bifurcated into two realms. In the first set of statements, fundamental religious truths are passed down faithfully in *paramparā* because those truths are based fundamentally in *śabda* (scriptural authority), following Jīva Gosvāmin's classical formulation of Caitanya Vaiṣṇava epistemology. In the second set of statements, the *ācārya* may express his opinions about other matters, but he may be wrong. Gupta uses this theology of the guru to explain some of Prabhupāda's statements about women, Africans, and people of low caste.[26] In this regard, a Vaiṣṇava can accept what Kṛṣṇadāsa wrote that falls under the first set of statements. For example, the extensive theological discussions at the beginning of *Ādi Līlā* can remain as is, verbatim, as expressions of a distinctive Caitanya Vaiṣṇava theological truth. Kiyokazu Okita identifies six distinctive features of the Caitanya *sampradāya*, and the first is Caitanya's divinity.[27] Kṛṣṇadāsa faithfully establishes the distinctive theology of Caitanya Vaiṣṇavism, in keeping with the paramount importance of the guru in delivering "the grace of God *to* humans in the world [and delivering] humans *from* the world of suffering to God."[28] But in regard to the dialogue with Chand Kazi, a Vaiṣṇava interested in theological discussions with a Muslim would be well served to adopt the recommended strategy of interpreting Kṛṣṇadāsa's rendering of the event as containing a mixture of both types of statements.

For example, the theological declaration by Caitanya of the severe and long-lasting punishments that await any Muslim who eats *ḥalāl* beef can be bucketed under the first set. There is no need for a Vaiṣṇava to soften their convictions regarding the eschatological consequences of certain actions in their theological tradition. But when Chand Kazi tries to interpret the Qur'an using Sanskritic concepts such as *pravṛtti* and *nivṛtti* in a way that concedes *a priori* that not eating meat is a higher spiritual path, we can just leave that aside as either a mistake by Kṛṣṇadāsa in his understanding of the Islamic tradition or a purposeful distortion of Islamic thought for some other didactic purpose meant for a Vaiṣṇava readership.

By using a bifurcated hermeneutical model to interpret the dialogue, interreligious scholarship between Muslims and Vaiṣṇavas can preserve the requirement for Muslims to speak authoritatively about their own tradition and also preserve the need for Vaiṣṇavas to believe that Caitanya accomplished something meaningful in this particular dialogue. As stated before, if we take the dialogue at face value, Caitanya does not encounter and defeat an authoritative representation of the Islamic tradition. Of course, no matter what actually happened, he was able to continue his preaching, which involved public singing, chanting, and dancing. As such, the whole event can reasonably be read as an act of "civil disobedience" with contemporary implications.[29] But the dialogue in particular can also be read as serving a different purpose—a manifest victory over Islamic theology.

In order for the text to retain the possibility that that is indeed what happened, someone needs to be blamed for failing to narrate the story in a way that could convince an educated Muslim scholar. Kṛṣṇadāsa is the best candidate, and Gupta's account of the "epistemic authority" of Caitanya Vaiṣṇava gurus makes this an acceptable hermeneutical strategy. This corresponds with Bohanec's recommendation in regard to Buddhist-Vaiṣṇava dialogue to, "afford other traditions with the maximum valuation allowable without compromising one's own theological 'non-negotiables.'"[30] Otherwise one might end up with an epistemic divide so wide that engagement is impossible.

To be clear, this does not mean that we cannot criticize each other's traditions and the positions that we adhere to as representatives of our traditions. Rather, it means we have to take seriously *how we represent other people's traditions.* Kṛṣṇadāsa and the rest of the *sampradāya* have faithfully conveyed the threat from Caitanya to me as an eater of *ḥalāl* beef. There is no reason for me to doubt, as a Muslim, that this threat is a real one from within the theology that the *Caitanyacaritāmṛta* was composed to convey. I am merely pointing out that Chand Kazi does not speak for me, nor could I imagine any Muslim scholar I have ever studied with, accepting him as an adequate representative of Islam. I have been to Chand Kazi's *samādhi* in Mayapur, and I recognize it as one of many important places in India that serve as reminders of centuries of Hindu-Muslim encounter. But if we really want to talk about the issue of vegetarianism in the 21st century, it would be better to leave aside Chand Kazi and start with Kenneth Valpey's contemporary argument for cow protection.[31] It seems that a main purpose of *paramparā* is to always make available to the people living representatives of the tradition who address the concerns of the age adequately. Perhaps Chand Kazi served a useful purpose in past centuries, but in the 21st century it is hard to take seriously the perspectives of Vaiṣṇavas who repeat the exchange more or less verbatim.[32]

On the other side, Muslims have also not adequately represented the Hindu tradition in numerous ways. Muslims in general are much more knowledgeable about Advaita Vedānta than Vaiṣṇava theology, whether one is talking about a famous premodern scholar like Dara Shukoh or a widely-published contemporary theorist like Reza Shah-Kazemi.[33] Sufi *shaykhs* superimposed Islamic theological categories onto the Hindu tradition without ever having studied it systematically.[34] Muslims interpreted the *Bhagavad Gītā* according to their own perspectives, without any evidence of them consulting the Vaiṣṇava commentarial tradition.[35] Of course, it is encouraging, on the one hand, that there is ample evidence of South Asian Muslims taking an interest in the scholarship of their Hindu neighbors. Yet, it also must be pointed out clearly when their scholarly efforts do not do justice to the traditions they are representing. For interreligious scholarship to flourish in the 21st century, those on both sides of the divide need to be willing to embrace critiques of their own textual traditions, when and where appropriate.

Vaiṣṇava-Muslim dialogue has already happened, and this article is written in the hope that it continues around the world.[36] Undoubtedly there is a place for everyday Vaiṣṇavas and Muslims to get to know each other, and each other's texts. This paper should not be taken as an argument meant to exclude the presentation of *Caitanyacaritāmṛta* to Muslims. Rather, it is meant for those who seriously want to explore the contours of the two traditions in scholarly dialogue with one another. A secular historical perspective can be, and has been, used to delegitimize sacred biographies in many traditions. Interreligious scholarship should, in contrast, look for ways that accommodate coherent and acceptable norms of scholarly discourse amenable to both religious traditions. This is especially important when contemporary Vaiṣṇavas and Muslims, each heirs of traditions subject to colonization and orientalism, both struggle to help others recognize, "the possibility that other-than-Western religious, ecological, aesthetic and economic knowledge systems have something valuable to teach us."[37] It is not helpful for either of us to recreate distortions of each other from centuries ago, especially in a matter so continuously charged as the Hindu-Muslim divide.

Undoubtedly, *Caitanyacaritāmṛta* is only one source to explore in order to understand early Vaiṣṇava perceptions of Muslims, and the Chand Kazi story is only one moment in a rich and complicated text.[38] But each step towards mutual understanding and respectful scholarly exchange is meaningful, as it lays down building blocks of an interreligious discourse that has the possibility of outliving our short lives. The *Caitanyacaritāmṛta*, as well as the famous biographies of the Prophet Muhammad (peace and blessings upon him and his family), will remain central to each religious community in the future. But we can do work now that helps those who come after us appreciate how neither textual tradition truly exists in isolation, but is part of our shared heritage and future as human beings on planet Earth. Our traditions speaks through us, and we hope to emphasize the best of it as we pass it on to those who will discuss and debate about it long after we are gone.

Endnotes

1. Mikel Burley, "Sāṃkhya," in *History of Indian Philosophy*, ed. Purushottama Bilimoria (Abingdon: Routledge, 2018), 122–30.

2. Kenneth Valpey, "Caitanya," in *Brill's Encyclopedia of Hinduism*, vol. 4, 6 vols. (Leiden: Brill, 2012), 193–200.

3. Steven J. Rosen, "Who Is Shri Chaitanya Mahaprabhu?," in *The Hare Krishna Movement: The Postcharismatic Fate of a Religious Transplant*, ed. Edwin F. Bryant and Maria L. Ekstrand (New York: Columbia University Press, 2004), 63.

4. Jonathan Edelmann, "The Cause of Devotion in Gauḍīya Vaiṣṇava Theology: Devotion (Bhakti) as the Result of Spontaneously (Yadṛcchayā) Meeting a Devotee (Sādhu-Saṅga)," *Journal of the American Oriental Society* 135, no. 1 (2015): 65.

5. Alan Megill, "Recounting the Past: 'Description,' Explanation and Narrative in Historiography," *The American Historical Review* 94, no. 3 (1989): 627–53.

6. Jonathan A. C. Brown, *Muhammad: A Very Short Introduction* (Oxford: Oxford University Press, 2011); Robert G. Hoyland, *Seeing Islam As Others Saw It: A Survey and Evaluation of Christian, Jewish, and Zoroastrian Writings on Early Islam* (Piscataway: Gorgias Press, 2019).

7. Tony K. Stewart, *The Final Word: The Caitanya Caritāmṛta and the Grammar of Religious Tradition* (Oxford: Oxford University Press, 2010).

8. Valpey, "Caitanya," 193.

9. Stewart, *The Final Word*, 21.

10. Stewart, 99–138.

11. Valpey, "Caitanya," 194–95.

12. Shukavak N. Dasa, *Hindu Encounter with Modernity: Kedarnath Bhatta Bhaktivinoda, Vaiṣṇava Theologian* (Los Angeles: Sanskrit Religions Institute, 1999), 90–91.

13. Richard M. Eaton, *The Rise of Islam and the Bengal Frontier: 1204-1760* (Berkeley: University of California Press, 1993), 110; Mohammad Elius et al., "Muslim Treatment of Other Religions in Medieval Bengal," *SAGE Open* 10, no. 4 (2020): 7.

14. The online Vedabase of Prabhupāda's collected works is the most easily accessible version globally to reference his texts, and so I am providing a reference here to the initial verse of the relevant section of Prabhupāda's translation and commentary. All subsequent citations will simply reference the verse number in the main body of the article: "CC Ādi 17.123," accessed February 13, 2023, https://vedabase.io/en/library/cc/adi/17/123/

15. R. David Coolidge, "Dharma of Bhakti, Dharma of Mlecchas: Muslim Engagement with Gauḍīya Vaiṣṇavism as a Living Tradition," *Journal of Dharma Studies* 3, no. 1 (2020): 128.

16. Joseph T. O'Connell, *Caitanya Vaiṣṇavism in Bengal: Social Impact and Historical Implications*, ed. Rembert Lutjeharms (London and New York: Routledge, 2019), 212.

17. "CC Ādi 17.128," accessed February 13, 2023, https://vedabase.io/en/library/cc/adi/17/128/.

18. Ayesha A. Irani, *The Muhammad Avatāra: Salvation History, Translation, and the Making of Bengali Islam* (New York: Oxford University Press, 2021).

19. Momtazur Rahman Tarafdar, *Husain Shahi Bengal: 1494-1538 A.D., A Socio-Political Study* (Dhaka: Asiatic Society of Pakistan, 1965), 237.

20. O'Connell, *Caitanya Vaiṣṇavism in Bengal*, 82.

21. Steven Rosen, *India's Spiritual Renaissance: The Life and Times of Lord Chaitanya* (Brooklyn: Folk Books, 1988), 93–100.

22. O'Connell, *Caitanya Vaiṣṇavism in Bengal*, 178.

23. Supriya Gandhi, *The Emperor Who Never Was: Dara Shukoh in Mughal India* (Cambridge: Harvard University Press, 2020), 4–5.

24. In the spirit of dialogue, I would like to include this Vaiṣṇava perspective generated in the process of editing an earlier draft of this article: "If Kavirāja Gosvāmī is to be believed, then Chand Kazi may have been subject to two interrelated factors: exuberance and being overwhelmed in the presence of God. Indeed, who doesn't have the experience of relating an interreligious dialogue to one's own cohort and, due to exuberance or overzealousness, leave out certain details that favor the opposing side? This is not a good practice, of course, but far from uncommon, even among the most accomplished practitioners. Similarly, if we consider that the Kazi was in the actual presence of Śrī Chaitanya, whom the tradition views as God Himself, how would he not be overwhelmed to the point of being dumbfounded and unable to think properly? I usually think of these two factors, which are interrelated, when considering the slim possibility that Kavirāja Gosvāmī accurately presented the dialogue." (Personal correspondence with Steven J. Rosen, May 23, 2023)

25. A critical reading of the text could also contend that the sources Kṛṣṇadāsa used for the dialogue are the foundation of the problem. But that still would not resolve the issue, because Kṛṣṇadāsa's authorship inherently includes the responsibility to sort through the available sources. It only might shed some light on *why* Kṛṣṇadāsa wrote what he did.

26. Akshay Gupta, "Is a Guru as Good as God? A Vedāntic Perspective," *Journal of Dharma Studies* 5 (2022): 153–65.

27. Kiyokazu Okita, "The Theology of the Caitanya Sampradāya: Six Distinctive Features," *Journal of Vaishnava Studies* 29, no. 2 (2021): 5–24.

28. Graham M. Schweig, "Viśvanātha's Gurvaṣṭakam and the Understanding of Guru in Chaitanyaite Vaishnavism," *Journal of Vaishnava Studies* 12, no. 1 (2003): 119.

29. Steven J. Rosen, *Chaitanyology: A Collection of Essays on Śrī Chaitanya* (Charlottesville: Bookwrights Press, 2023), 57–84.

30. Cogen Bohanec, "Bhaktivedānta Swami and Buddhism: A Case Study for Interfaith Dialogue and Peacebuilding," *Journal of Dharma Studies* 4 (2021): 92.

31. Kenneth R. Valpey, *Cow Care in Hindu Animal Ethics* (Cham: Palgrave Macmillan, 2020).

32. Akif Manaf J., *Chand Kazi & Chaitanya: Muslim-Vaishnava Unification, Unity in Diversity* (Vrindavan: Traveling Sankirtan Party, 2012), 16–48.

33. Gandhi, *The Emperor Who Never Was: Dara Shukoh in Mughal India*; Reza Shah-Kazemi, *Paths to Transcendence: According to Shankara, Ibn Arabi, and Meister Eckhart* (Bloomington: World Wisdom, 2006).

34. Sher Ali Tareen, "Translating the 'Other': Early-Modern Muslim Understandings of Hinduism," *Journal of the Royal Asiatic Society* 27, no. 3 (2017): 436–60.

35. Ilyse R. Morgenstein Fuerst, "A Muslim Bhagavadgītā: 'Abd al-Rahman Chishti's Interpretive Translation and Its Implications," *Journal of South Asian Religious History* 1 (2015): 1–29.

36. Anuttama Dasa and Sanaullah Kirmani, "Vaiṣṇava-Muslim Dialogue in the United States: A Model," *The Muslim World* 107, no. 2 (2017): 211–21.

37. Rita D. Sherma, "Critical Interreligious Interdisciplinary Theological Reflection: Methodological and Hermenutical Considerations for Interreligious Studies," in *The Georgetown Companion to Interreligious Studies*, ed. Lucinda Mosher (Washington D.C.: Georgetown University Press, 2022), 489.

38. Joseph T. O'Connell, "Vaiṣṇava Perceptions of Muslims," *The Muslim World* 107, no. 2 (2017): 170–90.

Caitanya and the Mādhvas: An Argument for *Viśeṣa*

Gerald Surya

Abstract

In this article, I explore seven basic subjects: (1) There is an ongoing controversy about the link between Mādhvas and Gauḍīyas originating in the earliest days of the Gauḍīya *sampradāya*. (2) Indeed, there are two instances in Caitanya's life that appear to deny the link outright. (3) One instance occurring at Uḍupī has often been translated as meaning that Caitanya makes an emphatic distinction between the two traditions by his repeated use of the phrase "your *sampradāya*" and, furthermore, that he appreciates only *one* aspect of their tradition—Deity or image worship (based on misapplications of the words *eka* and *vigraha*). (4) A more thoughtful translation of the key verse would indicate instead that he appreciates a unique (*eka*) feature regarding ontology (*sambandha-jñāna*), and that the word *sampradāya* here carries no sectarian implications at all. (5) A critical question then arises: What is that feature that is unique to both traditions (as opposed to other Vaiṣṇava traditions) and is also mentioned in the verse? (6) The answer points to a conceptual understanding of God as having a form, and that each aspect of that form is absolutely real and ontologically nondifferent from every other aspect and, indeed, from his very self. (7) This nondifference is an application of a very specific doctrine called *viśeṣa*, the elucidation of which is unique to the Mādhva and Gauḍīya traditions, suggesting a deep foundational, theological relation between the two.

Throughout the ages, the Gauḍīya Vaiṣṇava *sampradāya* has had an ambiguous relationship with the Mādhva *sampradāya*. The variety of opinions on the issue of a link includes affirmation,[1] denial,[2] a mixed view affirming the historical connection but denying a doctrinal one,[3] and finally a general silence. On the one hand, both traditions worship Kṛṣṇa as the supreme reality through *bhakti* based on commonly revered texts; on the other, the distinctive features of Gauḍīya Vaiṣṇava tradition bear no resemblance to those of the Mādhva tradition.[4] This essay, however, attempts to seek answers on a possible link by going to the former tradition's source—Caitanya himself.

Two instances of dismissal?

Because Caitanya authored very little, we have to resort to his hagiographies to probe his perspectives. In one of them, the *Caitanya-candrodaya-naṭaka* of Kavi Karṇapūra (16th cent.), Caitanya makes a single negative comment to his close associates about the philosophy (*mata*) of the Mādhvas—one which arguably extends to the Śrī Vaiṣṇava philosophy as well:

> I have seen some Vaiṣṇavas, but they indeed were worshipers of Nārāyaṇa. Others were *tattvavādīs*; they were indeed of the same category. Their philosophy is not blameless. ... But Rāmānanda's philosophy is pleasant to me, O Bhaṭṭācārya.[5]

A later hagiography by Kṛṣṇadāsa Kavirāja (17th cent.), *Caitanya caritāmṛta*, relates an actual encounter between Caitanya and the Mādhvas themselves (2.9.245-278)—a narrative spanning over thirty verses (*payāra*-s). During his South India pilgrimage (c. 1510-1512 CE), Caitanya visited Uḍupī, the headquarters of the Mādhva *sampradāya*, and the narrative of that exchange can be divided into three parts: Firstly, he participates in the ritual observance of the original Kṛṣṇa deity or image consecrated in 1278 CE by Madhva himself at Uḍupī, an experience that inspires him to sing and dance in the ecstasy of *prema*. After an initial period of avoidance (in which they suspect him of being a follower of Advaitavāda), the followers of Madhva, known as Tattvavādīs, finally recognize him as a genuine Vaiṣṇava and offer him a proper reception.

In the second and most extensive section, Caitanya—noticing their pride—makes an inquiry into their view on *sādhya* (the goal) and *sādhana* (the means). He disputes their responses by referring to the *Bhāgavata-purāṇa* and the *Bhagavad-gītā*, emphasizing the conceptual distinctions between *dharma* and *bhakti*, and *mukti* and *bhakti*, respectively. It concludes with a final statement by Caitanya—designated in this essay as the third part. The adversarial character of the middle-part encounter dominates many academic comments on the entire episode. For example, Kenneth Valpey writes:

> Caitanya lectures him from the *Bhāgavata Purāṇa*, concluding with a rather blunt dismissal [of the Mādhva lineage].[6]

S. K. De notes:

> He [Jiva Gosvami] speaks of Madhvacarya ... as *Tattva-vāda-bhaṣya-kṛt*; [this is the] Tattva-vada Caitanya is said to have discredited at Udipi [sic] in his South Indian pilgrimage.[7]
>
> ... Madhvaism or affiliation to the Madhva sect is never acknowledged in the several authoritative lives of Caitanya ...[8]

Kiyokazu Okita writes:

> There is one incident which suggests Caitanya may have had neither formal nor theological affiliations with the Mādhva tradition. In his tour to South India, Caitanya met some Mādhvas. In his conversation with them, he recognized the Mādhvas as belonging to a different sect by referring to their tradition as 'your *sampradāya*'. Furthermore, in the same conversation, Caitanya at least partially rejects the teachings of the Mādhvas. Even though this incident does not exclude the possibility that Caitanya may have accepted some elements of the Mādhva tradition, as far as Caitanya's hagiographies are concerned there is no positive evidence that he had a theological affiliation with the Mādhvas.[9]

The general impression conveyed by the translations and scholarly assessments of this episode is that Caitanya substantially distances himself from the Mādhvas, and concludes with an acknowledgement of their *bhakti* as a token gesture. Thus, the scholarly consensus on the overall encounter from the *Caitanya-caritāmṛta* is largely one of dismissal, suggesting that Caitanya disavows any connection with the Mādhva tradition. IBased on these two sources, a Mādhva-Gauḍīya link of any substantial kind seems implausible.

A Second Look at the Two Cases

That said, Kostiantyn Perun argues for a more careful approach in interpreting the former example mentioned above:

> ... it is clear that while speaking about *tattvavādīs*, Śrī Caitanya expresses his striving for Vraja-*bhakti* and worship of Kṛṣṇa in that particular mood that he valued the most. That is why he preferred the association of Rāmānanda Rāya to the association of those Vaiṣṇavas who worshiped Nārāyaṇa in the mood of awe and reverence.[10]

This is a more thoughtful assessment pointing to Caitanya's absorption at the time in a very particular form of worship along with its supportive theological background. In fact, even from the Mādhva perspective, there is the sense that one's practice of *bhakti* is influenced by one's own particular spiritual constitution, and, therefore, the experiences in *bhakti* are not simply interchangeable amongst practitioners.

Similarly, this essay takes a deeper look into the episode at Uḍupī—particularly its third part in *Caitanya-caritāmṛta* 2.9.277.[11] The purpose is to challenge the above impressions by taking a fresh exegetical look at that final statement and then examining its theological content from the perspectives of *both* traditions, Mādhva and Gauḍīya.

In the narrative, Caitanya's concluding statement consists of the following Bengali couplet:

sabe, eka guṇa dekhi tomāra sampradāye
satya-vigraha kari' īśvare karaha niścaye[12]

This statement by Caitanya has been translated in various ways, the earliest one being: "I see only one merit in your order, you have fixed upon the true God."[13] Also, there are three printed versions of the second line that I have encountered as well: Rādhā Govinda Nāth's edition and Bhaktivedanta Swami Prabhupāda's edition include the word *kari'* ("accepting") after *satya-vigraha*, unlike the Gauḍīya Vedānta Samiti edition which omits *kari'*.[14] Nāth's version, unlike the others, has *niścaya* in place of *niścaye*.

The goal here is to interpret each word and the whole statement according to the principle of charity in order to account for the advanced intellectual statures of *both* Caitanya and his Mādhva interlocutor.

Sabe

The statement opens with this term—corresponding to *sarve* ("in all") in Sanskrit—and is explained by Edward C. Dimock:

> ... although you, like the followers of *jñāna*, consider that *mukti* is the desirable end of men, you do not, as the followers of *jñāna* do, consider that the image is merely *māyā*; you consider it as true, made up of *sat*, *cit*, and *ānanda*.[15]

Here he follows Nāth's interpretation of the word in terms of "all the followers of *jñāna*." However, the preceding verse has referred to the paths of both *karma* and *jñāna*, and, therefore, there is no reason to restrict the word "all" only to the practitioners of *jñāna*. Alternatively, Perun translates it as "now" which helps signal a sense of transition or contrast from the critical tone of the prior verse.

Tomāra sampradāya

In the narration of this episode, the phrase ("your *sampradāya*") actually appears twice—in the current verse and in the one immediately preceding it. Haripriya dāsa[16] points out that although much is made of this phrase to differentiate the two *sampradāyas* (i.e., Caitanya's vs. the Tattvavādīs'), the *Caitanya-caritāmṛta* never uses the term in such a specific sectarian way. Rather, it is always used in the sense of "group" or "subgroup"—as seen in, for instance, the various groups of *kīrtana*, or chanting parties, formed by the followers of Caitanya during the Ratha-yātrā festival at Purī.[17] Furthermore, taking into account that the Tattvavādīs didn't see Caitanya as one of their own, it is quite natural for Caitanya to simply say "your group" in a conventional way without any sectarian implications.

Guṇa

The word "*guṇa*" is simply translated as "quality" by Dimock and as "merit" by Sarkar. Prabhupāda's commentary glosses it as "the great qualification." In light of the harsh criticism given in the second part of the episode and the contrast drawn here, the most positive sense of the word *guṇa* fits best. Monier-Williams includes "good quality, virtue, merit, excellence ... the merit of composition (consistency, elegance of expression)." Utilizing these various senses of the words involved, Caitanya is then seen as preparing to announce something both special and unique.

Satya-vigraha (kari')

The word *kari'* ("accepting") creates a dependent clause with *satya-vigraha*, separating it from the remaining words in the second line. If it is not included in translation, that line becomes a single independent clause. The term *vigraha*, meaning "form," is interpreted by Rādhā Govinda Nāth and Dimock as referring to the image or *mūrti* mentioned in the opening of the episode (2.9.249). Valpey also explains the term *vigraha* as "physical temple image of the deity, Kṛṣṇa."[18]

However, Perun explains why this interpretation is most likely incorrect:

> Additionally, this statement is sometimes interpreted to refer to the form of a deity—*mūrti* or *arcā-vigraha*. However, such interpretation is not persuasive because, ironically, in the Mādhva tradition the form of a deity (*mūrti*) is considered to be a temporary representation of God (*pratimā*), made of matter, in which he simply resides after installation and thus is by no means identical with God himself.[19]

Similarly, Prabhupāda explains the term *vigraha* as being "the transcendental form of the Lord." This interpretation has the advantage of introducing the only one of the three Vedāntic subjects that has *not* been mentioned so far—*sambandha*, or divine ontology—into the discussion. Note that Caitanya elsewhere acknowledges that the *Vedas* cover three subjects (*sambandha*, *abhidheya*, and *prayojana*[20]), and that in this episode, until now, he has only raised the latter two using the equivalent terms, *sādhana* and *sādhya*, respectively.[21]

Prabhupāda notes that all Vaiṣṇavas (not only the Tattvavādīs) accept this same principle:

> Nonetheless, Caitanya Mahāprabhu was pleased that the Madhvācārya *sampradāya*, or the Tattvavāda-*sampradāya*, accepted the transcendental form of the Lord. This is the great qualification of the Vaiṣṇava *sampradāyas*.[22]

However, he points out the practical reality that there are various opinions among Vaiṣṇavas with an "impersonal attitude" who do not properly recognize the divine form of the Lord and who, therefore, are implicitly excluded here.

Another thing to note is that "*satya*" in a Mādhva context means "absolutely," "spiritually," or "real," without implying secondary realities envisaged in other systems.

Eka

The word *eka* has been translated as "one" by Dimock. However, because the term *vigraha*, as discussed above, does *not* convincingly refer to the worshippable image, this episode reveals not one but *two* features of Tattvavāda that Caitanya appreciates: the service to the image in part one, *and* the understanding about the Lord's form in part three. Therefore, translating the word "*eka*" as "one" is contextually inappropriate.

In contrast, Sarkar and Prabhupāda translate the word *eka* as "only one" and "only," respectively, thereby conveying a sense of distinctiveness. Monier-Williams Sanskrit-English dictionary defines *eka*, not only as "one," but also as "single of its kind, unique, singular, chief, pre-eminent, excellent"—therefore, it can be justifiably construed as "exclusive" or "unique."

Karaha niścaya
Sarkar translates the word *niścaya* as "fixed." However, the root of the word *niścaya* also includes the active sense of investigation, determination, or resolution thereby insinuating some form of a positive philosophical contribution. Furthermore, *karaha* being a verb meaning "to do" can be understood as an ongoing activity or practice rather than as a past or singular event. Therefore, Dimock's translation employing "established" is more suggestive of ongoing intellectual activity. Overall, his translation of the second line is commendable for showing how the two clauses make a clear identification of the two subjects—the Lord (*īśvara*) and his form (*vigraha*).

Discussion

Taking into account the above considerations, here are two alternate translations of the verse in question.

The first line:

> However, I see a unique specialty in your group.

or

> Among all [groups], I see a unique specialty in your group.

The second line:

> With regard to the Lord, you are demonstrating the absolute spiritual reality of (his) form.

or

> Accepting (*kari'*) the absolute spiritual reality of his form, you are establishing it as the Lord (himself).

These translations avoid all the contextual incongruities of other translations as described above. However, they pose a new challenge: What is the unique specialty (*eka-guṇa*) that Caitanya is highlighting?

Note that the other interpretations don't face this challenge because they have overlooked the sense of exclusivity inherent in the verse. This omission is what prompts the following assessment by Perun (emphasis added):

> Although this and preceding statements by Śrī Caitanya indicate that he distinguished his tradition from the *tattvavāda* school, and although he criticized *tattvavādīs* for practicing mixed *bhakti*, he nevertheless appreciated that they accept God's form as eternal. This statement refers to the general concept of the Supreme as having a form or being formless. Śaṅkara's school of extreme monism (*kevalādvaita*) subscribes to the latter view, rejecting any notion of a form in Brahman as a temporary product of *māyā*, whereas *all* major Vaiṣṇava traditions vehemently oppose such understanding and hold that the scriptures refer to the eternal *spiritual* form of God, free from any tinge of *māyā*. Thus, this statement cannot be taken as definitive evidence to suggest that this was the reason why Śrī Caitanya favored the Mādhva *sampradāya*—the eternality of the Lord's form is not an idea peculiar only to Madhva's tradition, but a common fundamental concept of all Vaiṣṇava traditions.[23]

This mistaken impression that this verse has nothing to say about a Mādhva-Gauḍīya link is primarily rooted in the common misunderstandings of the terms "*vigraha*" as the image and "*eka*" as "one."

Therefore, the final question, stated more precisely, is this: what unique specialty is (1) possessed by the Mādhva tradition, (2) shared with the Gauḍīyas, but *not* found in the other Vaisnava traditions, and (3) indicated in the second line of this verse?

The only possible answer is as follows: we see here the doctrine that the Lord has a body that is substantially real; and that the form *is the Lord himself* as determined by decisive hermeneutics and scriptural exegesis (*niścaya*). In Mādhva Vedānta, the concept of the complete identity of the Lord's body and his self is a specific case of a doctrine known as *viśeṣa*. This doctrine exists in the works of Gauḍīya Vaiṣṇava authors through the ages as well. Furthermore, the doctrine is *not* shared by the other Vaiṣṇava traditions. To discuss *viśeṣa* in detail is outside the scope of this essay, but some salient points can be made.

The Viśeṣa Doctrine of Madhva

The concept of *viśeṣa* addresses the problem of dualism in any given individual substance, an issue faced in all systems of thought. Mentally, one makes distinctions, for example, between a particular object's color, shape, size, function, and so on, even though all these components may be observed at once, and all function together to compose the reality of a given entity. In this way, according to the notion of *viśeṣa*, all permanent aspects of anything that exists are to be considered nondifferent.

Madhva defines *viśeṣa* as "the potency of things in themselves which determines the use of non-synonymous expressions in predicating something of them, provided however that in such cases, there is no absolute difference between the given thing and its predicates."[24] B. N. K. Sharma, a prominent scholar on Mādhva Vedānta, explains further:

> Viśeṣa is thus the same as the principle of identity-in-difference ... [It is] the peculiar characteristic or potency of things which makes description and talk of difference possible, where as a matter of fact only identity exists.[25]

It should be noted that *viśeṣa* is not to be confused with the Advaita-Vedānta principle of identity (*abheda*), for the latter refers to the ultimate oneness of *all* entities. In contrast, in the context of *viśeṣa*, the "oneness" is restricted to all the inherent features of a specific entity under discussion, whether it be the Lord, a particular soul, and so on.[26]

Madhva provides explicit references from the Vedic literature that specify it by name—one from the *śruti* (*Parama Upaniṣad*) and another from the *smṛti* (*Brahma-tarka*).[27] Both works are untraceable, and these specific references are currently known only via Madhva's own work, the *Viṣṇu-tattva-vinirṇaya.* A lengthier quote from the *Brahma-tarka* in his *Bhāgavata-purāṇa* commentary on verse 11.7.49 provides an explanation of the doctrine in conjunction with the term *acintya*:[28]

> Everything regarding Janārdana (Viṣṇu), such as the limbs of his body and his body itself; his qualities and [he as] their possessor; his energies and [he as] their possessor; his activities and [he as] the performer; his personal parts (*svarūpāṁśa*) and [he as] their whole—as well as the same things related to the *svarūpas* of the *jīvas* and to the sentient *prakṛti*—have an eternal exclusive non-difference (*nitya-abheda*) between them. But because of non-difference and because of the absence of separate qualities etc., and because of the eternality of the two [the part and the whole, the qualities and their possessor, the limbs and the body, etc.], they are said to be bereft of parts, qualities, activity and limbs. Everything is indeed possible due to Viṣṇu's inconceivable energy [*acintya-śakti*]. Even with regards to the eternality of activities etc. [of Īśvara, *jīva* and *cit-prakṛti*], either manifested or

> unmanifested—the attitude, modified by either existence or non-existence, is similar. The non-difference between the relative particulars (*viśeṣa*) and the composite whole (*viśiṣṭa*) is exactly the same. Because of the inconceivable energy everything suits the Supreme Lord. Only by his energy [this is also true] even for the *jīvas* and sentient *prakṛti*. Everywhere else there is certainly difference and non-difference (*bhedābheda*) because they both are seen. This is also true for the cause and effect, except for [Brahman as] the instrumental cause (*nimitta-kāraṇa*).[29]

Furthermore, Madhva recognizes *viśeṣa* in the well-known Upaniṣadic dictums ("one only, without a second"[30]; and "there is no plurality here whatsoever"[31]), the *Bhagavad-gītā's* narration of the *viśvarūpa*,[32] and the *Vedānta-sūtras* 3.2.28-31 in his respective commentaries.

The significance of this doctrine is also brought out by B. N. K. Sharma:

> This concept of Viśeṣas is thus Madhva's most original and substantial contribution to the problem of substance and attributes in Indian ontology.[33] ... The relation between substance and attributes is one of the intriguing problems of philosophy. It has well-nigh taxed the ingenuity and resources of philosophers in the East and in the West. Madhva's contribution to the solution of this problem is both original and significant.[34] ... This is no small service to scientific thinking and metaphysics.[35]

The above phrase "a distinction of reference, without one ... of essence" neatly captures the essence of *viśeṣa*.

The Viśeṣa Doctrine in Gauḍīya Vaiṣṇavism

The *viśeṣa* doctrine is found by name throughout the Gauḍīya tradition, particularly in the works of Baladeva Vidyābhūṣaṇa—for example, in his *Govinda-bhāṣya, Brahma-sūtra-kārikā-bhāṣyam, Gītā-bhūṣaṇa*, and frequently in his *Siddhānta-ratna*. It is also identified by Jīva Gosvāmī in his commentary on the *Bhagavat-sandarbha* via his explicit approval of Madhva's commentary to *Vedānta-sūtra* 3.2.28.[36] Bhaktivinoda Ṭhākura's subcommentary on Baladeva's *Gītā-bhūṣaṇa* also names and discusses this doctrine.[37]

An explanation more recognizable to practicing Gauḍīya Vaiṣṇavas, however, occurs in the text called the *Brahma-saṁhitā*, an otherwise unknown Vaiṣṇava compendium (and distinct from a *Pañcarātra* text bearing the same name). Caitanya is said to have encountered it on his South India pilgrimage. The verse in question states:

> I worship Govinda, the primeval Lord, whose transcendental form is full of bliss, truth, substantiality and is thus full of the most dazzling splendor. Each of the limbs of that transcendental figure possesses in Himself, the full-fledged functions of all the other organs, and eternally sees, maintains and manifests the infinite universes, both spiritual and mundane.[38]

In this articulation, each limb of the Lord's body possesses the power of all his other limbs: in other words, each limb contains the whole body. This corresponds perfectly with the part-whole identification made in the *Brahma-tarka* passage cited earlier (*avayavy-avayavānāṁ*), encapsulating the same doctrine in a form readily appreciated by Gauḍīya Vaiṣṇavas.

It should be underlined that the view expressed by Caitanya about the identity of the Lord and his absolute spiritual body differs sharply not only with views of the unorthodox but with the views of other Vaiṣṇava traditions. For example, although followers of Viśiṣṭādvaita accept both the Lord and his form as eternal, they consider them as two distinct (though inseparable) entities. The former is God himself, but the latter is made of a substance that is definitely non-conscious (*acetana*) and, in some cases, considered to be material in character (*jaḍa*).[39]

Conclusion

In summary, regarding the Caitanya narrative under discussion, let us consider the words of Tony K. Stewart: "This episode is perhaps significant in light of the later and still divisive controversy surrounding attempts by a small minority to affiliate the Gauḍīya Vaiṣṇava *sampradāya* with the Madhva *sampradāya*."[40] His words ring true to me, although not in the sense he likely intended them. Although there are many differences between the two traditions, the *viśeṣa* doctrine in conjunction with the concept of *acintya* provide a deep theological infrastructure that they share. This in turn has ramifications for the understanding of other theological topics, such as the nature of soul, the functioning of *bhakti*, and the nature of the liberated state. Therefore, Caitanya's affirmation of *viśeṣa* provides a meaningful basis to begin acknowledging a doctrinal affiliation between the Mādhva and Gauḍīya traditions.

Endnotes

1. This is seen most prominently in the works of Baladeva Vidyābhūṣana. A more recent work in Hindi, *Kumata Kālānala* (Delhi: Siddhanta Saraswati Prakashan, 2016)

by Haripriya dāsa argues extensively for a historical and theological affiliation. Dr. Demian Martins, in the introductions to several of his works, also provides useful data supporting a link.

2. Martins provides the relevant information in the introductions to his translations of (1) Baladeva Vidyabhūṣaṇa's first *Vedānta-sūtra* commentary, the *Brahma-sūtra-kārikā-bhāṣyam* (Vrindavan: Jiva Institute, 2017), and (2) Viśvanātha Cakravartī's *Gaura-gaṇa-svarūpa-tattva-candrikā* (Vrindavan: Jiva Institute, 2015) including the following: Śyāmacaraṇa Śarma, head priest at the Gopinātha temple in Jaipur (from 1697 to 1730 CE), wrote a letter to the Sawai Jai Singh II about the independence of the Gauḍīya *sampradāya* having had its origins with the Lord Himself. Ānandī, a commentator on Prabhodhānanda Sarasvatī's *Caitanya-candrāmṛta*, also emphasized this independence in his commentary dated 1723 CE.

Stuart Elkman's *Jiva Gosvamin's Tattvasandarbha: A Study on the Philosophical and Sectarian Development of the Gaudiya Vaisnava Movement* (Delhi: Motilal Banarsidass Publishers, 1986) notes that later, Rādhāmohana dāsa (c. 1740 CE), a leading pandit at Śāntipur, Bengal, and a descendant of Advaita Ācārya in the Advaita-parivāra, wrote a commentary on *Tattva sandarbha* countering the pro-Madhva orientation of Baladeva's existing commentary. More recently, scholars such as S. K. De, B. B. Majumdar, Rādhāgovinda Nāth, and Sundarānanda Vidyāvinoda, have been dismissive of a connection with the Madhva *sampradāya*, but they are well countered within the tradition itself.

3. Kapoor, O. B. L., *The Philosophy and Religion of* Śrī *Caitanya* (Delhi: Munshiram Manoharlal, 1976), 37-52, 171. See also on p. 171 regarding Baladeva: "[he] does not represent the true spirit of the philosophy of Śrī Caitanya and, in certain respects, his views are influenced by Madhvācārya."

4. Okita, Kiyokazu. "The Theology of the Caitanya Sampradāya: Six Distinctive Features," *Journal of Vaishnava Studies* (29:2, Spring 2021), 5-24.

5. *iyanta eva vaiṣṇavā dṛṣṭās te 'pi nārāyaṇopāsakā eva | apare tattvavādinas te tathāvidhā eva | niravadyaṁ na bhavati teṣāṁ matam | ... kintu bhaṭṭācārya rāmānanda-matam eva me rucitam* (chapter 8), translation reproduced from Perun, Kostiantyn. "The Gauḍīya Tradition as a Distinct Sampradāya," *Journal of Vaishnava Studies* (29:2, Spring 2021), 25-56.

6. Valpey, Kenneth R. "Circling in On the Subject: Discourses of Ultimacy in Caitanya Vaiṣṇavism" in *Caitanya Vaiṣṇava Philosophy: Tradition, Reason and Devotion*, ed., Ravi M. Gupta (New York: Routledge, 2016), 11.

7. De, Sushil Kumar. *Early History of the Vaisnava Faith and Movement in Bengal* (Calcutta: General Printers and Publishers Ltd, 1942), 16-17, fn. 3.

8. *ibid.*, 11.

9. Okita, Kiyokazu, *Hindu Theology in Early Modern South Asia: The Rise of Devotionalism and the Politics of Genealogy* (Oxford, UK: Oxford University Press, 2014), 55.

10. Perun, *op. cit.*, 34.

11. All verses quoted from the *Caitanya-caritāmṛta* in this essay are numbered according to Prabhupāda's edition.

12. This version is from Prabhupāda's edition.

13. Sarkar, Jadunath. *Chaitanya's Life and Teachings: from his contemporary Bengali biography the Chaitanya-charitamrita*, 2nd edition, revised and enlarged, with topographical notes. (Calcutta: M. C. Sarkar & Sons, and London: Luzac & Co., 1922), 87. Other translations of the statement are: "The only qualification that I see in your *sampradāya* is that you accept the form of the Lord as truth" (Prabhupāda, *op. cit.*, 62); "In all, I see one quality in your *sampradāya*: having considered the *vigraha* as true, you have established it as Īśvara" See Dimock, Edward C., ed., Tony K. Stewart, *Caitanya Caritāmṛta of Kṛṣṇadāsa Kavirāja: A Translation and Commentary* (Cambridge, MA:, Department of Sanskrit and Indian Studies, Harvard University, 1999), 478; and "Now, I see one good quality in your *sampradāya*: accepting that God's form is real, you maintain that with certainty." (Perun, *op. cit.*, 37)

14. The Śrī Gauḍīya Vedānta Samiti edition of *Caitanya caritāmṛta* was published in Navadvīpa in 2004. Radha Govinda Nath's edition of *Caitanya caritāmṛta* is published by Sanskrit Book Depot in Kolkata in 2015.

15. Dimock, *op. cit.*, 478, fn. 250.

16. Dāsa, *op. cit.*, division 2, chapter 17.

17. *Caitanya caritāmṛta* 3.7.72.

18. Valpey, *op. cit.*, 11.

19. Perun, *op. cit.*, 37.

20. *Caitanya-caritāmṛta* 2.20.124.

21. *Caitanya-caritāmṛta* 2.9.255.

22. Prabhupāda, *op. cit.*, 63.

23. Perun, *op. cit.*, 37.

24. *bhedahīnetva-paryāśabdāntara-niyāmakaḥ viśeṣo nāma kathitaḥ so›sti vastuṣvasheṣataḥ* (Madhva's *Anu-vyākhyāna* 1.1.1). Sharma, B. N. K. *Philosophy of Madhvacarya* (New Delhi: Motilal Banarsidass, 1986), 87.

25. Sharma, *op. cit.*, 87.

26. In fact, the Mādhvācārya doctrine of *viśeṣa* should not be confused with the Gauḍīya doctrine of Acintya-bhedābheda ("Inconceivable and simultaneous oneness and difference"). This is because the latter doctrine chiefly refers to the relationship of the Lord and his potency, whereas the former focuses more on the internal characteristic of oneness in relation to a given individual or substance, i.e., all parts of God's form are equal to any other part of his form. *Viśeṣa* should also not be confused with either (1) the same term used by other schools such as Nyāya-Vaiśeṣika, nor (2) the concept of *samavāya* (sometimes translated as "inherence") because the latter involves at least *two* distinct entities—a substance and its qualities, whereas with *viśeṣa*, the substance and its qualities are all identical with each other as a single entity.

27. *guṇakriyādayo viṣṇoḥ svarūpaṁ nānyadiśyate | ato mitho'api bhedo na teṣāṁ kaścit kadācana | svarūpe'api viśeṣo 'asti svarūpatvavadeva tu | bhedābhāve'api tenaiva vyavahāraśca sarvataḥ || iti paramopaniṣadi*

The *Paramopaniṣad* states: "The attributes, activities, etc. of Viṣṇu constitute his very nature. They are not different from him. There is no mutual difference whatsoever among them (or between them and the essential nature). In the nature itself, there is *viśeṣa* as there is substantiality in the substance. Though there is no difference, by virtue of *viśeṣa*, the conventional distinction within language is possible." (This translation is my adaptation from those of K.T. Pandurangi [*Viṣṇu-tattva-vinirṇaya*, Dvaita Vedanta Studies and Research Foundation, Bangalore, 1991] and S.S. Raghavachar [Bangalore, third edition of his English translation as reproduced at https://sites.google.com/site/harshalarajesh/vishnutatvanirnaya 1959])

abhinnatvamabhedaśca yathā bhedavivarjitam | vyavahāryaṁ prithak ca syādevaṁ sarve guṇā hareḥ | abhedābhinnayoḥ bhedo yadi vā bhedabhinnayoḥ | anavasthitireva syāt na viśeṣaṇatā matiḥ | mūlasambandhamajñātvā tasmādekamanantadhā | vyavahāryaṁ viśeṣeṇa dustarkabalato hareḥ | viśeṣo'api svarūpaṁ sa svanirvāhakatāsya cha" || -iti brahmatarke

The *Brahma-tarka* states: "Just as being non-different and non-difference are not different, but still can be treated as different in language, even so are all the qualities of Hari. If difference were to be postulated between the non-different and non-difference and between the different and difference, there results infinite regress. The quality cannot be apprehended as adjectival to an entity, if the fundamental relation between the entity and its quality is not apprehended before. Therefore the single substantive essence lends itself to be spoken of as if it were a manifold consisting of substance, quality, etc., through the principle of Viśeṣa. All this is made possible by the power of Viṣṇu which transcends human reason. Viśeṣa itself is the substantive essence and also lends itself to be spoken of as if it were different therefrom. It functions with reference to itself as it does with reference to rest of the features of the substance." (Translation by S. S. Raghavachar op. cit.)

28. *avayavy-avayavānāṁ ca guṇānāṁ guṇinas tathā śakti-śaktimatoś caiva kriyāyās tadvatas tathā svarūpāṁśāṁśinoś caiva nityābhedo janārdane jīva-svarūpeṣu tathā tathaiva prakṛtāv api cid-rūpāyām ato'naṁśā aguṇā akriyā iti hīnā avayavaiś ceti kathyante te hy abhedataḥ pṛthag-guṇādy-abhāvāc ca nityatvād ubhayor api viṣṇor acintya-śakteś ca sarvaṁ sambhavati dhruvam kriyāder api nityatvaṁ vyakty-avyakti-viśeṣaṇam bhāvābhāva-viśeṣeṇa vyavahāraś ca tādṛśaḥ viśeṣasya viśiṣṭasyāpy abhedas tadvad eva tu sarvaṁ cācintya-śaktitvād yujyate parameśvare/ tac-chaktyaiva tu jīveṣu cid-rūpaprakṛtāv api/ bhedābhedau tad anyatra hy ubhayor api darśanāt kārya-kāraṇayoś cāpi nimittaṁ kāraṇaṁ vinā.*

29. Translation reproduced from Perun, *op. cit.*, 27.

30. *ekamevādvitīyaṁ* (*Chandogya Upaniṣad* 6.2.1).

31. *neha nānāsti kiñcana* (*Katha Upaniṣad* 2.1.11).

32. Madhva's *Gītā-tātparya* 11.1-15.

33. Sharma, *op. cit.*, 99-100.

34. Sharma, *op. cit.*, 82.

35. Sharma, *op. cit.*, 92.

36. "The Lord is both knowledge itself and qualified with knowledge, like a snake

and its coils because scriptures say the Lord is both. (*Brahma-sūtra* 3.2.28) We explain this *sūtra* according to what Madhva says. ... Brahman is both knowledge and knowing, bliss and blissful. The word *tu* in the *sūtra* indicates that *śruti* is the proof." See Swami, Bhanu (tr.), *Bhagavat Sandarbha with Sarva-samvadini by Jīva Gosvāmī* (Chennai: Sri Vaikunta Enterprises), 2013, 344.

37. *Śrīmad Bhagavadgītā* (Navadvīpa: Śrī Sārasvata-Gauḍīyāsana Miṣan Pratiṣtānataḥ, 1999), 3.

38. *aṅgāni yasya sakalendriya-vṛtti-manti paśyanti pānti kalayanti ciraṁ jaganti ānanda-cinmaya-sad-ujjvala-vigrahasya govindam ādi-puruṣaṁ tam ahaṁ bhajāmi* (5.32) Translation from Bhaktisiddhānta Sarasvatī Goswami, *Brahma-saṁhitā* (Los Angeles: Bhaktivedanta Book Trust, 1972).

39. S. M. S. Chari, in *Fundamentals of Viśiṣṭādvaita Vedānta: A Study based on Vedānta Deśika's Tattva-muktā-Kalāpa* (New Delhi: Motilal Banarsidass, 2004), writes (emphasis added): "The bodily form assumed by Īśvara in His eternal abode is *nitya*. It is constituted of pure *sāttvika* stuff known as *śuddha-sattva*." (232) "It is also described as that which possess the quality of *sattva* being at the same time self-luminous in character. According to the above definitions, the *śuddha-sattva* has two important features. First, it is *ajaḍa*, or non-material in the same way as Īśvara, *jīva* and *jñāna* are. *Ajaḍa* implies it is spiritual in character and like *jñāna* it is self-luminous (*svayam-prakāśa*). The second important feature is that *śuddha-sattva* is *acetana* like *dharma-bhuta-jñāna*. That is, unlike self it cannot know but manifests itself always for others (*parāk* or *parasmā eva bhāsamāna*). In this respect, it is different from Īśvara and *jīva* which are self-revealed." (340-341) "According to some Viśiṣṭādvaitins, *śuddha-sattva* is *jada* or material in character." (343)

40. Dimock, *op. cit.*, 478, fn. 250.

Prema-Vilāsa-Vivarta-Mūrti: Śrī Chaitanya as the Embodiment of the Highest Love

Steven J. Rosen

"Those who say 'I love you' know nothing about *prema*, for in *prema* there is no other." – Swami B.V. Tripurari[1]

Introduction

The primacy of love is appreciated by many, both as a concept and as a way of life. Most people, in fact, would say that it is love, first and foremost, that gives life meaning. This same truth is fundamental to the world's major world religions, regardless of the particular tradition. For example, the Bible says, "Beloved, let us love one another, for love is from God, and whoever loves has been born of God and knows God. Anyone who does not love does not know God, because God is love." (See 1 John 4:7-8) Jesus goes further, quoting the tradition of Leviticus: "You must love the Lord your God with all your heart, all your soul, and all your mind.' This is the first and greatest commandment. A second is equally important: 'Love your neighbor as you love yourself.'" (See Matthew 22:37-39)

Yet what, exactly, is meant by love?[2] Religious traditions acknowledge that love exists with both a lowercase "l" and a capital "L," referring to our relationships with man and God, respectively. And both are important, the Vaishnava sages tell us, even if love of God is considered particularly indispensable, in the sense that it is life's ultimate goal. A traditional analogy might serve to clarify: God is like the root of the tree of life, while all other living beings are compared to twigs and branches. If we water any of the tree's appendages separately, the tree will quickly die, but if we water her roots, perhaps spraying the twigs and branches as well, life-giving sustenance is enjoyed by all.

Regarding love of both man and God, there is also a second category of lower and upper: One can love individual beings with selfish motivation, merely trying to satisfy personal urges, or one can love more fully, selflessly, more in tune with the beloved's desires than one's own, though such love is said to be rare. Similarly, in terms of love of God, one can love God minimally, with one's own wants and desires taking a prominent role, or one can love "with heart, mind, and soul," considering God before oneself.

Gauḍīya Vaishnavism teaches adherents how to love in this more holistic way, both in interpersonal relationships and in terms of loving the Supreme. Indeed, it teaches how to be a *sāragrāhin*, that is, one who reaches for the essence, looking into the heart of love, as opposed to a *bhāravāhin*, wherein one settles for superficials, allowing surface affections to predominate.

All of this may serve as background to the kind of love witnessed in the person and teachings of Śrī Chaitanya Mahāprabhu (1486–1534), seen by his followers as Krishna himself in the mood of his female counterpart, Rādhā. Chaitanya promulgated a love that is "unmotivated and uninterrupted," and thus completely pure. (See *Śrīmad-Bhāgavatam* 1.2.6-7) Gauḍīya tradition teaches that he brought to this world an *ultimate* form of love (*prema*) illuminated as a detailed science (*tattva*), with methodical approach and procedure (*sādhana*), and concrete, analytical ways of gauging progress and accomplishment (*pragati-māpinī viśleṣaṇātmaka-praṇāli*).

Although Śrī Chaitanya left only eight devotional verses in writing, he instructed his chief followers to compile literature that would thoroughly explain the Vaishnava tradition, with special attention to the philosophy and theology of love. Śrī Rūpa Gosvāmī's *Bhakti-rasāmṛta-sindhu* and its appended text *Ujjvala-nīlamaṇi*, for example, stand supreme in this realm of devotional writing, detailing specifics of divine love as never before. The *Bhakti-rasāmṛta-sindhu* (1.3.1) compares love of God to the rays of the sun, whose warmth softens the devotee's heart without limit. Such a devotional heart, the tradition teaches, lies far beyond the best that this world has to offer. Indeed, it is a transcendental phenomenon, understood only by those who receive Krishna's grace.

In Śrī Rūpa's work, he articulates both a vocabulary and method for understanding divine love in all its forms. For example, he outlines *bhakti-rasa* theory, through which his readers can explore the various kinds of relationships one may have with God (*mukhya-bhakti-rasa-nirūpaṇa*).[3] Such relationships manifest in either neutrality (*śānta-rasa*); the mood of a loving servant (*dāsya-*

rasa); fraternity (*sakhya-rasa*); parenthood or a similar nurturing love (*vātsalya-rasa*); and, finally, conjugal affection (*mādhurya-rasa*), according to one's interaction with Krishna in the spiritual realm.[4] It is *mādhurya*, the last and highest form of love, that concerns us here, with its numerous levels of intimacy leading to a stage called *prema-vilāsa-vivarta*, which we will define below.

It should be noted, too, that *mādhurya* accommodates the qualities of all the rest. To clarify, *Caitanya-caritāmṛta* (Madhya 8.86) tells us: "As the qualities increase, so the taste also increases in each and every relationship. Therefore, the qualities found in *śānta-rasa, dāsya-rasa, sakhya-rasa* and *vātsalya-rasa* are all manifested in conjugal love (*mādhurya-rasa*)." In the words of Tony K. Stewart: "While *dāsya* may include elements of *śānta, sakhya* will embrace both, and *vātsalya* all four. Only *śṛṅgāra* [*mādhurya*] can range through the full permutation of forms, for lovers variously experience the feelings of friendship, of being a parent or a child, of being a servant, and even being overawed by the mate."[5] In fact, a brief look at the lexicon found in Rūpa Gosvāmī's *Ujjvala-nīlamaṇi* (chapters 14 and 15) should lay bare the depth and profundity of Śrī Chaitanya's approach to love of God. It will show how such love develops in the heart of the spiritual adept—particularly in the hearts of Rādhā and the *gopīs*, its ultimate exemplars.

Although exploring the minutiae of this love may seem a circuitous way of discussing the central theme of our essay—*prema-vilāsa-vivarta*, particularly in relation to Śrī Chaitanya—it will later be seen that perusing this terminology can heighten one's understanding and appreciation of this love as markedly distinct from love in the material sphere. For this reason, among others, Gauḍīya *ācāryas* enriched their literature with these elaborate details to facilitate deeper entry into the topic at hand.

Part I: Divine Love in the Gauḍīya Tradition

We begin with the Sanskrit *rati*, which means "attraction" or "pleasure," but which culminates in the concept of the purest love. "When *rati* is firm, it becomes *prema*," says Śrī Rūpa in his *Ujjvala-nīlamaṇi* (UN). "This then morphs into *sneha*, followed by *māna, praṇaya, rāga, anurāga*, and *mahābhāva*." (UN 14.59)

He defines these terms at length.

In summary, *sneha* is fully developed *prema*, when love is at its peak—it is a level of love that fully illuminates its central object of adoration, melting the hearts of both lover and beloved. (UN 14.79)

But this is just the beginning. Recognizing the intricacies of love—including the apparent reverses that ultimately deepen our emotional response—the tradition tells us that *māna*, or righteous indignation, comes next. When overcome by feelings of *māna*, one may exhibit a form of non-cooperation (*vāmyam*), even feigning disinterest, just to get the beloved's attention; by doing this, one increases the thrill of the exchange. (UN 14.96)

Through these methods, one gradually achieves *praṇaya*, the deepest of intimate feelings, unattainable through the kind of mutual respect and polite consideration one finds in more formal relationships. *Praṇaya* engenders a type of closeness known only by the most intimate of lovers, even if, externally, they might seem as if they are taking each other for granted. In fact, they simply feel that they are one and the same person, i.e., closer than humanly possible, and thus can take unspeakable liberties with each other. (UN 14.108)[6] As we will see, this has a certain resonance with the *prema-vilāsa-vivarta* concept, to be explained in due course.[7]

Praṇaya gives birth to *rāga*, the level of love where any tinge of discontent is eclipsed by inner happiness, creating a deep level of passion and leading to union. (UN 14.126) One becomes intensely determined or even "greedy" (*lobha*) to achieve the beloved, with a deep and insurmountable hankering for consummation. Such intensity leads to a type of ingenuity, in which one conceives ever-fresh ways of pleasing their beloved; at this point, one has reached *anurāga*. (UN 14.146) While in this state, one has an intense desire to be controlled by their lover, fearing their absence even while in their presence (*prema-vaicittya*); and, sometimes, the reverse is true: one sees them as present even during separation. (UN 14.149). Here too one finds intimations of *prema-vilāsa-vivarta*, even if one is still far away from that highest level.

As our mood deepens, we approach the dawn of the highest love, described as *bhāva* and *mahābhāva*. To begin, *bhāva* is achieved when *anurāga* reaches its most mature state, which is difficult for the body to contain. That is, one is forced to exhibit *sāttvika-bhāvas*, or uncontrollable, overt bodily symptoms of love, such as profuse weeping or cold shivers. (UN 14.154)[8]

Mahābhāva, which comes next, is described as being the essence of love's nectar, totally absorbing the mind and soul, and those who are privy to it are unable to focus on anything else. In its higher stages, *prema-vilāsa-vivarta* begins to manifest. Indeed, *mahābhāva* appears in two forms: *rūḍha* and *adhirūḍha* (UN 14.157-158), and the distinction should be understood.

Briefly, *rūḍha mahābhāva* can be called love's highpoint, which is free from any sense of awe and reverence and expectation of return. One simply wants to please the beloved. One's love becomes like a blazing, uncontrollable fire. If one finds that their desired object of affection is gone for even a zeptosecond, they become mad with the mood of separation. For example, the *gopīs* bemoaned the nature of the eye—which blinks—for this necessitates losing sight of Krishna, if even for a brief moment.[9]

As for *adhirūḍha mahābhāva*, it may be understood as an amplified version of *rūḍha-bhāva*, and it is only found in the hearts of the *gopīs*. (UN 14.170) Here there is inconceivable and simultaneous happiness and suffering caused by both union and separation, the merger of which is said to cause incomparable joy—with separation enhancing eventual union. (see UN 14.171, along with commentary of Viśvanātha Cakravartī) Indeed, this level of love is characterized by the feeling that each moment of being separated from the beloved is like an eternity, and each moment in his or her presence is conversely far too swift or short.

Adhirūḍha mahābhāva exists in two varieties: *modana* and *mādana*. (UN 14.172) Madness, indescribable bliss, and emotional trembling are the chief characteristics of both, catapulting one into the highest state of divine intoxication. (UN 14.173, with the commentary of Jīva Gosvāmī) The *modana* variety appears only among Rādhā's group of *gopīs*, as opposed to the other groups who express their love for Krishna in a more mild way. *Modana* is the ultimate expression of *hlādinī-śakti*, Krishna's internal energy. (UN 14.176) But it goes on from there.

Modana transforms into *mohana*, a yet higher stage, wherein one experiences intense moods of separation, intolerable for the soul. (UN 14.179) In such a state, Krishna's happiness becomes one's foremost concern, and to this end, his lover is willing to accept untold suffering for the sake of the Lord's pleasure. For such a *gopī*, *divyonmāda*, or divine madness, is never far away, often engulfing both lover and beloved in a river of ecstasy. (UN 14.181-183) Still greater is *mādana-bhāva*, also referred to as *mādanākhya-mahābhāva*. This is an experience that occurs at the time of perfect union, where love in separation finds its ultimate repose. Indeed, this highly esoteric dimension of love is associated only with Śrī Rādhā, who loves Krishna like no other.[10] It is from these higher platforms that we gain our first true glimpse of *prema-vilāsa-vivarta*.

The Vraja *gopīs*, being portions of Śrī Rādhā, are therefore portions of *mahābhāva*. Nevertheless, because they lack the essential characteristic called *mādana*, a quality found only in Rādhikā, they are never identified with *mahābhāva* in its fullness. It is Rādhā, and she alone, who is known as Mahābhāva-svarūpiṇī—the personification of the highest love. Indeed, rivers, streams, and ponds are bodies of water. Yet they are distinct from the ocean, whose magnitude can effortlessly accommodate not only these tributary rivulets, but so much more. This analogy attempts to shed light on the *gopīs' mahābhāva* in relation to Rādhā's.

With these love-specific categories to inform our understanding, we may proceed to explore the subject at hand, which is exceedingly esoteric. To my knowledge, the phrase "*prema-vilāsa-vivarta*" is only mentioned in the *Caitanya-caritāmṛta*, at least as far as premodern Gauḍīya texts go, and that only in a single verse (Madhya 8.192). This is saying quite a bit, since Rūpa Gosvāmī, Jīva Gosvāmī, and others provide an incalculably rich literature on the various levels of mystical love, as summarized above.[11]

As a side note, it may be mentioned that there are several 17th-century Gauḍīya Vaishnava classics, roughly contemporaneous with the *Caitanya-caritāmṛta*, that have names such as the *Prema-vilāsa* (Nityānanda Dāsa) *Prema-vivarta* (Jagadānanda Paṇḍita), and *Vilāsa-vivarta* (Akiñcana Dāsa).[12] These texts, profound though they are, tend to circumvent the full phrase "*prema-vilāsa-vivarta*," both in book title and in terms of the subjects explored in their pages. But *prema-vilāsa-vivarta*, as a specific book, is conspicuous by its absence. The one reference we have to a volume with all three words in the title is mentioned by Śrīla A. C. Bhaktivedanta Swami Prabhupāda (*Caitanya-caritāmṛta* 2.8.193, purport), and ascribed to Rāmānanda Rāya himself, but this might merely refer to the brief verse that Rāmānanda sings in the Madhya-līlā, soon to be discussed. That said, an entire book by that name, at least today, seems no longer extant.

Part II: My Introduction to the Subject

In 1984, while I was in India, noted Gauḍīya Vaishnava scholar O. B. L. Kapoor (1909–2001) expressed a desire to meet with me. He had become aware of a soon-to-be-published book that I was writing on the life and times of Śrī Chaitanya, and he wanted to advise me in a specific way. I was surprised, though, when I discovered exactly what he wanted to say: he asked me to include in my book a section on *prema-vilāsa-vivarta*. Although I was of course familiar with the *Caitanya-caritāmṛta* and the tradition surrounding it, the topic he raised was one I knew nothing about.

Then he explained. *Prema-vilāsa-vivarta*, he told me, was the highest stage of divine love, and its inner dimensions were tasted by Mahāprabhu himself. Indeed, Kapoor was emphatic that *prema-vilāsa-vivarta* comprised the summit of Mahāprabhu's blissful experience of divine love. How could I not be intrigued? And as he spoke, my fascination increased more and more.

Here's how he introduced the subject: "In the *Caitanya-caritāmṛta*, Rāmānanda Rāya responds to Śrī Chaitanya's request: 'Recite a verse from the revealed scriptures to elucidate the ultimate goal of life.' Rāma Rāya began by quoting a text in support of Varnāśrama-dharma, but Mahāprabhu asked him to go further. Accordingly, he moved on, quoting verses that espoused the virtues of karma; the rejection of karma; knowledge mixed with devotion (*bhakti*); *bhakti* that was not diluted by knowledge; *prema-bhakti*; and *Rādhā-prema*. In this section of the *Caitanya-caritāmṛta*, called 'Rāmānanda Samvāda,' we also find profound details about Krishna-tattva, Rādhā-tattva, Rādhā-Krishna-prema-tattva, and finally *prema-vilāsa-vivarta*." And Kapoor concluded that there is nothing beyond *prema-vilāsa-vivarta. This, he said, is the last word in love of God.*

Dr. Kapoor's conclusion that *prema-vilāsa-vivarta* is the highest level of love is confirmed by scholarly stalwarts in the tradition.[13] The first and most significant evidence, of course, is in the *Caitanya-caritāmṛta* itself (2.8.196), where Mahāprabhu says, "This is the topmost limit, or the ultimate goal of human life (*prabhu kahe—'sādhya-vastura avadhi' ei haya*).

The build-up to this is also fascinating: In 2.8.192, Rāmānanda suggests that the subject is so esoteric that Mahāprabhu may not want to hear it. And, sure enough, in the next verse, Chaitanya physically covers Rāmānanda's mouth (*mukha ācchādila*), stopping him from uttering more than he already has. The tradition avers that the reasoning for this physical action is twofold, with one exoteric explanation and the other esoteric: (1) *prema-vilāsa-vivarta* is a highly confidential subject—the pinnacle of divine love—and the tradition forbids non-devotees and neophytes from prematurely availing themselves of such advanced topics, lest they misunderstand it. Covering Rāma Rāya's mouth, therefore, is almost a symbolic gesture, meant to remind those who have not qualified themselves that they should instead focus on more rudimentary subjects; and, on a more confidential level, (2) the truth of *prema-vilāsa-vivarta* hints at Mahāprabhu's distinct *avatāra*—he is Rādhā and Krishna combined—and, though we will define it more thoroughly below, *prema-vilāsa-vivarta* basically refers to the paradoxical oneness that the Divine Couple experience due to their profound love. Mahāprabhu wanted to keep his identity as

Rādhā and Krishna a secret (for his mission was to experience the *bhāva* of a devotee, self-consciously underplaying his manifestation as God). To be sure, the revelation of Rādhā and Krishna's oneness, as espoused in the doctrine of *prema-vilāsa-vivarta,* would point in the direction of Mahāprabhu's purposely undisclosed identity; he was thus naturally resistant to its being articulated.[14] Nonetheless, Rāmānanda sang the truth of *prema-vilāsa-vivarta* for posterity, as preserved in the *Caitanya-caritāmṛta,* and Chaitanya eventually revealed himself as the combined form of Rādhā and Krishna, specifically to Rāmānanda.

"How could I write about this?" I asked Dr. Kapoor. "The subject is light-years beyond my pay grade."

Beaming with compassion, he laughed as he assured me that I would be guided by Krishna. But then his face turned grave, and he added that I should thoroughly read the texts passed down in the tradition. Moreover, he emphasized that I should also make good use of the *ācāryas'* writing. They have analyzed the subject in great depth, he continued, and expressed its complexities in a way that makes this otherwise abstruse knowledge completely accessible. He went further, advising me to consult peers and experts, both devotees and scholars, whose realization and command of the subject would surely help me to write about it in a lucid way.[15]

Over the years, I followed those instructions as best I could, studying the *Caitanya-caritāmṛta* and related texts by Gauḍīya *ācāryas,* tracking down obscure literature on the subject, and consulting with experts. Apropos of this, I sincerely hope that what I write here contains some measure of accuracy, capturing both the content and spirit of the subject under discussion.

All of this said, it must be remembered that this level of divine love is extremely nuanced, making its full comprehension somewhat evasive. In Viśvanātha Cakravartī's *Śrī Prema-sampuṭa* (51), Rādhikā herself tells us that people who talk about *prema,* or intellectualize about it, will likely miss the point. And in Bhaktivinoda Ṭhākura's *Jaiva Dharma,* toward the end of Chapter Two, we again read that words themselves are insufficient when it comes to *prema.* Rather, one must have the *adhikāra* (qualification) to understand it, and this comes from practice (*sādhana*) and grace (*kṛpā*). Still, it must also be noted that we study it as part of that practice, and we read about it to attain that grace.

Part III: Prema-Vilāsa-Vivarta Defined

Before defining *prema-vilāsa-vivarta,* there is one other highly esoteric term that will prove useful to our study: *sva-saṁvedya-daśā*. *Sva* means "one's self," *samvedya* means, "capable of being realized," and *daśā* means "a state of consciousness." In our present context, it is a type of all-encompassing self-awareness that subsists within the highest reaches of love. When Rādhikā serves Śrī Krishna, for example, she is fully in this *sva-saṁvedya* state, i.e., aware of every facet of her loving service. Thus, she loses herself in serving Krishna, without ever focusing on her own desires—her only interest is in pleasing him. Because of this unique level of intensity, the Divine Couple begin to feel that their minds and bodies are one, to the point where they lose awareness of their individuality. Since love itself has captured their full attention, it effectively becomes yet another self-aware experience (*sva-saṁvedya daśā*), as if taking on a life of its own—and gaining complete control of the Divine Couple themselves.[16]

To be sure, the primary *gopīs* and even Krishna himself are not devoid of this *sva-saṁvedya-daśā*, though they experience it to different degrees and in different ways. That said, Rādhikā's sense of *sva-saṁvedya-daśā* is supreme, even if the foremost *gopīs* may approximate this level due to their being her direct expansions, and Śrī Krishna, God himself, also has a means of experiencing it: he appears as Śrī Chaitanya Mahāprabhu and tastes this highest level of *sva-samvedya-daśā*, usually reserved only for Rādhā (for he fully adopts her *bhāva*). We will address this more fully below, but for now, we turn to defining the phrase at the heart of this essay.

In its most simple expression, *prema-vilāsa* means "playful, divine pastimes that are generated by love," and *vivarta*, which is a bit more complicated, refers to "changing from one state to another, modification, alteration, transformation, altered form or condition" and even "mistaking one thing for something else"[17]—we will soon see how these cryptic meanings play into the pastimes of Rādhā and Krishna.

The term *prema-vilāsa-vivarta*—considering all that has been written about it—could more meaningfully be understood as follows: "the topmost evolution (*paripāka*) of Krishna's divine play (*vilāsa*), which arises from a form of spiritual love (*prema*) that is so intense, it causes 'identity inversion' (*viparīta*), a form of spiritual alchemy that leads to transformation (*vivarta*) or even a type of confusion (*bhrānti*), where lover and beloved are merged as one (*paraikya*)." How one arrives at this longer definition involves an in-depth study of *Caitanya-caritāmṛta* commentaries, along with the exegesis of Kavi Karṇapūra, Jīva Gosvāmī and Viśvanātha Cakravartī, in particular.

The latter two *ācāryas* tell us that *prema-vilāsa* means "loving pastimes," as is commonly understood.[18] But *vivarta*, they say, is the telling word, for in this context it includes a sense of *paripāka* (fully mature), *bhrama* or *bhrānti* (bewilderment), and *viparīta* (reversal), along with its usual sense of transformation. As we will see, this same terminology informs the explanation of modern-day Gauḍīya writers as well, who trace these definitions to the *ācāryas*, and depending on how one defines the word *vivarta*, a given instance of *prema-vilāsa-vivarta* will have specific meaning or a more general one.

To begin, then, let us look at the primary definition of the phrase in terms of the present context: in the full maturity of their love, Rādhā and Krishna cannot distinguish between themselves; their sense of individuality is effectively obliterated, for their love has made them one. From Rādhā's point of view, in particular, her love is so total that she sees the two of them as fundamentally nondifferent. In other words, there is a type of role reversal (*viparīta*), or, in the extreme, a complete merger of identities (*paraikya*), brought on by a transcendental form of confusion (*bhrānti*).[19] This is the essence of *prema-vilāsa-vivarta*. That is to say, there is a certain oneness that exists between the Divine Couple, and in the height of their supreme love, this truth becomes prominent, eclipsing the fact that they are two distinct entities.

The "oneness" of Rādhā and Krishna, as referenced in *prema-vilāsa-vivarta*, should be clearly understood: As Dr. Rādhāgovinda Nāth (1879–1970), the much lauded contemporary scholar of Gauḍīya Vaishnavism, reminds us, "Here the *bheda-rāhitya* ('absence of distinction') is not the *bheda-rāhitya* of *jñāna-mārga* practitioners, who are seeking the impersonal Brahman."[20] Rādhāgovinda Nāth goes on for some pages in his *Caitanya-caritāmṛta* commentary to explain that Rādhā and Krishna are forever two beings, who subsist in eternity in loving relationship. It is their minds and hearts, if you will, that meld into one, and this occurs only in the sense that their love is so complete that they can no longer see distinction, even if said distinction is prerequisite for that very same love. (This distinction between the oneness propounded by Advaitins and that found in the doctrine of *prema-vilāsa-vivarta* is so important that we will return to it throughout this essay, particularly in our conclusion.)

Rādhāgovinda Nāth further explains that "neither Rādhā nor Krishna are *nirviśeṣa-brahma* covered by *ajñāna*, as Māyāvādīs or followers of Śaṅkara would argue. Rather, they are *anāvṛta* ('non-covered') *saviśeṣa-brahma*. They are eternal, and their *vilāsa* is also eternal. Compelled by *prema's* supremely ripened state, their minds and hearts have achieved *ekātmatā*, 'one-soul-ness,' and because of this absorption and sense of oneness, they are deprived of proper awareness of '*ke ramaṇa, āre ke ramaṇī*—i.e., who is the lover, and who is the beloved.' Neither *ramaṇa* nor *ramaṇī* disappear; only the awareness or mental comprehension of who is who disappears. This is the fruit of the ultimate ripeness of love."[21] Rādhāgovinda Nāth continues:

> Śrī Śrī Rādhā-Krishna's bodies are separate, the minds within their bodies are also separate; only the moods of their minds become one. The *jñāna-mārga sādhakas*, or the Advaitins, desire no individual existence in their perfected state. They do not have any sense of experience, because in their perfection, there is no knower, nothing to be known, and no knowledge. All is one. However, in *prema-vilāsa-vivarta*, Śrī Śrī Rādhā-Krishna have individual existences, and they have an awareness or experience of being keen on the joy of *vilāsa*. Their efforts for *vilāsa* endure, as does the *vilāsa* itself.[22]

In fact, Rādhāgovinda Nāth takes great care to fully explain the mysteries of *prema-vilāsa-vivarta*, specifically in his gloss of Madhya 8, *payāra* 150 (which corresponds to text 192 in the Bhaktivedanta Book Trust edition), where he quotes both Jīva and Viśvanātha to good effect. This is found in the third volume (Madhya, Part 1) of his six-volume series. He also begins his massive commentary with a 450-page *Bhūmika*, an introductory volume, in which he further illuminates the subject.

His initial point is that *prema-vilāsa-vivarta* focuses on the highest stage of love, *adhirūḍha-mahābhāva*. He also notes that although other levels of *prema* may share some of the same characteristics as those found in *prema-vilāsa-vivarta*—and so, too, might mundane love—*prema-vilāsa-vivarta* stands countless miles above either of them. He reminds us that *prema-vilāsa-vivarta* is not the sort of *vilāsa* that is inspired by desires for one's own happiness; that sort of *vilāsa* is called *kāma-vilāsa*, he says, or the pastimes of material enjoyment. As he points out, the tradition draws a considerable distinction between the two, with spiritual *prema* as the ultimate goal of life.

After this, he explains that the word *vivarta* is highly mysterious (*rahasya-maya*) and filled with the utmost significance (*viśeṣa-gurutva-pūrṇa*). This is where he gives us Viśvanātha Cakravartī's gloss that the word means *viparīta*, i.e., "inverted" or "reversed," as stated above. So, too, does he refer to Jīva Gosvāmī's commentary on *Ujjavala-nīlamaṇi*, *Uddīpana-vibhāva-prakaraṇa*, verse 37, where we learn that the word *vivarta* is also understood to mean *paripākaḥ*, or "fully ripened," "completely evolved," or "uniquely transformed," also indicated above. And still again he informs us that the word *vivarta* can refer to *bhrama*, "perplexity," or *bhrānti*, "confusion," although, in this context, it refers only to a perplexity and confusion that is steeped in the topmost spiritual love. With these meanings as our starting point, Rādhāgovinda Nāth now directs us to the two statements of the Rāmānanda-samvāda, which is the main source for understanding *prema-vilāsa-vivarta* in the Chaitanya tradition.

At the height of his conversation with Mahāprabhu, Rāmānanda explains *prema-vilāsa-vivarta* with two examples: (1) a poem that he composed in the Bengali vernacular, using the voice of Rādhā (*Caitanya-caritāmṛta* 2.8.194); and (2) a Sanskrit verse originally penned by Rūpa Gosvāmī in his *Ujjvala-nīlamaṇi* 14.155. (*Caitanya-caritāmṛta* 2.8.195) Here are those two verses in full:

> "Alas, before We met there was an initial attachment between Us brought about by an exchange of glances. In this way attachment evolved. That attachment has gradually grown, and there is no limit to it. Now that attachment has become a natural sequence between Ourselves. It is not that it is due to Kṛṣṇa, the enjoyer, nor is it due to Me, for I am the enjoyed. It is not like that. This attachment was made possible by mutual meeting. This mutual exchange of attraction is known as *manobhava*, or Cupid. Kṛṣṇa's mind and My mind have merged together. Now, during this time of separation, it is very difficult to explain these loving affairs. My dear friend, though Kṛṣṇa might have forgotten all these things, you can understand and bring this message to Him. But during Our first meeting there was no messenger between Us, nor did I request anyone to see Him. Indeed, Cupid's five arrows were Our via media. Now, during this separation, that attraction has increased to another ecstatic state. My dear friend, please act as a messenger on My behalf, because if one is in love with a beautiful person, this is the consequence."[23]

And then:

> "O my Lord, You live in the forest of Govardhana Hill, and, like the king of elephants, You are expert in the art of conjugal love. O master of the universe, Your heart and Śrīmatī Rādhārāṇī's heart are just like shellac and are now melted in Your spiritual perspiration. Therefore one can no longer distinguish between You and Śrīmatī Rādhārāṇī. Now You have mixed Your newly invoked affection, which is like vermilion, with Your melted hearts, and for the benefit of the whole world You have painted both Your hearts red within this great palace of the universe."[24]

References to Cupid are common in Vaishnava literature, and it is often used as a catchword to indicate an assortment of love-inflected deities, according to context.[25] It is especially interesting in the above verse. In his commentary, Bhaktivinoda Ṭhākura suggests that during those moments that Rādhā and Krishna actually come together in union, the resultant attachment and depth of love might be compared to the work of Cupid. So, too, is this the case—if counterintuitively—during the period of separation, when Cupid becomes a messenger of an even higher order. Accordingly, Śrī Rādhikā addresses this messenger *as a friend*, indicating that she relishes separation as much as union, if in a different way. As Śrī Rūpa informs us elsewhere (*Padyāvali* 240), Rādhā's perspective on separation is as follows: "[In certain respects] I prefer separation to union, because in union I see Krishna only in one place, whereas in separation, I see him everywhere." In *prema-vilāsa-vivarta*, she has gone even further, becoming one with him.

The tradition refers to this oneness as "*paraikya*," a word that conveys total harmony or uniformity—fundamental unity.[26] Although I have explained this subject earlier (when discussing the difference between this kind of oneness and that promulgated by the Advaitins), it should be understood in the current context as well. In fact, this oneness is artfully elaborated upon in 2.8.195 by the shellac or wax (*lākṣa*) analogy, above. As stated in this verse, under the influence of *prema*, both Rādhā and Krishna's minds melt and mix (*miśiyā*), and have thus become indistinguishable. That is to say, they have attained the state of *nirdhūta-bheda-bhramam*—a sort of spiritual confusion wherein all sense of separateness is washed away. They are described as being like two pieces of wax that have melted and become one under intense heat (*tīvra-tāpa*). And yet they remain two individuals.

Commenting on these verses, Vaishnava scholar and guru, Gour Govinda Swami Mahārāja (1929–1996), shares his insights:

> This is *prema-vilāsa-vivarta*. There is no difference between *ramaṇa*, the enjoyer, and *ramaṇī* the enjoyed. *Ramaṇa* is Krishna. *Ramaṇī* is Rādhā. In *prema-vilāsa-vivarta* there is oneness. *Nā so ramaṇa, nā hāma ramaṇī*—"It is not that He is the enjoyer and I am the enjoyed." *Duṅhu-mana manobhava peṣala*—"His mind and My mind have became one." This is the last stage known as *mādanākhya-mahābhāva*. *Mādanākhya-mahābhāva* is Rādhārāṇī's attitude. There is no difference between the lover and the beloved. The minds of these two, Krishna and Rādhā, are crushed together. *Peṣala* means crushing. Then it is transformed into a form known as *praṇaya*. This is the

> explanation. *Mano dadhāno viśrambhaṁ praṇayaḥ procayate budhaiḥ.* That means, when *māna* becomes more condensed it becomes *praṇaya*, the stage of *viśrambha*. *Viśrambha* means a feeling of oneness between *kānta*, the lover, and the *kāntā*, the beloved. They are crushed together, "His mind and My mind became one." *Nā so ramaṇa, nā hāma ramaṇī duṅhu-mana manobhava peṣala jāni.* This is the activity of *hlādini-śakti*. There is a difference between *śakti*, the energy, and *śaktiman*, the energetic source. But in *praṇaya-vikṛtir*, there is oneness between the *āsvādika*, the enjoyer, and the *āsvādita*, the enjoyed. ... Rādhā and Lord Krishna are one, yet They have taken two forms to enjoy the mellows of pastimes.[27]

To make it clearer still, O. B. L. Kapoor offers the following analogy:

> It is, as Jīva Gosvāmī explains, like the union between fire and a piece of iron. A piece of iron, when put for a long time in fire, becomes red-hot like the fire. Every part of it is animated by fire and acquires the characteristics of fire. Still, iron remains iron and fire remains fire. Similarly, both Krishna and Rādhā retain their identity. They are so absorbed in each other's love and lost in each other's thoughts that there is hardly any room in their hearts for the thought of anything else.[28]

In summary, then, *prema-vilāsa-vivarta* in its highest form is understood as an inversion of sorts that is created by the most acute form of love. Along these lines, in Vaishnavism's most esoteric literature, particularly in the poetry of the Vrindavan Gosvāmīs, we see Rādhā and Krishna lose their sense of individuality and mistake one for the other. He thinks he is Rādhā, and she thinks she is Krishna, resulting in a sort of merging of the two, where their two hearts, again, melt into one. Ultimately, *prema-vilāsa-vivarta*, at least according to its primary definition, means "the culmination of loving pastimes in which the hero and heroine exchange roles," a phenomenon also known as *viparīta-kāma-krīḍā*.

Perhaps the best summation of the subject as a whole, at least in regard to the special oneness that Rādhā and Krishna feel in relation to each other, can be found in Viśvanātha Cakravartī's *Śrī Prema-sampuṭa*, although the phrase *prema-vilāsa-vivarta* does not appear in this text:

> *anyonya-citta-viduṣau nu parasparātma-*
> *nitya-sthiter iti nṛṣu prathitau yad āvām*
> *tac-caupacārikam aho dvitayatvam eva*
> *naikasya sambhavati karhicid ātmano nau* (107)

Śrī Rādhikā then spoke: "Common people say, 'Rādhā and Kṛṣṇa are eternally present in each others' hearts, and that is why They know each others' minds.' Factually, the real truth is this: We are one soul. It is not possible for one soul to become two.

ekātmanīha rasa-pūrṇatame 'tyagādhe
ekā susaṅgrathitam eva tanu-dvayaṁ nau
kasyiṁścid eka-sarasīva cakāsad eka-
nālottham abja-yugalaṁ khalu nīla-pītam (108)

"In a lake, two lotuses—one blue and one yellow—may bloom from a single stem. In the same way, Our two bodies, one blue and one yellow, are connected as one life. They are one supremely profound soul composed of topmost *rasa*. As bodies, We are separate, but by nature, We are one. Kṛṣṇa is by nature blissful (*ānanda*) and I by nature am joyful (*hlādinī*). Just as fire and its burning potency are one, there is no difference between the potency (*śakti*) and the possessor of the potency (*śaktimān*). We cannot be distinguished from each other when seen as a person and the person's potency, but for the sake of *rasa*, We manifest in separate forms as Rādhā and Kṛṣṇa. Without pastimes, We cannot relish each other; and without form, We cannot perform pastimes."

Part IV: The Black Tamāla Tree and the Switching of Clothes

A related phenomenon, inseparable from our subject, addresses how this transcendental merger might be seen externally, resulting in action that has resonance with *prema-vilasa-vivarta*. Indeed, some may even call it a second-tiered instance of *prema-vilasa-vivarta*. In other words, there are other forms of divine bewilderment that attest to *prema-vilāsa-vivarta* as well.

For example, when Rādhārāṇī sees a black *tamāla* tree, thinking it to be Krishna, and she embraces it with heart and soul—her spiritual delirium has reached a pitch that involves mistaken identity, even if she is not personally identifying with the tree. Such pastimes echo the truth of *prema-vilāsa-vivarta* and so, in this section, we will briefly explore them.

Given our essential definition—that *prema-vilāsa-vivarta* is a product of the topmost love (*adhirūḍha-mahābhāva*); that it manifests as a type of confusion (*bhrānti*); and that it includes a sense of mistaken identity (*viparīta*)—let us consider Rādhārāṇī misconstruing a black *tamāla* tree for Krishna and whether it has any relation to what we now know about the subject.

The story is told throughout the Purāṇas and Gosvāmī literature. We find a prominent version of it in Śrīla Viśvanātha Cakravartī Ṭhākura's *Śrī Krishna-Bhāvanāmṛta Mahākāvya.*[29] In this text, during the Divine Couple's evening pastimes, we meet Rādhā as she enters the magical forest of Vraja. There, she notes that everything she sees, hears, smells, and feels reminds her of Krishna, i.e., every sound is his flute, every scent is his fragrance, every tree his form, and so on. The text then focuses on a particular *tamāla* tree: Its blackish form gives her shivers, and she is not able to contain herself in its presence. She embraces the tree with a heart full of love. "Thus, Krishna became just like the *tamāla* tree and Rādhikā like the golden vine who embraced him."[30]

Another example of the *tamāla* tree "illusion" is found in Rūpa Gosvāmī's *Vidagdha-mādhava.* Although this distinct arboreal lookalike appears throughout the play, with numerous poetic comparisons between the tree and Krishna's form, it relates to our subject most effectively in Act Six, where Lalitā says in a matter-of-fact tone: "This girl sees a *tamāla* tree and thinks it is Krishna!"[31] Donna Wulff comments on the incident as a whole:

> The intense preoccupation of Rādhā and Kṛṣṇa with one another is indicated by another set of parallel passages with similar metaphysical overtones. So obsessed with Kṛṣṇa does Rādhā become that she sees him everywhere; when she mistakes a black *tamāla* tree for her dark lover, Viśakhā asks her how it is that the three worlds have become Kṛṣṇa for her. Kṛṣṇa poses the corresponding question for himself as he eagerly awaits Rādhā at their point of rendezvous: "Rādhā appears before me on every side; how is it that for me the three worlds have become Rādhā?" (V.18). Rūpa seems to have been especially taken with this mode of indicating Kṛṣṇa's infatuation, for on two additional occasions he has other characters make virtually the same observation about Kṛṣṇa's "delusion" (III.18; VI.23. 20-21). Moreover, it is not only Rādhā in her obsession with Kṛṣṇa who is explicitly termed "mad," but also Kṛṣṇa in his unbridled passion for her. At one point, as Kṛṣṇa is rushing headlong to meet her, Madhumaṅgala, steadying him, asserts that he has been "driven mad (*unmādita*) by an evil spell [uttered] by the wicked *gopīs*." (VI.14.3-4)."[32]

Acknowledging Śrī Rādhā's love-mad misapprehensions, Bhaktivinoda Ṭhākura singles out the black *tamāla* tree incident as a form of *prema-vilāsa-vivarta.* In his *Amṛta-pravāha-bhāṣya* to *Caitanya-caritāmṛta* (2.8.194), he writes: "In seeing the *tamāla* tree as Krishna, Rādhikā is subject to a type of *sambhoga* [union] in *vipralambha* [separation], particularly in the form of *vivarta-*

bhāvāpanna adhirūḍha-mahābhāva [i.e., *prema-vilāsa-vivarta*]."[33] Further drawing on Bhaktivinoda's insights, Śrīla A. C. Bhaktivedanta Swami Prabhupāda says it even more directly: "When Śrīmatī Rādhārāṇī was fully absorbed in love of Kṛṣṇa, She mistook a black *tamāla* tree for Kṛṣṇa and embraced it. Such a mistake is called *prema-vilāsa-vivarta*."[34] Thus, we have identified what might be considered a secondary tier of *prema-vilāsa-vivarta,* without *viparīta* in the sense of complete identity inversion or *paraikya* in the form of an identity merger between Rādhā and Krishna. Yet there is, in this instance, still a case of mistaken identity based on the topmost love. And one must always ask, since Krishna is ultimately everything: Is this indeed a case of mistaken identity, or is Rādhā merely seeing things as they truly are?

Another example—as ubiquitous as the black *tamāla* tree narrative—would be when Rādhikā mistakenly adorns herself with Krishna's yellow cloth, or he, her blue *sari*. This almost comical state of affairs points to the same kind of misidentification or confusion (*bhrānti*) we see in other examples of *prema-vilāsa-vivarta*, for it too takes place as a result of the highest love. We even see here a case of mistaken identity (*viparīta*), though it is not exactly a merging of hearts, at least not in the same way.

Indeed, this pastime might be regarded, again, as suggestive of *prema-vilāsa-vivarta*. As Shrivatsa Goswami, head priest and eminent scholar at Vrindavan's famous Radha-ramana temple, eloquently writes, "She wears his peacock feather, he dons her lovely, delicate crown; she sports his yellow garment, he wraps himself in her beautiful *sari*. How charming the very sight of it . . . The daughter of Vṛṣabhānu [Rādhā] turns [into] Nanda's son [Krishna], and Nanda's son, into Vṛṣabhānu's girl."[35]

These truths are conspicuous in the switching of clothes: On one occasion, the *gopīs*, seeing that Krishna is wearing Rādhikā's blue cloth and not his usual yellow *dhoti*—and not wanting his mother to find out that he and Rādhā had slept together—make excuses for him; they point out to Mother Yaśodā that on this day Krishna seems to have chosen Balarāma's clothes (for the latter, too, wears blue, like Rādhikā). In this way, they had hoped to deceive Mother Yaśodā, distracting her from the truth that her son had spent the evening with Rādhā.[36] This "unconscious" switching of clothes is indicative of an "identity switch," and is thus suggestive of *prema-vilāsa-vivarta*.

We see a similar scene, too, in Śrī Raghunātha Dāsa Gosvāmī's *Prārthanā* (from *Śrī Stavāvalī*), specifically in a song called "*Prātaḥ pīta-paṭe kucopari.*" Therein, he tells us that one day, in early morning, Jaṭilā-devī, Śrī Rādhā's mother-in-law, met Rādhā and her friend Lalitā on the road. Jaṭilā noticed that Rādhā was wearing a yellow garment on her upper chest, which was unusual, and that she seemed overly sleepy as well. Jaṭilā thus made innuendos that Rādhā had perhaps spent the night with Krishna. Although frightened that she had been found out, Rādhā externally assumed a confident pose, as Lalitā composed a network of believable lies to help her transcendental friend. When it was over, Rādhikā glorified Lalitā for her skillful help.

Or consider Krishnadāsa Kavirāja Gosvāmī's *Govinda-līlāmṛta* 1.79-80: "Krishna, seeing that Rādhārāṇī's restless eyes were accosted by fear, nervously donned her fine blue cloth, quickly arising from bed. Wearing each other's clothes, Rādhā and Krishna held each other's hands and emerged from the *kuñja*." We find much the same, and perhaps a summation of all that precedes this, in Jīva Gosvāmī's *Gopāla-campū* (*Pūrva* 15.9):

> *imau gaurī-śyāmau manasi viparīrtau bahir api*
> *sphurat tad tad vastrāv iti budha-janair niścitam idam*
> *sa ko 'py accha-premā vilasad ubhayoḥ sphūrtikatayā*
> *dadhan mūrttī-bhāva-pṛthag-apṛthag apy āvirudabhūt*

> These two, Rādhā and Krishna, are *gaura-varṇa* (gold complexion) and *śyāma-varṇa* (blue complexion), respectively. But in their minds, it is the opposite. In other words, Śrī Rādhikā's mind fully reflects Śrī Krishna, and so it is *śyāma-varṇa*, whereas Śrī Krishna's mind has likewise mirrored Śrī Rādhikā and is thus *gaura-varṇa*. Additionally, their minds are manifesting outwardly, too, which is why their garments are gold and blue. In other words, Śrī Krishna's *pītāmbara* is reflecting his own mind, which is *vibhāvita*, or overwhelmed, by Śrī Rādhā's *varṇa*. And Śrī Rādhikā's blue *sari* is providing a *sphūrti*, or glimpse, of her mind, as it is absorbed in Śrī Krishna's complexion. Wise persons have determined the nature of this matter accordingly. Because that indescribable, pristine *prema* manifests in two different forms to perform enchanting pastimes, it is understood that these forms are both different and nondifferent (*pṛthag-apṛthag*).

Part V: Śrī Chaitanya as Prema-Vilāsa-Vivarta-Mūrti

When those familiar with Gauḍīya Vaishnavism consider the words *gaura-varṇa*, as in the above verse, their minds naturally turn to Śrī Chaitanya Mahāprabhu, who is famously the same golden color as Śrī Rādhikā. Indeed, the truth of Śrī Chaitanya's person, identity, and reason for appearance is the very essence of *prema-vilāsa-vivarta*, for he is the ultimate manifestation of Rādhā and Krishna becoming one. As Krishnadāsa Kavirāja's *Caitanya-caritāmṛta* (Ādi 1.5) reminds us:

> *rādhā kṛṣṇa-praṇaya-vikṛtir hlādinī śaktir asmād*
> *ekātmānāv api bhuvi purā deha-bhedaṁ gatau tau*
> *caitanyākhyaṁ prakaṭam adhunā tad-dvayaṁ caikyam āptaṁ*
> *rādhā-bhāva-dyuti-suvalitaṁ naumi kṛṣṇa-svarūpam*
>
> "The loving exchanges between Rādhā and Krishna are completely spiritual, a product of the Lord's *hlādinī-śakti*. Indeed, although Rādhā and Krishna are one, they exist as separate entities. Now, in the form of Śrī Chaitanya, these two divine entities have again become one. I offer obeisance to him [Śrī Chaitanya], who manifests [in the world] with the sentiment and complexion of Śrī Rādhā, although he is Krishna himself."

The implicit message of this verse is that Rādhā and Krishna unify in the person of Śrī Chaitanya, and yet, inconceivably, they never lose their "two-ness." The verse begins by affirming their oneness (*ekātmānāv*), and then moves on to their obvious duality (*deha-bhedaṁ*)—and then returns to inevitable unity (*aikyam āptaṁ*) in the form of Śrī Chaitanya. And Chaitanya himself, as has been well recorded, spent his entire lifetime longing for Krishna, thus reaffirming a sense of duality yet again. Indeed, the cycle goes ever on, for as soon as one affirms one side (*bheda*), one must immediately acknowledge the other (*abheda*), a truth confirmed by Chaitanya and his followers in various ways.[37]

Moreover, the notion of *prema-vilāsa-vivarta* is indirectly mentioned in this verse: *Praṇaya* (love) is a synonym for *prema*, and *vikṛtiḥ* (transformation) is another way of saying *vivarta*. Accordingly, when the verse tells us that Rādhā and Krishna are in fact one, even if they exist as two separate entities—and that they unite once again in the form of Śrī Chaitanya—it is inadvertantly expressing the truth of *prema-vilāsa-vivarta*. Thus, according to this verse, Mahāprabhu is the ultimate manifestation or culmination of Rādhā and Krishna's union, and thus, extrapolating freely, he may be seen as the very "embodiment" of *prema-vilāsa-vivarta*, i.e., the Prema-Vilāsa-Vivarta-Mūrti, a phrase to which we will return in a few moments.

In the context of our present subject, the ontological position of Śrī Chaitanya, in which he partakes of the moods and intensity of Śrī Rādhā, must be clear. Along these lines, the Vaishnava poet-saint, Śrīla B. R. Śrīdhara Dev-

Goswāmī Mahārāja (1895–1988), famously referred to Chaitanya as a "golden volcano of divine love," making explicit Mahāprabhu's divine connection to Rādhā-bhāva:

> Diving deep into the reality of His own beauty and sweetness, Krishna stole the mood of Rādhāraṇī and, garbing Himself in Her brilliant luster, appeared as Śrī Chaitanya Mahāprabhu. . . . He was deeply absorbed in the mood of union and separation and shared His heart's inner feelings with His most confidential devotees. In the agony of separation from Krishna, volcanic eruptions of ecstasy flowed from His heart, and His teachings, known as *Śikṣāṣṭakam*, appeared from His lips like streams of golden lava. I fall at the feet of Śrī Chaitanya Mahāprabhu, the Golden Volcano of Divine Love.[38]

The overarching and complete correlation between Śrī Rādhā and Śrī Chaitanya is thus critical for understanding Mahāprabhu as the epitome of *prema-vilāsa-vivarta*. This is because the "misapprehension" or "illusion" that is so much a part of *prema-vilāsa-vivarta* must take place as a result of *adhirūḍha-mahābhāva*, and, at its peak, *mādanākhya-mahābhāva*, a level of love known only to Śrī Rādhā. As we will see, Mahāprabhu exhibits such misapprehension in abundance, and for the same reasons as Rādhā does.

The tradition takes great pains to show that Mahāprabhu experiences the depth of Rādhā's love, since he is said to be Krishna himself specifically incarnating to realize that purpose—to feel the love that his devotees feel for him, especially that of Śrī Rādha, the topmost devoteē.[39] And, as the tradition makes clear, he is successful in his purpose.

With that much as a backdrop, one can understand Śrī Chaitanya as the very form of *prema-vilāsa-vivarta*, i.e., the Prema-Vilāsa-Vivarta-Mūrti.

I initially discovered this phrase in an article by Vaishnava scholar Śrī Prem Prayojan Prabhu.[40] Of course, as I looked more carefully, I could see that numerous variations were to be found in most any thorough book on Śrī Chaitanya. Indeed, in the first volume of Rādhāgovinda Nāth's 450-page *Bhūmika*—the introductory volume for his commentary on the *Caitanya-caritāmṛta*—he writes, "For all these reasons, it has been said that Śrī Śrī Gaurasundara [Chaitanya] is the *mūrta-rūpa* (personified form) of *prema-vilāsa-vivarta*."[41] Or, as O. B. L. Kapoor articulates it, "Śrī Caitanya is the substantial or personalized form of this union."[42]

And why not? If we look into many of Śrī Chaitanya's later life narratives, we can identify at least certain elements of *prema-vilāsa-vivarta*, especially if we consider that his inner identity was more and more ensconced in Rādhā-bhāva—and the texts indeed tell us that it was. For example, the whole 14th chapter of *Caitanya-caritāmṛta*'s Antya-līlā, which culminates in Mahāprabhu running like a madman to "Govardhana," seems dependent on him being so focused on Krishna that he forgets himself, identifying instead with Rādhā, overtaken with her *adhiruḍha-mahābhāva*. Thus, he finds himself in a state of divine madness (*divyonmāda*) or bewilderment (*mohana-bhāva*), clearly reminiscent of Krishna's divine consort.

When Mahāprabhu finally sees Caṭaka-parvata, the sand dune he "mistakes" (*bhrānti, vivarta*) for Govardhana Hill, it acts as an *uddīpana* to stimulate his remembrance of the actual mountainous region of Krishna's pastimes, triggering his transition from external consciousness to a more internal or transcendent realm. Halfway through the transition, he sees Govardhana in his mind's eye while his outer senses still act out on the physical plane, resulting in incoherent behavior. While Krishnadāsa Kavirāja Gosvāmī does not term this *prema-vilāsa-vivarta*, it has enough of its pertinent elements to be seen as at least a pointer in that direction.

In fact, there are numerous examples in Chaitanya-līlā of a type of love-filled madness, wherein the Lord found it difficult to distinguish one thing from another, overtaken, as he was, by various cases of mistaken identity (*viparīta*). These cases are very much like the incident of Śrī Rādhā mistaking the black *tamāla* tree for Krishna, and so could indeed play a role in our understanding of *prema-vilāsa-vivarta*. Moreover, we see examples of this phenomenon engaging each of Mahāprabhu's five senses:

> Antya 17 – "Hearing": Śrī Chaitanya **heard** and followed the sound of Krishna's flute in the night (which no one else heard), as well as the tinkling of Rādhā and Krishna's foot ornaments. He also heard the sound of Krishna and the *gopīs* joking, with their laughter, until he arrived at the sound's source and found nothing more than a group of cows. He was later found in the shape of a turtle (*kūrmera ākāra*), and then that of a pumpkin (*kuṣmāṇḍa-phala*), next to the Jagannātha temple.

> Antya 14 – "Seeing": He **looked upon** the Deity of Jagannātha, but instead **saw** the beautiful humanlike figure of Krishna in Vrindavan. After his divine reverie was broken, he **saw** Jagannātha of Purī/Kurukṣetra and lamented for having lost his vision of Vrindavan Krishna. In the same chapter, Śrī Chaitanya **saw** the sand dune that he mistook for Govardhana Hill.

Antya 18 — "Touching": He saw the ocean at Purī and mistook it for the Yamunā, where he saw Rādhā-Krishna and the *gopīs* engaged in mock fighting, playfully expressing their love for each other. He watched as they "splashed water on one another. Then they fought **hand to hand**, then face to face, then chest to chest, teeth to teeth and finally nail to nail."

Antya 19 — "Smelling": He saw Krishna standing beneath an Ashoka Tree in the Jagannātha Vallabha gardens at Purī, and when he ran to embrace him, he was disappointed that Krishna had disappeared—even if the **fragrance** of Krishna's body lingered. Śrī Chaitanya lost consciousness due to its otherworldly aroma.

Antya 16 — "Tasting": He **tasted** the flavor of Krishna's lips when he tasted Jagannātha *prasāda.*[43]

Although it can be argued that these examples are not technically direct instances of *prema-vilāsa-vivarta*—that is to say, they are not described as such in the text itself—we see here clear examples of divine bewilderment, all based on Śrī Chaitanya's overflowing love in the mood of Rādhā.[44] Whether they are direct instances or just pointers to the larger ideal is a matter for experts in *rasa*. But since Mahāprabhu is universally viewed by such experts as Prema-Vilāsa-Vivarta-Mūrti, we feel justified in bringing these examples to our readers' attention. At the very least, they can serve as indicators of his pure, otherworldly love, which ensconced him in a type of divine intoxication (*pramattatā*) that is wholly reminiscent of Krishna's divine lover, Śrī Rādhā.

The notion of Rādhā and Krishna becoming one in the form of Śrī Chaitanya is the capstone of *prema-vilāsa-vivarta*, whose central quality involves an inner perception of mystical unity (*paraikya*). Indeed, it is this unity, forged through the overpowering mood of Śrī Rādhikā, outstripping the heart of Śrī Krishna himself, that allows Mahāprabhu to experience the mystical illusions (*bhrānti*) depicted in Antya-līlā, wherein perceived transformations (*vivarta*) seem to occur in natural phenomenon due to the presence of an overpowering love.

Conclusion

Śrī Chaitanya's very existence is the ultimate expression of *prema-vilāsa-vivarta*, for just as the Lord originally manifests as two beings—Rādhā and Krishna—to taste *rasa*, or loving relationship, that same love intensifies to the point of making them one, a position which they also share in eternity. This, the tradition teaches, is the inner position of Śrī Chaitanya, and it is from this fact that we derive the term "Prema-Vilāsa-Vivarta-Mūrti."

Dr. Rādhāgovinda Nāth again offers insight along these lines, which I paraphrase: He tells us that generally, the enamored *nāyaka* (hero) embraces the enamored *nāyikā* (heroine), and he leads her in a dance of love. But in *prema-vilāsa-vivarta*, the *nāyikā* takes the lead and embraces the *nāyaka*. In other words, Rādhā is in charge, taking the first step, and in doing so, she makes the *nāyaka* dance like a puppet.[45]

When Krishna adopts the form of Śrī Chaitanya, we see that Nāyikā Śrī Rādhā has eternally and uninterruptedly embraced Nāyaka Śrī Krishna and caused him to become absorbed in her moods, thereby enacting various forms of uncontrollable *līlā*, a new dance, as it were, wherein reality itself is turned on its head. By the influence of her moods, Śrī Krishna, God, has forgotten his own identity, his *svarūpa-jñāna*. This leads to *vaiparītya* (a reversal of behavior), and *bhrānti* (illusion), which are considered the pinnacle of this level of love, and the very stuff of *prema-vilāsa-vivarta*.[46]

But the unprecedented characteristic of this higher level, Rādhāgovinda Nāth continues, is that while there is a deep appreciation of being united with one's beloved—because such union is the supreme, ultimate perfection and maturation of *prema*—one finds that there is also deep appreciation of *viraha* (separation) as well—on a par with the thrill of being together (*milana*)—for the Divine Couple herein experience how it is actually both states, separation and union, that lead to the ultimate achievement in divine love. In a word, union has greater meaning *after* separation.[47]

"This truth," Rādhāgovinda Nāth continues, "is fundamental to the manifestation of Śrī Chaitanya, and it exists in him in its most radiant and radical configuration, for he is none other than the full amalgamation of Rādhā and Krishna in one form. More, even within this eternal, uninterrupted union (*sambhoga*), which is his very essence, the supreme manifestation of separation (*viraha*) is manifest, too, and to an overwhelming degree, as seen in his Gambhirā-līlā, the pinnacle of his confidential pastimes of pining for the Lord. For all these reasons, it has been said that Śrī Chaitanya is the personified form of *prema-vilāsa-vivarta*."[48]

We sum up with the words of Professor Abhishek Ghosh, noted scholar of Gauḍīya Vaishnavism: "Reversals in love that enhance passion are known as *prema-vivarta*. For example, when Śrī Caitanya Mahāprabhu, from far away in Puri, was experiencing his deepest love for Śrī Kṛṣṇa and his hamlet Vrindavan, he would mistake a rock to be a Govardhana-śilā, or ordinary forests to be the forests of Vraja. We witness here God making mistakes. How is it possible? It is a 'mistake' born of the highest love, which he allows himself in order to enhance the flavors of transcendental enjoyment. In this experience, Mahāprabhu functions at a highly liminal stage of existence, completely spiritual, where he feels not only separation from Kṛṣṇa, but also simultaneous union with him. Similarly, in Kṛṣṇa-līlā, Rādhārāṇī is sometimes in distress, even while in Kṛṣṇa's presence, knowing that no matter how prolonged those moments of togetherness may be, by the wish of Yoga-māyā, these moments will not last, and thus she starts feeling separation from Kṛṣṇa even while gazing at his moonlike face. Such is the pain of real love, which can only be found, at its highest pitch, in the exchanges of the Divine Couple, Rādhā and Kṛṣṇa.

"It is a great mystery," concludes Dr. Ghosh, "and it is hinted at in the *Bhagavad-gītā*, which teaches us in its fifteenth chapter that this world is like a warped reflection, an inverted reality—Kṛṣṇa gives the example of a banyan tree, whose roots point upward and branches face down. When next to a pond, such a tree indeed looks upside down. Yet, we know, we are observing only its reflection. So it is in this world, which is a reflection of the spiritual world. We are further told that the leaves of this mystical tree are the verses of the Vedas, and thus, stretching this most appropriate metaphor to its limit, *prema-vilāsa-vivarta*, the *vilasa* of inversion, could be seen as the pinnacle of all *līlā*, for it is the ultimate fruit of the 'Vedic tree' of knowledge. It is, so to speak, the culmination of Vedānta, and therefore what Vedānta is to the Vedas—i.e., its very essence—so, too, is *prema-vilāsa-vivarta* the essence of esoteric Gauḍīya *siddhānta*. It is the Vedānta within Vedānta, we might say. In the same way, Gauḍīya *rasikas* know that Caitanya Mahāprabhu is the *prema-vilāsa-vivarta-mūrti*, for he is the inner portion of Krishna himself in the mood of Rādhā. He is Kṛṣṇa within Kṛṣṇa. Thus, the *akhila-rasāmṛta-mūrti* known as Śrī Kṛṣṇa manifests as the *prema-vilāsa-vivarta-mūrti*: Caitanya Mahāprabhu, the representative of the highest love."[49]

Endnotes

1. From personal correspondence with Swami B. V. Tripurari (4-24-23). The notion of oneness in regard to lovers—how they both crave and experience it—is found throughout Western literature and philosophy as well, especially in the work of the poets. But it is nowhere as developed as in the narratives of Rādhā and Krishna. For

Western examples we may look to E. E. Cummings' "i carry your heart with me (i carry it in my heart)" and Emily Brontë's *Wuthering Heights*, specifically Catherine's expression of love for Heathcliff. As Aaron Ben-Zeév Ph.D. writes, ". . . Plato claimed that love is essentially the process of seeking our missing half. In the same vein, the psychoanalyst Eric Fromm argued that erotic love 'is the craving for complete fusion, for union with one other person. It is by its very nature exclusive and not universal.' Likewise, the philosopher Robert Nozick said that in romantic love, 'it feels to the two people that they have united to form and constitute a new entity in the world, what might be called a we.'" See Aaron Ben-Zeév "Are Lovers Two Faces of the Same Coin?" *Psychology Today* (https://www.psychologytoday.com/ca/blog/in-the-name-of-love/200901/are-lovers-two-faces-of-the-same-coin).

2. In Jagadānanda Paṇḍita's 16th-century work *Śrī Śrī Prema-vivarta*, Chapter Sixteen, the Gauḍīya tradition highlights this important question: "What is Love?" The query comes from the lips of Gauḍīya Vaishnavism's quintessential mystic, Raghunātha Dāsa Gosvāmī, who asks the question of Svarūpa Dāmodara, one of Chaitanya Mahāprabhu's most intimate associates. The answer is initiated in Text 21: "Those who are intoxicated by the vulgar pleasures of this world do not attain the essence of love of Krishna, and the divine flute player never becomes the object of their love. ..." This, of course, only tells us what love is not. The author elaborates on a more positive definition as well, revealing in no uncertain terms that, in its ultimate form, real love is found in the writings of great Vaishnava poets, such as Jayadeva, Vidyāpati, and Caṇḍīdāsa—that is, real love is nothing more or less than the sweet love of Krishna. Although such love may externally appear nondifferent from lust, it is nonetheless something far more refined, like the difference between iron and gold. Briefly, love is summed up in the *Bhakti-rasāmṛta-sindhu* (1.1.11) as follows: "One should render devotional service to Lord Krishna favorably and without desire for material profit or gain, whether gross or subtle. That is called pure bhakti, or devotional love." (*anyābhilāṣitā-śūnyaṁ jñāna-karmādy-anāvṛtam ānukūlyena kṛṣṇānu-śīlanaṁ bhaktir uttamā*)

3. *Rasa* theory is an ancient system of Indian aesthetics that describes audience reaction to any visual, literary, or musical work, specifically one that evokes an ineffable emotion or feeling. The concept is originally associated with Bharata's *Nāṭya Śāstra*, and was later developed by Abhinavagupta (c. 950–1016 CE) and King Bhoja (circa, 11th century), among others. But according to the Gauḍīya perspective, its full theological dimensions were not revealed until the work of Śrīla Rūpa Gosvāmī.

4. Interestingly, Greek philosophers identified six forms of love, though not exactly in line with Rūpa's Sanskrit categories: love of family (*storge*), friendly love (*philia*), amorous love (*eros*), narcissistic love (*philautia*), love of strangers (*xenia*), and divine love (*agape*).

5. See Tony K. Stewart, *The Final Word: The Caitanya-caritāmṛta and the Grammar of Religious Tradition* (New York: Oxford University Press, 2010), 211.

6. See also Viśvanātha Cakravartī's commentary on this verse. Interestingly, the

tradition teaches that the earlier stages of love, like *praṇaya*, find themselves in the higher stages as well, if in a more developed form. It is a phenomenon that we also see in the five primary *rasas*, whose characteristics all appear in some form in *mādhurya*, the highest stage, as mentioned above. In other words, each iteration of love contains elements of the former iteration, as suggested in UN 14.60: "[In this way, the progressive stages of love] may be compared to a seed, the sugar cane plant, sugar cane juice, molasses, solidified molasses, granulated sugar, refined sugar and rock candy." Commenting on this verse, Viśvanātha Cakravartī illuminates the analogy: "One object, by changing its previous state, takes on a new name according to its more developed level of excellence. This is shown with the example of a seed, which becomes a sprout and, soon, a stalk. Similarly, *rati* becomes *prema*. This produces juice, which is analogous to *sneha*. Juice produces molasses, *māna*, which eventually becomes solid, i.e., *praṇaya*. After this, it becomes sugar, or *rāga*, and then refined sugar, or *anurāga*. Finally, it becomes rock candy, which is comparable to *mahābhāva*." See also UN 14.219 (along with the commentaries of Jīva and Viśvanātha): "*Mādana*, the essence of *hlādinī-śakti*, is superior to *mohana*, and it makes all prior *bhāvas* blossom as never before; these qualities are fully present in Rādhā."

7. Of course, one can say that *praṇaya* is a more fundamental level than *prema-vilāsa-vivarta*. But it should be remembered, too, that there is necessarily a form of *praṇaya* in the higher stages as well, as per endnote 6. According to the saint-scholar Ananta Dāsa Bābājī (1925–2018), "When *praṇaya* becomes intense, then mind and intelligence become one, and a sweet meeting takes place. *Praṇaya* is an essential ingredient in *prema-vilāsa-vivarta*. If there was no loving intimacy and a feeling of union devoid of awe and reverence under all circumstances, how could such pastimes exist?" (https://gaudiyadiscussions.gaudiya.com/topic_23.html)

8. The standard *sāttvika-bhāvas*, or the outward manifestation of spiritual emotion, are usually delineated as follows: *stambha* (paralysis), *sveda* (perspiration), *romāñca* (horripilation, or hair standing on end), *svarabheda* (voice change), *vepathu* (trembling), *vaivarṇya* (bodily color change), *aśru* (weeping), and *pralaya* (fainting).

9. See *Śrīmad Bhāgavatam* 10.31.15. Also see Śrīla Bhaktivinoda Ṭhākura, *Jaiva Dharma, Our Eternal Nature*, Bhaktivedānta Nārāyaṇa Mahārāja, Araṇya Mahārāja, et. al., translation (Mathura: Gauḍīya Vedānta Publications, 2002), Chapter 36.

10. Although most of these higher levels of love are within the provenance of *mādhurya-rasa*, they sometimes manifest in other *rasas* as well. For example, Krishna's intimate cowherd playmates, such as the *priya-narma-sakhās*, are known to experience a similar mood in relation to Krishna. Specifically, Subāla and others in his camp are privy to (*rūḍha*) *mahābhāva*, a level often said to be unique to the *gopīs*. (14.233, see also *Jaiva Dharma*, Chapter 36) Still, *mādanākhya-mahābhāva*, the highest level of love, is found only in the heart of Rādhikā, though it expands into the hearts of her personal *sakhīs* as well, for they are her *kāya-vyūha*, or immediate expansions and assistants—they are said to be alternate versions of her very self. Thus, like Rādhā, they relish

an inconceivably high form of *mahābhāva*. And under their guidance, the *mañjaris*, too, experience such divine affection to the fullest. In fact, the tradition teaches that because of their relation to Rādhā, the *sakhīs* and *mañjaris* can experience even more than Krishna, as suggested in the *Caitanya-caritāmṛta* (Madhya 8.210): "When the nectar of Krishna's pastimes is sprinkled on that creeper, the happiness derived by the twigs, flowers and leaves is ten million times greater than that derived by the creeper itself." Consequently, in Gaura-līlā, Krishna himself falls at their feet and even takes *śikṣā* from them. Parenthetically, the tradition avers that Śrī Chaitanya Mahāprabhu, who partakes of Rādhā's nature, also naturally experiences the highest levels of *mahābhāva*; this will be the subject of our paper's latter portion.

11. Śrī Rūpa makes it clear in *Ujjvala-nīlamaṇi* (15.182) that, in this work, he abbreviated the various levels of divine love, hoping that the finished volume would not be too unwieldy: "The states of love described herein are ordinary for the different types of *prema*. The extraordinary states have not been described for fear of making the volume too large." (*etās tu prema-bhedānām anubhāvatayā daśāḥ / sādhāraṇyaḥ samastānāṁ prāyaśaḥ sambhavanty api*) This may be a partial explanation of why *prema-vilāsa-vivarta* is not directly mentioned in the UN. That said, it is clearly alluded to in various texts, such as 14.155 (the one quoted by Rāmānanda Rāya), where we may especially note Viśvanātha Cakravartī's commentary: "Their hearts are like lac, melted by the heat of *prema*, or have become liquid by the heat of fire. This indicates *sneha* ... The hearts merge (*yunjan*)."

12. Of the three, Jagadānanda's work comes closest to discussing the subject at hand, though in a somewhat disguised format. The first three introductory sequences of *Śrī Śrī Prema-vivarta* evoke the "*rādhā-kṛṣṇa-praṇaya-vikṛtir* ..." verse (*Caitanya-caritāmṛta*: Ādi-līlā, 1.5), wherein we learn about the oneness of Rādhā and Krishna, how they become two, and then become one again in Śrī Chaitanya. I have elaborated on this verse elsewhere in this article. The second verse again tells us, "The Absolute is sometimes two, as Rādhā and Krishna, and sometimes one, as Śrī Chaitanya, the Supreme Being." (*sei tattva kabhu dui rādhā-kṛṣṇa-rūpe kabhu eka parātpara chaitanya-svarūpe*) This articulation hints at *prema-vilāsa-vivarta*. Chapter Five is called "*Vivarta-vilāsa-sevā*," and Chapter Fourteen, "*Viparīta Vivarta*"—thus we see quite a bit of the same terminology one finds in discourses on *prema-vilāsa-vivarta*. In this way, Jagadānanda introduces his readers to the concept in a nutshell. Even so, conceptually, one has to read between the lines to find it in this particular text, and the phrase itself is never mentioned.

13. Here are but a few examples: Sudhindra Chandra Chakravarti, *Philosophical Foundations of Bengal Vaiṣṇavism* (Calcutta: Academic Publishers, 1969), 352, writes: "While closing his account of the highest stage of *Mādhurya-bhakti* with a song composed by him, Rāmānanda designates this experience as *Prema-vilāsa-vivarta* (maturing of the display of love)." Similarly Bhaktivinoda Ṭhākura writes in his *Amṛta-pravāha-bhāṣya* (commentary) to *Caitanya-caritāmṛta* 2.8.194: "This highest platform of divine love

is the messenger of *prema-vilāsa-vivarta*, in which there is an experience of union even during separation." Finally, Śrīla A. C. Bhaktivedanta Swami Prabhupāda, in his book, *Śrī Rāmānanda Samvāda: In Search of the Ultimate Goal of Life* (California: Mandala Publishing, 2004), 70, writes: "This sort of feeling during separation of the lover and the beloved is called *prema-vilāsa-vivarta*, which is the topmost sentiment in loving affairs." And also, p. 72: "In concluding this explanation of *prema-vilāsa-vivarta*, the highest stage of transcendental relationships, Lord Caitanya said ... 'Now I understand the topmost limit of the ultimate goal of life. This has been possible by your grace. The goal cannot be reached without the endeavor of the devotee and the mercy of a pure devotee. Please therefore let me now know the means of reaching this topmost goal.'"

14. The exoteric reason for Mahāprabhu covering Rāmānanda Rāya's mouth is found in the *Caitanya-caritāmṛta* (2.8.193), particularly in Prabhupāda's commentary. The esoteric reason is related in Śrī Śrīmad Bhaktivedānta Nārāyaṇa Gosvāmī Mahārāja, *Śrī Rāya Rāmānanda Samvāda* (Vrindavan: Gaudiya Vedanta Publications, 2009), 177: "Śrī Gaurahari wished to conceal His nature as being Śrī Kṛṣṇa internally, covered by a golden complexion. He did not want Śrī Rāmānanda Rāya to reveal His identity, so He covered Rāmānanda's mouth before he could utter this fact." This view is also suggested in the writings of Śrīla B. R. Śrīdhar Mahārāja. See Swami B. R. Śrīdhar, *Encounters with Divinity: The Path of Dedication, Vol. II* (Bangalore: Gosai Publishers, 2005), 199.

15. In addition to the traditional texts on the subject and the commentaries of the *ācāryas*, what follows is a partial list of devotees, friends, and scholars that I consulted as well: Śrīla B. V. Nārāyaṇa Mahārāja, Prem Prayojan Prabhu, Bhanu Swami, Tripurāri Mahārāja, Rasikānanda Swami, Dhanurdhara Swami, Śrīvāsa Prabhu, Revatī Devī Dāsī, Uttamaśloka Prabhu, Mukunda Prabhu, Jan Brzezinski (Jagadānanda), Abhishek Ghosh, Śyāmarāṇī Dāsī, Satyanārāyaṇa Dāsa Bābājī, Navadvīpa Prabhu, Advaita Prabhu, Reverend David Carter, H. D. Resnick, Joshua Greene, and others. Special thanks to Śrīvāsa Prabhu, for his help with Dr. Rādhāgovinda Nāth's Bengali text.

16. The tradition asserts that Rādhā and Krishna are actually embodied forms of this omnipotent love—the energies of *hlādinī* (blissful experience) and *saṁvit* (cognition) combined. Accordingly, they allow their love to actually exert control over them (*prema-vaśyaḥ*). Indeed, according to the *Bhakti-rasāmṛta-sindhu* (1.1.41), "Having made Hari [Krishna] the vessel of love, along with his dear ones, this *prema-bhakti* is called *śrī-kṛṣṇākarṣiṇī* [the attractor of Krishna]—verily, it brings him under its complete control." (*śrī-kṛṣṇākarṣiṇī—kṛtvā hariṃ prema-bhājaṃ priya-varga-samanvitam / bhaktir vaśīkarotīti śrī-kṛṣṇākarṣiṇī matā*) That is to say, in the Gauḍīya tradition, divine love (*prema*) is supreme. What does that mean in the present context? Following Viśvanātha Cakravartī's commentary on *Ujjvala-nīlamaṇi* 14.154 (see full verse below), we learn that the word "*sva*" in the compound phrase *sva-saṁvedya-daśā* refers to *anurāga* as it expands into *mahābhāva*, thus becoming "self-aware." To say that the Divine Couple's love becomes self-aware is to say that they lose their sense of individu-

ality and instead identify with that love, almost as an entity unto itself. And as they become fully absorbed in that experience, it is as if they are becoming a third person. In other words, love itself becomes the dominant force, overtaking both Rādhā and Krishna according to their implicit desire.

All of this is based on Śrīla Rūpa Gosvāmī's *Ujjvala-nīlamaṇi*, with particular attention to 14.154, cited here with the incorporated commentaries of Jīva and Viśvanātha: "When *anurāga* reaches a special state of intensity, it is known as *bhāva*. This state of intensity has three characteristics: (1) *anurāga* reaches the state of *sva-saṁvedya, which means that it becomes the object of its own experience* (italics added), (2) it becomes *prakāśita*, radiantly manifest, which means that all eight *sāttvika-bhāvas* become prominently displayed, and (3) it attains *yāvad-āśraya-vṛtti*, in which the previous stages of *praṇaya* and *rāga*—especially the oneness of body and mind felt in *praṇaya*—come to their crescendo, catapulting *anurāga* into *bhāva*. It then spreads its influence to all devotees who are ready to embrace it."

The significance of this verse in terms of *prema-vilāsa-vivarta* is as follows: It immediately precedes the verse quoted in the *Caitanya-caritāmṛta* (from the same *Ujjvala-nīlamaṇi*) by Rāmānanda Rāya, wherein he succinctly utters the truth of *prema-vilāsa-vivarta* and establishes its conceptual framework for the tradition. That is to say, Text 154 cites the essential characteristics of the highest love, including its ever-growing transformations, while 155, cites an example of this love in terms of Rādhā and Krishna, thus offering a complete overview of the subject.

17. In Indian philosophy, one typically encounters the notion of *vivarta*, or "transformation," within a Śaṅkarite or Advaitin context. That particular school of thought, known as Vivartavāda, centers on the idea that the visible world is nothing more than an illusion, an unreal manifestation or transformation of Brahman (spiritual substance). This understanding is fostered by the traditional "rope-snake analogy," which runs as follows. Imagine, if you will, that a person enters a dark room and suddenly sees a snake. He draws back in fear, but then, upon turning on the lights, he sees that the "snake" is actually just a large curled up piece of twined rope. In this analogy, the snake represents the material world, which is illusory, while the rope represents the overarching truth of Brahman. The light that helps us distinguish truth from illusion comes from spiritual aids, such as scripture or the guru, which allow us to see the truth as it is, to distinguish the snake from the rope. Extrapolating from this example, Vivartavādīs say that the varieties we see around us, which are part of our darkened world, are false, just as the snake in the analogy is false. When we are enlightened, they say, we see that all varieties are just illusions, that they are simply unreal. Vaishnava philosophers, however, point out that while the rope is certainly not a snake, snakes as such are not false. That is, in reality, both snakes and ropes exist, and the illusion is merely when we mistake one for the other. Similarly, this world, which is full of varieties, is not a mere illusion, as the Vivartavādīs say; instead, it is a reflection of the reality in the Vaikuṇṭha world, the spiritual world, which is also full of variety.

The *Śrīmad Bhāgavatam*, in fact, includes numerous examples that use the analogy in a Vaishnava way (see, for instance, 4.22.38, 6.9.37, and 10.6.8). While the above is a summary of the standard rope-snake analogy as expressed in various schools of Indian thought, Bhaktivinoda Ṭhākura, in his commentary on the *Caitanya-caritāmṛta*, Madhya 8.194 (*Amṛta-pravāha*), goes further, fully reclaiming the analogy for Vaishnavas by using it to describe the profound illusion produced by the highest levels of love, specifically *prema-vilāsa-vivarta*, wherein Rādhā and Krishna lose their sense of self-identity, thinking each is the other. It is to be noted that while the usual snake-rope analogy focuses on *jaḍa-vivarta* (mundane delusion), *prema-vilāsa-vivarta* focuses on *divya-vivarta* (divine delusion).

18. The words *vilāsa* and *līlā* are interrelated, although likely derived from completely different roots (√las & √lī respectively). Some argue that the root of the word *līlā* remains unknown. That said, vi+√lās, like *līlā*, means "to play, sport, dally, and to be amused or delighted." Thus, *vilāsa* can, by way of a general, initial definition, be interchangeable with *līlā*, but *līlā* more suggests play, imitation, etc., while *vilāsa* moves more towards sensuality, erotic dance, and even lovemaking. To summarize: In common parlance, *līlā* refers to play or sport, and *vilāsa* is the enjoyment of that play.

19. It may be questioned how a divinity like Rādhā or Krishna can fall into "illusion." This is a complex subject, and many Vaishnava writers attempt to explain it to practitioners' satisfaction. Suffice it to say, God's illusion is unlike ours. When we fall into illusion, it takes us away from reality. This is known as *mahā-māyā*. But God's "illusion," and that of his close associates, bring them closer to each other, closer to ultimate reality. It is the opposite of illusion as we know it. This is called *yoga-māyā*. Expressed another way, the word *tattva* represents "hard fact," or "truth," *līlā* means "the Lord's play," and *rasa* means "relationship" (through which he plays). From the Gauḍīya perspective, *līlā* and *rasa* are higher than *tattva*, for *līlā* and *rasa* allow practitioners to partake of a yet higher truth. For more on this subject, see Viśvanātha Cakravartī Ṭhākura, *Rāga-vartma-cāṇḍrikā*, Second Illumination, Text 6, where this is elucidated with graphic examples. Starting in verse 1 of that section we learn that Krishna can simultaneously be both bewildered and omniscient, for he is unlimited and inconceivable, and thus need not adhere to our laws of logic. For the sake of his pastimes, in which he interacts with his close associates, he is both *mugdhatā* (innocently unaware) and *sarvajñatā* (all-knowing), and in this way he relishes exchange with his devotees. Otherwise, it would not be possible for an unlimited being to function in a world of three dimensions. Again, one must keep in mind the distinction between *jaḍa-vivarta* and *divya-vivarta*.

20. See Krishnadāsa Kavirāja, *Caitanya-caritāmṛta*, edited with the commentary *Gaura-kṛpā-taraṅgiṇī-ṭīkā* by Rādhāgovinda Nātha, 4th ed., 6 vols. (Kalikātā: Sādhanā Prakāṣanī, 1952), Vol 1, pp. 231-232.

21. *ibid.*

22. *ibid.*

23. I am here using the translation of His Divine Grace A. C. Bhaktivedanta Swami Prabhupāda, translation, and commentary, Krishnadāsa Kavirāja Goswāmī's *Śrī Caitanya-caritāmṛta*, 9-volume set (Los Angeles, California, 1996, reprint), 2.8.194.

24. *ibid.*, 2.8.195.

25. Cupid (from the Latin *cupido*, meaning "desire") is the god of erotic love, traceable to Roman and Greek mythology. In the Indic tradition, he is sometimes identified with the demigod Kāmadeva, though the name is also periodically used for Krishna's son, Pradyumna. It is also used as a name for Krishna himself, and sometimes, as in the *Caitanya-caritāmṛta*, as a divine messenger who instigates loving emotions.

26. For the significance of the word "*paraikya*," or "supreme oneness," see Kavi Karṇapūra, *Kṛṣṇa-Caitanya Caritāmṛtam Mahākāvyam*, edited with an introduction and Bengali translation by Prāṇa-kiśora Gosvāmī (Kolkata: Śrī Gaurāṅga Maṇḍira, n.d.), Verse 13.45. See also Śrī Kavi Karṇapūra, *Caitanya-candrodaya-nāṭaka* (7.83 and 87), for the oneness of Rādhā and Krishna. Although he doesn't use the term *prema-vilāsa-vivarta*, he describes its essence: "Śrī Rādhā says: 'I no longer think in terms of, 'I am your beloved and you are my lover.' For us, the conception of 'I' and 'you' has been macerated. I no longer sense any distinction between us. It seems like Cupid has ground our hearts together in the most intense way, dusting them with the nectar of perfect love."

27. See Śrī Śrīmad Gour Govinda Swami Mahārāja, *Mathura Meets Vrindavan* (Bhubaneswar, Orissa, Gopal Jiu Publications, 2003), 111-112.

28. O. B. L. Kapoor, *Śrī Chaitanya and Rāgānuga Bhakti* (Vrindavan U.P.: The Vaishnava Book Trust, 1995), 3-4.

29. See Viśvanātha Cakravartī Ṭhākura, *Śrī Kṛṣṇa-Bhāvanāmṛta*, translated by Advaita Dāsa (Vrindavan U.P: Ras Bihari Lal and Sons, 2000), Chapter 18, Texts 37, and 45-57.

30. *ibid.*

31. Wulff, Donna M., *Drama as a Mode of Religious Realization: the Vidagdhamādhava of Rūpa Gosvāmī*, American Academy of Religion, Academy Series (Chico, CA: Scholars Press, 1984), Act Six: See especially Text 7.

32. *ibid.*, 123-124.

33. See Bhaktivinoda Ṭhākura, *Amṛta-pravāha-bhāṣya* to *Caitanya-caritāmṛta* (2.8.194).

34. See His Divine Grace A. C. Bhaktivedanta Swami Prabhupāda, *Caitanya-caritāmṛta*, Madhya 8.194, purport.

35. See Shrivasta Goswami, "Rādhā: The Play and Perfection of Rasa," in John Stratton Hawley and Donna Marie Wulff (eds.), *The Divine Consort: Rādhā and the Goddesses of India* (Berkeley religious studies series, 1982), 87.

36. See Viśvanātha Cakravartī Ṭhākura, *Śrī Kṛṣṇa-Bhāvanāmṛta, op. cit.*, Chapter Three, Texts 14, 38-64. It starts in chapter 1, when the Divine Couple initially wake up, and then again when they get caught in chapter 2, exposed for wearing each other's clothes.

37. Of course, the subject of *bhedābheda* is vast, spanning the entire gamut of Indian philosophy, but it exists in a distinct form in the Gauḍīya tradition, as conceived by Jīva Goswāmī in his auto-commentary to *Paramātmā Sandarbha* (Anuccheda 77, 78). For

an in-depth view of the notion of *acintya-bhedābheda*—Śrī Jīva's particular version of "inconceivable and simultaneous oneness and difference"—as an explanation for all reality, with special attention to the interrelation of Krishna and his various energies, see Steven J. Rosen, "Deferring to Difference: The Essence of Śrī Chaitanya's Acintya-Bhedābheda Vedānta," *Journal of Vaishnava Studies*, Volume 25, No. 1 (fall 2016), 223-248.

38. B. R. Śrīdhara Swami, *The Golden Volcano of Divine Love* (Nadiya, West Bengal: Sri Chaitanya Saraswat Math, 1996, reprint), 10.

39. In addition to *Caitanya-caritāmṛta* Ādi 1.5, already quoted, see Ādi 4.230: "Desiring to (1) understand the depth of Rādhā's love, (2) the incomparable sweetness of Krishna's nature through her eyes, and (3) the bliss that Rādhā feels due to that sweetness, the Supreme Lord Hari, draping himself in her emotions, appeared from Śacī-devī's womb [as Chaitanya] just as the moon appears from the ocean." Also see Madhya 2.80: "During his previous incarnation in Vṛndāvana, Lord Krishna wanted to enjoy these three forms of ecstasy, but despite his best efforts, they evaded him, for they are solely tasted by Śrī Rādhā. Therefore, Śrī Krishna accepted her mood of love in the form of Śrī Chaitanya." There are numerous verses to this effect.

40. "On the one hand," writes Vaishnava scholar Prem Prayojan Prabhu, "Kṛṣṇa is consumed with greed to taste the highest love, in which Rādhā loses awareness of her individuality. And on the other, Rādhā ardently dreams of fulfilling all of Kṛṣṇa's desires. Inevitably, their mutual emotions arising from *samvit* and *hlādinī*, find the support of *sandhinī* (being), resulting in the coming into being of a combined form of Rādhā and Kṛṣṇa, in which Kṛṣṇa takes on the golden complexion of Rādhā and experiences her otherwise inaccessible sentiments. This *prema-vilāsa vivarta mūrti*, the extraordinary form in which Kṛṣṇa finally fulfills his desire to experience *prema-vilāsa vivarta*, is Śrī Chaitanya Mahāprabhu." See Prem Prayojan Dāsa, "The Ontology of a Tīrtha: Śrī Navadvīpa Dhāma in Gauḍīya Vaiṣṇavism," in *Journal of Vaishnava Studies*, Volume 27, No. 1 (Fall 2018), 120.

41. See Krishnadāsa Kavirāja, *Caitanya-caritāmṛta*, edited with the commentary *Gaura-kṛpā-taraṅgiṇī-ṭīkā* by Rādhāgovinda Nātha, op. cit., Volume 1 (*Bhūmika*), 239.

42. See O. B. L. Kapoor, *Śrī Chaitanya and Rāgānuga Bhakti* (Vrindavan U.P.: The Vaishnava Book Trust, 1995), 4.

43. I am indebted to Śrī Prahlāda (Ace Simpson) for the specifics in this list. (personal correspondence, 3-8-23)

44. It is our thesis that *prema-vilāsa-vivarta* can exist in various iterations, as we have seen in the example of Rādhārāṇī mistaking the black *tamāla* tree for Krishna. In other words, certain qualities normally associated with this highest stage of love, such as inversion (*viparīta*), or the absence of distinction (*bheda-rāhitya*), might be unavailable in a given pastime, but that need not disqualify it from being an instance of *prema-vilāsa-vivarta.* To wit: Regarding the black *tamāla* tree incident, we may note the following. While Śrī Rādhā saw the tree as Krishna, she did not personally identify with it, nor did she become one with it. Yet the pastime is still cited by Gauḍīya

authorities as an example of *prema-vilāsa-vivarta*. With this in mind, let us consider that Mahāprabhu is known to have experienced all aspects of Rādhā-bhāva. In general, it is said that these higher moods of love are peculiar to Rādhā, but in as much as the *gopīs* and Mahāprabhu take part in Śrī Rādhā's inner moods, they too can partake of *prema-vilāsa-vivarta*, if not to the same degree or in the same way that Rādhā does.

It might be argued that I am being too liberal with my extension of *prema-vilāsa-vivarta*, and that it should solely be used in ways that align with its primary definition as per the *Caitanya-caritāmṛta*. To be sure, Kavirāja Gosvāmī uses the term in a specific way, but there are more general ways that the term can be used, too, as when Bhaktivinoda and Śrīla Prabhupāda apply it to the black *tamāla* tree. One further example may be cited as well: Śrīla Nārāyaṇa Mahārāja writes: "When Madhu-maṅgala says, 'O Rādhā, Madhusūdana has gone away,' Śrī Rādhā begins to lament in separation from Him, even though Śrī Kṛṣṇa is right next to Her. This is *prema-vilāsa-vivarta*." He further writes, "*Prema-vilāsa* means 'loving pastimes,' and *vivarta* indicates '*prema-vaicittya*.'"

Of course, *prema-vaicittya* constitutes a separate area of *prema* altogether, as defined in the *Ujjvala-nīlamaṇi* (see 15.4, 15.147, 150, 151). But Nārāyaṇa Mahārāja finds enough resonance to acknowledge its kinship to *prema-vilāsa-vivarta*, indicating that there are both primary and secondary definitions of the term. See Śrī Śrīmad Bhaktivedānta Nārāyaṇa Gosvāmī Mahārāja, *Śrī Rāya Rāmānanda Samvāda* (Vrindavan: Gaudiya Vedanta Publications, 2009), 173. Incidentally, Nārāyaṇa Mahārāja is here following Śrīla Bhaktisiddhānta Sarasvatī, who aligns the two in the following way in his *Caitanya-caritāmṛta* commentary (*Anubhāṣya* on Madhya 8.191): "The *vilāsa-vaicitrya* and *vilāsa-vivarta* of *mohana-mādanādi adhirūḍha-mahābhāva* that exists within *prema-vaicittya* [that is *antargata* to *prema-vaicittya*] is expressed in Śrī Rāmānanda Rāya's song."

45. See Krishnadāsa Kavirāja, *Caitanya-caritāmṛta*, edited with the commentary *Gaura-kṛpā-taraṅgiṇī-ṭīkā* by Rādhāgovinda Nātha, *op. cit.*, Volume 1 (Bhūmika), 238-239.

46. *ibid.*

47. *ibid.*

48. *ibid.*

49. Personal correspondence with Abhishek Ghosh (June 14, 2023). For more on *prema-vilāsa-vivarta*'s connection to Vedānta, also see Haridāsa Dāsa, *Gauḍīya Vaiṣṇava Abhidhāna* (Navadvīpa: Haribola Kuṭīra, 1957, reprint, Kolkata, Sanskrit Pustak Bhandar, 2014), especially Vol. 1, p. 506, a special entry on *prema-vilāsa-vivarta*.

Bibliography

Brzezinski, Jan K., "Jīva Gosvāmin's *Gopāla-campū*," Ph.D. thesis, School of Oriental and African Studies, University of London, 1992.

———. "Does Kṛṣṇa Marry the Gopīs in the End? The *Svakīya-vāda* of Jīva Gosvāmin." in *Journal of Vaishnava Studies*, vol. 5, issue 4 (Fall, 1997), 49–110.

Chakravarti, Ramakanta, *Vaiṣṇavism in Bengal: 1486–1900* (Calcutta: Sanskrit Pustak Bhandar, 1985).

Chakravarti, Sudhindra Chandra, *Philosophical Foundations of Bengal Vaiṣṇavism* (Calcutta: Academic Publishers, 1969).

———. "Bengal Vaiṣṇavism," in K. R. Sundararanjan and Bithika Mukerji, eds. *Hindu Spirituality: Postclassical and Modern* (New York: The Crossroad Publishing Company, 1997), 47–62.

Dasa, Gopīparāṇadhana, trans., *Śrī Bṛhad Bhāgavatāmṛta of Śrīla Sanātana Gosvāmī*, 3 vols. (Los Angeles: Bhaktivedanta Book Trust, 2002–2003).

Dāsa, Haridāsa, *Gauḍīya Vaiṣṇava Abhidhāna*, 4 parts in 2 vols. (Navadvīpa: Haribola Kuṭīra, 1957, reprint, Kolkata, Sanskrit Pustak Bhandar, 2014).

Dāsa, Kuśakratha, translated, *Śrīla Vṛndāvana Dāsa Ṭhākura's Śrī Caitanya-bhāgavata* (Alachua, Florida: The Kṛṣṇa Institute, 1994).

Dasa, Navadvipa, "Prema-vilāsa-vivarta—Śrī Kṛṣṇa's divine play with Śrī Rādhā," Parts 1 and 2 (https://www.jiva.org/prema-vilasa-vivarta-sri-kṛṣṇas-divine-play-with-sri-radha-part-1/).

Dāsa, Ravīndra Svarūpa [William H. Deadwyler III], "Rādhā, Kṛṣṇa, Caitanya: The Inner Dialectic of the Divine Relativity." in *Journal of Vaiṣṇava Studies*, vol. 10, issue 1 (Spring, 2001), 5–26.

Delmonico, Neal, "Sacred Rapture: A Study of the Religious Aesthetic of Rūpa Gosvāmin," Ph.D. Dissertation, The University of Chicago, 1990.

Dimock, Edward C., Jr., translated, and Stewart, Tony K. (ed.), *Caitanya-caritāmṛta* of *Kṛṣṇadāsa Kavirāja: A Translation and Commentary*, Harvard Oriental Series, Vol. 56 (Cambridge, MA: The Department of Sanskrit and Indian Studies, Harvard University, 1999).

Gosvāmī, Kṛṣṇadāsa Kavirāja, *Caitanya-caritāmṛta,* edited with the commentary *Gaura-kṛpā-taraṅgiṇī-ṭīkā* by Rādhāgovinda Nātha, 4th ed., 6 vols. (Kalikātā: Sādhanā Prakāṣanī, 1952), 338-343. See especially the third volume (Madhya, Part 1) of his six-volume series, as well as his 450-page Bhūmika, or introductory volume.

Gosvāmī, Kṛṣṇadāsa Kavirāja, *Govinda-līlāmṛta,* translated by Advaita Dāsa (Vrindavan U.P: Ras Bihari Lal and Sons, 2000).

Gosvāmin, Rūpa, *Bhakti-rasāmṛta-sindhu*, with the commentaries of Jīva Gosvāmin, Mukundadāsa Gosvāmin, and Viśvanātha Chakravartin (Navadvīpa: Haribol Kuṭhīr, 1945).

———. *Padyāvali of Rūpa Gosvāmin: An Anthology of Vaishnava Verses in Sanskrit,* ed. Sushil Kumar De (Dacca: University of Dacca, 1934).

———. *Ujjvalanīlamaṇi*, ed. Bengali translation by Haridasa Dāsa, with the *Svātmapramodinī ṭīkā* of Viṣṇudāsa (Navadvīpa: by the editor at Haribola Kuṭīra, 1955).

Gosvāmin, Rūpa, *The Bhaktirasāmṛtasindhu of Rūpa Gosvāmin*, David Haberman, trans. (Delhi: Motilal Banarsidass (May 1, 2002).

Goswami, Shrivasta, "Rādhā: The Play and Perfection of Rasa," in John Stratton Hawley and Donna Marie Wulff (eds.), *The Divine Consort: Rādhā and the Goddesses of India* (Berkeley religious studies series, 1982).

Kapoor, O. B. L. *Śrī Chaitanya and Rāgānuga Bhakti* (Vrindavan U.P.: The Vaishnava Book Trust, 1995).

Karṇapūra, Kavi, *Chaitanya-candrodaya-nātaka* (Benares: Chowkhambha, 1966).

———. *Śrī Kṛṣṇa-Caitanya Caritāmṛtam Mahākāvyam,* edited with an introduction and Bengali translation by Prāṇa-kiśora Gosvāmī (Kolkata: Śrī Gaurāṅga Maṇḍira, n.d.)

Maharaja, B. R. Sridhar Swami, *Encounters with Divinity: The Path of Dedication, Vol. II* (Bangalore: Gosai Publishers, 2005).

Mahārāja, Śrī Śrīmad Bhaktivedānta Nārāyaṇa Gosvāmī, *Śrī Rāya Rāmānanda Samvāda* (Vrindavan: Gaudiya Vedanta Publications, 2009).

Mahārāja, Śrī Śrīmad Gour Govinda Swami, *Mathura Meets Vrindavan* (Bhubaneswar, Orissa, Gopal Jiu Publications, 2003).

Maharaja, Swami B. P. Puri, *The Art of Sadhana: Guide to Daily Devotion* (San Francisco: Mandala Publishing, 1999).

Mitra, Khagendranātha. "*Premavilāsa-vivarta,*" *Bharata-varṣa* 25 (in Bengali), no. 1 (1344 BS, i.e., 1937 CE), 17-20.

Padmanābha, Swāmī Bhakti Praṇaya, "Ramananda-samvada & the Ontological Ultimacy of Gaura Lila"in *The Harmonist*, May 19, 2022.

Prabhupāda, A. C. Bhaktivedanta Swami, translation and commentary, Krishnadāsa Kavirāja Goswāmī's *Śrī Caitanya-caritāmṛta*, 9-volume set (Los Angeles, California, 1996, reprint).

———. *Teaching of Lord Chaitanya* (Boston: ISKCON Press, 1968). Reprinted as *Teachings of Lord Caitanya, the Golden Avatar* (Los Angeles: Bhaktivedanta Book Trust, 1988).

———. *The Nectar of Devotion* (California: Bhaktivedanta Book Trust, 1970).

Prayojan Prabhu, Prem, "Catching the Jivas" in *Yoga Vidya*, February 25, 2009 (https://my.yoga-vidya.org/profiles/blogs/catching-the-jivas-artilce-by).

———. "The Ontology of a Tīrtha: Śrī Navadvīpa Dhāma in Gauḍīya Vaiṣṇavism," in *Journal of Vaishnava Studies*, Volume 27, No. 1 (Fall 2018), 117–122.

Roberts, Michelle Voss, *Dualities: A Theology of Difference* (Louisville, Kentucky: Westminster John Knox Press, 2010).

Rosen, Steven J., "Who is Shri Chaitanya Mahaprabhu?" in *The Hare Krishna Movement: The Postcharismatic Fate of a Religious Transplant*, eds. Edwin F. Bryant and Maria Ekstrand (New York: Columbia University Press, 2004), 63–72.

———. *Śrī Chaitanya's Life and Teachings: The Golden Avatāra of Divine Love* (Lanham, MD: Lexington Books, 2017).

———. *Chaitanyology: A Collection of Essays on Śrī Chaitanya* (Charlottesville, Virginia: Bookwrights Press, 2023).

Stewart, Tony K., *The Final Word: The Caitanya Caritāmṛta* and the Grammar of Religious Tradition (New York and London: Oxford University Press, 2010).

Swami, B. R. Śrīdhara, *The Golden Volcano of Divine Love* (Nadiya, West Bengal: Sri Chaitanya Saraswat Math, 1996, reprint).

Ṭhākura, Bhaktivinoda, *Shri Chaitanya Mahaprabhu, His Life and Precepts*, originally published in 1896 (Nabadwip: Shri Goudiya Vedanta Samiti, 1981, reprint).

———. *Shri Chaitanya Shikshamritam*, Bijoy Krishna Rarhi, translation (Madras: Sri Gaudiya Math, 1983, reprint).

———. *Śrīla Bhaktivinoda Ṭhākura's Gaurāṅga-līlā-smaraṇa-maṅgala-stotra—Auspicious Meditations on Lord Gaurāṅga*, Kuśakratha dāsa, translation (Los Angeles: Kṛṣṇa Institute, 1988).

———. *Jaiva Dharma, Our Eternal Nature*, translated by Bhaktivedānta Nārāyaṇa Mahārāja, Araṇya Mahārāja, (Mathura: Gauḍīya Vedānta Publications, 2002).

Ṭhākura, Viśvanātha Chakravartī, *Rāga Vartma Chandrikā: A Moonbeam to Illuminate the Path of Spontaneous Devotion*, translated by Narayana Maharaja (Mathura: Gaudiya Vedanta Publications, 2001).

Ṭhākura, Viśvanātha Cakravartī, *Śrī Kṛṣṇa-Bhāvanāmṛta*, translated by Advaita Dāsa (Vrindavan U.P: Ras Bihari Lal and Sons, 2000).

———. *Śrī Prema-samputa*, translation and commentary by Bhaktivedānta Nārāyaṇa Mahārāja (Vrindavan, U.P.: Gaudiya Vedanta Publications, 2011).

Thakura, Vrndavana dasa, *Sri Caitanya Bhagavata with commentary of Bhakti-*

siddhanta Sarasvati Gosvami Maharaja Prabhupada, Bhumipati Dasa, translation, 7 vols. (New Delhi: Vrajraj Press. 1998–2005).

Wulff, Donna M., *Drama as a Mode of Religious Realization: the Vidagdhamādhava of Rūpa Gosvāmī*, American Academy of Religion, Academy Series (Chico, CA: Scholars Press, 1984).

———. "Radha: Consort and Conqueror of Krishna." in *Devi: Goddesses of India*, ed. John Hawley and Donna Wulff (Berkeley: University of California Press, 1998).

Chaitanya, Popular Culture, and Amar Chitra Katha Comic Books

David Mason

I'm opposed, generally, to definitions. It seems to me that language is a fundamentally creative mechanism that is always out ahead of *definitive* declarations of the meanings of this or that word or phrase. And the efforts to define the things that we say can too easily slip into a militant insistence on what words and phrases are allowed to do. Definitions are fascists.

But before I bore anyone with a homily on *Chaitanya in Popular Culture*, I might do well to show that I have some idea as to where exactly *popular culture* is, as the grounds for locating Chaitanya in it. And a person could say that *popular culture* is not a *where*, with geographic borders, like Sweden, but a *what*, with particular characteristics, like a cardboard box or a swimming pool. Obviously, *popular culture* might both a *where* and a *what*. The concept of *popular culture* is not monolithic. I do know that much. Anyway, first, some attempt to identify what I'm talking about. Not a definition, but a genuine *essai*.

There's a simplistic understanding of *popular culture*, of course. We could simply say that *popular culture* is comprised of things that lots of people like. But *culture* can't really be reduced to *things*. Not even to things that are people. A pile of stones—which a lot of people might like—doesn't have *culture*, popular or otherwise. So, when we discuss *pop culture* we can't elide the *liking* part. The *liking* is a human activity, or maybe quality, that provides for the possibility of culture and, thus, for culture's iteration as *pop*. To the extent that *lots of people* are crucial to the *pop* concept, it must be that the *liking* part foments some kind of relation between lots of people. Lots of people, in *pop*, like things, and also like those things, *together*.

There's an anticipation of this sort of popular culture in the stories that comprise Chaitanya's own histories, which valorize Chaitanya's devotion as especially seductive. In proximity, people could not resist Chaitanya. One after another, his first disciples fell under Chaitanya's spell, even folks who enter the Chaitanya history as his enemies. Madhāi and Jagāi wreak violence on Chaitanya's followers and then, in Chaitanya's presence, almost immediately transform into devotees, themselves. People just really liked Chaitanya, and they liked him *together*, so that, even in his own day, he was a kind of pop phenomenon.

This simplistic explication of *pop culture* as simply the liking that a lot of people do would tip toward the Frankfurt School, and when we tip that direction, we find people like Theodor Adorno arguing that there's nothing simple about it. Adorno and his Frankfurt friends worried over what inspires this *liking* element of *pop culture*. What *exactly*. If you like something—a movie, say, or a song—you, as an individual, might simply say that there's no special reason that you like it. You just *do*. Chaitanya's hagiographies are mostly content to chalk his appeal up to a natural charisma and his divine nature. Miraculous, that is. Not really having a reason.

But the Frankfurt School thinkers weren't so content with rationalizing the popular appeal of a Sarah Bernhardt or Gertie the Dinosaur as something that just happens. It might be that the liking that you do, especially of something that lots of people like, is motivated, and not by a natural urge that is in, and is part of, you, but something that is outside of you. Something that imposes itself on you and directs your interests in order to realize its own goals. Something that gets something out of the fact that you like that movie that lots of people like. For Adorno and the Frankfurt folks, that outside thing is capitalism, which benefits from the feeling that lots of people might have that they all like the same thing and that they are, consequently, all alike each other. The outcome is a *mass*: a collective identity that presents itself as a naturally-occurring reality—because what could be more natural than that I just like what everyone just likes, and vice-versa? To this end, capitalism creates—perhaps, *manufactures*—the conditions in which lots of people like things, together, and experience that together-liking as a common identity.

Popular Culture, in this deeply suspicious view, is the manifestation of our duped-ness. The things, themselves, of popular culture—the movies, the songs, the diets, etc.—come to us in order to forge and to sustain our sense that we are one on the basis of these *things*, so that the things *are*, in a not trivial way, our identity, and we feel that our very existence depends on them. Pop things, thus, can be seen as thieves of agency. The widely-liked movies, the widely-liked songs, made available by mass production to lots and lots of people in infinite, exact copies, reveal that we can be made to surrender our selves—our individual selfhood—to be subsumed in a broadly-collective, and not at all autonomous, togetherness.

That's one view of *popular culture*, anyway. To the extent that this view holds, the examination of Chaitanya in popular culture would have to wrestle with the extent to which Chaitanya's appearance in one of these pop *things* contributes to a mass de-selfing, in the service of capitalism's own purposes. I think it would not be a disservice to Chaitanya to make such an argument, insofar as the implication might be that capitalism is capable of appropriating *anything* for its purposes. The claim, for example, that Chaitanya's appearance in a popular, mass-marketed movie ultimately serves an end that is not especially devotional would not be an effort to undermine Chaitanya, so much as an effort to show how material interests always threaten spiritual pursuits.

But maybe there is yet another layer of complexity, even within this Marx-inspired, Frankfurt School understanding of *popular culture*. After all, if an external agency can wield *things* to create a mass of people that it can move in its own, desired direction, we might look for agencies apart from capitalism that also labor in this regard, agencies that might pose their own, contrary threat to capitalism, or that might be revolutionary, otherwise. This view might be inherent in Varuni Bhatia's 2017 study *Unforgetting Chaitanya*, since Bhatia argues that prominent individuals in nineteenth-century Bengal sought to elevate Chaitanya in the popular imagination precisely to combat what could be read as the *pop culture* forged in the region by western colonialism.[1]

One of western philosophy's most important theorists of *popular culture*, or, at least, of the technology of popular culture, seems similarly to have intuited the dual possibility in *pop* for undermining and also for activating individuality and the revolutionary potential that goes with it.[2] Walter Benjamin's ubiquitously cited essay "The Work of Art in the Age of Mechanical Reproduction" calls us to consider a subtle force in the mass production of *things* that might be understood as *art*. Technical reproduction, Benjamin reasons, saps the work of art of what, in history, had been its especial quality: the essential uniqueness of the artwork, as an object. The artwork's peculiar ability to grab attention, to awe, to inspire, and to sustain a kind of ritual authority—the art's "aura," as Benjamin terms it—depends on this uniqueness.

Mass reproduction puts itself between an individual and the religio-historical context in which the artwork, as a unique thing, had significance. One consequence, for Benjamin, is "a tremendous shattering of tradition," amounting to "the liquidation of the traditional value of... cultural heritage."[3] So, in the machine age that provides for the production of thousands, or millions, of copies of an image, the image has no path to being genuinely *present* to an individual. The reproduction establishes itself as present, in the place of the unique artwork, and the technology that makes the reproduction establishes itself as the thing with which a person has a relationship. In mass reproduction, Benjamin writes, the quality of the artwork's presence "is always depreciated."[4]

On the other hand, Benjamin intuits that reproduction provides an original work with a new force, one that is not necessarily negative, by putting "the copy of the original into situations which would be out of reach for the original itself."[5] In this case, the reproduced artwork meets a person "in his own particular situation . . . [and] it reactivates the object reproduced."[6]

If Benjamin is, in this "other hand" point, articulating his appreciation for the way in which a reproduction can, in spite of itself, bring the thing that the reproduction reproduces into a person's presence—at least, sort of—then Benjamin has sensed that quality of *popular culture* that holds more promise than despair, even if he can't quite commit himself to it. Perhaps, on the positive possibility of the mechanisms that ground popular culture, Benjamin is speaking in spite of himself, since he wants very much to warn everyone of the terrible use to which fascism can put the force that mass-produced imagery exerts on the world. Even so, in Benjamin we see a glimmer of something apart from, or in addition to, a confirmed view about *popular culture* that comes to us through Adorno and his Frankfurt comrades. When everyone seems to like the (reproducible) things that everyone else likes, because everyone has a kind of equal access to those things, then the things will make a common identity that subsumes everyone's existence; but there nevertheless remains a possibility for the reproduced thing to facilitate a genuine presence that might not be available to a particular person, otherwise.

Krishna, after all, does not look at the viewer.[7]

I'm talking about the image on the cover of the very first Amar Citra Katha (ACK) comic, published back in the year I was born, 1969. This first incidence of the facet of popular culture in India that is ACK comic books turned Krishna's eyes sharply aside. The choice was deliberate. ACK's founder Anant Pai (1929–2011) thought he should disrupt the possibility of the comic book's ritual, religious force.[8] There's no escaping the correlation of Pai's objective with Benjamin-ian theory, here, which claims that mechanical reproduction divests the art-image of its cult or ritual value. Pai seems to have exactly the aim of divesting the reproducible image of its religious potential, but by way of his design choice, his deliberate intervention, as though the machine reproduction wouldn't do the job. For Pai, the mechanical reproduction itself would not strip a cover image of Krishna of its Benjamin-esque *aura*. Without Pai's direction to his artist, apparently, the cover image could overlap with the ritual, religious value of a *mūrti*.

Before we conclude that Pai's Krishna-themed comic book shows that popular culture operates differently and has a different character in India, let us just acknowledge that Pai's decision to turn Krishna's eyes can be read as intending to fill the undeniably capitalist purpose of maximizing the comic's popular appeal. Karline McLain reports that Pai "did not want to run the risk of offending any orthodox Hindus."[9] Popular culture, as a concept in Europe and in India, turns out to be convoluted. To be fair to Benjamin, the cover of Pai's 1969, mass-produced comic book does, in fact, intervene between viewers and the presence of illustrator Yusuf Bangalorewala's original cover art. *That* thing—the singular sheet of paper or Bristol board on which Bangalorewala laid down pencil and ink—does not itself arrive in the hands of readers.[10]

Still, Pai's decision to make sure that, in his cover image, Krishna looks askance indicates something that Benjamin did not—perhaps could not—quite grasp, however much he sensed it. Pai's concern was not merely over divine presence in the cover of his comic book, but over the possibility of divine presence in *each* cover of *each* mass-printed reproduction of the issue. To whatever extent that Pai had reason to worry, we see that the mechanically reproduced image might very well operate, on a mass scale, as a ritual or cult object.

The reason is the population, itself, which is not and has never been, anywhere, merely a passive screen onto which culture and value and the like are projected. I wouldn't deny capitalism's ability to fashion culture, nor the plain evidence that people, en masse, can be seduced, duped, and manipulated. But, just as Marx figured that capitalism creates the conditions of its own destruction, I would argue that people are always the creative agency of things like *tradition* and *culture*, even of those that might turn on them.[11]

Benjamin, et. al., do not consider the possibility that *tradition* does not really *exist*. No tradition ever *existed*, in a consummate form. Tradition only *persists*, in a flow, in and by what people do. Not even in the primitive past of Benjamin's imagination can we find *tradition* that *is*, like a house in which people live and that can be handed down as a heritage from ancestor to heir. What people might regard as a tradition of the past, a tradition that was in history and that, perhaps, comes down to the present from history, is always and ever made *as* a tradition by a present population's regard for historical matters as indicative of a whole and by how that population acts that regard. Living people *do* tradition, as something in the present and also as a relic, recognized and perhaps longed-for, in the past.[12]

Tradition, with the religio-historical qualities that Benjamin identifies with it, comes not like a house but rather like the games that we play. If you know how to play Hearts, you've picked up its rules and its aims from the past, so that you affirm and perpetuate the tradition whenever you play. And it doesn't matter, much, which deck of cards you use. It's the *game*, not a particular *deck*, that has *presence*. Better still: playing the game *makes* presence, so that any particular deck can become the game's immediate embodiment. Considered in this way, mechanically reproduced works do not *necessarily* liquidate traditional value, since a populace always has the means to invest or to inject traditional value into reproduced works. A populace always *is* the means.

A few years after ACK's launch, Pai modified his policy to allow some front-facing, front-looking images of divine figures, as with Shiva in 1976's *Sati and Shiva*, and Krishna himself in ACK's 1977 adaptation of the Bhagavad Gītā. McLain notes that these sorts of images "do not derive from the American comic book formula, but are instead . . . influenced by Hindu ritual practices and ways of seeing." McLain goes on:

> Such iconic panels within the *ACK* comic books, in combination with the visual and textual narrativization of sacred Hindu stories, open up space for their Hindu readers to view them as something sacred, even if they do not ritually worship them.[13]

On the cover of that first ACK comic book, Pai felt that he had to turn Krishna from the viewer, because the populace of viewers to whom the comic was geared knew how to play Krishna's presence, even in a reproduction.

They were heirs of a tradition that the reproduced image could not shatter because the tradition itself provided the parameters for encountering divinity—or *aura*—in a reproduced image. ACK comics entered into popular culture in India, quickly and solidly, on account of a mixture of reasons. Among those reasons was the aptitude, broadly conserved in the culture, for finding God in things.

Apparently, I've said almost nothing about Chaitanya. But Chaitanya made a significant contribution to this cultural aptitude, particularly with regard to things like *books*.

One of the things we can attribute to Chaitanya is the demonstration of personal, embodied enactment of divine presence. Chaitanya seems to have known how to play in and with the world in such an earnest way as to transform how the world showed up. Anant Pai's comic book biography of Chaitanya, "Chaitanya Mahaprabhu: The Miracle Messenger of Love," published in 1975, intimates this crucial quality.[14] Within four pages of the comic's conclusion, Chaitanya is shown in the bucolic landscape of early sixteenth-century Braj, arms above his head, staring at a peacock that is perched on a tree branch above him. In a word balloon, Chaitanya says, "O MY LORD KRISHNA."[15]

This pop history recognizes Chaitanya's inclination to see God everywhere and in everything, but it also hints that the inclination didn't arise spontaneously. The written narration for this panel: "As usual, Chaitanya Dev went barefoot. The bellowing of a cow or the sight of a peacock would arouse in him the thought of Lord Krishna." The first sentence doesn't necessarily offer the ground for the second, but it might. *As usual*, that is, Chaitanya undertook some specific sort of embodied practice, and the manifestation of God followed. Indeed, the panel shows the person who had been Nimāi now with a shaven head and wearing saffron—choices that Nimāi makes for how to do his material body. For that matter, this panel is part of the comic book's account of Chaitanya's pilgrimage throughout the subcontinent, each barefoot step marking Chaitanya's enactment of a certain reality. Christian Novetzke notes how central such embodied practice is to *bhakti*:

> [The] publics of *bhakti* in South Asia require "embodiment". . . . The manifestation of *bhakti* not only in performance through song or literacy, but also through all those actions and bodily displays that make up *bhakti* in the broadest sense, such as . . . pilgrimage, *pūjā*, *darśan*, the wearing of signs on the body, and so on.[16]

If doing *bhakti* can tune a person to find God in a peacock, then, no doubt, in *any* peacock. Perhaps there are distinct differences between individual peacocks that would manifest to the familiar, expert eye, so that one peacock does not look just like another. Otherwise, for folks not tuned in to peacock peculiarities, one peacock might as well be a copy of another. And where one can find God in any functionally-identical peacock, one might, by the same operation, find God in any and all animals, in any and all trees, in any *thing*, including things mass manufactured in the age of machines.

"*Bhakti* traditions," writes Barbara A. Holdrege, "foster a variety of notions in which the deity assumes corporeal form in a human body."[17] Which is, perhaps, only pointing out the obvious. But "the deity" also assumes form in objects, like books. Jīva Gosvāmī regarded the Bhāgavata Purāṇa as "*non-different* from Kṛṣṇa."[18] The importance to the *bhakti* tradition of reciting the Bhāgavata Purāṇa would affirm an understanding that it is the book's *content* that matters and that the book's *content* invites a view of the book as divine. But Jīva seems to have the book, as a book, in mind. In the *Tattva Sandarbha*, he characterizes the Bhāgavata as a *pratinidhi-rūpa* or "representative embodiment."[19] Jīva's not alone. Chaitanya himself, according to Vrindāvana Dāsa Ṭhākura's sixteenth-century biography, identified the Bhāgavata Purāṇa as "an *avatāra* of Kṛṣṇa in the form of a text." And Krishnadāsa Kavirāja reports Chaitanya as characterizing the Bhāgavata as a *svārupa* of God, "identical with Kṛṣṇa."[20] The Bhāgavata is not just any book, of course, so it's not like the content doesn't have something to do with how devotees experience it. But note: if the *material* thing that is the Bhāgavata Purāṇa book can be divine, it follows that divinity can appear in *each* and *any* copy of that book. The multiplication of copies does not impair any particular copy's potentially divine aura.

The thing is knowing how to play the game. As Holdrege accounts for it, the Padma Purāṇa, in its Bhāgavata Mahātmya portion, does not merely regard the Bhāgavata Purāṇa as divine. It prescribes a method for ritually reciting the Bhāgavata, and also for ritually venerating it *as a book*, including a prayer that addresses the book: "You are Kṛṣṇa himself visible to the eyes."[21] In the *Tattva Sandarbha* and also the *Bhakti Sandarbha*, Jīva identifies a battery of practices "through which *bhaktas* can engage the Bhāgavata in both its oral-aural and written-visual forms."[22] The same playing would be applicable with any physical copy of the book, so that, when mass printing shows up, some two hundred years later, it does not shatter the tradition, in

Benjamin's terms, that holds the book as sacred.

In the case of the first ACK comic, Waeerkar's original cover art, on its own in 1969, long before ACK had established itself in India's popular imagination, could have little in the way of traditional value. In the 1960's, when Pai launched ACK, the "comic book,' as such, was only two or three decades old, and hadn't yet claimed for itself a status as *art*, anywhere on the globe.[23] But each of the thousands of "Krishna" covers, on the other hand, each precisely repeating the others, even before they rolled off the press, were already primed for a traditional value—a unique presence, in each case, and a uniquely founded *aura*—because the capacity to enact that value, to *play* it in whichever copy of the comic their hands found, was already in the people to whom the comic would be available.

Maybe I'm finally getting to the point where I say something about ACK's Chaitanya comic book, as a comic book. Krishna appears with Chaitanya on the cover of this 1975 publication. As on the cover of ACK's first comic, Krishna's eyes do not look forward. Neither do Chaitanya's. He stands in front of and to the right of Krishna, turned slightly to the right, his hands raised above his shoulders, and his face and eyes turned upwards. An iconic posture of devotion. For his part, Krishna's eyes are on Chaitanya. By 1975, Pai had allowed front-facing, front-looking figures on covers. The "Ayyappan" issue, no. 85, published in 1975, presents Ayyappan riding a tiger directly toward readers. Both Ayyappan's and the tiger's eyes engage the viewer's. Issue 89, published immediately prior to the Chaitanya issue, offers a distinctly devotional image of Ganesha, almost indistinguishable in posture and mien from a *mūrti* that one might find in the shrine of any shop or home. So, the enterprise had crossed that line that Pai had drawn at the outset, in acknowledgment that, without care, the comic's cover images might call for religious veneration. For issue 90, both of the cover's figures retreat back across that line, affirming, perhaps, a special consideration for the potential of images of Krishna and Chaitanya to radiate divinely.

The comic book's interior content is artistically conservative. Each page offers a few, sharply squared panels that firmly contain the action of each scene they present. Most pages have considerable narration, in the form of simple prose in text boxes that are almost always set at the top of a panel so that the narration is the first thing in each panel on which a reader's eye will fall. The ACK comics, in this way, privilege the written word, and the visual art mostly shows up to illustrate the text.

But it's worth noting that each panel in this "Chaitanya Mahaprabhu" issue—with only one or two exceptions—places the viewer at the eye level of the people whom the visual art presents. That is to say, the very first panel, which presents a half-page scene of the village of Nabadwip and Jagannath Mishra seated in the near foreground, places the viewer on eye-level with Mishra, as though standing just behind him and looking down at the village from his elevated perch. In the first page's final panel, Mishra is turned toward the viewer. Rather than placing the view of Mishra at a point above him, or below him, the panel again gives Mishra to the viewer at Mishra's own eye level. All of the panels that follow, all the way to the very end, are roughly the same. Whatever is happening in a panel, the art places the viewer at eye level of the panel's principal figures.[24]

Intentional or accidental, I can't say, but keeping the comic's viewer at eye level with the comic's people does a couple of things. First, that eye-level perspective undermines comic art's capacity to create the experience of the miraculous. The super-hero comics that dominate the market commonly tilt, drop, raise, and skew the viewer's approach to a scene, which help human(oid) figures to appear as more-than-human: bigger, stronger, faster, more heroic. Even *miraculously* heroic (which only makes sense, since comic book super-powers are, essentially, miracles). The eye-level design of each panel in ACK #90 keeps Chaitanya very human. The avoidance of the miraculous was certainly intentional. Pai's original policy for ACK comics was "minimizing the miraculous."[25] Comic #90 avoids illustrating the miraculous, even when there's a call for it, as when Nimāi rushes to punish Madhāi and Jagāi for injuring Nityānanda, Chaitanya's elder and one of his most important followers. Common renderings of this episode call up a supernatural *chakra*-weapon on Nimāi's finger. Pai's comic keeps the *chakra* entirely out of the story. The eye-level perspective reinforces the experience of the story as about real people in the real world.

That's a world that is shared by a viewer, which is the second thing that the eye-level perspective accomplishes. The fantastic points-of-view that superhero comics give to viewers put the viewers at some distance from what happens in these stories, as the point-of-view is itself a bit miraculous. One couldn't *really* view Batman on the top of a building from high above. That point-of-view would cast the viewer as miraculously capable of hovering flight. Or, at least, that top-down perspective creates a view that would be possible from a hovering drone with a camera—that is, the view would imply that the viewer is not present in Batman's happening space and time, but receiving the image remotely, as through a movie or television screen. Aligned with some of the comic book storytellers who are the most capable of developing human rapport between comic characters and viewers—Will Eisner, Gilbert Hernandez, Marjane Satrapi—Pai's artists, under his demands for a staid naturalism, provide for viewers to be with the characters in the comics, in those characters' worlds, as co-players in those worlds.

And there's a devotional advantage in this. Eschewing the miraculous and imposing an eye-level view of things emulates Krishna's own mercy in the Bhagavad Gītā, when, as Arjuna swoons under the vision of Krishna's transcendent form, Krishna recovers himself in a human form that Arjuna can comprehend and with which he can have a human relationship.[26] What Pai's non-miraculous telling of Chaitanya sacrifices, it claims again in its invitation to viewers to know Chaitanya, as a person and personally.

Which might bring us back to Chaitanya in popular culture. We can certainly see how Pai's ACK project not only found a market, but then operated to shape that market, even to create the population for whom ACK comics would be a crucial commodity. McLain provides a clear account of the strategies that Pai employed to do just this, until, by 1986, ACK was selling lakhs of copies of its books, every month, in a gamut of languages.[27] We can even see how, in a Benjamin-ian way, ACK comics came to take the place of the divine and human figures whose stories they told.[28] In this view, ACK #90 would erase Chaitanya. In his place would be the comic itself, dearly paid for, dearly read, dearly kept, dearly remembered.

But *bhakti* and Chaitanya himself established, long ago, a doctrine of genuine divinity in a book and its copies. The regard for the book—dearly kept, dearly remembered, in ritual reverence—can provide access to divine presence. Even while ACK #90 shapes and motivates a mass of people to accomplish its self-serving purposes, it nevertheless also gives itself to shaping and motivating that mass for divine purpose. In the *bhakti* tradition, the capitalism that seeks its own ends in ACK's success can itself be seen as a tool of an even grander force.

Perhaps, then, we can see ACK's "Chaitanya Mahaprabhu" comic book as not especially threatening to devotion. The comic book, as a medium, has been regarded for all of its short life as trivial, at best, and as dangerously subversive. And one doesn't need to know much about comic book history to know that certain artists have wielded the medium, deliberately, for both trivial and subversive ends. But with an acknowledgment of Marshall McLuhan's insight, the medium is not necessarily the message. At least, every medium has always been suspect, at one point or another in its history, regardless of the messages they might have been carrying. The four Vedas, for instance, were not written down for centuries, for fear of the damage that a written form would do to them. Audio recording and photographing rās-līlā theatre in Vrindavan was generally prohibited until the late twentieth century. People accommodated themselves to these media as the media showed what they could contribute. ACK #90 can contribute, positively, to a person's devotion. The crucial thing is knowing how to play with the book.

Endnotes

1. While Bhatia especially connects the nineteenth-century effort to remember, or "to unforget," Chaitanya with the aspirations of the region's *bhadralok* bourgeoisie, she nevertheless identifies a link between the development of Bengali Vaishnavism with "the cultural apparatus deployed by the Communists in Bengal." At least the communists in Bengal, at one time, recognized Chaitanya's revolutionary potential. See Varuni Bhatia, *Unforgetting Chaitanya: Vaishnavism and Cultures of Devotion in Colonial Bengal* (Oxford: Oxford University Press, 2017), 19.

2. Benjamin begins his essay with a preface that notes Marx's own insight that capitalism creates "conditions which would make it possible to abolish capitalism itself." See Walter Benjamin, *Illuminations*, Hannah Arendt, ed. (New York: Mariner Books, 2019), 167.

3. Benjamin, 171.

4. Benjamin, 170.

5. Benjamin, 170.

6. Benjamin, 171.

7. From a devotional point-of-view, Krishna certainly *does* look at the viewer, all the time, whatever the form of an illustration might suggest, otherwise.

8. Karline McLain, *India's Immortal Comic Books: Gods, Kings, and Other Heroes* (Bloomington: Indiana University Press, 2009), 16.

9. McLain, 17. McLain also argues that Pai conceded to market forces by deciding to publish ACK comics in English. Pai knew, McLain writes, "that the market for such comic books was the rapidly growing English-speaking middle classes of urban India" (25). ACK comics do not contradict the understanding of popular culture as a particularly capitalist phenomenon. But ACK does show that the satisfaction of capitalist demands is not the only force behind popular culture.

10. Indeed, the original art for the "Krishna" issue—which, at this point would probably have a considerable monetary value—might have been lost forever in a 1994

fire that consumed much of ACK's archive of original work.

11. What I've written here can be construed as victim blaming. But I don't have the interaction of particular individuals in mind. And, anyway, I'm not excusing or justifying the exploitation of popular imagination.

12. A nod, again, to Varuni Bhatia, whose book is founded on her recognition of nineteenth-century efforts to renew, or to newly do—*to unforget*, as Batia would have it—Chaitanya as (a) tradition.

13. McLain, 17.

14. The 1975 issue of the Chaitanya comic is number 90. ACK initiated a reprint series when the company stopped producing new titles, in 1991. The reprint series gives new numbers to all of ACK's titles, beginning with the first "Krishna" issue from 1969, re-numbered as #501. In the reprint series, the "Chaitanya Mahaprabhu" issue is #631. Wikipedia provides a comprehensive list of all ACK issues, with original and reprint numbers: https://en.wikipedia.org/wiki/List_of_Amar_Chitra_Katha_comics.

15. In my copy of this comic book, the pages have not been printed with numbers. Also, all the written text, including all of the spoken dialogue, is rendered in all-caps. I decided to keep the capitalization, here, rather than decide which of these four words ought to be capitalized, even though the all-caps might make it seem like Chaitanya is screaming his devotion.

16. Quoted in Barbara A. Holdrege, *Bhakti and Embodiment: Fashioning Divine Bodies and Devotional Bodies in Kṛṣṇa Bhakti* (New York: Routledge, 2017), 24.

17. Holdrege, 23.

18. Holdrege, 152.

19. Holdrege, 77.

20. Quoted in Holdrege, 140.

21. Quoted in Holdrege, 137.

22. Holdrege, 140.

23. I recognize that dating the invention of the "comic book" depends on a theory of what constitutes a comic book, and that these theories vary widely. Among the many treatments of the history of comic books, and of the theory of what they are, one might consult Scott McCloud's *Understanding Comics: The Invisible Art* (New York: HarperPerennial, 1994).

24. The notable exceptions are, perhaps, only two. The first is a middle panel, a few pages in, in which Nimāi, a teenage troublemaker, does a cannonball into the water at a *ghat*, splashing the priests in their ritual labor at the water's edge. This panel gives the reader a unique view from above, looking down on Nimāi's explosive splash. The only other exception is late in the story, when Nimāi leaves Nabadwip by swimming across the Ganges. Here, a panel offers another look-from-above, as Nimāi emerges from the water at Katwa.

25. McLain, 30.

26. In the tradition that recognizes Chaitanya's own divinity—as the *channa* or hid-

den *avatāra*—Chaitanya had his own reason for assuming human-ness. The tradition teaches that he wanted to experience being "human" inasmuch as he wanted to "taste the love of Rādhā, and know her Rādhā-bhāva, or the love of a perfect devotee." For this purpose, as Nimāi, he often kept his divinity a secret and interacted as a devotee rather than as God. See Steven J. Rosen, "'I am He': The Unique Secret of Mahāprabhu's Divinity," in *Chaitanyology: A Collection of Essays on Śrī Chaitanya* (Charlottesville, VA: Bookwrights Press, 2023), 28–41.

27. McLain, 41-45. McLain, on page 45, quotes some data provided by Vikram Doctor, in a 1997 article for *Businessworld*.

28. McLain offers the representative testimony of one reader: "Growing up as a kid in India, my memories and knowledge of Indian mythology and history are constructed solely of the numerous *Amar Chitra Katha* books that were my staple diet for reading" (22).

Bibliography

Benjamin, Walter. *Illuminations.* Edited by Hannah Arendt. New York: Mariner Books, 2019.

Bhatia, Varuni. *Unforgetting Chaitanya: Vaishnavism and Cultures of Devotion in Colonial Bengal.* Oxford: Oxford University Press, 2017.

Holdrege, Barbara A. *Bhakti and Embodiment: Fashioning Divine Bodies and Devotional Bodies in Kṛṣṇa Bhakti.* New York: Routledge, 2017.

McLain, Karline. *India's Immortal Comic Books: Gods, Kings, and Other Heroes.* Bloomington: Indiana University Press, 2009.

McCloud, Scott. *Understanding Comics: The Invisible Art.* New York: HarperPerennial, 1994.

Rosen, Steven J., "'I am He': The Unique Secret of Mahāprabhu's Divinity." In *Chaitanyology: A Collection of Essays on Śrī Chaitanya.* Charlottesville, VA: Bookwrights Press, 2023.

A Temple That is Not a Temple: The Sri Chaitanya Mahaprabhu Museum in Kolkata

Måns Broo and Sourish Das (Sundar Gopal Das)

Introduction

A visitor to the beautiful and historical Baghbazar Gaudiya Math in north Kolkata would not fail to notice the futuristic, gold-colored building standing right next to the famous marble temple belonging to the Gaudiya Mission. This is the Sri Chaitanya Mahaprabhu Museum, a landmark achievement of the Gaudiya Mission in recent years. In this article, we will describe some of the thought and plans that went into this very interesting museum, offering not only a description of the museum itself, but also some general reflections on the construction of religious space in urban India today.

The architecture of Kolkata in general has of course been studied before. Siddharta Sen (2017) offers a fascinating overview of the architecture and urban planning of this city, from its beginnings in the late 17th century until today, noting the unique character of its city planning post-independence and until the 1990s, as the massive influx of Bangladeshi refugees, the growth of slums and a resulting near collapse of urban infrastructure left the local government with policy planning as the only available option. Civil unrest and fighting between Naxalite revolutionaries/terrorists and communists ended with the advent of the Left Front government in 1977, but this regime, which remained in power until 2011, led Kolkata to become "a stagnant city, shunned by outsiders, a 'black hole' in the eyes of foreigners. It remained a city of traffic jams, poverty, squalor, and slums" (Sen 2017: 238). Since the 1990s, Kolkata has seen rapid development, as the city authorities began to open up to global trends, though many hurdles remain. Often this has led to the demolishing of colonial architecture; Shivashish Bose (2015) has noted the difficulties inherent in conserving old buildings in Kolkata since the 1990s.

Deonnie Moodie (2019) has in an excellent monograph studied the Kālī temple at Kālīghaṭ in south Kolkata, providing a wealth of ethnographic information on the processes of pushing for and resisting modernization (meaning breaking the power of the local Brahmin priests) at this important shrine. She shows further how since the 1990s, temples have once again regained their popularity among the Hindu urban middle classes, but that these people want a particular kind of temples—clean, orderly and serene temples.

Now, the Sri Chaitanya Mahaprabhu Museum is not a temple; it is self-consciously a museum with an educational rather than a religious mission. Nevertheless, as we shall see, it is run by a religious organization with an explicit religious mission, and much of it fits very well into Moodie's description of the modern Hindu temple.

The Baghbazar Gaudiya Math

When Gauḍīya Vaiṣṇava reformer Bhaktisiddhānta Sarasvatī (b. Bimalā Prasāda Datta, 1874–1937) first began his outreach in Kolkata in 1918, he did so in rented premises at nr 1, Ultadanga Junction Road in Manicktala. It was here that in 1922 he first met the young Abhay Charan De (1896–1977), who much later became Bhaktivedanta Swami Prabhupāda, the founder of ISKCON, but more important for the present article is Bhaktisiddhānta's meeting, at this same place, with Jagabandhu Datta in 1925.

Jagabandhu Datta (1872–1930) was born in Banaripara in today's Bangladesh and came to the then Calcutta as a half-deaf, destitute and unhappy young man, but through hard work and an uncommonly acute business sense, he made a fortune by manufacturing and selling silver jewelry, ink, scented oils and other products. Datta first met disciples of Bhaktisiddhānta in 1919; he later credited them with curing him of a serious leg infection. On the advice of these disciples, Datta began studying the literature of Bhaktisiddhānta and his father Bhaktivinoda (1838–1914), finding particularly much happiness in Bhaktivinoda's didactic novel *Jaivadharma* (1893). He began spending time with Bhaktisiddhānta's disciples whenever he could, becoming particularly close to Kuñjavihārī Vidyābhūṣaṇa (1894–1976). Datta was impressed by the sincerity and dedication of Bhaktisiddhānta's followers, and when he finally met Bhaktisiddhānta himself, he felt that he had met his eternal spiritual master, and that the depression that had been plaguing him for years finally disappeared (Anon 1928).

Jagabandhu Datta had two wives but no offspring. After lengthy discussions with Kuñjavihārī Vidyābhūṣaṇa, he decided to spend the lion's share of his fortune on a grand temple for his guru. In 1928, he bought a piece of land close to his own residence in Baghbazar, Kolkata. The ground-breaking ceremony for the new temple that fall was covered in *The Bengalee*, one of the leading newspapers of the time.

> On Wednesday last, the 26th ultimo, the ceremony for laying the foundation of the proposed Temple for the Gaudiya Math, Calcutta, was performed with great eclat. The plot of land at 16, Kali Prosad Chakravarty Street, Bagbazar, recently secured for the Gaudiya Math, was very beautifully decorated with a pandal in the middle. At 7 A.M. the big procession with *Sankirtan* from the present Math arrived on the spot under the lead of Pandit Kunja Behari Vidyabhusan, whose whole-hearted labour brought the whole function to a successful end. Large number of people from various parts of Calcutta had already assembled there and the whole plot was overcrowded. His Divine Grace Paramahansa Sri Srimad Bhakti Siddhanta Saraswati Goswami Maharaj entered the pandal amidst hearty cheers of the whole assembly. At the auspicious moment, the necessary Puja and other ceremonials were duly performed. Sree Paramhansa Thakur solemnly laid the foundation-stone in the midst of loud and prolonged cries of "Haribol." The ceremony being over Pandit Sundarananda Vidyavinode, B.A. delivered an interesting lecture tracing out therein the History of the Gaudiya Math since its inception, it aims objects and its special line of activities as distinct from other Institutions of the kind in doing real and eternal good to the humanity at large. In the course of his speech he went on to say that the Gaudiya Math implores the whole people of the world without any distinction whatsoever to suspend their present activities in all forms, to halt for a while in their breathless race only to listen for the moment to the message of the Math. The Math has taken upon itself the task of solving all problems in connection with it in the light of *Sanatan Shastras* and to remove all possible doubts and misgivings that stand in the way of accepting the message of Math. This is how the Math has arranged to do eternal good to one and all good not only at the present life alone, but of the eternal life for all time to come. His Divine Holiness Sri Srimad Bhakti Siddhanta Saraswati Goswami Maharaja in a neat little speech explained the significance and value of activities of the Math-members, who are engaged in preaching the true teachings of Sriman Mahaprabhu Sri Sri Chaitanya Deva, who alone has

> kindly chalked out the royal road to eternal good for every being—which fact was so long not only unknown to the world but was perverted in its entirety.
>
> Everybody present showed cordial benedictions upon the benevolent donor Jagadbandhu Datta, who was garlanded by Srila Paramhansa Thakur Himself.[1]

On the 21st of April 1929, the construction work began. Jagabandhu Datta would personally be present and supervise the construction work at the site. The temple itself became 85 feet tall, topped with nine graceful domes in the Bengali style. Around the temple, Datta constructed living quarters and a large kirtan hall so that many people could be accommodated during the Mission's many festivals to sit and listen to the lectures. Datta bore all the costs for the temple construction and without depending on anyone would visit the markets and personally get the best materials for building the formidable structure. Despite his physical illness during that time, he would still be present at the construction site to supervise the work from early morning to late into the night.

The temple was ready in the fall of 1930, when Bhaktisiddhānta and his followers shifted from Ultadangi Road to the new temple in a large and festive procession. Shortly after this, Jagabandhu Datta passed away, but the legacy of his temple remained. After Bhaktisiddhānta passed away on the first of January 1937, his movement soon splintered into many factions. The Bagbazaar temple became the headquarters of what was arguably the main branch, the Gaudiya Mission (Sardella 2013: 129–132).

The Genesis of the Chaitanya Museum

In 2008, the then general secretary of the Gaudiya Mission, Swami Bhakti Sundar Sannyasi Maharaj, felt the need for a museum in reverence to the contributions of Bhaktivinoda and his disciples to the Chaitanya movement. The importance of Bhaktivinoda towards Gauḍīya Vaiṣṇavism in the modern period has been noted by many scholars (see e.g., Ghosh 2014; Okita 2010; Wong 2014 and 2018), but he is of particular note for the followers of his son Bhaktisiddhānta, as his songs and writings form a central part of their liturgy and theology, and since he discovered the birthplace of Chaitanya that they now administer (see Bhatia 2017: 161–199).

The museum was to be constructed in Swarupganj, Navadwip, close to

Bhaktivinoda's residence and *samādhi* memorial. Sannyasi Maharaj remembers,

> At that time I was in Nabadwip and at one point within a dream I had been given the glimpse and inspiration to somehow come up with the idea of a Vaishnava museum in the name of Bhaktivinoda Thakur. Later, I proposed the idea to [the then president of the Gaudiya Mission] Bhakti Suhrid Parivrajak Maharaj and with his permission and spiritual blessings, I could go forward with the idea, to apply the inspiration that I got from Bhaktivinoda Thakur and build a museum.[2]

Nevertheless, when the Gaudiya Mission held its annual meeting in 2011, its governing committee raised some doubts about the plan. Firstly, focusing on Bhaktivinoda felt too restricting in terms of reaching a broader audience, and secondly, Svarupganj is not easy to reach, since it is out in the countryside. The idea instead was to broaden the scope of the museum to focus on Caitanya, and to place the museum in Kolkata instead of rural Swarupganj. Parivrajak Maharaj felt that this would be a fitting tribute to Caitanya on the event of his 525th birth commemoration that year.[3]

In the years since the founding of the temple, the area around it has been extensively developed. While the temple and associate buildings have been periodically renovated, the area itself was not enlarged before 1999, when Parivrajak Maharaj acquired 4 *kathas* of land (ca. 268 m2) adjacent to the temple. Again in 2010, another 5.5 *kathas* (ca. 369 m2) were purchased. Nevertheless, this new land formed a narrow strip right between existing buildings, some of which were deemed protected heritage buildings. The new land was only 55 feet wide, and after accommodating mandatory open spaces around the building, only 25 feet remained.

The late Dr. Gopal Mitra, a member of the design team of the World Trade Centre and a pioneer of multi-storied housing complexes in Kolkata, accepted the challenge to design the museum building. Dr. Gopal Mitra proposed a three-story (49.5 feet high) building design in 2013, fulfilling all space requirements but following the stringent building rules of the local municipality. Special permission for the desired building height was obtained with the help of the Chief Minister of West Bengal (Roy 2019: 39).

In his design, Gopal Mitra was inspired by organic forms, such as those of the Guggenheim Museum in New York, but space restraints led him to more of a ramped gallery. The facade is finished with golden tinted Aluminum cladding, matching the yellow surface of the older buildings. A continuous horizontal recessed glazed window with a greenish tint looks like a loop of golden ribbon gradually wider at the top (Roy 2019: 39).

On the 16th of September 2013, the foundation stone of the museum was laid by the former President of India, Sri Pranab Mukherjee. In his talk, the President said,

> I call Sri Chaitanya a magician and a revolutionary. He lived here 526 years ago, when Bengal was going through one of its most turbulent times. The society was at a strange crossroads, on the one hand reeling under the ruthless diktats of the Brahmins, and on the other hearing about the message of equality and harmony that Islam had brought into the country. It was then the Chaitanya emerged with his message of peace and love and shook the Hindu society out of its stupor.[4]

An important factor in the construction and design of the museum was the desire of the Gaudiya Mission to co-operate with various Indian state agencies. The design of the museum itself was undertaken by the National Council of Science Museums (NCSM) under the guidance of Saroj Ghose, an Indian science popularizer, museum maker and the introducer of the concept of high-tech storytelling museums in India. He was the museum advisor to the President of India and the Former President of ICOM (International Council of Museums), as well as the former director of NCSM (National Council of Science Museum). Ghose guided the museum in preserving and exhibiting valuable artefacts, manuscripts, and other evidence of Chaitanya and his associates (Roy 2019: 38).

This co-operation also led to state funds. Through the recommendation of Pranab Mukherjee and Mamata Banerjee, the prime minister of the state of West Bengal, the NCSM invested 4 crores (40 million) rupees in the Museum. Another 5 crores was received from the Department of Information and Culture, Government of India. The museum also received what is called Corporate Social Responsibility (CSR) funds, that is, funds that Non-Profit Organizations (NGOs) can get from the corporate sector. Under the Indian Companies Act, 2013, it is a mandatory provision to provide a contribution of 2 percent of the average net profits of companies. CRS funds were donated to the Museum by companies such as Coal India Ltd., Indian Peerless Co., Dalmia Cement, Syntex, and LIC (Life Insurance Corporation of India).[5]

The largest private donation—3 crores rupees—came from Manju Mitra of

Golders Green, London. Manju Mitra's father, Kali Mitra, had been the attorney for the Gaudiya Mission in the United Kingdom. After his demise, Manju Mitra took over his work for the Mission and also became the president of the Gaudiya Mission Vidya Mandir School at Swarupganj, Navadwip.[6]

The building of the museum began in July 2014 and was supposed to last three years, but because of various ensuing problems—not the least the almost impossible task of convincing illegal squatters to vacate such a valuable space—the construction took five years. The input of Dr. Himadri Guha, an eminent civil engineer must also be mentioned, for he took charge of the project at a very critical time (Roy 2019: 40). Finally, on the 13th of August 2019, the museum was officially inaugurated by the Chief Minister of West Bengal, Mamata Banerjee.

Contents of the Museum

The ground floor of the museum focuses on the life of Caitanya Mahāprabhu. The first hall ("meditation hall") houses a life-size statue of Mahāprabhu built in Jaisalmer stone along with replicas of his wooden sandals. The idea of this hall is that the visitor can sit here in some modicum of comfort before entering further.

The second hall ("*mānava līlā*") focuses on the first 24 years of Mahāprabhu's life. Here, traditional Bengali art forms such as *paṭuya* painting and terracotta reliefs have been used. The third and final hall of the first floor ("*prema dāna līlā*") narrates the post-initiation life of Mahāprabhu in the form of life-size dioramas, tableaux, and virtual reality.

On the first floor (one flight up), the fourth hall ("*jīva uddhara līlā*") depicts Mahāprabhu's travel to Vrindavan through the forests of Jharikhand, where he is supposed to have made wild animals dance in ecstatic love for Kṛṣṇa. Here, the museum uses both lights and sounds to create an immersive experience. The fifth hall shows Mahāprabhu and his associates, both those in Puri and those in Vrindavan.

On the second floor, the focus shifts to the post-Caitanya era. Hall number six focuses on the Viśva Vaiṣṇava Rāja Sabhā, as founded by Jīva Gosvāmin in the 16th century and then revived by Bhaktivinoda and Bhaktisiddhānta in the 19th and 20th centuries. The museum here exhibits artefacts connected with the two latter saints, such as fans, walking sticks, water pots, pens, manuscripts, and printed books. The seventh hall focuses on the impact of Caitanya on Bengali culture, such as various temples, musical instruments, and visual arts. Here also books and manuscripts are displayed and there is an interactive multimedia show for those who wish to learn more.

The third and final floor houses the eighth hall, focusing on Bhaktisiddhānta. It contains his life-size image, pictures of him and his chief disciples, articles he used, handwritten letters, and some of his clothing. On this floor one also finds an auditorium seating 140 spectators, equipped with state-of-the-art facilities. The auditorium is used for organizing workshops, seminars, and other programs relating to the museum.

The museum exhibits some 70 items, many of them pieces of ancient Gauḍīya Vaiṣṇava temples or places of special significance, such a terracotta panel from the prison of Hussain Shah where Sanātana Gosvāmin was incarcerated, but many also associated with important Gauḍīya Vaiṣṇava leaders, such as a cup used by Rasikānanda Deva or a broach used by Miss Daisy Bowtell (Vinodavāṇī Dāsī), one of the first Western converts to the faith.

Of perhaps the greatest interest to Gauḍīya Vaiṣṇavas is a fragment of Bengali handwriting purported to belong to Caitanya himself, and the Adhokṣaja Viṣṇu image held to have been worshipped by Jagannātha Miśra, Caitanya's father, and which was found when excavating Caitanya's birthplace.

Impact of the Museum

The media team of the Gaudiya Mission has been active during the whole process of establishing and nurturing the museum, making sure to keep media updated and well-informed. For example, the opening of the museum was covered online alone by *The Times of India* (9.8.2019),[7] *Millenium Post* (10.8.2019),[8] *The Siasat Daily* (12.8.2019),[9] *One India* (13.8.2019),[10] *Hindustan Times* (14.8.2019),[11] and other news sources. As but one example, the *The New Indian Express* (8.8.2019) wrote,

> The museum is the dream project of Gaudiya Mission, which will be a reality after its inauguration on August 13. Amidst the prevalent cruelty, clashes or say intolerant situations in our society, we wish to showcase Mahaprabhu's teachings and vision and serve the society," Bhakti Nishtha Madhusudan Maharaj, the mission's assistant secretary and museum in-charge told IANS.
>
> The Gaudiya Mission, a spiritual and philanthropic organisation established in 1935, propagates the teachings of Sri Chaitanya and the Vaishnava faith. It has many centres in India and temples in London and New York.
>
> He said that they aimed at spreading the message across society and not just keep it restricted to the devotees. They want researchers,

> intellectual and scholars to avail of the library facilities and experience a detailed life of Mahaprabhu by visiting the museum.
>
> The museum is a three-storey structure built on an area of approximately 1,350 square metres and includes galleries, public utility areas and a library. Each floor is dedicated to different phases of the saint's life starting from his birth, his marriage with Vishnupriya, journey throughout the country up to the period after he attained "Sanyasa" (sainthood).
>
> Life-size models, 3D films, audio tracks and animatronics will ensure maximum engagement of the visitors. The museum has been designed by the National Council of Science Museums (NCSM). "While the museum seeks to play a key role in creating awareness among the present generations, its primary objective is to preserve all the evidence of Vaishnava heritage, living traditions as well as the intangible heritage which are disappearing very fast," the official page of the museum said.[12]

Some researchers have already availed themselves to the facilities offered by the museum. For example, on the 21st of August, 2021, a seminar on "The Role of Chaitanya Mahaprabhu in Modern Society" was held at the museum, with speakers including Dr. Sk. Makbul Islam of Saint Paul's Cathedral Mission College. Many other scholars have given guest lectures at the venue. For example, on the 10th of May, 2022, Dr. Abhishek Ghosh spoke on the *Amrita Bazaar Patrika* in the history of Vaiṣṇavism.

The general public appears to have taken well to the museum. On the 24th of May, 2023, Google gave the museum a rating of 4.5 based on 139 reviews. Many reviewers comment on the cleanliness and peacefulness of the establishment (in particular contrast with the chaotic and congested streets in Baghbazar just outside). Judging from the pictures uploaded, many did not visit the museum alone but also the temple next door. Interestingly, the ratings for the temple itself (Sri Gaudiya Math Baghbazar) are even higher (4.6 based on 537 reviews); again, people liked the peacefulness and friendliness of the resident monks—though some did complain about the quality of the food!

These reviews can be compared to those of the famous Kālīghaṭ Kālī temple, which has a rating of 4.2 based on 507 reviews. Confirming the views voiced in Moodie's study (2019), many remark on the powerful spiritual energy present but also warn against the "scams" of local shopkeepers, the "money-grabbing" Brahmins, the crowds, and the general lack of order. Some write that they will never visit again. On the other hand, the Dakṣineśvara

Kālī temple, where Rāmakṛṣṇa Paramahaṃsa lived, has a rating of 4.7 based on no less than 74,283 reviews! The Sri Chaitanya Mahaprabhu museum has a long way to go to reach such popularity.

Concluding Reflections

The fact that the Gaudiya Mission, an explicitly religious organization, decided to build a museum rather than a temple, and to do so in co-operation with government agencies such as the Indian National Council of Science Museums, can be understood in many different ways. One is a pragmatic consideration. The leaders of the Gaudiya Mission are well connected within the Indian political landscape (for example, the Baghbazar temple has in recent years been officially visited both by Mamata Banerjee and by Narendra Modi, fierce political opponents of each other), and by downplaying the religious aspect of the project, they managed to secure state funding for it.

Nevertheless, at least as important a motive is surely the wish of the Gaudiya Mission to spread the message of Caitanya in new and innovative ways, a legacy of theirs from the time of Bhaktisiddhānta himself, who, though going to great lengths to demonstrate his fidelity to the teachings of the first followers of Caitanya, consciously made use of technical advances such as mass communication like newspapers and the radio, slideshow presentations, and exhibitions to spread his teachings. A futuristic, aluminum-cladded golden building fits perfectly into this mode of Gauḍīya Vaiṣṇavism.

Somtimes, museums have been seen as the paradigmatic "secular space," where religious artefacts are stripped of their original meaning and transformed into powerless objects to be seen by mildly interested onlookers (see e.g., Reeve 2012). In a place where the boundaries between different religions can be so hotly contested as in India, this makes a museum a safe space, as it were, where anyone can visit.

Still, as noted by scholars such as Crispin Pain (2013), in many locations, the status of the museum as a purely secular location is being renegotiated, with many museums opening up to the idea of allowing visitors to treat some exhibits as objects of devotion. This can be seen in the Chaitanya Mahaprabhu museum as well, where visitors are encouraged to bow down to the large image of Caitanya in the first hall and to sit and meditate on his unique gift to mankind. At the same time, the guidelines of the museum[13] make it clear that visitors are expected to behave in a calm and dignified way—as are the staff, who are forbidden from, for example, soliciting funds from visitors, one of the things that urban Hindus find most offensive at traditional religious sites such as Kālighaṭ or the Jagannātha temple at Puri (Moodie 2019).

The Sri Chaitanya Mahaprabhu Museum at Baghbazar, Kolkata, thus represents much of what urban Hindus want today: to learn about their religious history, culture, and heritage in a peaceful and dignified way, far away from avaricious Brahmin priests, bloody animal sacrifices, and messy food offerings. The danger with this sanitized Hinduism is of course that it looses its "feeling" (*bhāv*), as noted by Moodie (2019: 129); how the Sri Chaitanya Mahaprabhu Museum will fare only time will tell.

Endnotes

1. Quoted in *Sree Sajjana Toshani or The Harmonist*, 26/4 (1928), p. 100.

2. Personal communication from B. S. Sannyasi Maharaj to Måns Broo, 19.5.2023.

3. Personal communication from B. S. Sannyasi Maharaj to Måns Broo, 19.5.2023.

4. Cited in https://timesofindia.indiatimes.com/city/kolkata/new-chaitanya-museum-coming-up-in-kolkata/articleshow/22645685.cms

5. Personal communication from B. S. Sannyasi Maharaj to Sundar Gopal Dasa, 16.5.2023

6. Personal communication from B. S. Sannyasi Maharaj to Måns Broo, 19.5.2023.

7. https://timesofindia.indiatimes.com/city/kolkata/texts-artefacts-throw-light-on-vaishnav-heritage/articleshow/70595045.cms

8. https://www.millenniumpost.in/kolkata/mamata-to-inaugurate-worlds-1st-museum-on-sri-chaitanya-368314?infinitescroll=1

9. https://www.siasat.com/mamata-opens-worlds-1st-museum-chaitanya-mahaprabhu-1581794/

10. https://www.oneindia.com/india/mamata-banerjee-arrives-to-inaugurate-sri-chaitanya-mahaprab-2933484.html

11. https://www.hindustantimes.com/india-news/better-for-me-to-die-than-prove-my-religion-before-entering-a-hindu-temple-mamata-banerjee/story-msAP0aY3GlvYqzWQyy17PP.html

12. https://www.newindianexpress.com/cities/kolkata/2019/aug/08/kolkata-to-get-worlds-first-museum-on-chaitanya-mahaprabhu-2015979.html

13. https://www.chaitanyamuseum.org/visitor-guidelines/

Bibliography

Anon 1928. Prākṛta Jagabandhu. *Gaudiya* 7/6, pp. 88–93.

Bhatia, Varuni 2017. *Unforgetting Chaitanya: Vaishnavism and Cultures of Devotion in Colonial Bengal*. New York: Oxford University Press.

Bose, Shivashish 2015. State and management of architectural heritage in Kolkata. *Journal of Architectural Conservation*, 21/3, pp. 178–194.

Ghosh, Abhishek 2014. *Vaiṣṇavism and the West: A Study of Kedarnath Datta Bhaktivinod's Encounter and Response, 1869-1909*. PhD dissertation, University of Chicago.

Moodie, Deonnie 2019. *The Making of a Modern Temple and a Hindu City: Kālīghaṭ and Kolkata*. New York: Oxford University Press.

Okita, K. K. 2010. A Caitanya Vaisnava Response to the Nineteenth-century Bengal Renaissance Movement According to the Works of Bhaktivinoda Thakura. *Religions of South Asia*, 2/2), pp. 195–214.

Pain, Crispin 2013. *Religious Objects in Museums. Private Lives and Public Duties*. London: Bloomsbury.

Reeve, John 2012. A question of faith: the museum as a spiritual or secular space. In *Museums, Equity, and Social Justice*, eds. Richard Sandell & Eithne Nightingale. London: Routledge.

Roy, Kalyani 2019. Sri Chaitanya Mahaprabhu Museum: A Critical Apprisal. *Special Issue on Inauguration of Sri Chaitanya Mahaprabhu Museum*. Bagbazaar: Gaudiya Mission.

Sardella, Ferdinando 2013. *Modern Hindu Personalism. The History, Life, and Thoughts of Bhaktisiddhānta Sarasvatī*. New York: Oxford University Press.

Sen, Siddhartha 2017. *Colonizing, Decolonizing, and Globalizing Kolkata*. Amsterdam: Amsterdam University Press.

Wong, Lucian 2014. Negotiating History in Colonial Bengal: Bhaktivinod's *Kṛṣṇa-saṁhitā*. *Journal of Hindu Studies* 7/3, pp. 341–370.

Wong, Lucian 2018. Universalising Inclusivism—and its Limits: Bhaktivinod and the Experiential Turn. *Journal of South Asian Intellectual History* 1/2, pp. 221–263.

Personalism, Impersonalism, and Beyond: Reflections on Swami Vivekananda and Śrī Caitanya Mahāprabhu

Jeffery D. Long

"He is eternal and immortal.
He is within this world and beyond it.
He is the Creator,
Both universal and transcendental.
Personal and impersonal,
With form and without,
God the Supreme
Encompasses all.
Who is God? God is an infinite Consciousness.
He is also the self-illumining Light.
There is no human being who does not own within this infinite Consciousness and this self-illumining Light.
God is Delight. Delight is the source of existence. Delight is the meaning of existence. Delight is the language of Infinity, Eternity, and Immortality.
God is all Love. Love is God's Life-Breath in us."
–Sri Chinmoy[1]

Acknowledging Difference and Looking Beyond It

Though in some ways seeming opposites, given the very real differences in their respective views of the nature of ultimate reality, Swami Vivekananda (1953-1902), a modern-day proponent of Advaita Vedānta, and Śrī Caitanya Mahāprabhu (1486–1533), the founder of the Gauḍīya Vaiṣṇava tradition, share a number of important affinities. Though Swami Vivekananda expresses his views in terms of non-dualism, his cosmopolitan philosophy affirms the equal validity of the paths of *bhakti* and *jñāna* as ways to the highest realization. Similarly, Śrī Caitanya Mahāprabhu's philosophy of *Acintya Bhedābheda* is a path that affirms the literally inconceivable truth of the simultaneous duality and non-duality of the individual soul (*jīva*) and the Supreme Being (Īśvara). This essay will ultimately argue for the importance of a philosophy built upon the common ground of an understanding of ultimate reality as capable of being perceived and approached in many ways, drawing upon elements of both of these thinkers.

Swami Vivekananda: A Non-Dualist with a Difference

Swami Vivekananda is widely credited with first bringing the philosophy of non-dual (Advaita) Vedānta to the Western world. As the first Hindu teacher to come to the West and develop a major following, Swami Vivekananda paved the way for subsequent teachers from an array of *saṃpradāyas* to share their wisdom with Americans, Europeans, and others whose knowledge of Hindu traditions would otherwise be entirely dependent on books (or would require them to travel to India themselves).[2]

The characterization of Swami Vivekananda as a non-dualist comes chiefly from two sources. The first is his own words and pronouncements. There is abundant evidence scattered throughout his *Complete Works* to establish that he certainly saw himself as teaching non-duality, and that he saw non-duality as representing the highest truth of existence. The second is the considerable literature that has emerged from monastic scholars within the Ramakrishna Order, which he established after the passing of his guru, Sri Ramakrishna Paramahamsa, in 1886.

There is also, however, abundant evidence that Swami Vivekananda's philosophy was not simply a restatement of the Advaita Vedānta of Śaṅkara: that is, of the Advaita Vedānta that a wide array of Vaiṣṇava scholars have critiqued for many centuries. To be sure, there is plenty in the teaching of Swami Vivekananda with which Vaiṣṇavas will disagree. Most fundamentally, the personhood of the ultimate Reality is seen by Vivekananda, as it is seen by Śaṅkara, as an effect of the way in which we approach a Reality which is Itself beyond all qualities. This "impersonalism" is contrary to the "personalism" that is foundational to Vaiṣṇava philosophy.[3]

As pointed out, however, by Vivekananda scholars such as Anantanand Rambachan and, recently, Swami Medhananda (himself a monk of the Ramakrishna Order), important dimensions of Swami Vivekananda's thought depart in some significant ways from at least a standard interpretation of the Advaita Vedānta of Śaṅkara.[4] I would argue that the current of Swami Vivekananda's thought that Swami Medhananda, in particular, emphasizes, places his philosophy closer to that of Śrī Caitanya than one might otherwise suspect.

Specifically, Swami Vivekananda strongly emphasizes the idea of the four yogas as independently valid and efficacious paths to God-realization and liberation.[5] This is a contrast with both classical Advaita Vedānta, which emphasizes the path of knowledge alone—*jñāna yoga*—as the one effective path to liberation, and the teachings of the various Vaiṣṇava *ācāryas*, which emphasize the path of devotion alone—*bhakti yoga*—as the one effective path to liberation. In classical Advaita Vedānta, yogas other than *jñāna—bhakti*, as well as *karma yoga* (the path of action) and *rāja yoga* (the path of meditation)—are seen merely as preparatory and purificatory practices, beneficial to creating conditions in the practitioner's consciousness for the emergence of liberating knowledge, but not as separate paths to liberation in their own right. Similarly, in the Vaiṣṇava traditions, yogas other than *bhakti-jñāna yoga, karma yoga,* and *rāja yoga*—are also seen as preparatory and purificatory, but not as, in the end, constitutive of liberation.

One could of course argue that Swami Vivekananda's doctrine of the four yogas puts him at odds with both Advaita Vedānta and with the teachings of the Vaiṣṇava *ācāryas*, and this is certainly, in one sense, the case. But the fact that he does see *bhakti* as an independent and effective path to the ultimate goal does place his view closer to that of Vaiṣṇava teachers like Śrī Caitanya than were he to affirm the efficacy of *jñāna yoga* alone, in the vein of classical Advaita. In other words, when Śrī Caitanya and other Vaiṣṇava teachers affirm that *bhakti* is sufficient to bring about realization and liberation, Swami Vivekananda, unlike what one would expect of an "impersonalist," is in full agreement with them. He would not, however, say that only *bhakti* has this capability.

Sri Ramakrishna:
The Bridge Between Swami Vivekananda and Śrī Caitanya Mahāprabhu

Why does Swami Vivekananda make this departure from a hardline view about the path to God-realization? What is the source of his yogic pluralism?

To answer these questions, it is important that we turn to the teachings of Swami Vivekananda's guru, Sri Ramakrishna Paramahamsa (1836-1886). One of the most noteworthy characteristics of the teaching of Sri Ramakrishna is his radical pluralism. Sri Ramakrishna, according to all of the primary sources available on his life, practiced in succession (not all at once) a wide array of paths, each of which he claimed led him to an experience of God-realization. These paths included the various forms of Hinduism available to him in his time and place, as well as Christianity and Islam:

> 'I have practiced,' said he, 'all religions—Hinduism, Islam, Christianity—and I have also followed the paths of the different Hindu sects. I have found that it is the same God toward whom all are directing their steps, though along different paths. ... The substance is One under different names, and everyone is seeking the same substance; only climate, temperament, and name create differences. Let each man follow his own path. If he sincerely and ardently wishes to know God, peace be unto him! He will surely realize Him.[6]

Sri Ramakrishna's religious experiences were not simply identical to one another, but he saw them all as stemming from a common divine source. On the basis of his experiences of diverse paths, he rejected dogmatism and any claim that only one religion or philosophy is in possession of saving truth:

> It is not good to feel that one's own religion alone is true and all others are false. God is one only, and not two. Different people call Him by different names; some as Allah, some as God, and others as Kṛṣṇa, Śiva, and Brahman. It is like the water in a lake. Some drink it at one place and call it "*jal*," others at another place and call it "*pānī*," and still others at a third place and call it "water." The Hindus call it "*jal*," the Christians "water," and the Muslims "*pānī*." But it is one and the same thing. Views are but paths. Each religion is only a path leading to God, as rivers come from different directions and ultimately become one in the one ocean.[7]

As Swami Medhananda explains:

> From Sri Ramakrishna's perspective, religious exclusivism and fanaticism stem from limiting God dogmatically to what one has understood or experienced of Him. Since "there is no limit to God," we should humbly acknowledge that God may have various aspects and forms of which we cannot conceive ... [A]ll religions are salvifically effective, since all of them ... make contact with a real aspect of God, though none of them encompasses the *whole* of God, who is infinite and illimitable.[8]

Why could Sri Ramakrishna be characterized as a bridge between the thought of Śrī Caitanya and that of Swami Vivekananda? In order to answer this question, let us turn to the teachings of Śrī Caitanya himself.

Ultimate Reality as Acintya-Bhedābheda: Inconceivable Unity in Diversity

In the Vedāntic teaching of Śrī Caitanya Mahāprabhu, the founder of the Gauḍīya Vaiṣṇava tradition, the question of the relationship between God and the rest of reality is addressed in a profound way. This relationship is described, first of all, as *acintya*—that is, inconceivable. The human mind literally cannot grasp this relationship in its totality (just as, according to the teaching of Sri Ramakrishna, the human mind cannot grasp the totality of God). It is secondly, *bhedābheda*. *Bheda*, in Sanskrit, means "distinct" or "separate." *Abheda* is its opposite: that is, "not distinct, not separate." Non-dual! *Bhedābheda* therefore means that reality is in a sense distinct from, but in a sense one with, God. It is, in part, the seeming contradiction between "distinct" and "not distinct" that makes this relationship *acintya*—inconceivable.

This is beautifully explained by Vaiṣṇava scholar Steven Rosen:

> Acintya-bhedābheda refers to the sphinxlike relationship between the Lord (*śaktiman*) and his energies (*śakti*), which exists in a perpetual state of simultaneous oneness and difference. This is supported by an age-old Vedāntic aphorism: "There is no difference between potency and the possessor of potency" ... Yet the possessor of potency is unquestionably prior, the source, and also distinguished as an independent entity. The potency, on the other hand, is not distinguished in the same way, but rather manifests as both the cosmos and as spiritual beings who are dependent on the source as his separated and individualistic parts. ... They are both distinct (*bheda*) and non-distinct (*abheda*) from the Lord, inconceivably (*acintya*), and hence the term *acintya-bhedābheda*. ... Thus, what reality sets before us is God and all things directly related to God, on the one hand, and, simultaneously, it gives us those things that are *not* God, that emanate from him but ony partially exhibit his spiritual nature, on the other. Both "God" and "not God," Vaishnava texts tell us, are in some sense one, if also obviously different.[9]

In a similar vein, Sri Ramakrishna teaches that Brahman and Śakti are also one, yet distinct. "Like fire and its power to burn, Brahman and Śakti mutually entail each other."[10] "One cannot think of Brahman without Śakti, or of Śakti without Brahman. One cannot think of the *nitya* [the eternal, God] without the *līlā* [the divine play, or in Rosen's terms, "not God"], or of the *līlā* without the *nitya*."[11] And yet these words—Brahman and Śakti, *nitya* and *līlā*—do have distinct meanings and it is possible to differentiate one from the other. Their relationship is one of *bhedābheda*.

This same analogy is used in the Gauḍīya Vaiṣṇava tradition. Steven Rosen cites Gauḍīya Vaiṣṇava theologian O. B. L. Kapoor (1909-2001) in this regard:

> We cannot think of fire without the power of burning; similarly, we cannot think of the power of burning without fire. Both are identical. Fire is nothing except that which burns; the power of burning is nothing except fire in action. At the same time, fire and its power of burning are not absolutely the same. If they were absolutely the same, there would be no sense in saying "fire burns." It would be enough to say "fire." "Fire burns" would involve needless repetition, for "fire" would mean the same thing as "burns."[12]

Acintya-Bhedābheda and Pluralism

A direct logical link can be discerned between the *acintya-bhedābheda* metaphysics shared by both Śrī Caitanya and Sri Ramakrishna (the latter of whom, though many may not know it, was steeped in Gauḍīya Vaiṣṇava practice, having grown up in a devout Vaiṣṇava family in rural Bengal)[13] and the latter's pluralistic stance on religion.[14] If the reality of God is ultimately inconceivable (*acintya*), due to the finite nature of the ordinary human mind, then it would be the height of arrogance to say that God is only *this* and not *that*: in short, that the infinite Reality upon which all of existence depends must conform to *my* particular view of how things should be. And given the *bhedābheda* relationship between God and the totality of being, it is not possible to affirm dogmatically *only* that God is distinct from all which is not God, *or* that God is one with all things. God is both. And neither. And more which we cannot even conceptualize or formulate in language. And entire religions and philosophies exist which are built on each of these possibilities.

This does not mean, however, that all is lost. For an essential aspect of the divine Reality which is affirmed as a core teaching of all Vaiṣṇava traditions is that God is a being of pure love. As B. R. Śrīdhara Mahārāja, cited by Steven Rosen, explains:

> There are channels by which the infinite descends. ... The infinite cannot be contained in a limited sphere ... but if He really is infinite, then He has the power of making Himself known in all His fulness to the finite mind. When

> out of His own prerogative, he takes the initiative and reveals Himself to the devotee, there is actual perception of Godhead, self-realization, transcendental revelation.[15]

Revelation occurs. God can be experienced directly. This is also a core teaching of Ramakrishna. Our attempts to reduce this divine experience to a simple philosophical formula or to insist that our way alone can lead to God—whose grace more than any particular effort on our part is the key factor in the revelatory experience—are an effect of our human vanity. And our infliction of violence on those who disagree with us stems from our tragic failure to see the divine presence in all beings.

Conclusion

Swami Vivekananda, who inherited Sri Ramakrishna's teaching, also inherited his pluralism and his aversion to dogmatism and fanaticism. In his teaching of the efficacy of many paths, he humbly affirms that the divine *śakti* is unlimited, and that all sincere attempts to reach the infinite are to be respected: an attitude which we can see has its roots, via Ramakrishna, in the *acintya-bhedābheda* philosophy of Śrī Caitanya. Such an attitude is essential to human survival, as Vivekananda himself expressed in the closing words of his renowned welcome address at the World Parliament of Religions in Chicago in 1893:

> Sectarianism, bigotry, and its horrible descendant, fanaticism, have long possessed this beautiful earth. They have filled the earth with violence, drenched it often and often with human blood, destroyed civilization and sent whole nations to despair. Had it not been for these horrible demons, human society would be far more advanced than it is now. But their time is come; and I fervently hope that the bell that tolled this morning in honour of this convention may be the death-knell of all fanaticism, of all persecutions with the sword or with the pen, and of all uncharitable feelings between persons wending their way to the same goal.[16]

Regarding Advaita Vedānta and the various systems of Vedānta developed by Vaiṣṇava scholars, including Śrī Caitanya Mahāprabhu, it needs to be pointed out that the arguments in favor of both the impersonalist and personalist philosophies have been generated by highly qualified spiritual adepts over many centuries. It would certainly not do justice to minimize or trivialize either set of views in any way. What we do in this article, in terms of resolution, is to seek a brief overview, narrowing down their respective arguments to their essence, while at the same time hopefully offering all due appreciation to both positions. Clearly, Vaiṣṇava and Advaitic philosophers have thoroughly thought out their positions with respect to both logic and scriptural knowledge, and they have presented them in various complex and nuanced ways that are beyond the scope of this essay to explore in great depth. Our attempt here is merely to summarize the end points and explore areas of harmony for those so inclined.

Endnotes

1. Kusumita Pedersen, *The Philosophy of Sri Chinmoy: Love and Transformation* (Lanham, MD: Lexington Books, 2021), 23. These verses are drawn together from various publications of Sri Chinmoy, as Pedersen describes in her end notes.

2. Though Swami Vivekananda would be the first teacher to come to the West *and develop a major following*, he was not technically the first. He was preceded by Pratap Majumdar, a representative of the Brahmo Samāj. Jeffery D. Long, *Hinduism in America: A Convergence of Worlds* (London: Bloomsbury, 2020), 92.

3. Recently characterized as "radical personalism" by Vaiṣṇava monastic scholar Swami Padmanabha in his book of the same name. Swami Padmanabha, *Radical Personalism: Revival Manifesto for Proactive Devotion* (Mill Spring, NC: Inword Publishers, 2023).

4. See Anantanand Rambachan, *The Limits of Scripture: Vivekananda's Reinterpretation of the Vedas* (Honolulu, HI: University of Hawaii Press, 1994) and Swami Medhananda, *Swami Vivekananda's Vedāntic Cosmopolitanism* (New York: Oxford University Press, 2022).

5. See Jeffery D. Long, "A Complex Ultimate Reality: The Metaphysics of the Four Yogas," *Religions* 11 (12), 655 (2020), and "Religions as Yogas: How Reflection on Swami Vivekananda's Theology of Religions Can Clarify the Threefold Model of Exclusivism, Inclusivism, and Pluralism," *International Journal of Hindu Studies* 1-26 (2022).

6. Swami Nikhilananda, trans., *The Gospel of Sri Ramakrishna* (New York: Ramakrishna Vivekananda Center, 1942), 35.

7. Nikhilananda, 264-265.

8. Ayon Maharaj, *Infinite Paths to Infinite Reality: Sri Ramakrishna and Cross-Cultural Philosophy of Religion* (New York: Oxford University Press, 2018), 92. Ayon Maharaj was the name of Swami Medhananda before he took his monastic vows.

9. Steven J. Rosen, *Śrī Chaitanya's Life and Teachings: The Golden Avatāra of Divine Love* (Lanham, MD: Lexington Books, 2017), 123-124.

10. Maharaj, 38.

11. Nikhilananda, 134.

12. O. B. L. Kapoor, *The Philosophy and Religion of Śrī Caitanya* (New Delhi: Munshiram Manoharlal, 1977), 153, cited in Rosen, 125.

13. Sri Ramakrishna's parents were devout Gauḍīya Vaiṣṇavas. All their children

had Vaiṣṇava names. Ramakrishna was originally named Gadadhāra, but eventually came to be referred to as Ramakrishna. In fact, he did not become affiliated with the Śakta tradition until he was appointed a priest at the Dakshineswar Kālī Mandir at the age of nineteen. Mahendranath Gupta always believed that Ramakrishna was fundamentally a Vaiṣṇava. He has also been regarded as a Śakta, an Advaitin—even a Christian! For more, see Saradananda, Swami (Swami Chetanananda, trans.), *Sri Ramakrishna and His Divine Play (Śrī Śrī Rāmakṛṣnalīlāprasṅga)* (St. Louis: Vedanta Society of St. Louis, 2018).

14. Sri Ramakrishna's direct disciple and chronicler, Mahendranath Gupta, argued that Sri Ramakrishna's philosophy was closest to the Viśiṣṭādvaita of Rāmānuja, while others have sought to place him in a Tāntric framework, and others within the framework of Advaita Vedānta. His thought, being deeply pluralistic, has affinities with all of these views.

15. Śrīla B. R. Śrīdhara Mahārāja, "The Descent of the Holy Name: A Gauḍīya Vaiṣṇava Perspective" (http://bvml.org/SBRSM/tdothn.html), cited in Rosen, 128.

16. Swami Vivekananda, *Complete Works* (Volume One), (Mayavati Memorial Edition) (Mayavati: Advaita Ashrama, 1979), 3-4.

Bibliography

Kapoor, O. B. L., *The Philosophy and Religion of Śrī Caitanya* (New Delhi: Munshiram Manoharlal, 1977).

Long, Jeffery D., *Hinduism in America: A Convergence of Worlds* (London: Bloomsbury, 2020a).

———., "A Complex Ultimate Reality: The Metaphysics of the Four Yogas," *Religions* 11 (12), 655 (2020b).

———., "Religions as Yogas: How Reflection on Swami Vivekananda's Theology of Religions Can Clarify the Threefold Model of Exclusivism, Inclusivism, and Pluralism," *International Journal of Hindu Studies* 1-26 (2022).

Medhananda, Swami, *Swami Vivekananda's Vedāntic Cosmopolitanism* (New York: Oxford University Press, 2022).

Nikhilananda, Swami, trans., *The Gospel of Sri Ramakrishna* (New York: Ramakrishna Vivekananda Center, 1942).

Padmanabha, Swami, *Radical Personalism: Revival Manifesto for Proactive Devotion* (Mill Spring, NC: Inword Publishers, 2023).

Pedersen, Kusumita P., *The Philosophy of Sri Chinmoy: Love and Transformation* (Explorations in Indic Traditions: Ethical, Philosophical, and Theological) (Lanham, MD: Lexington Books, 2021).

Rambachan, Anantanand, *The Limits of Scripture: Vivekananda's Reinterpretation of the Vedas* (Honolulu, HI: University of Hawaii Press, 1994).

Rosen, Steven J., *Śrī Chaitanya's Life and Teachings: The Golden Avatāra of Divine Love* (Explorations in Indic Traditions: Ethical, Philosophical, and Theological) (Lanham, MD: Lexington Books, 2017).

Saradananda, Swami (Swami Chetanananda, trans.), *Sri Ramakrishna and His Divine Play (Śrī Śrī Rāmakṛṣṇalīlāprasṅga)* (St. Louis: Vedanta Society of St. Louis, 2018).

Śrīdhara Mahārāja, Śrīla B. R., "The Descent of the Holy Name: A Gauḍīya Vaiṣṇava Perspective" (http://bvml.org/SBRSM/tdothn.html)

Vivekananda, Swami, *Complete Works* (Mayavati Memorial Edition) (Mayavati: Advaita Ashrama, 1979).

Book Reviews

1.

Eben Graves, *The Politics of Musical Time: Expanding Songs and Shrinking Markets in Bengali Devotional Performance*. Bloomington, IL: Indiana University Press, 2022.

Review by Aniket De, Harvard University

Far from its medieval origins as slow-moving devotional music, *padabali kirtan* in twenty-first century West Bengal has emerged as a robust commercial affair, complete with new performance arenas and networks of circulation. Those acquainted with *kirtan* from scriptural sources alone are bound to be baffled at the quick tempo and versatile storytelling of contemporary performances. This new, fast-paced form of the performance, as Eben Graves argues, must be understood with reference to the political economy of market pressures, time constraints, and advertisement strategies that have shaped contemporary Bengali *kirtan.*

The Politics of Musical Time combines archival, ethnographic, and musicological research methods to trace the changing timescales of contemporary Bengali *padabali-kirtan.* While Graves provides some overview of the origins of the genre in medieval Braj and Bengal (p. 69-89), the work, on the whole, is concerned with modern lineages of performers in the city of Calcutta. This genealogy is traced out in detail in the first part of the book, with chapter-length sections on the role of temporality in Bengali Vaishnava devotional performances; the early modern seeds of kirtan in the works of Rupa Gosvamin and Narottama Dasa; the modern institutionalization of *kirtan* performers in colonial Calcutta by Nabadwip Chandra Brajabasi, Chitta Ranjan Das, and Khagendranath Mitra; and the contemporary networks of instruction and performance in Kolkata, centering on the performer Nimai Mitra, his family, and their students.

Part II offers nuanced textual and musicological analyses of mood and meaning through "word pictures" in kirtan (chapter 5); the centrality of *taal* theory in kirtan (chapter 6); and interpretation and storytelling in a contemporary performance of the "Divine Play of the Tax Collector" by Dyuti Mitra (chapter 7). This section is the analytical heart of the book, informed by the author's long and painstaking training in *taal* under Nimai Mitra's tutelage. Part III shows how these aesthetics of musical expansion have been affected by what the author calls "shrinking markets," not only in present-day music festivals, such as the one in Joydeb Kenduli (chapter 8), but also in choreographed and recorded performances in VCDs (chapter 9) and websites (chapter 10).

The book's focus on the political economy of contemporary *kirtan* performances is an important contribution to the fields of Vaishnava Studies, histories of performance in South Asia, and the cultural histories of modern Bengal. The author's multi-disciplinary approach—informed by his keen ethnographic eye and training in *taal*—provides a welcome departure from the purely phenomenological and textual approaches that have hitherto structured the study of *padabali kirtan*. Indeed, it is this innovative approach that makes the present volume stand out from other recent works on modern Bengali Vaishnavism (see, for instance, Sarbadhikary 2015; Bhatia 2017). Conceptually, Graves has creatively blended multiple "layers" of time, such as the divine time of *lila*, the historical time of *kirtan* institutionalization in Calcutta, and the contemporary social time of performances and markets. While the work is primarily ethnographic and musicological in nature, the historical section of the book has managed to recover little-known characters like Nabadwip Chandra Brajabasi and Khagendranath Mitra, along with gesturing at Chitta Ranjan Das' role in instituting *kirtan* in modern Calcutta (92, 118).

Yet, the author's argument would have been more compelling had he treated "politics" as a broader category beyond the market imperatives of shrinking time. There is, for instance, a tantalizing reference in the final pages of the book of a YouTube Channel called "Jago Hindu," (Awake, Hindu) established in 2018, featuring songs over 5.2 and 5.8 million views within a few months. Graves correctly notes the "growing interest" in these channels, but, alas, can only explain the interest as a result of "new forms of distribution" in a global technoscape (355-7). A very different picture would have emerged had he taken into consideration the robust rise of Hindu sectarian politics in West Bengal around that time, as is obvious from the name of the channel. Indeed, it is possible to argue that the market for *kirtan*, as well as other performances patronized as "Hindu" has *expanded* in twenty-first century West Bengal due to the increased patronage from all-India Hindu sectarian politics. The author's sustained silence on the question of the politics of religious identity is baffling, especially given the book's promise to analyze the political economy of devotional performances. Similarly, the inclusion of snippets of Hindi popular songs within Bengali performances (308-11), which Graves interprets as a performer's strategy to attract new audiences, is better understood in relation to the gradual hegemony of Hindi and the concomitant marginalization of regional cultures. A more sophisticated understanding of politics, especially in relation to questions of power, dominance, and hegemony, would have greatly added to the analysis of market pressures in the book.

That said, *The Politics of Musical Time* is an impressively researched and elegantly written book that effortlessly transcends disciplinary boundaries. The book will serve as a worthy introduction to modern *kirtan* for specialists and non-specialists alike, and will be of especial interest to musicologists and scholars of religious performance in modern South Asia.

Bibliography

Bhatia, Varuni. 2017. *Unforgetting Chaitanya: Vaishnavism and Cultures of Devotion in Colonial Bengal.* New York: Oxford University Press.

Sarbadhikary, Sukanya. 2015. *The Place of Devotion: Siting and Experiencing Divinity in Bengali Vaishnavism.* Berkeley: University of California Press.

2.
Simon Brodbeck, *Divine Descent and the Four World-Ages in the* Mahābhārata—*or, Why Does Kṛṣṇa* Avatāra *Inaugurate the Worst* Yuga? Cardiff: Cardiff University Press, 2022.

Review by André Couture, Laval University, Québec, Canada

Simon Brodbeck, the well-known Indologist, recently published a translation of the *Mahābhārata* including the *Harivaṃśa* (Oxford University Press, 2019). Brodbeck is a specialist of this literature and a recognized expert in Epic genealogies. The subtitle of his new book is: "*Why Does Kṛṣṇa* Avatāra *Inaugurate the Worst* Yuga?" He discusses the apparent contradiction between the *yugas*, a cycle of four periods characterized by a gradual decay of order (*dharma*), and the notion of *avatāra*, that is, the descent or manifestation of Viṣṇu as he comes into the world of men as Kṛṣṇa to destroy the wicked King Kaṃsa in Mathurā, and, afterwards, to take part in the terrible fight that brings the Dvāparayuga to a close. The new proposal explores how the world could be rescued by divine intervention at that point in the cycle where things are actually getting worse. (p. 3). While this problem has already been raised by other specialists (see for example, *The* Mahābhārata *and the Yugas*, a 2002 book by Luis González-Reimann, which deals rather with the Hindu System of World Ages), Brodbeck's text is the first exhaustive treatment of the problem and the first monograph devoted entirely to it.

The book is divided into seven chapters. After a first chapter dedicated to "Preliminaries" (an expanded table of contents and methodology), Chapter 2 (p. 13-46) describes the *yuga* cycle in detail, surveying the oldest descriptions of the system. Chapter 3 (p. 47-61) addresses the problem that lies at the heart of the book, that is, the appearance of Kṛṣṇa at the point of transition from the Dvāpara- to the Kaliyuga, a period during which *dharma* has nearly completely disappeared. Chapter 4 (p. 63-87) explains the word *yugānta*, the end of a *yuga*, a compound that takes on different meanings, depending on the context. Chapter 5 (p. 89-140), rightly entitled: "The Kurukṣetra *Avatāra* and the Divine Plan," discusses the functions of the *avatāra*, the presence of death on the Earth, the various accounts of Earth's problems, the attitudes of the gods concerning these problems, and finally the *avatāra*'s function in the great battle. Chapter 6 explores the transition to the *Kṛtayuga*, a renewed world, and Chapter 7 brings together the conclusions and analyses of the book. While the book has no thematic index, it does include a "Glossary of Sanskrit Words" (p. 177-180), a "Bibliography" (p. 181-196) and an "Index of Passages Cited" (p. 197-202).

The topic explored in this book is expertly managed. I have not personally examined in depth the specific question explored in the book, and I would simply like to add a few comments and share some references.

First of all, Brodbeck largely limits his analysis to the critical texts of the *Mahābhārata* and *Harivaṃśa* that he places on an equal footing. He considers the critical text of both texts as "an integrated whole" (p. 9). "A proto-*Mahābhārata* excluding the *Harivaṃśa* would be of much the same type as a proto-*Mahābhārata* excluding the various substories (*upākhyānas*), or excluding Bhīṣma's voluminous post-war teaching to Yudhiṣṭhira, or excluding the frame-story of Janamejaya and his snake sacrifice: that is, it would be an unavailable text" (*ibid.*). As such, a *khila*, or *pariśiṣṭa*, or *śeṣa*, is a supplement to a text, used to complement another text, adding, for example, the mythological support needed for its full understanding. It does not imply later or earlier dating, which is an altogether separate issue.[1] What Brodbeck proposes is a literary approach (p. 7), trying to understand the critically constituted text as an integrated whole, and I agree with the relevance of such a perspective.

Brodbeck tries to explain why *avatāras* generally appear at *yugāntas*. He identifies three senses for *yugānta*: the end of each of the four *yugas*, the end of a *mahāyuga*, that is, the four *yugas* considered as a whole, and the end of all the *yugas* in a much larger unit, that is, a Brahmā's day or *kalpa* (p. 68-75). In a compound like *yugānta*, the word *yuga* can be either singular or plural, meaning "the end of a specific *yuga* or the *yugas* (those in a *mahāyuga*, or even the thousand *mahāyugas* of a *kalpa*), depending on the context. This particularity of the Sanskrit language, that could have been more clearly explained, does not solve all the problems aptly raised by Brodbeck, but rather helps explain certain ambiguities within the text. Closely related is the question of the *yugānta* as a period of instability (p. 75-83). While appreciating the commentaries given by the author, I would like to add that the "instability" of the Earth appears to me to be immediately linked, directly or indirectly, to the ancient myth of winged mountains. Shaken by these huge birds, the Earth was at first chaotic, that is, unstable and insecure (*śithira/śithila*), as well as empty and arid. Indra clipped the wings of these birds with his thunderbolt and transformed their bodies into massive pillars in order to fix the Earth. He also transformed their wings into rain clouds, thereby converting the barren Earth into a fertile space where people can live. Elliptical references to this creation myth are found occasionally in the Epics. Throughout the *yugas*, there is an incessant danger of going back to the former state without mountains and clouds, a possibility expressly alluded to in the story of the Mount Govardhana according to the *Harivaṃśa*.[2]

The reader will perhaps be impressed by the number of graphs (Figures 3 to 13, and 15) used to highlight the structure of the time-cycle. The pedagogical value of such charts is evident. However, I also see the risk of confusing what I would describe as a mythological problem with a quasi-mathematical vision of the scale of time. The problem increases with a section called "the *yuga* machine" (chap. 4) or the "celestial mechanic" (p. 166). It is probably important to address the *yuga* as a scale of time and the reasons for the manifestation of the deity separately. I agree that time schemes hide various approaches to the significance of human life, including time as a sort of automatic device. Nevertheless, to my mind, the four-*yuga* graphs do not stand by themselves. In the Epic context, the *yugas* remain a sort of chronological projection of throws of dice.

The game of dice, so important in the Epics, is needed to make sense of the *yugas*, even though we do not know the precise rules of the game. The *yugas* also need the *sabhā*, a hall dedicated to dice play, where the ritual of royal consecration or *rājasūya* takes place in the *Sabhāparvan* (Book 2 of the *Mahābhārata*). Even if the ritual is not described as such in the book, the Earth (or Draupadī herself) remains the real issue behind all these fights. Even though Biardeau's analyses are not always convincing as regards the fine details, her vision of the problem, occasionally alluded to by Brodbeck, and indirectly in references drawn from Hiltebeitel's works, remains a valuable contribution. Of particular significance is the 1976-article, quoted here, and the self-assessment of her research on the *Mahābhārata* that she offers in the 2-volume *Le Mahābhārata. Un récit fondateur du brahmanisme et son interprétation* (Paris, Seuil, 2002).

Finally, Brodbeck's reflections about the problems faced by the Earth, decoded in terms of *jāmi* (under-differentiation) and *pṛthak* (over-distinction) (p. 116-122) are particularly welcome. The references to Verpoorten ("Unité et distinction ...", 1977) and to B. K. Smith (*Reflections on resemblance ...*, 1989) were essential. An important work cited by both Verpoorten and Smith, however, receives no mention in Brodbeck. I am referring to the pioneering book by Lilian Silburn (*Instant et cause. Le discontinu dans la pensée philosophique de l'Inde* [Instant and Cause. The Discontinuous in the Philosophical Thought of India], Paris, Vrin, 1955). Silburn already studied some important *Brāhmaṇa* passages dealing with Prajāpati, identified with the year. He is a god who is split into pieces, disjointed, and scattered (Prajāpati-the-Time in his germinal dispersion ("en sa dispersion germinale"), but also considered as identical to destructive time or death ("Le temps destructeur. La mort") as well as a god who has to be ritually reconstructed ("Prajāpati-le-Temps en sa reconstruction"). I would have expected her research to have been included here.

Does the Kṛṣṇa *avatāra* do what any *avatāra* is required to do at the end of a *yuga*, that is, to lighten the Earth's burden, or does Kṛṣṇa's descent rather encapsulate the dynamic of the four yugas (a *mahāyuga*) as a whole? The book's conclusion suggests that there is apparently no causal link between the transition to the Kaliyuga and the complexity of the Earth's affliction in face of death, only a sort of chronological marker of an epoch where *dharma* is decaying and during which salvation has become easier to realize thanks to Kṛṣṇa's teaching to his devotees or *bhaktas* (see notably p. 173-175).

Endnotes

1. See A. Couture, "The Harivaṃśa. A Supplement to the *Mahābhārata*," *Journal of Vaiṣṇava Studies* (1996, 4.3, p. 127-38).

2. A. Couture, "The Winged Mountains: Variations on a Vedic Theme," in *Kṛṣṇa in the Harivaṃśa*, Vol. I, Delhi, DK Printworld, 2015, pp. 277-300 (first published in French, 2008).

CONTRIBUTORS

Ferdinando Sardella (PhD 2010, University of Gothenburg, Sweden) is Associate Professor at the Department of Ethnology, History of Religions and Gender Studies at Stockholm University. He is the co-director of the project "Bengal Vaishnavism in the Modern Period" at the Oxford Centre for Hindu Studies, where he is a research fellow. His field is South Asian studies, Bengal studies, yoga, new religious movements and the history and sociology of religion. His area of specialization is modern Hinduism. He is the author of the monograph *Modern Hindu Personalism: The History, Life and Thought of Bhaktisiddhānta Sarasvatī* (2013), and has coedited *The Sociology of Religion in India: Past, Present and Future* (with Ruby Swain 2013), *The Legacy of Vaiṣṇavism in Colonial Bengal* (with Lucian Wong 2020) and *Handbook of Hinduism in Europe* (with Knut A. Jacobsen 2020). He has published several articles in international journals about modern Vaishnavism.

Tony K. Stewart retired from teaching in 2021 and is now the Gertrude Conaway Vanderbilt Chair in Humanities, *Emeritus*, at Vanderbilt University. In his early career, his research focused on the creation of the Gauḍīya Vaiṣṇav movement of the 16th and 17th centuries, the results of which can be found in his monograph, titled, *The Final Word: The Caitanya Caritāmṛta and the Grammar of Religious Tradition* (Oxford 2010). This work was preceded by a translation of *The Caitanya Caritāmṛta of Kṛṣṇadāsa Kavirāja*, translated with the late Edward C. Dimock, Jr. (Harvard Oriental Series 1999). Followers of the Vaiṣṇav traditions also recognize Satya Pīr, who is considered an *avatār* of Nārāyaṇ or Kṛṣṇa as well as a Sufi saint. Publications focusing on these *pīr kathās* include *Witness to Marvels: Sufism and Literary Imagination* (California 2019), which was awarded the Ananda Kentish Coomaraswamy Prize by the Association for Asian Studies. Relevant unabridged translations include two anthologies: *Fabulous Females and Peerless Pīrs: Tales of Mad Adventure in Old Bengal* (Oxford 2004), and just this year, *Needle at the Bottom of the Sea: Bengali Tales from the Land of the Eighteen Tides* (California 2023).

Katrin Stamm takes care of the private Sadānanda-Archive in Flensburg, Germany and is a research associate at the Europa-Universität Flensburg. Her MA and BA theses were written in the field of Philosophy of Language. She also studied Indology under Prof. Dr. Albrecht Wezler (Sanskrit) and Prof. Dr. Monika Boehm-Tettelbach (*bhakti* theology), with a special focus on Gauḍīya Vaiṣṇavism. The Sadānanda Archive contains the literary estate of the German scholar and Vaiṣṇava, Svāmī Sadānanda dāsa (Ernst Georg Schulze), and some of his disciples, such as Walther Eidlitz (Vamandās), Marthe Calmbach, Georg Wagner, and Mario Windisch. Her main tasks are conservation, editing, and publishing of the materials. Contact can be made via the website sadananda.com or directly via contact@sadananda.com

Gerald T. Carney is Professor Emeritus of South Asian Religions at Hampden-Sydney College in Virginia. Jerry continues research on Baba Premananda Bharati and on the writings of his disciple Krishna Gopal Duggal. Recent publications have concerned Govindadeva Mandir, Mahanambrata Brahmachari, and Sri Yashoda Ma. Since 1980 he has practiced documentary photography to explore the evolving religious ecology of contemporary Vrindaban. He is a participant in the Vaishnava-Christian dialogue.

Dr. Guy L. Beck is an historian of religions, musicologist, and musician affiliated with Tulane University, Loyola University New Orleans, and the Oxford Centre for Hindu Studies. A regular contributor to JVS, Beck has written *Sonic Theology: Hinduism and Sacred Sound* (1993), *Sonic Liturgy: Ritual and Music in Hindu Tradition* (2012), and *Musicology of Religion: Theories, Methods, and Directions* (2023). He also edited an anthology and CD archive of Bhakti devotional music, *Vaishnava Temple Music in Vrindaban: The Rādhāvallabha Songbook* (2011), as well as the popular textbook with CD, *Sacred Sound: Experiencing Music in World Religions* (2006).

David Buchta, Ph.D. (2014), University of Pennsylvania, is Senior Lecturer in Classics at Brown University where he heads the Sanskrit language program. His courses range from elementary to advanced language study and include topics such as Pāṇinian linguistics, Nyāya and Vedānta theology, and the *Bhāgavata Purāṇa* commentarial tradition. His published scholarship primarily focuses on Vaiṣṇava Vedānta, Sanskrit devotional poetry, and the theistic adaptation of *rasa* theory, especially focusing on the writing of

Rūpa Gosvāmin and Baladeva Vidyābhūṣaṇā. His recent paper on horror (*bhayānaka-rasa*) as devotion was published in the *Journal of Dharma Studies.*

Sugopi Palakala is a doctoral student at the University of Texas at Austin, pursuing a Ph.D. in Asian Languages and Cultures. Before joining UT, she earned a Master of Arts in Asian Religions at the Yale Divinity School. Her research interests include Gauḍīya Vaishnavism and Bhakti movements in early modern India.

Cogen Bohanec currently holds the position of Assistant Professor in Jain Studies at Arihanta Academy and is a Visiting Assistant Professor at Claremont School of Theology (CST). He has taught numerous classes on South Asian Culture & Religions and Sanskrit language at the Graduate Theological Union (GTU) in Berkeley. Dr. Bohanec specializes in comparative *dharma* traditions, philosophy of religion, and Sanskrit language and literature, and has numerous publications in those areas. He has a Ph.D. in "Historical and Cultural Studies of Religion" with an emphasis in Hindu Studies from GTU, where his research emphasized ancient Indian languages, literature, and philosophical systems. He also holds an M.A. in Buddhist Studies from the Institute of Buddhist Studies at GTU where his research primarily involved translations of Pāli Buddhist scriptures in conversation with the philology of the Hindu Upaniṣads.

R. David Coolidge received his Ph.D. from the Graduate Theological Union in 2023. He is visiting faculty at Bayan Islamic Graduate School. From 2014-17, he was an adjunct at New York University, where he taught an undergraduate course on Islamic law and ethics. From 2009-13 he worked as the Muslim chaplain at Brown University, and before that at Dartmouth College. He has also served on the boards of various American Muslim institutions, including Zaytuna College and Taleef Collective.

Gerald Surya, MD is a health and spiritual educator based in New York, He has been consulted by many authors for assistance in research, editorial services, and publication in electronic and audiobook formats. As a student and practitioner of Indian spirituality, he is a contributor to the *Journal of Vaishnava Studies* and the associate editor of *Studies in the Ontology of the Bhagavad Gita: What is One's View of God, the Universe, and the Soul?* (Edwin Mellen Press, 2015).

Steven J. Rosen is a disciple of A. C. Bhaktivedanta Swami Prabhupāda. He is also the founding editor of the *Journal of Vaishnava Studies* and associate editor of *Back to Godhead* magazine. His thirty-plus books include *Essential Hinduism* (Rowman & Littlefield); *Yoga of Kīrtan: Conversations on the Sacred Art of Chanting* (FOLK Books); *Krishna's Other Song: A New Look at the Uddhava Gītā* (Praeger-Greenwood); and *Śrī Chaitanya's Life and Teachings: The Golden Avatāra of Divine Love* (Lexington Books).

David Mason is editor of the performance studies journal *Ecumenica*. Twice a Fulbright Fellow, he is the author of the books *Theatre and Religion on Krishna's Stage*, *Brigham Young: Sovereign in America*, and *The Performative Ground of Religion and Theatre*. He is co-convenor of the Performance, Religion, and Spirituality working group of the International Federation for Theatre Research.

Måns Broo, Ph.D. (2003, Åbo Akademi University, Finland) is a senior lecturer at Åbo Akademi and an affiliated research fellow at the Oxford Centre for Hindu Studies. His research interests are mainly focused on yoga, modern Hindu movements, and Gauḍīya Vaiṣṇavism. His most recent book is the first volume of a critical edition and annotated translation of the 16th-century Gauḍīya Vaiṣṇava ritual text, *Haribhaktivilāsa* (Brill 2023).

Sourish Das (Sundar Gopal) is a disciple of Śrīla Bhakti Ballabh Tīrtha Gosvāmī Mahārāja. He is also the Research Assistant at the Bhaktivedanta Research Center in Kolkata, India. After completing his studies in Mass Comm. Journalism from Delhi University, he extensively studied the history, culture, and tradition of Gauḍīya Vaishnavism. He has been working with several national and international scholars worldwide, assisting them in their research work by providing research materials from various sources, translating classical Bengali texts into the English language, as well as conducting extensive fieldwork on their behalf. He also led the entire effort of curating a museum (1, Ultadanga Junction aka Bhaktivinoda Asan) for a heritage project in Kolkata. In 2020 he worked with Nathan Hartley for his publication "The Hare Krishnas in Britain" and is currently assisting Katrin Stamm with the biography of Ernst Georg Schulze/Swami Sadānanda Dāsa, the German disciple of Bhaktisiddhānta Sarasvatī Ṭhākura.

Jeffery D. Long is the Carl W. Zeigler Professor of Religion, Philosophy, and Asian Studies at Elizabethtown College, in Pennsylvania, where he has taught since receiving his doctoral degree from the University of Chicago Divinity School in the year 2000. He has authored, among other works, *Hinduism in America: A Convergence of Worlds* (2020), *Jainism: An Introduction* (2009), and, with Michael Long, *Nonviolence in the World's Religions: A Concise Introduction* (2021). In 2021, Dr. Long received the Ranck Award for Research Excellence from Elizabethtown College, and in 2022, he received an Ahimsa Award from the International Ahimsa Foundation for his work to promote nonviolence through his scholarship. In 2022, he also received the Rajinder and Jyoti Gandhi Award for Excellence in Philosophy, Theology, and Critical Reflection from DANAM (the Dharma Academy of North America) for *Hinduism in America.* Dr. Long has spoken at a wide variety of prestigious venues, including three talks at the United Nations. He is the editor of the Lexington Books series *Explorations in Indic Traditions: Ethical, Philosophical, and Theological.* Dr. Long has been a practitioner of Hinduism throughout his adult life, in the tradition of Sri Ramakrishna, and is an active member of the HARI temple (Hindu American Religious Institute) located in New Cumberland, Pennsylvania.

Made in the USA
Las Vegas, NV
10 December 2023

82469073R00163